GO MATH!

HOUGHTON MIFFLIN HARCOURT

HOUGHTON
MIFFLIN
HARCOURT

Dear Students and Families,

Welcome to **Go Math!**, Grade 6! In this exciting mathematics program, there are hands-on activities to do and real-world problems to solve. Best of all, you will write your ideas and answers right in your book. In **Go Math!**, writing and drawing on the pages helps you think deeply about what you are learning, and you will really understand math!

By the way, all of the pages in your **Go Math!** book are made using recycled paper. We wanted you to know that you can Go Green with **Go Math!**

Sincerely,

The Authors

Made in the United States
Text printed on 100% recycled paper
By using this paper in a typical print run,
we achieved the following environmental benefits:*
• Trees Saved: 345
• Air Emissions Eliminated: 36,645 pounds
• Water Saved: 185,503 gallons
• Solid Waste Eliminated: 28,390 pounds

*Environmental impact estimates calculated using
 the Environmental Defense Fund Paper Calculator.
 For more information, visit www.papercalculator.org

GO MATH!

Authors

Juli K. Dixon
Professor of Mathematics Education
University of Central Florida
Orlando, Florida

Matt Larson
Curriculum Specialist for Mathematics
Lincoln Public Schools
Lincoln, Nebraska

Miriam A. Leiva
Founding President, TODOS:
    Mathematics for All
Distinguished Professor
    of Mathematics Emerita
University of North Carolina Charlotte
Charlotte, North Carolina

Thomasenia Lott Adams
Professor of Mathematics Education
University of Florida
Gainesville, Florida

Contributing Author

Anne M. Goodrow
Associate Professor, Elementary Mathematics
Rhode Island College
Providence, Rhode Island

Decimal and Fraction Operations

 DIGITAL PATH Go online! Your math lessons are interactive. Use *i*Tools, Animated Math Models, the Multilingual *e*Glossary, and more.

Big Idea

1

Focal POINT

Developing an understanding of and fluency with multiplication and division of fractions and decimals.

Look for these:

BIG IDEA Project — Sweet Success

REAL WORLD

H.O.T. — Higher Order Thinking

Connect to Science
pp. 8, 52, 74

Use every day for Standards practice.

Look for these:

REAL WORLD

H.O.T.
Higher Order Thinking

Connect to Health
p. 132

GO MATH!

Use every day
for Standards practice.

Ratio, Proportional Reasoning, and Percent

 DIGITAL PATH Go online! Your math lessons are interactive. Use *i*Tools, Animated Math Models, the Multilingual *e*Glossary, and more.

Big Idea 2

Connecting ratio and rate to multiplication and division.

Focal POINT

Look for these:

BIG IDEA Project — Meet Me in St. Louis

REAL WORLD

H.O.T.
Higher Order Thinking

Connect to Art
p. 196

Connect to Science
p. 240

Use every day for Standards practice.

Look for these:

REAL WORLD

H.O.T.
Higher Order Thinking

Connect to Social Studies
p. 280

Connect to Science
p. 294

GO MATH!

Use every day
for Standards practice.

Algebra: Expressions, Equations, and Functions

DIGITAL PATH Go online! Your math lessons are interactive. Use *i*Tools, Animated Math Models, the Multilingual eGlossary, and more.

Big Idea 3

Focal POINT

Writing, interpreting, and using mathematical expressions and equations.

Look for these:

BIG IDEA Project — This Place is a Zoo!

Higher Order Thinking

Connect to Science
p. 340

Use every day for Standards practice.

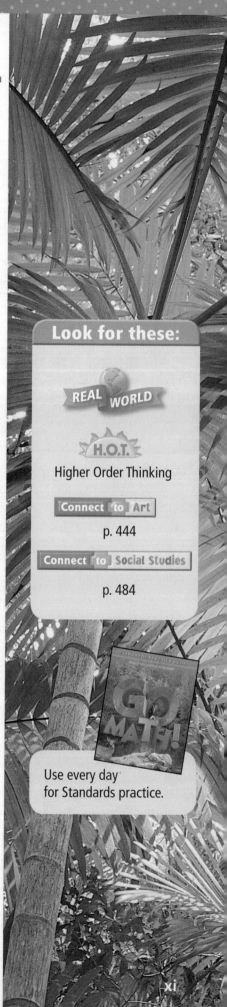

Look for these:

REAL WORLD

H.O.T.
Higher Order Thinking

Connect to Art
p. 444

Connect to Social Studies
p. 484

Use every day
for Standards practice.

BIG IDEA 1

Decimal and Fraction Operations

Focal POINT Number and Operations: Developing an understanding of and fluency with multiplication and division of fractions and decimals

Pennsylvania is one of the nation's largest growers of apples.

Project

Sweet Success

Businesses that sell food products need to combine ingredients in the correct amounts. They also need to determine what price to charge for the products they sell.

Project

You will begin to learn about the Big Idea when you work on this project.

A company sells Apple Cherry Mix. They make large batches of the mix that can be used to fill 250 bags each. Determine how many pounds of each ingredient should be used to make one batch of Apple Cherry Mix. Then decide how much the company should charge for each bag of Apple Cherry Mix, and explain how you made your decision.

Important Facts

Ingredients in Apple Cherry Mix (1 bag)
- $\frac{3}{4}$ pound of dried apples
- $\frac{1}{2}$ pound of dried cherries
- $\frac{1}{4}$ pound of walnuts

Cost of Ingredients
- dried apples: $2.80 per pound
- dried cherries: $4.48 per pound
- walnuts: $3.96 per pound

Completed by _____

Show What You Know

Check your understanding of important skills.

Name _____

▶ **Factors** **Find all of the factors of each number.**

1. 16 _____

2. 27 _____

3. 30 _____

4. 45 _____

▶ **Repeated Multiplication** **Find the product.**

5. $8 \times 8 \times 8$ _____

6. $3 \times 3 \times 3 \times 3$ _____

7. $4 \times 4 \times 4$ _____

8. $6 \times 6 \times 6 \times 6$ _____

▶ **Use Parentheses** **Identify which operation to do first.**
Then find the value of the expression.

9. $5 \times (3 + 6)$ _____

10. $(24 \div 3) - 2$ _____

11. $40 \div (20 - 16)$ _____

12. $(7 \times 6) + 5$ _____

MATH DETECTIVE

WITH

CARMEN SANDIEGO™

Mr. Pilcher spilled ink on the paper containing the
combination to his safe. One of the digits is now unreadable.
Be a Math Detective and help him figure out the missing digit.
What is the missing digit in the combination?

Top Secret
Safe Combination
9 5 4 6 3 ● 2

Hint: The combination
is divisible by 4 and 9.

Vocabulary Builder

▶ **Visualize It** ••••••••••••••••••••••••••••••••••

Sort the review words into the bubble map.

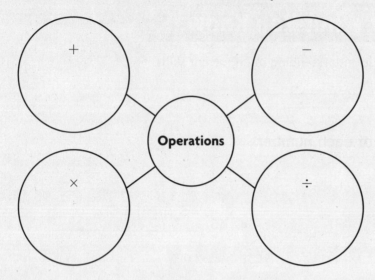

Review Words

addition

difference

division

multiplication

product

quotient

subtraction

sum

Preview Words

algebraic expression

base

divisible

numerical expression

prime factorization

terms

variable

whole number

▶ **Understand Vocabulary** •••••••••••••••••••••••••

Complete the sentences using the preview words.

1. An exponent is a number that tells how many times a(n)

   _____ is used as a factor.

2. A number is _____ by a whole
   number greater than zero if the quotient is a(n)

   _____ with no remainder.

3. A number written as the product of its prime factors is the

   _____ of the number.

4. A mathematical phrase that uses only numbers and operation

   symbols is a(n) _____.

5. A letter or symbol that stands for one or more numbers is a(n)

   _____.

6. The parts of an expression that are separated by an addition

   or subtraction sign are the _____ of the
   expression.

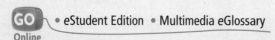 • eStudent Edition • Multimedia eGlossary

Name _____

Exponents

Essential Question How can you represent numbers by using exponents?

You can use an exponent and a base to show repeated multiplication of the same factor. An **exponent** is a number that tells how many times a number called the **base** is used as a repeated factor.

$$\underbrace{5 \times 5 \times 5}_{\text{3 repeated factors}} = 5\overset{\leftarrow \text{ exponent}}{\underset{\nwarrow \text{ base}}{3}}$$

UNLOCK the Problem REAL WORLD

The table shows the number of bonuses a player can receive in each level of a video game. Use an exponent to write the number of bonuses a player can receive in level D.

Use an exponent to write $3 \times 3 \times 3 \times 3$.

The number _____ is used as a repeated factor.

3 is used as a factor _____ times.

Write the base and exponent. _____

So, a player can receive _____ bonuses in level D.

Level	Bonuses
A	3
B	3×3
C	$3 \times 3 \times 3$
D	$3 \times 3 \times 3 \times 3$

Math Talk Explain how you know which number to use as the base and which number to use as the exponent.

Try This! Use one or more exponents to write the expression.

A $7 \times 7 \times 7 \times 7 \times 7$

The number _____ is used as a repeated factor.

7 is used as a factor _____ times.

Write the base and exponent. _____

B $6 \times 6 \times 8 \times 8 \times 8$

The numbers _____ and _____ are used as repeated factors.

6 is used as a factor _____ times.

8 is used as a factor _____ times.

Write each base with its own exponent.   6 _____ × 8 _____

🔑 Example 1 Find the value.

Ⓐ 10^3

STEP 1 Use repeated multiplication to write 10^3.

The repeated factor is _____. 10^3 = _____ × _____ × _____

Write the factor _____ times.

STEP 2 Multiply.

Multiply each pair of factors, working from left to right. $10 \times 10 \times 10$ = _____ × 10

= _____

Ⓑ 7^1

The repeated factor is _____. 7^1 = _____

Write the factor _____ time.

> **Math Talk** In Part A, does it matter in what order you multiply the factors? **Explain.**

🔑 Example 2 Write 81 with an exponent by using 3 as the base.

STEP 1 Find the correct exponent.

Try 2. $3^2 = 3 \times 3$ = _____

Try 3. 3^3 = _____ × _____ × _____ = _____

Try 4. 3^4 = _____ × _____ × _____ × _____ = _____

STEP 2 Write using the base and exponent.

81 = _____

1. **Explain** how to write repeated multiplication of a factor by using an exponent.

_____

_____

2. Is 5^2 equal to 2^5? **Explain** why or why not.

_____

3. Describe how you could have solved the problem in Example 2 by using division.

_____

_____

_____

Name _____

Share and Show [MATH BOARD] . . . .

1. Write 2^4 by using repeated multiplication. Then find the value of 2^4.

$2^4 = 2 \times 2 \times$ _____ $\times$ _____ $=$ _____

Use one or more exponents to write the expression.

2. $7 \times 7 \times 7 \times 7$

_____

✓ **3.** $5 \times 5 \times 5 \times 5 \times 5$

_____

4. $3 \times 3 \times 4 \times 4$

_____

Find the value.

5. 11^2

_____

✓ **6.** 9^3

_____

7. 4^4

_____

8. Write 64 with an exponent by using 4 as the base.

_____

Math Talk List two ways that you can read the answer to Problem 8.

On Your Own . . . .

Use one or more exponents to write the expression.

9. $25 \times 25 \times 25$

_____

10. $2 \times 2 \times 2 \times 4 \times 4$

_____

11. $8 \times 8 \times 8 \times 8 \times 8$

_____

Find the value.

12. 20^2

_____

13. 82^1

_____

14. 3^5

_____

15. Write 32 with an exponent by using 2 as the base.

_____

Complete the statement with the correct exponent.

16. $5^{\boxed{}} = 125$

17. $16^{\boxed{}} = 16$

18. $30^{\boxed{}} = 900$

Bacterial Growth

Bacteria are tiny one-celled organisms that live almost everywhere on Earth. Although some bacteria cause disease, other bacteria are helpful to humans, other animals, and plants. For example, bacteria are needed to make yogurt and many types of cheese.

Under ideal conditions, a bacterium cell grows larger and then splits into two "daughter" cells. After 20 minutes, the daughter cells split, resulting in 4 cells. This splitting can happen again and again as long as conditions remain ideal.

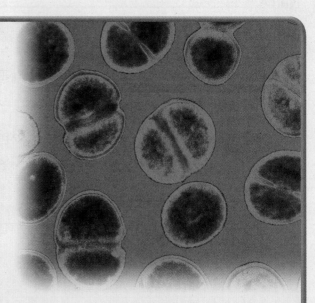

Complete the table.

Bacterial Growth	
Number of Cells	Time (min)
1	0
$2^1 = 2$	20
$2^2 = 2 \times 2 = 4$	40
$2^3 = \underline{} \times \underline{} \times \underline{} = \underline{}$	60
$2^{} = 2 \times 2 \times 2 \times 2 = 16$	80
$2^5 = \underline{} \times \underline{} \times \underline{} \times \underline{} \times \underline{} = \underline{}$	100
$2^{} = \underline{} \times \underline{} \times \underline{} \times \underline{} \times \underline{} \times \underline{} = \underline{}$	120
$2^7 = 2 \times 2 \times 2 \times 2 \times 2 \times 2 \times 2 = \underline{}$	\underline{}

Extend the pattern in the table above to answer 19 and 20.

19. What power of 2 shows the number of cells after 3 hours? How many cells are there after 3 hours?

20. How many minutes would it take to have a total of 4,096 cells?

_____   _____

Name _____

Divisibility

Essential Question How can you determine whether one number is divisible by another number?

Whole numbers are the number 0 and the counting numbers 1, 2, 3, 4, and so on. A number is **divisible** by a whole number greater than 0 if the quotient is a whole number with no remainder.

$20 \div 2 = 10$ 20 is divisible by 2 because the quotient 10 is a whole number.

> **! ERROR Alert**
>
> The terms "divisible" and "divided by" do not have the same meaning. The number 18 can be *divided by* 4, but it is not *divisible* by 4 because the remainder is not 0.

🔑 UNLOCK the Problem   REAL WORLD

A marching band has 140 musicians. The musicians form lines with the same number of musicians in each line. Can the musicians be arranged in 2 lines? In 3 lines? In 4 lines? In 5 lines? In 10 lines?

Divisibility Rules
A whole number is divisible by...
2 if the last digit is even.
3 if the sum of the digits is divisible by 3.
4 if the last two digits are divisible by 4.
5 if the last digit is 5 or 0.
10 if the last digit is 0.

🔑 **Tell whether 140 is divisible by 2, 3, 4, 5, or 10.**

Check 2.   The _____ digit of 140 is even, so 140 is divisible by _____.

Check 3.   The sum of the digits of 140 is 1 + _____ + 0 = _____.

The sum of 5 is _____ by 3, so 140 is

_____ by 3.

Check 4.   The last two digits are _____. Because 40 is divisible by

_____, 140 is _____ by 4.

Check 5.   The last digit of 140 is _____, so 140 is _____ by 5.

Check 10.   The _____ digit of 140 is 0, so 140 is divisible by _____.

So, the musicians can be arranged in _____ lines, _____ lines,

_____ lines, or _____ lines, but not in _____ lines.

> **Math Talk** Describe what you can tell about the divisibility of a number by looking at its last digit.

Chapter 1 9

🔒 Activity Use the chart to write divisibility rules for 6 and 9.

Number	Divisible by						
	2	3	4	5	6	9	10
312	✓	✓	✓		✓		
3,488	✓		✓				
918	✓	✓			✓	✓	
1,464	✓	✓	✓		✓		
1,881		✓				✓	
1,224	✓	✓	✓		✓	✓	
344	✓		✓				
3,360	✓	✓	✓	✓	✓		✓

- Look at the numbers divisible by 6. Each of these numbers also has

  the divisors _____ and _____ in common.
- Write a divisibility rule for 6.

  _____

- Complete the table below for the numbers divisible by 9.

Divisibility by 9		
Number	Sum of digits	Is the sum divisible by 9?
918		
1,881		
1,224		

Math Talk Explain how you can check your divisibility rule for 9 by using the numbers in the chart above that are not divisible by 9.

- Write a divisibility rule for 9.

  _____

🔒 Example Tell whether 6,852 is divisible by 6 or 9.

Check 6.   6,852 is _____ by 2.   The last digit is even.

6,852 is _____ by 3.   The sum of the digits is _____, which is divisible by 3.

So, 6,852 is _____ by 6 because it is _____ by both 2 and 3.

Check 9.   The sum of the digits of 6,852 is _____. The sum of the digits is

_____ by 9, so 6,852 is _____ by 9.

Share and Show [MATH BOARD] ·························

1. Complete the table to decide whether 2,385 is divisible by 2, 3, 4, 5, 6, 9, or 10.

Last digit	Last 2 digits	Sum of digits

2,385 is divisible by _____.

Tell whether the number is divisible by 2, 3, 4, 5, 6, 9, or 10.

2. 45

✓ 3. 201

✓ 4. 916

Math Talk Explain why a number that is divisible by 9 is also divisible by 3.

On Your Own ·····························

Tell whether the number is divisible by 2, 3, 4, 5, 6, 9, or 10.

5. 48

6. 135

7. 320

Write a four-digit number that fits the description.

8. The number is divisible by 4 and 9.

9. The number is divisible by 3 but not by 9.

10. The number is divisible by 4 but not by 6.

Problem Solving 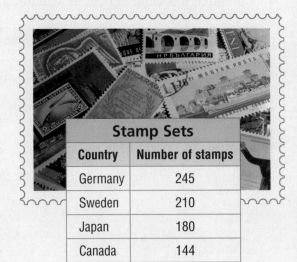 REAL WORLD

Use the table for 11–15.

11. Reggie buys the set of stamps from Canada. Could he put 2 stamps on each page of his stamp book without having any left over? 3 stamps? 4 stamps? 5 stamps? 10 stamps?

_____

_____

_____

Stamp Sets	
Country	**Number of stamps**
Germany	245
Sweden	210
Japan	180
Canada	144

12. Kirk buys a set of stamps. He can put the same number of stamps on each page of his stamp book if he uses 4, 5, 6, or 10 stamps per page. Which set did Kirk buy?

_____

13. Zoe buys the set of stamps from Germany. Can she put 7 stamps on each page of her stamp book without having any left over? Tell how you know.

_____

14. **H.O.T.** Tina plans to buy two different sets of stamps. She wants to put 9 stamps on each page of her stamp book and not have any stamps left over. Which two sets should Tina buy?

_____

15. **Write Math** ➤ Geri wants to put 10 stamps on some pages of her stamp book and 6 stamps on other pages. **Explain** one way Geri could do this with the stamp set from Sweden.

_____

_____

_____

········· **SHOW YOUR WORK** ·····

16. ⭐ **Test Prep** There will be 196 cars on display at a car show. The cars will be in rows with the same number in each row. Which could be the number of rows?

(A) 3   (C) 6

(B) 4   (D) 9

FOR MORE PRACTICE:
Standards Practice Book, pp. P5–P6

Name _____

Prime Factorization

Essential Question How do you write the prime factorization of a number?

🔑 UNLOCK the Problem REAL WORLD

Secret codes are often used to send information over the Internet. Many of these codes are based on very large numbers. For some codes, a computer must determine the prime factorization of these numbers to decode the information.

The **prime factorization** of a number is the number written as a product of all of its prime factors.

🔓 One Way Use a factor tree.

The key for a code is based on the prime factorization of 180. Find the prime factorization of 180. Use exponents if possible.

Choose any two factors whose product is 180. Continue finding factors until only prime factors are left.

Remember

A prime number is a whole number greater than 1 that has exactly two factors: itself and 1.

A Use a basic fact.

Think: 10 times what number is equal to 180?

10 × _____ = 180

```
            180
           /    \
         10      [ ]
        /  \    /  \
       2   [ ] 6   [ ]
      / \  / \ / \  / \
     2 [ ][ ] 3 [ ]
```

180 = _____ × _____ × _____ × _____ × _____

180 = _____ × _____ × _____

B Use a divisibility rule.

Think: 180 is even, so it is divisible by 2.

2 × _____ = 180

```
            180
           /    \
          2     [ ]
               /  \
              2    2   [ ]
             / \  / \  / \
           [ ][ ][ ] 3 [ ]
          [ ][ ][ ][ ][ ]
```

List the prime factors from least to greatest.

Use exponents to write repeated factors.

So, the prime factorization of 180 is _____ × _____ × _____.

Math Talk Explain how to find factors of a number.

Another Way Use a ladder diagram.

The key for a code is based on the prime factorization of 140. Find the prime factorization of 140. Use exponents if possible.

Choose a prime factor of 140. Continue dividing by prime factors until the quotient is 1.

A Use the divisibility rule for 2.

Think: 140 is even, so 140 is divisible by 2.

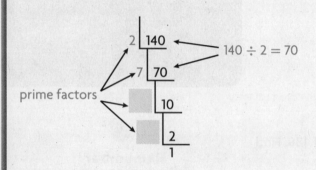

$140 \div 2 = 70$

prime factors

140 = _____ × _____ × _____ × _____

140 = _____ × _____ × _____

So, the prime factorization of 140 is _____ × _____ × _____.

B Use the divisibility rule for 5.

Think: The last digit is 0, so 140 is divisible by 5.

List the prime factors from least to greatest.

Use exponents to write repeated factors.

Math Talk How can you check whether the prime factorization of a number is correct?

Share and Show MATH BOARD ·····························

Find the prime factorization. Use exponents if possible.

1. 18

18 = _____ × _____

2. 42

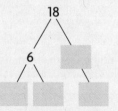

42 = _____ × _____ × _____

Name _____

Share and Show

Find the prime factorization. Use exponents if possible.

3. 75

✓ **4.** 12

✓ **5.** 65

Math Talk Explain why a prime number cannot be written as a product of prime factors.

On Your Own

Find the prime factorization. Use exponents if possible.

6. 104

7. 225

8. 306

Write the number whose prime factorization is given.

9. $2^3 \times 7$

10. $2^2 \times 5^2$

11. $2^4 \times 3^2$

Practice: Copy and Solve Find the prime factorization. Use exponents if possible.

12. 45

13. 50

14. 32

15. 76

16. 108

17. 128

Problem Solving

Use the table and the information below for 18–20.

Agent Sanchez must enter a code on a keypad to unlock the door to her office.

18. In August, the digits of the code number are the prime factors of 150. What is the code number for the office door in August?

_____

19. In September, the digits of the code number are the prime factors of 375. What is the code number for the office door in September?

_____

20. **H.O.T.** One day in October, Agent Sanchez enters the code 3477. How do you know that this code is incorrect and will not open the door?

_____

_____

Code Number Rules

1. The code is a 4-digit number.

2. Each digit is a prime number.

3. The prime numbers are entered from least to greatest.

4. The code number is changed at the beginning of each month.

21. **Write Math** The prime factorization of 24 is $2^3 \times 3$. **Explain** how to find the prime factorization of 48 without using a factor tree or a ladder diagram.

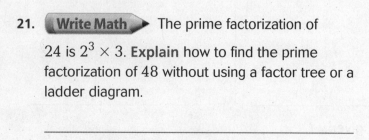

_____

_____

_____

_____

. . . . **SHOW YOUR WORK** . . . . . .

22. ⭐ **Test Prep** The key for a security code is based on the prime factorization of 90. What is the prime factorization of 90?

Ⓐ $2^3 \times 3 \times 5$ Ⓒ $3 \times 5 \times 6$

Ⓑ $2 \times 5 \times 9$ Ⓓ $2 \times 3^2 \times 5$

FOR MORE PRACTICE:
Standards Practice Book, pp. P7–P8

Name _____

Order of Operations

Essential Question How do you use the order of operations to evaluate expressions?

A **numerical expression** is a mathematical phrase that uses only numbers and operation symbols.

$$3 + 16 \times 2 \qquad 4 \times (8 + 5) \qquad 2^3 + 4$$

You **evaluate** a numerical expression when you find its value. To evaluate an expression with more than one operation, you must follow a set of rules called the **order of operations**.

Order of Operations

1. Perform operations in parentheses.
2. Find the values of numbers with exponents.
3. Multiply and divide from left to right.
4. Add and subtract from left to right.

 UNLOCK the Problem REAL WORLD

An archer shoots 6 arrows at a target. Two arrows hit the ring worth 8 points, and 4 arrows hit the ring worth 6 points. Evaluate the expression $2 \times 8 + 4 \times 6$ to find the archer's total number of points.

Follow the order of operations.

Write the expression.	$2 \times 8 + 4 \times 6$
There are no parentheses or exponents.	$2 \times 8 + 4 \times 6$
_____ from left to right.	_____ $+ 4 \times 6$
	$16 +$ _____
Then add.	_____

So, the archer scores a total of _____ points.

Math Talk Tell what order you should perform the operations to evaluate the expression $30 - 4 \times 5 + 2$.

Try This! Evaluate the expression $20 - 10 \div 2$.

There are no parentheses or exponents.	$20 - 10 \div 2$
Divide.	$20 -$ _____
Then subtract.	_____

🔑 Example 1 Evaluate the expression $72 \div (13 - 4) + 5 \times 2^3$.

Write the expression.	$72 \div (13 - 4) + 5 \times 2^3$
Perform operations in _____.	$72 \div \text{_____} + 5 \times 2^3$
Find the values of numbers with _____.	$72 \div 9 + 5 \times \text{_____}$
Multiply and _____ from left to right.	$\text{_____} + 5 \times 8$
	$8 + \text{_____}$
Then add.	_____

🔑 Example 2

The cheerleading team is buying new uniforms. Each uniform consists of a top and a skirt. Tops cost $12 each, and skirts cost $18 each. How much will it cost the cheerleading team to buy 9 uniforms?

STEP 1 Write an expression.

- Write the cost for 1 uniform.

- Then write the cost for 9 uniforms.

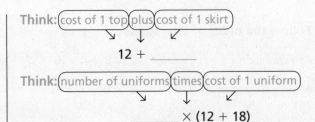

Think: cost of 1 top plus cost of 1 skirt

$12 + \text{_____}$

Think: number of uniforms times cost of 1 uniform

$\text{_____} \times (12 + 18)$

STEP 2 Evaluate the expression.

Write the expression.	$9 \times (12 + 18)$
Perform operations in _____.	$9 \times \text{_____}$
Multiply.	_____

So, the cost of 9 uniforms is _____.

 ERROR Alert

When you write an expression to represent a problem, be sure to put parentheses around the operation that should be performed first.

- **Explain** why the order of operations is necessary.

_____

_____

_____

Name _____

Share and Show

1. Evaluate the expression $9 + (5^2 - 10)$.

$9 + (5^2 - 10)$	Write the expression.
$9 + (\underline{} - 10)$	Follow the order of operations within the parentheses.
$9 + \underline{}$	
$\underline{}$	Add.

Evaluate the expression.

2. $6 + 24 \div 3 \times 4$

✓ 3. $(15 - 3)^2 \div 9$

✓ 4. $(8 + 9^2) - 4 \times 10$

Math Talk Explain how the parentheses make the values of these expressions different: $(18 \div 6) - 3$ and $18 \div (6 - 3)$.

On Your Own

Evaluate the expression.

5. $10 + 6^2 \times 2 \div 9$

6. $6^2 - (2^3 + 5)$

7. $16 + 18 \div 9 + 3^4$

 Place parentheses in the expression so that it equals the given value.

8. $10^2 - 50 \div 5$
value: 10

9. $20 + 2 \times 5 + 4$
value: 38

10. $28 \div 2^2 + 3$
value: 4

Problem Solving REAL WORLD

Use the table for 11–13.

11. Camilla is buying cell phone charms to give as gifts. She buys 2 heart charms and 3 star charms. Write and evaluate an expression to find how much Camilla's charms cost.

_____

Cell Phone Charms	
Type	**Price**
Dollar sign	$7
Guitar	$9
Heart	$8
Kitten	$8
Star	$6

12. Jake buys a guitar charm and a star charm and pays with a $20 bill. Write and evaluate an expression to find how much change Jake should receive.

_____

13. **H.O.T. Pose a Problem** Use the data in the table to write a new problem that involves using the order of operations. Then solve the problem.

_____

_____

_____

_____

_____

········· **SHOW YOUR WORK** ·········

14. **What's the Error?** Joel wrote
17 − 5 × 2 = 24. **Explain** his error.

_____

_____

_____

15. ⭐ **Test Prep** A banquet hall has 23 square tables that can seat 2 people on each side. On Friday night, 104 people attend a banquet. How many seats are empty?

Ⓐ 12 seats   Ⓒ 80 seats

Ⓑ 58 seats   Ⓓ 150 seats

FOR MORE PRACTICE:
Standards Practice Book, pp. P9–P10

Work Backward · Order of Operations

Essential Question How can working backward help you solve problems?

🔑 UNLOCK the Problem · REAL WORLD

A song in a musical has two verses. At the beginning of the song, several dancers are onstage. Two groups of 5 dancers enter the stage during the first verse, and 8 dancers leave during the second verse. At the end of the song, there are 20 dancers onstage. How many dancers were onstage at the beginning of the song?

Use the graphic organizer to help you solve the problem.

Read the Problem	Solve the Problem
What do I need to find? I need to find _____ _____.	• Work backward to write an expression. End of song:　　　　20 **Think:** Dancers leave during the second verse. So, there are more at the start than at the end. Use addition. Start of second verse: 20 + _____
What information do I need to use? I need to use the number of dancers who _____ or _____ the stage. I also need to use the number of dancers at the _____ of the song.	**Think:** Dancers enter during the first verse. So, there are fewer at the start than at the end. Use subtraction. Start of first verse:　　20 + 8 − (_____ × _____) • Evaluate the expression. $20 + 8 - (2 \times 5)$
How will I use the information? I can work backward to find the number of _____ at the start of each _____.	$20 + 8 -$ _____ _____ $- 10$ _____

So, there were _____ dancers onstage at the beginning of the song.

1. **Explain** how you could check your answer to the problem and show that your answer is correct.

_____

_____

_____

🔑 Try Another Problem

An airplane descends 2,000 feet to avoid a cloud. It then ascends 1,400 feet to an altitude of 28,000 feet. What was the plane's altitude before it descended to avoid the cloud?

Use the graphic organizer to help you solve the problem.

Read the Problem	Solve the Problem
What do I need to find?	
What information do I need to use?	
How will I use the information?	

So, the plane's altitude before it descended was _____ feet.

> **Math Talk** Explain how the strategy of working backward helped you solve the problem.

2. How did you decide which operations to use when solving the problem above?

_____

_____

_____

Name _____

Share and Show

? UNLOCK the Problem Tips

√ Underline the important information.
√ Check your answer.

1. Olivia used some of her savings to buy 2 novels for $7 each. Then she bought a bookmark for $3. After these purchases, she had $32 left in her savings. How much money did Olivia have in her savings before she bought the novels and the bookmark?

   First, write an expression for the original amount in

   Olivia's savings. _____

   Next, evaluate the expression. _____

   So, Olivia had _____ in her savings before she made her purchases.

2. **H.O.T.** **What if** Olivia had $46 left in her savings after her purchases? How much money would she have had in her savings before she bought the novels and the bookmark?

   _____

3. A baker puts out a tray of muffins. The first customer who enters the bakery buys 3 muffins. The second customer buys 2 boxes of 6 muffins each. After the second customer, there are 21 muffins left. How many muffins were there before any were bought?

   _____

4. The table shows the number of tickets each game costs at a carnival.

Carnival Games	
Game	Number of Tickets
Ring toss	1
Strike zone	2
Basketball toss	2
Dunk tank	3

   Rob plays the strike zone game 3 times. Then he plays the dunk tank game once. Afterward he has 6 tickets left. How many tickets did Rob have before he played the carnival games?

   _____

SHOW YOUR WORK

On Your Own

Choose a STRATEGY

Work Backward
Solve a Simpler Problem
Choose an Operation
Use a Model
Use a Formula
Draw a Diagram

5. Marco received a gift card. He used it to buy 2 bike lights for $10 each. Then he bought a handlebar bag for $18. After these purchases, he had $2 left on the gift card. How much money was on the gift card when Marco received it?

Sea snail shells

_____

6. Lydia collects shells. She has 24 sea snail shells, 16 conch shells, and 32 scallop shells. She wants to display the shells in equal rows, with only one type of shell in each row. What is the greatest number of shells Lydia can put in each row?

Conch shell   **Scallop shell**

_____

7. ⭐H.O.T.⭐ There are 18 players on a soccer team. There are 2 more girls on the team than boys. How many girls are on the team?

_____

SHOW YOUR WORK

8. **Write Math** ➤ On one day, Keri received 6 emails in her inbox, and she deleted 13 emails from her inbox. At the end of the day, she had 38 emails in her inbox. **Explain** how you could find the number of emails Keri had in her inbox at the beginning of the day.

_____

_____

_____

_____

9. ⭐ **Test Prep** A scientist adds 30 grams of a powder to a container. Then she adds 50 grams of water. After these steps, the container has a mass of 104 grams. What was the mass of the container before the scientist added anything to it?

Ⓐ 24 grams   Ⓒ 74 grams

Ⓑ 54 grams   Ⓓ 184 grams

FOR MORE PRACTICE:
Standards Practice Book, pp. P11–P12

✓ Mid-Chapter Checkpoint

▶ **Vocabulary**

Choose the best term from the box.

Vocabulary
exponent
numerical expression
prime factorization

1. A(n) _____ tells how many times a base is used as a factor. (p. 5)

2. The mathematical phrase $5 + 2 \times 18$ is an example of a(n)

   _____. (p. 17)

▶ **Concepts and Skills**

Find the value. (pp. 5–8)

3. 5^4

4. 21^2

5. 8^3

Tell whether the number is divisible by 2, 3, 4, 5, 6, 9, or 10. (pp. 9–12)

6. 85

7. 284

8. 1,428

Find the prime factorization. Use exponents if possible. (pp. 13–16)

9. 44

10. 36

11. 90

Evaluate the expression. (pp. 17–20)

12. $9^2 \times 2 - 4^2$

13. $2 \times (10 - 2) \div 4$

14. $30 - (3^3 - 8)$

Fill in the bubble to show your answer.

15. The bill with the greatest value ever printed in the United States was worth 10^5 dollars. Which of the following is equal to the value of the bill? (pp. 5–8)

Ⓐ $10,000

Ⓑ $50,000

Ⓒ $100,000

Ⓓ $500,000

16. There are 63 students taking part in a scavenger hunt. The students are divided into teams, with the same number on each team. Which could be the number of students on each team? (pp. 9–12)

Ⓐ 2

Ⓑ 3

Ⓒ 5

Ⓓ 6

17. Kendra bought 2 magazines for $3 each and 3 paperback books for $4 each. She paid for her purchases with a $20 bill. How much change should Kendra receive? (pp. 17–20)

Ⓐ $2

Ⓑ $3

Ⓒ $5

Ⓓ $6

18. The high temperature on Monday was 8 degrees higher than on Sunday. The high temperature on Tuesday was 5 degrees lower than on Monday. The high temperature on Tuesday was 78 degrees. What was the high temperature on Sunday? (pp. 21–24)

Ⓐ 65 degrees

Ⓑ 75 degrees

Ⓒ 81 degrees

Ⓓ 91 degrees

Name _____

Properties

Essential Question How can you use properties of operations to solve problems?

You can use properties of operations to help you evaluate numerical expressions more easily.

Properties of Addition

Commutative Property of Addition If the order of addends changes, the sum stays the same.	$12 + 7 = 7 + 12$
Associative Property of Addition If the grouping of addends changes, the sum stays the same.	$5 + (8 + 14) = (5 + 8) + 14$
Identity Property of Addition The sum of 0 and any number is that number.	$0 + 13 = 13$

Properties of Multiplication

Commutative Property of Multiplication If the order of factors changes, the product stays the same.	$4 \times 9 = 9 \times 4$
Associative Property of Multiplication If the grouping of factors changes, the product stays the same.	$11 \times (3 \times 6) = (11 \times 3) \times 6$
Identity Property of Multiplication The product of 1 and any number is that number.	$1 \times 4 = 4$

🔑 UNLOCK the Problem REAL WORLD

The table shows the number of bones in several parts of the human body. What is the total number of bones in the ribs, the skull, and the spine?

Part	Number of Bones
Ankles	14
Ribs	24
Skull	28
Spine	26

 Use properties to find 24 + 28 + 26.

$24 + 28 + 26 = 28 + $ _____ $ + 26$ Use the _____ Property to reorder the addends.

$= 28 + (24 + $ _____ $)$ Use the _____ Property to regroup the addends.

$= 28 + $ _____   Use mental math to add.

$= $ _____

So, there are _____ bones in the ribs, the skull, and the spine.

Math Talk Explain why grouping 24 and 26 makes the problem easier to solve.

Chapter 1 27

Distributive Property

Multiplying a sum by a number is the same as multiplying each addend by the number and then adding the products.	$5 \times (7 + 9) = (5 \times 7) + (5 \times 9)$

The Distributive Property can also be used with multiplication and subtraction. For example, $2 \times (10 - 8) = (2 \times 10) - (2 \times 8)$.

🔑 Example 1 Use the Distributive Property to find the product 8 × 59.

One Way Use addition.

$8 \times 59 = 8 \times (\underline{\hspace{1cm}} + 9)$ Use a multiple of 10 to write 59 as a sum.

$= (\underline{\hspace{1cm}} \times 50) + (8 \times \underline{\hspace{1cm}})$ Use the Distributive Property.

$= \underline{\hspace{1cm}} + \underline{\hspace{1cm}}$ Use mental math to multiply.

$= \underline{\hspace{1cm}}$ Use mental math to add.

Another Way Use subtraction.

$8 \times 59 = 8 \times (\underline{\hspace{1cm}} - 1)$ Use a multiple of 10 to write 59 as a difference.

$= (\underline{\hspace{1cm}} \times 60) - (8 \times \underline{\hspace{1cm}})$ Use the Distributive Property.

$= \underline{\hspace{1cm}} - \underline{\hspace{1cm}}$ Use mental math to multiply.

$= \underline{\hspace{1cm}}$ Use mental math to subtract.

🔑 Example 2 Complete the equation, and tell which property you used.

A $23 \times \underline{\hspace{1cm}} = 23$

Think: A number times 1 is equal to itself.

Property: _____

_____

B $47 \times 15 = 15 \times \underline{\hspace{1cm}}$

Think: Changing the order of factors does not change the product.

Property: _____

_____

Math Talk Explain how you could find the product 3 × 299 by using mental math.

© Houghton Mifflin Harcourt Publishing Company

Name _____

Share and Show [MATH BOARD] ·

1. Use properties to find $4 \times 23 \times 25$.

23 $\times$ _____ $\times$ 25   _____ Property of Multiplication

23 $\times$ (_____ $\times$ _____)   _____ Property of Multiplication

23 $\times$ _____

_____

Use properties to find the sum or product.

2. $89 + 27 + 11$

3. 9×52

✔ **4.** $107 + 0 + 39 + 13$

Complete the equation, and tell which property you used.

5. $9 \times (30 + 7) = (9 \times \underline{\hspace{1cm}}) + (9 \times 7)$

✔ **6.** $0 + \underline{\hspace{1cm}} = 47$

Math Talk Describe how you can use properties to solve problems more easily.

On Your Own ·

Practice: Copy and Solve Use properties to find the sum or product.

7. 3×78

8. $4 \times 60 \times 5$

9. $21 + 25 + 39 + 5$

Complete the equation, and tell which property you used.

10. $11 + (19 + 6) = (11 + \underline{\hspace{1cm}}) + 6$

11. $25 + 14 = \underline{\hspace{1cm}} + 25$

12. [H.O.T.] Show how you can use the Distributive Property to evaluate $(32 \times 6) + (32 \times 4)$.

_____

Problem Solving REAL WORLD

13. Three friends' meals at a restaurant cost $13, $14, and $11. Use parentheses to write two different expressions to show how much they spent in all. Which property does your pair of expressions demonstrate?

_____

_____

14. Jacob is designing an aquarium for a doctor's office. He plans to buy 6 red blond guppies, 1 blue neon guppy, and 1 yellow guppy. The table shows the price list for the guppies. How much will the guppies for the aquarium cost?

_____

Fancy Guppy Prices

Blue neon	$11
Red blond	$22
Sunrise	$18
Yellow	$19

15. Sylvia bought 8 tickets to a concert. Each ticket cost $18. To find the total cost in dollars, she added the product 8×10 to the product 8×8, for a total of 144. Which property did Sylvia use?

_____

SHOW YOUR WORK

16. **H.O.T.** **Sense or Nonsense?** Julie wrote $(15 - 6) - 3 = 15 - (6 - 3)$. Is Julie's statement sense or nonsense? Do you think the Associative Property works for subtraction? **Explain.**

_____

_____

_____

17. ⭐ **Test Prep** Canoes rent for $29 per day. Which expression can be used to find the cost in dollars of renting 6 canoes for a day?

Ⓐ $(6 + 20) + (6 + 9)$

Ⓑ $(6 \times 20) + (6 \times 9)$

Ⓒ $(6 + 20) \times (6 + 9)$

Ⓓ $(6 \times 20) \times (6 \times 9)$

FOR MORE PRACTICE:
Standards Practice Book, pp. P13–P14

Name _____

Write Algebraic Expressions

Essential Question How do you write an algebraic expression to represent a situation?

An **algebraic expression** is a mathematical phrase that includes at least one variable. A **variable** is a letter or symbol that stands for one or more numbers.

$x + 10$ $3 \times y$ $3 \times (a + 4)$

↑   ↑   ↑

variable   variable   variable

> ### Math Idea
> There are several ways to show multiplication with a variable. Each expression below represents "3 times y."
>
> $3 \times y$ $3y$ $3(y)$ $3 \cdot y$

UNLOCK the Problem ⟩ REAL WORLD

An artist charges a fee of $10 for drawing a cartoon picture plus $5 for each person in the drawing. Write an algebraic expression for the total amount in dollars that the artist charges for a drawing that includes p people.

 Write an algebraic expression for the total charges.

Think: (a fee of $10) plus ($5 for each person)

        ↓   ↓   ↓

    _____ + (_____ × p)

So, the total amount in dollars is _____.

Math Talk Discuss why p is an appropriate variable for this problem.

Try This! A football team scores t touchdowns, f field goals, and e extra points. Write an algebraic expression for the team's total score.

Think: (touchdown points) (plus) (field goal points) (plus) (extra points)

      ↓   ↓   ↓   ↓   ↓

    $(6 \times t) + ($ _____ $\times$ _____ $) + ($ _____ $\times$ _____ $)$

Football Scoring	
Type	Points
Touchdown	6
Field goal	3
Extra point	1

So, the team's total score is _____.

🔑 Example 1   Write an algebraic expression for the word expression.

A   **30 more than the product of 4 and x**

Think: Start with the product of 4 and *x*. Then find 30 more than the product.

the product of 4 and *x*   _____ × _____

30 more than the product   _____ + **4x**

B   **4 times the sum of x and 30**

Think: Start with the sum of *x* and 30. Then find 4 times the sum.

the sum of *x* and 30   _____ + _____

4 times the sum   _____ × (*x* + 30)

🔑 Example 2   Write two word expressions for the algebraic expression.

A   *b* + 17

• *b* _____ than 17

• the _____ of *b* and 17

B   13*s* − 4

• 4 _____ than 13 _____ by *s*

• 4 _____ from the _____ of 13 and *s*

1. When you write an algebraic expression with two operations, how can you show which operation to do first?

_____

2. One student wrote 4 + 2*x* for the word expression "4 more than the product of 2 and *x*." Another student wrote 2*x* + 4 for the same word expression. Are both students correct? Justify your answer.

_____

_____

3. **Explain** why the expression 1 × *m* is equal to *m*.

_____

_____

Name _____

Share and Show

1. Write an algebraic expression for the product of 6 and p.

What operation does the word "product" indicate?

_____

The expression is _____ $\times$ _____.

Write an algebraic expression for the word expression.

2. 11 more than the product of 7 and e

3. 9 less than the quotient of n and 5

_____

Write a word expression for the algebraic expression.

4. $x \div 2$

5. $2 \times (m - 6)$

_____

Math Talk Explain why $3x$ is an algebraic expression.

On Your Own

Write an algebraic expression for the word expression.

6. 7 less than 5 multiplied by d

7. 20 more than y plus 5

_____

8. 20 divided by the sum of c and 10

9. 8 times the product of 5 and t

_____

Write a word expression for the algebraic expression.

10. $w - 8$

11. $2n + 3$

_____

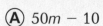

12. Martina signs up for the cell phone plan described at the right. Which expression gives the total cost of the plan in dollars if Martina uses it for *m* months?

SPECIAL OFFER
CELL PHONE PLAN!

Pay a low monthly fee of **$50.**

Receive **$10** off your first month's fee.

- (A) $50m - 10$
- (B) $50m + 10$
- (C) $50 \times (m - 10)$
- (D) $50 \times (m + 10)$

a. What information do you know about the cell phone plan?

_____

_____

b. Write an expression for the monthly fee in dollars for *m* months.

_____

c. What operation can you use to show the discount of $10 for the first month?

_____

d. How do you know that the correct answer cannot be choice B?

_____

_____

_____

e. Write an expression for the total cost of the plan in dollars for *m* months.

_____

f. Fill in the bubble for the correct answer choice above.

13. The Computer Club has 4 fewer than twice the number of students in the band. Let *n* represent the number of students in the band. Which expression gives the number of students in the Computer Club?

- (A) $4n - 2$
- (B) $2n - 4$
- (C) $2 \times (n - 4)$
- (D) $4 \times (n - 2)$

14. At a bookstore, comic books are on sale for $2 each and graphic novels are on sale for $8 each. Which expression gives the cost in dollars of *c* comic books and *g* graphic novels?

- (A) $(2 + c) + (8 + g)$
- (B) $(2 + c) \times (8 + g)$
- (C) $2c + 8g$
- (D) $2c \times 8g$

Name _____

Evaluate Algebraic Expressions

Essential Question How do you evaluate an algebraic expression?

To evaluate an algebraic expression, substitute numbers for the variables and then follow the order of operations.

🔑 UNLOCK the Problem ▸ REAL WORLD

Mitchell is saving money to buy an MP3 player that costs $120. He starts with $25, and each week he saves $9. The expression $25 + 9w$ gives the amount in dollars that Mitchell will have saved after w weeks.

- Which operations does the expression $25 + 9w$ include?

_____

- In what order should you perform the operations?

_____

A How much will Mitchell have saved after 8 weeks?

🔑 **Evaluate the expression for $w = 8$.**

Write the expression.	$25 + 9w$
Replace w with 8.	$25 + 9 \times$ _____
Multiply.	$25 +$ _____
Add.	_____

So, Mitchell will have saved $ _____ after 8 weeks.

B After how many weeks will Mitchell have saved enough money to buy the MP3 player?

🔑 **Make a table to find the week when the amount saved is at least $120.**

Week	Value of $25 + 9w$	Amount Saved
9	$25 + 9 \times 9 = 25 +$ _____ $= 106$	
10	$25 + 9 \times 10 = 25 +$ _____ $=$ _____	
11	$25 + 9 \times 11 = 25 +$ _____ $=$ _____	

So, Mitchell will have saved enough money for the

MP3 player after _____ weeks.

Math Talk Explain what it means to substitute a value for a variable.

🔑 Example 1 Evaluate the expression for the given value of the variable.

A $4 \times (m - 8) \div 3$ for $m = 14$

Write the expression.	$4 \times (m - 8) \div 3$
Replace m with 14.	$4 \times (\rule{1cm}{0.4pt} - 8) \div 3$
Perform operations in parentheses.	$4 \times \rule{1cm}{0.4pt} \div 3$
Multiply and divide from left to right.	$\rule{1cm}{0.4pt} \div 3$
	$\rule{1cm}{0.4pt}$

B $3 \times (y^2 + 2)$ for $y = 4$

Write the expression.	$3 \times (y^2 + 2)$
Replace y with 4.	$3 \times (\rule{1cm}{0.4pt}^2 + 2)$
Follow the order of operations within the parentheses.	$3 \times (\rule{1cm}{0.4pt} + 2)$
	$3 \times \rule{1cm}{0.4pt}$
Multiply.	$\rule{1cm}{0.4pt}$

> ⚠ **ERROR Alert**
> When squaring a number, be sure to multiply the number by itself.
> $$4^2 = 4 \times 4$$

🔑 Example 2 Evaluate $2a + 3b$ for $a = 5$ and $b = 6$.

Write the expression.	$\rule{2cm}{0.4pt}$
Replace a with 5 and b with 6.	$2 \times \rule{1cm}{0.4pt} + 3 \times \rule{1cm}{0.4pt}$
Multiply from left to right.	$\rule{1cm}{0.4pt} + 3 \times 6$
	$10 + \rule{1cm}{0.4pt}$
Add.	$\rule{1cm}{0.4pt}$

1. **Describe** how evaluating an algebraic expression is different from evaluating a numerical expression.

_____

_____

2. **Identify** the variables in the expression $2w \times (h + 5)$.

_____

36

Name _____

Share and Show

1. Evaluate $5k + 6$ for $k = 4$.

   Write the expression.   _____

   Replace k with 4. $5 \times$ _____ $+ 6$

   Multiply.   _____ $+ 6$

   Add.   _____

Evaluate the expression for the given values of the variables.

2. $m - 9$ for $m = 13$

3. $16 - 3b$ for $b = 4$

4. $p^2 + 4$ for $p = 6$

5. $5 \times (h + 3)$ for $h = 7$

6. $2 \times (c^2 - 5)$ for $c = 4$

7. $4x + 5y$ for $x = 2$ and $y = 3$

Math Talk Tell what information you need to evaluate an algebraic expression.

On Your Own

Evaluate the expression for the given values of the variables.

8. $7s + 5$ for $s = 3$

9. $21 - 4d$ for $d = 5$

10. $(t - 6)^2$ for $t = 11$

Practice: Copy and Solve Evaluate the expression for the given values of the variables.

11. $6 \times (2v - 3)$ for $v = 5$

12. $2 \times (k^2 - 2n)$ for $k = 6$ and $n = 13$

13. $5 \times (f - 32) \div 9$ for $f = 95$

Problem Solving  REAL WORLD

The table shows how much a company charges for skateboard wheels. Each pack of 8 wheels costs $50. Shipping costs $7 for any order. Use the table for 14–16.

14. Complete the table.

15. A skateboard club has a budget of $200 to spend on new wheels this year. What is the greatest number of packs of wheels the club can order?

_____

16. **H.O.T.** **Pose a Problem** Use the data in the table to write a new problem that involves evaluating an expression. Then solve the problem.

_____

_____

_____

_____

Costs for Skateboard Wheels

Packs	50 × n + 7	Cost
1	50 × 1 + 7	$57
2		
3		
4		
5		

SHOW YOUR WORK

17. **H.O.T.** **What's the Error?** Bob used these steps to evaluate $3m - 3 \div 3$ for $m = 8$. **Explain** his error.

$$3 \times 8 - 3 \div 3 = 24 - 3 \div 3$$
$$= 21 \div 3$$
$$= 7$$

_____

_____

_____

_____

18. ⭐ **Test Prep** The expression $22g$ gives the distance a car can travel on g gallons of gasoline. How far can the car travel on 8 gallons of gasoline?

  (A) 30 miles   (C) 176 miles

  (B) 56 miles   (D) 228 miles

Name _____

Simplify Algebraic Expressions

Essential Question How do you simplify an algebraic expression?

The **terms** of an algebraic expression are the parts of the expression that are separated by an addition or subtraction sign. **Like terms** are terms that have the same variables with the same exponents.

Algebraic Expression	Terms	Like Terms
$5x + 3y - 2x - 7$	$5x$, $3y$, $2x$, and 7	$5x$ and $2x$
$8z^2 + 4z + 12z^2$	$8z^2$, $4z$, and $12z^2$	$8z^2$ and $12z^2$
$15 - 3x + 5$	15, $3x$, and 5	15 and 5

🔑 UNLOCK the Problem · REAL WORLD

Baseball caps cost $9, and logo patches cost $4. Shipping is $8 per order. The expression $9n + 4n + 8$ gives the cost in dollars of buying caps with logos for n players. Simplify the expression $9n + 4n + 8$ by combining like terms.

• In the expression $9n + 4n + 8$, which terms are like terms?

_____

🔓 One Way Use a model.

Draw a bar model to combine the like terms $9n$ and _____.

	$9n$								$4n$		

n	n	n	n	n	n	n	n	n	n	n	n	n

$9n + 4n + 8 =$

_____ $+ 8$

_____n

🔓 Another Way Use properties.

Use the Commutative Property of Multiplication to rewrite $9n$ and $4n$.

$9n + 4n + 8 = n \times$ _____ $+ n \times$ _____ $+ 8$

Use the Distributive Property to rewrite $n \times 9 + n \times 4$.

$=$ _____ $\times (9 + 4) + 8$

Add within the parentheses.

$= n \times$ _____ $+ 8$

Use the Commutative Property of Multiplication to rewrite $n \times 13$.

$=$ _____ $n + 8$

So, the simplified expression for the cost in dollars is _____.

🔑 Example 1 Simplify the expression $5a + 12 - 3a$ by combining like terms.

Use the Commutative Property of Addition to rewrite $5a + 12$.

$$5a + 12 - 3a = 12 + \underline{\hspace{2cm}} - 3a$$

Use parentheses to group like terms.

$$= 12 + (5a - \underline{\hspace{1.5cm}})$$

Combine like terms.

$$= 12 + \underline{\hspace{2cm}}$$

🔑 Example 2 Use properties to determine whether the expressions are equivalent.

Ⓐ $7y^2 + (x + 3y^2)$ and $10y^2 + x$

Simplify the first expression and compare it to the second expression.

Use the Commutative Property of Addition to rewrite $x + 3y^2$.

$$7y^2 + (x + 3y^2) = 7y^2 + (\underline{\hspace{1.5cm}} + \underline{\hspace{1.5cm}})$$

Use the _____ Property of Addition to group like terms.

$$= (\underline{\hspace{1.5cm}} + 3y^2) + x$$

Combine like terms.

$$= \underline{\hspace{1.5cm}} + x$$

So, the expressions $7y^2 + (x + 3y^2)$ and $10y^2 + x$ are _____.

Ⓑ $10 \times (m + n)$ and $10m + n$

Simplify the first expression and compare it to the second expression.

Use the Distributive Property.

$$10 \times (m + n) = (10 \times \underline{\hspace{1.5cm}}) + (10 \times \underline{\hspace{1.5cm}})$$

Multiply within the parentheses.

$$= 10m + \underline{\hspace{1.5cm}}$$

So, the expressions $10 \times (m + n)$ and $10m + n$ are _____.

---

1. Explain how you could evaluate $237x - 236x$ for $x = 9$ by using mental math.

_____

_____

2. Can you simplify the expression $2x + 2y$ by combining like terms? **Justify** your answer.

_____

_____

Name _____

Share and Show MATH BOARD ·

1. Simplify the expression $13k - 9k + 7$ by combining like terms.

   Use parentheses to group like terms. $13k - 9k + 7 = ($ _____ $-$ _____ $) + 7$

   Combine like terms. $=$ _____ $+ 7$

Simplify the expression by combining like terms.

2. $9 + 5x - 3x$

3. $10y + 5 + 6y + 4$

4. $2t + t^2 + 3t$

Use properties to determine whether the expressions are equivalent.

5. $3 \times (v + 2) + 7v$ and $16v$

6. $14h + (17 + 11h)$ and $25h + 17$

7. $4b \times 7$ and $28b$

Math Talk List three expressions with two terms that are equivalent to $5x$. Discuss your list with a partner.

On Your Own ·

Simplify the expression by combining like terms.

8. $15s + 15 - 12s$

9. $8d + 11 + 2d - 8$

10. $2n^2 + 3n^2$

Use properties to determine whether the expressions are equivalent.

11. $3a + (7a \times 0)$ and $10a$

12. $6 \times (w + 5w)$ and $36w$

13. $4a - a + 3$ and $3a + 3$

Problem Solving  REAL WORLD

 Sense or Nonsense?

14. Brooks and Jade are using what they know about properties to simplify the expression $2 \times (n + 6) + 3$. Whose answer makes sense? Whose answer is nonsense? **Explain** your reasoning.

I can start with the Associative Property of Addition.

I can start with the Distributive Property.

Brooks's Work	
Expression:	$2 \times (n + 6) + 3$
Associative Property of Addition:	$2 \times n + (6 + 3)$
Add within parentheses:	$2 \times n + 9$
Multiply:	$2n + 9$

Jade's Work	
Expression:	$2 \times (n + 6) + 3$
Distributive Property:	$(2 \times n) + (2 \times 6) + 3$
Multiply within parentheses:	$2n + 12 + 3$
Associative Property of Addition:	$2n + (12 + 3)$
Add within parentheses:	$2n + 15$

For the answer that is nonsense, correct the statement.

_____

_____

FOR MORE PRACTICE:
Standards Practice Book, pp. P19–P20

Name _____

Chapter 1 Review/Test

▶ **Vocabulary**

Choose the best term from the box.

Vocabulary
Associative Property of Addition
Commutative Property of Addition
Distributive Property

1. The _____ states that if the order of addends changes, the sum stays the same. (p. 27)

2. The _____ states that if the grouping of addends changes, the sum stays the same. (p. 27)

▶ **Concepts and Skills**

Use one or more exponents to write the expression. (pp. 5–8)

3. $4 \times 4 \times 4 \times 4 \times 4$

4. $8 \times 8 \times 8 \times 9 \times 9$

_____

Evaluate the expression for the given values of the variables. (pp. 35–38)

5. $(b - 2)^2 + 10$ for $b = 7$

6. $5f + 7g$ for $f = 4$ and $g = 10$

_____

Use properties to determine whether the expressions are equivalent. (pp. 27–30, 39–42)

7. $2 \times (m + 5)$ and $10 + 2m$

8. $5a + 3a + 0$ and $15a$

_____

Fill in the bubble to show your answer.

9. Rochelle is decorating a table by gluing small glass tiles to its top. She needs a total of 13^2 tiles. How many tiles does Rochelle need? (pp. 5–8)

  (A) 26

  (B) 139

  (C) 169

  (D) 213

10. Marcie was born in a year divisible by 9 but not by 6. Which could be the year in which Marcie was born? (pp. 9–12)

  (A) 1989

  (B) 1992

  (C) 1995

  (D) 1998

11. The combination for the lock to a storage room is a 5-digit number. The digits are the prime factors of 630 listed from least to greatest. What is the combination? (pp. 13–16)

  (A) 23335

  (B) 23357

  (C) 22357

  (D) 23557

12. Ben has $6 to spend on lunch at a taco stand. He can choose among the menu items shown in the table. Which combination of menu items does he have enough money to buy? (pp. 17–20)

Menu	
Item	**Price**
Taco	$2
Chips and salsa	$1
Burrito	$3
Drink	$1

  (A) 2 burritos and 1 drink

  (B) 1 burrito and 2 tacos

  (C) 3 tacos and chips and salsa

  (D) 2 tacos, chips and salsa, and 1 drink

Fill in the bubble to show your answer.

13. Tickets to an amusement park cost $35 for the first ticket and $25 for each additional ticket. Tickets for the Quinn family cost $160. How many tickets did the Quinn family buy? (pp. 21–24)

Ⓐ 4   Ⓒ 6

Ⓑ 5   Ⓓ 7

14. A painter bought 6 gallons of wall paint for $23 each and 6 gallons of ceiling paint for $12 each. The expression $6 \times 23 + 6 \times 12$ gives the total cost in dollars of the paint. Which is another way to write this expression? (pp. 27–30)

Ⓐ $6 + (23 \times 6) + 12$

Ⓑ $6 \times (23 + 6) \times 12$

Ⓒ $6 + (23 \times 12)$

Ⓓ $6 \times (23 + 12)$

15. There are 12 months in one year. Which expression gives the number of months in y years? (pp. 31–34)

Ⓐ $12 + y$

Ⓑ $y - 12$

Ⓒ $12y$

Ⓓ $y \div 12$

16. A department store is having a sale on coats. The sales clerks use the expression $2 \times (c - 10) \div 3$ to find the sale price of a coat that regularly costs c dollars. What is the sale price of a coat that regularly costs $82? (pp. 35–38)

Ⓐ $35   Ⓒ $51

Ⓑ $48   Ⓓ $55

17. Posters cost $15. Frames cost $12. The expression $15n + 12n$ gives the total cost for n posters and frames. Which is another way to write this expression? (pp. 39–42)

Ⓐ $27n$

Ⓑ $27n^2$

Ⓒ $180n$

Ⓓ $180n^2$

▶ Short Answer

18. Explain why the order of operations is important in mathematics. Use the expression $10 + 2 \times 3$ to support your answer. (pp. 17–20)

19. Use properties to write two expressions that are equivalent to $2 \times (a + 5)$. Tell which properties you used. (pp. 39–42)

▶ Performance Task

20. It costs $10 per month for membership at a gym. Yoga classes at the gym cost an extra $4 per class.

A Write an expression for the monthly cost in dollars, including the membership fee, for a person who takes y yoga classes at the gym.

B Use your expression from Part A to complete the table.

Monthly Gym Costs	
Yoga Classes Taken	**Total Cost**
1	
2	
3	
4	

C Ms. Vincent has budgeted $35 per month for the gym. Will she be able to take 7 yoga classes per month and stay within her budget? Explain how you determined your answer.

© Houghton Mifflin Harcourt Publishing Company

Decimal Operations

Show What You Know ✔

Check your understanding of important skills.

Name _____

▶ **Decimal Models** Shade the model to show the decimal.

1. 0.31

2. 0.7

3. 1.7

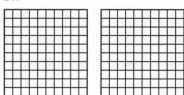

▶ **Round Decimals** Round to the place of the underlined digit.

4. 0.<u>3</u>23

5. <u>4</u>.096

6. 10.<u>6</u>7

7. 5.2<u>7</u>8

▶ **Division** Find the quotient.

8. 2,002 ÷ 91

9. 98)3,038

10. 24,487 ÷ 47

11. 22)2,332

MATH DETECTIVE WITH CARMEN SANDIEGO™

Maxwell saved $18 to buy a fingerprinting kit that costs $99. He spent 0.25 of his savings to buy a magnifying glass. Be a math detective and help Maxwell find out how much more he needs to save to buy the fingerprinting kit.

GO Online Assessment Options: Soar to Success Math

Vocabulary Builder

▶ **Visualize It** ••

Complete the Flow Map using the words with a ✓.

Estimation

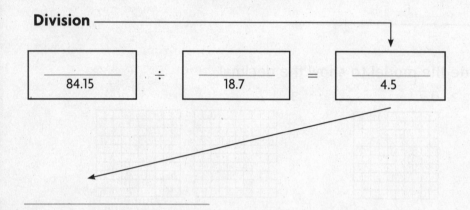

Division

| 84.15 | ÷ | 18.7 | = | 4.5 |

| 80 | ÷ | 20 | = | 4 |

▶ **Understand Vocabulary** •••••••••••••••••••••••••••••••

Complete the sentence.

1. One of one thousand equal parts is a _____.

2. Pairs of numbers that are easy to compute mentally are

   _____.

3. The _____ is the number that is to be divided in a division problem.

4. The _____ is the result when one number is divided by another.

5. The _____ is the number that divides the dividend.

GO Online • eStudent Edition • Multimedia eGlossary

© Houghton Mifflin Harcourt Publishing Company

Name _____

Add and Subtract Decimals

Essential Question How do you add and subtract decimals?

CONNECT The place value of a digit in a number shows the value of the digit. The number 2.358 shows 2 ones, 3 tenths, 5 hundredths, and 8 thousandths.

Place Value						
Thousands	Hundreds	Tens	Ones	Tenths	Hundredths	Thousandths
			2	3	5	8

 UNLOCK the Problem REAL WORLD

Amanda and three of her friends volunteer at the local animal shelter. One of their jobs is to weigh the puppies and kittens and chart their growth. Amanda's favorite puppy weighed 2.358 lb last month. If it gained 1.08 lb, how much does it weigh this month?

• Why is it important to line up the decimal points when you add decimals?

_____

_____

🔑 **Add 2.358 + 1.08.**

Estimate the sum. _____ + _____ = _____

Add the thousandths first.

Then add the hundredths, tenths, and ones.

$$\begin{array}{r} 2.358 \\ + 1.08 \\ \hline \end{array}$$

Regroup as needed.

Compare your estimate with the sum. Since the estimate,

_____, is close to _____, the answer is reasonable.

So, the puppy weighs _____ lb this month.

1. Is it necessary to add a zero after 1.08 to find the sum? **Explain.**

_____

2. Explain how place value can help you add decimals.

_____

🔑 Example 1

A bee hummingbird, the world's smallest bird, has a mass of 1.836 grams. A new United States nickel has a mass of 5 grams. What is the difference in grams between the mass of a nickel and the mass of a bee hummingbird?

Subtract 5 − 1.836.

Estimate the difference. _____ − _____ = _____

Think: 5 = 5._____

Subtract the thousandths first.

Then subtract the hundredths, tenths, and ones.

Regroup as needed.

$$\begin{array}{r} 5. \\ -1.836 \\ \hline \end{array}$$

Bee hummingbird

U.S. Nickel

Compare your estimate with the difference. Since the estimate,

_____, is close to _____, the answer is reasonable.

So, the mass of a new nickel is _____ grams more than the mass of a bee hummingbird.

Math Talk Explain how to use inverse operations to check your answer to 5 − 1.836.

🔑 Example 2 Evaluate 6.53 − s for s = 1.97.

Replace s with 1.97.   6.53 − _____

Estimate the difference.   _____ − _____ = 5

Subtract.

$$\begin{array}{r} 6.53 \\ -1.97 \\ \hline \end{array}$$

Compare your answer to your estimate. Since the estimate is _____, the answer is reasonable.

So, 6.53 − s = _____ for s = 1.97.

Math Talk Describe how adding and subtracting decimals is like adding and subtracting whole numbers.

Name _____

Share and Show

1. Find $3.42 - 1.9$.

Estimate. _____ _ _____ = _____

Subtract the _____ first.

$$\begin{array}{r} 3.42 \\ -1.90 \\ \hline \end{array}$$

Estimate. Then find the sum or difference.

☑ 2. $2.3 + 5.68 + 21.047$

☑ 3. $33.25 - 21.463$

4. Evaluate $82 - k$ for $k = 38.749$.

_____ | _____ | _____

Math Talk Explain why it is important to align the decimal points when you add or subtract decimals.

On Your Own

Estimate. Then find the sum or difference.

5. $57.08 + 34.71$

6. $20.11 - 13.27$

Practice: Copy and Solve Evaluate for the given value of the variable.

7. $8.01 - c$ for $c = 6.87$

8. $m + 7.787$ for $m = 54$

9. $t + 4.77$ for $t = 4.77$

10. $16.313 - d$ for $d = 0.92$

11. $h - 15.88$ for $h = 21.3$

12. $y + 116.75$ for $y = 12.7$

13. **H.O.T.** **What's the error?** A student subtracted $6.85 - 4.7$ and got 6.38. What is the correct answer? Explain the error.

_____

Comparing Eggs

Different types of birds lay eggs of different sizes. Small birds lay eggs that are smaller than those that are laid by larger birds. The table shows the average lengths and widths of five different birds' eggs.

Average Dimensions of Bird Eggs		
Bird	Length (m)	Width (m)
Canada Goose	0.086	0.058
Hummingbird	0.013	0.013
Raven	0.049	0.033
Robin	0.019	0.015
Turtledove	0.031	0.023

Canada Goose

Use the table for 14–17.

14. What is the difference in average length between the longest egg and the shortest egg?

_____

15. Which egg has a width that is eight thousandths of a meter shorter than its length?

_____

16. How many robin eggs, laid end to end, would be about equal in length to two raven eggs? Justify your answer.

_____

_____

_____

_____

17. A perfectly spherical egg would have an equal length and width. Which egg is closest to spherical? Justify your answer.

_____

_____

Model Decimal Multiplication

Essential Question How can you use a model to show multiplication of decimals?

Investigate

Materials ■ decimal models

Giant tortoises move very slowly. They can cover a distance of about 0.17 mile in 1 hour. At that rate, how far could a giant tortoise move in 4 hours?

A. Which operation should you use to find the distance? Why?

_____

_____

B. Use a decimal model. What does each small square represent?

_____

C. Start with the first column. Shade squares to represent the distance that a giant tortoise can move in 1 hour.

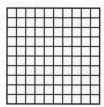

D. Shade additional squares to represent the distance that a giant tortoise can move in 4 hours. Describe your method.

_____

_____

E. How far could a giant tortoise move in 4 hours? Explain.

_____

_____

Draw Conclusions

1. **Explain** why you used only one decimal model to show the product.

   _____

   _____

2. **Comprehension** A student used this model to show 4×0.17. How does the model show the Distributive Property?

   _____

   _____

3. **Compare** the product of 0.17 and 4 with each of the factors. Which number has the greatest value? How does this compare to what happens when you multiply two whole numbers?

   _____

   _____

4. How is the problem 4×0.17 different than 4×1.7?

   _____

   _____

Make Connections

Jenna and her mom made a pan of cornbread. After Jenna's brother ate some of the cornbread, 0.8 of the pan was left. Jenna ate 0.2 of the leftover cornbread. How much of the pan of cornbread did Jenna eat?

Use a decimal model to find the product. 0.2×0.8

STEP 1

Shade columns to show 0.8 of the pan leftover.

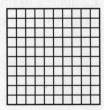

STEP 2

Double-shade 0.2 of 0.8.

Think: Shade 0.2 of each of the 0.1 already shaded.

STEP 3

To find how much of the pan of cornbread Jenna ate, count how many hundredths are double-shaded.

So, Jenna ate _____ of the cornbread.

Math Talk Why does it make sense that the product of 0.2 and 0.8 is less than the two factors, 0.2 and 0.8?

Name _____

Share and Show ·

Use the model to find the product.

1. $0.4 \times 0.8 =$ _____

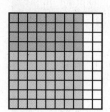

2. $0.8 \times 0.3 =$ _____

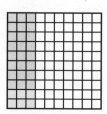

3. $0.6 \times 0.6 =$ _____

4. $0.5 \times 0.2 =$ _____

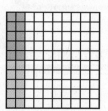

5. $0.7 \times 0.8 =$ _____

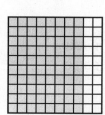

6. $0.9 \times 0.4 =$ _____

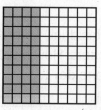

Write the multiplication problem shown by the model. Then find the product.

7.

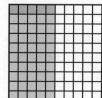

_____

8.

_____

9.

_____

Use a model to solve.

10. $3 \times 0.27 =$ _____

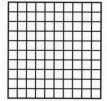

11. $0.5 \times 0.6 =$ _____

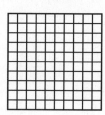

12. $4 \times 0.35 =$ _____

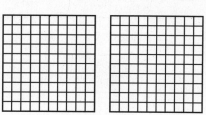

13. What's the Error? Fernando said that $0.4 \times 0.7 = 2.8$. Why does his answer not make sense? What is the correct answer?

_____

_____

_____

Problem Solving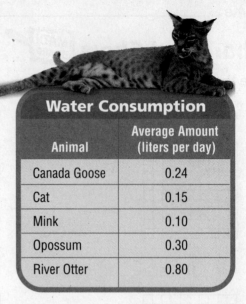

Use the table and decimal models for 14–16.

14. Each day, on average, a bobcat drinks 3 times the amount of water that a Canada goose drinks. How much water does a bobcat drink in one day?

Water Consumption	
Animal	**Average Amount (liters per day)**
Canada Goose	0.24
Cat	0.15
Mink	0.10
Opossum	0.30
River Otter	0.80

_____

15. Bald eagles drink water at a rate 0.2 times the rate of river otters. How much water does a bald eagle drink in one day?

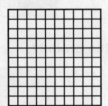

_____

····· SHOW YOUR WORK ·····

16. **Write Math ▶ Explain** how you could use a decimal model to find the amount of water that a river otter drinks in 6 hours.

_____

_____

_____

_____

_____

17. ⭐ **Test Prep** Jared has two pet snakes. His king snake is 0.9 meter in length. His corn snake is 0.8 times the length of his king snake. How long is his corn snake?

Ⓐ 0.63 meter   Ⓒ 1.7 meters

Ⓑ 0.72 meter   Ⓓ 7.2 meters

FOR MORE PRACTICE:
Standards Practice Book, pp. P27–P28

Name _____

Multiply Decimals

Essential Question How do you multiply decimals?

🔑 Activity

Materials ■ base-ten blocks

Use base-ten blocks to find the area of a bulletin board that is 1.2 meters wide by 1.3 meters long.

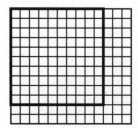

Think: Use ones, tenths, and hundredths to make a rectangle that is _____

units long and _____ units wide.

I used _____ one, _____ tenths, and _____ hundredths.

So, the area of the bulletin board is 1.2 × 1.3 = _____ square meters.

🔑 UNLOCK the Problem REAL WORLD

Last summer Rachel worked 38.5 hours per week at a grocery store. She earned $9.70 per hour. How much did she earn in a week?

> ● How can you estimate the product?
>
> _____
>
> _____

🔑 **Multiply** $9.70 × 38.5.

First estimate the product. $10 × 40 = _____

You can use the estimate to place the decimal in a product.

$$\begin{array}{r} \$9.70 \\ \times\,38.5 \\ \hline \end{array}$$

Multiply as you would with whole numbers.

The estimate is about $ _____,

so the decimal point should be

placed after $_____.

Compare your answer to your estimate.

Since the estimate is _____, the answer is reasonable.

So, Rachel earned _____ per week.

---

1. **What if** Rachel gets a raise of $1.50 per hour? How much will she earn when she works 38.5 hours?

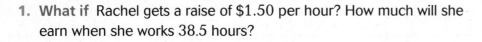

_____

Counting Decimal Places It is difficult to estimate the product of factors that are very small. Another way to place the decimal in a product is to add the numbers of decimal places in the factors.

 Example 1 Multiply 0.084 × 0.096.

$$\begin{array}{r} 0.084 \\ \times\, 0.096 \\ \hline \end{array}$$ _____ decimal places

_____ decimal places

Multiply as you would with whole numbers.

$$\begin{array}{r} \\ +\; \\ \hline \end{array}$$

_____ + _____, or _____ decimal places

Example 2 Evaluate 0.04n for n = 0.006.

$0.04n = 0.04\,(\underline{\hspace{2cm}})$ Substitute _____ for n.

$$\begin{array}{r} 0.006 \\ \times\; 0.04 \\ \hline \end{array}$$ _____ decimal places

_____ decimal places

_____ + _____, or _____ decimal places

So, 0.04n = _____ for n = 0.006.

Math Talk 0.04n is one way to write 0.04 times n. What are two other ways to write 0.04 times n?

---

2. Is the product of 0.5 and 3.052 greater than or less than 3.052? Explain.

_____

---

3. **H.O.T.** Look for a pattern. Explain.

0.645 × 1 = 0.645

0.645 × 10 = 6.45   The decimal point moves _____ place to the right.

0.645 × 100 = _____   The decimal point moves _____ places to the right.

0.645 × 1,000 = _____   The decimal point moves _____ places to the right.

_____

_____

Name _____

Share and Show

Estimate. Then find the product.

1. $12.42 × 28.6

_____ × _____ = _____

$$\begin{array}{r} \$12.42 \\ \times\ 28.6 \\ \hline \end{array}$$

Estimate.

Think: The estimate is about _____, so the decimal point should be placed after _____.

2. 32.5 × 7.4

_____

Algebra Evaluate the expression for $n = 9.4$.

3. 0.24n

4. 0.075n

5. 6.83n

_____   _____   _____

Math Talk Explain how estimation helps you know where to place the decimal in a product.

On Your Own

Estimate. Then find the product.

6. 29.14 × 5.2

7. 6.95 × 12

8. 0.055 × 1.82

9. 0.88 × 12.5

_____   _____   _____   _____

Algebra Evaluate the expression for $n = 7.2$.

10. 3.65n

11. 0.83n

12. 0.04n

13. 5.8n

_____   _____   _____   _____

UNLOCK the Problem REAL WORLD

Use the table for 14–16.

The table shows the major currency exchange rates for 2009. Read across each row to find equivalent amounts of each type of currency.

Different denominations of Euro

Major Currency Exchange Rates in 2009				
Currency	U.S. Dollar	Japanese Yen	European Euro	Canadian Dollar
U.S. Dollar	1	88.353	0.676	1.052
Japanese Yen	0.011	1	0.008	0.012
European Euro	1.479	130.692	1	1.556
Canadian Dollar	0.951	83.995	0.643	1

14. When Cameron went to Canada in 2007, he exchanged 40 U.S. dollars for 46.52 Canadian dollars. If Cameron exchanged 40 U.S. dollars in 2009, how much did he receive in Canadian dollars? Did he receive more or less than he received in 2007? How much more or less?

a. What do you need to find?

_____

_____

b. How will you use the table to solve the problem?

_____

_____

_____

_____

c. Complete the sentences.

40 U.S. dollars were worth _____ Canadian dollars in 2009.

So, Cameron would receive _____ (less or more) Canadian dollars in 2009.

15. 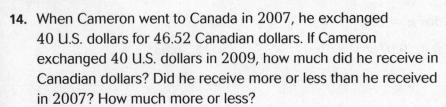 **H.O.T.** Based on the exchange rates in the table, which is more valuable, 1 U.S. dollar or 1 euro? **Explain**.

_____

_____

_____

16. ⭐ **Test Prep** Mr. Jackson needs to exchange his euros for yen. How many yen will he receive if he exchanges 30 euros? Round your answer to the nearest yen.

(A) 0.24 yen   (C) 3,921 yen

(B) 3,900 yen   (D) 16,337 yen

FOR MORE PRACTICE:
Standards Practice Book, pp. P29–P30

Name _____

✓ Mid-Chapter Checkpoint

▶ **Concepts and Skills**

1. Explain how to check the answer to 7.6 + 3.2 + 22.8 for reasonableness. (pp. 49–52)

_____

_____

_____

2. Find the product and explain how to place the decimal. 3.14 × 1.8 (pp. 57–60)

_____

_____

Estimate. Then find the sum or difference. (pp. 49–52)

3.   63.45
   + 17.65

_____

4. 22 + 6.7 + 4.159

_____

5.   9.18
  − 2.017

_____

6. 14.7 − 3.732

_____

Use a model to solve. (pp. 53–56)

7. 4 × 0.16

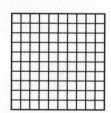

_____

8. 0.3 × 0.7

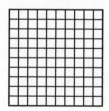

_____

9. 5 × 0.32

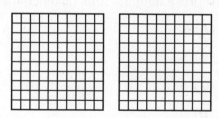

_____

Estimate. Then find the product. (pp. 57–60)

10. 1.4 × 3.9

_____

11. 0.07 × 0.03

_____

12. 0.44 × 16.2

_____

13. 118 × 1.6

_____

Fill in the bubble to show your answer.

14. Two samples of volcanic rock weighed 0.718 kilograms and 11.35 kilograms. What was the difference in the weights of the samples? (pp. 49–52)

Ⓐ 0.417 kilogram

Ⓑ 4.17 kilograms

Ⓒ 10.632 kilograms

Ⓓ 12.068 kilograms

15. At an electronics store, Ayana bought items priced at $14.98 and $129.95. The sales tax on her purchases was $7.25. What was the total charge for her purchases? (pp. 49–52)

Ⓐ $100.48

Ⓑ $137.68

Ⓒ $145.65

Ⓓ $152.18

16. Energy bars sell for $0.79 apiece. Find the total cost for 7 energy bars. (pp. 53–56)

Ⓐ $4.93

Ⓑ $5.53

Ⓒ $5.63

Ⓓ $55.30

17. A car traveled for 3.119 hours at an average rate of 53.797 miles per hour. How many decimal places are there in the number representing the total distance the car traveled? (pp. 57–60)

Ⓐ 3

Ⓑ 5

Ⓒ 6

Ⓓ 9

18. One dozen muffins cost $13.20. Elena needs 3.5 dozen muffins for the meeting. How much will the muffins cost? (pp. 57–60)

Ⓐ $16.70

Ⓑ $35.10

Ⓒ $45.20

Ⓓ $46.20

Name _____

Divide Decimals by Whole Numbers

Essential Question How do you divide a decimal number by a whole number?

🔑 UNLOCK the Problem · REAL · WORLD

Dan opened a savings account at a bank to save for a new snowboard. He earned $3.48 interest on his savings account for a 3-month period. What was the average amount of interest Dan earned per month on his savings account?

 Use a model to divide.

STEP 1

Finish shading the decimal models to show 3.48.

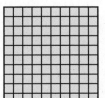 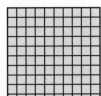 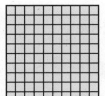 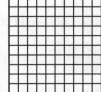

STEP 2

_____ the shaded

wholes into _____ equal

groups.

Divide _____

into _____ equal groups.

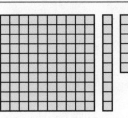

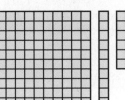

Each group contains _____ whole and _____ hundredths.

So, Dan earned an average of _____ in interest per month.

Math Talk Explain why your answer is reasonable.

- **What if** the same amount of interest was gained over 4 months? Explain how you would solve the problem.

_____

🔑 Example 1

Rachel and Desean received a tip of $6.34. How much will each receive if they split it evenly?

First estimate. 6 ÷ 2 = _____

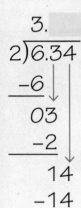

$$\begin{array}{r} 3. \\ 2\overline{)6.34} \\ -6\downarrow \\ \hline 03 \\ -2\downarrow \\ \hline 14 \\ -14 \\ \hline 0 \end{array}$$

Think: 6.34 is shared between 2 groups.

Divide the ones. Place a decimal point after the ones place in the quotient.

Divide the tenths and then the hundredths. When the remainder is zero and there are no more digits in the dividend, the division is complete.

So, each will receive _____.

🔑 Example 2 Divide 42.133 ÷ 7.

First estimate. 42 ÷ 7 = _____

$$\begin{array}{r} 6.0 \\ 7\overline{)42.133} \\ -42 \\ \hline 01 \\ -0 \\ \hline 13 \\ -7 \\ \hline 63 \\ - \\ \hline \end{array}$$

Think: 42.133 is shared among 7 groups.

Divide the ones. Place a decimal point after the ones place in the quotient.

Divide the tenths. Since 1 tenth cannot be shared among 7 groups, write a zero in the quotient. Regroup the 1 tenth as 10 hundredths. Now you have 13 hundredths.

Continue to divide until the remainder is zero and there are no more digits in the dividend.

Check your answer.

$$\begin{array}{r} 6.019 \\ \times7 \\ \hline \end{array}$$

Multiply the divisor by the quotient to check your answer.

So, 42.133 ÷ 7 = _____.

Math Talk Explain how to tell if your answer is reasonable.

Name _____

Share and Show

1. Jayla divided 2.48 decimal models into 4 equal groups. What decimal names each group? _____

  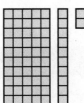 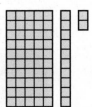

What is the quotient? _____

What is 2.48 ÷ 4? _____

Estimate. Then find the quotient.

2. 7)$17.15   ✓3. 4)1.068   4. 12)60.84   ✓5. 18.042 ÷ 6

_____ _____ _____ _____

Math Talk Explain how you know where to place the decimal point in the quotient when dividing a decimal by a whole number.

On Your Own

Estimate. Then find the quotient.

6. 9)461.7   7. 15)45.75   8. 8)0.744   9. 19)8.17

_____ _____ _____ _____

Practice: Copy and Solve Estimate. Then find the quotient.

10. $21.24 ÷ 6   11. 28.63 ÷ 7   12. 1.505 ÷ 35   13. 0.108 ÷ 18

Algebra Evaluate the expression.

14. $(3.11 + 4.0) ÷ 9$ 15. $(6.18 - 1.32) ÷ 3$ 16. $(18 - 5.76) ÷ 6$

_____ _____ _____

Problem Solving REAL WORLD

Pose a Problem

17. This table shows the average height in inches for girls and boys at ages 8, 10, 12, and 14 years.

Average Height (in.)				
	Age 8	Age 10	Age 12	Age 14
Girls	50.75	55.50	60.50	62.50
Boys	51.00	55.25	59.00	65.20

To find the average growth per year for girls from age 8 to age 12, Emma knew she had to find the amount of growth between age 8 and age 12, then divide that number by the number of years between age 8 and age 12.

Emma used this expression: $(60.50 - 50.75) \div 4$

She evaluated the expression using the order of operations.

Write the expression.	$(60.50 - 50.75) \div 4$
Perform operations in parentheses.	$9.75 \div 4$
Divide.	2.4375

So, the average amount of growth for girls ages 8–12 is 2.4375 inches.

Write a new problem using the information in the table for the average height for boys. Use division in your problem.

Pose a Problem	Solve Your Problem

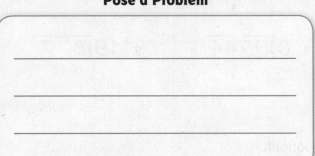

18. **H.O.T.** Wan Chen was 50.75 inches tall at age 8 and 60.50 inches tall at age 14. **Compare** her average amount of growth per year to the average shown on the chart.

_____

_____

_____

Name _____

Model Decimal Division

Essential Question How can you use a model to divide a decimal by a decimal?

Materials ■ decimal models, color pencils, scissors

The weight of an object depends on the pull of gravity where the object is located. An object that weighs 0.57 pound on the planet Mars will weigh 1.71 pounds on the planet Neptune. How many times greater is the pull of gravity on Neptune than the pull of gravity on Mars?

A. Which operation should you use to find the answer? Why?

_____

_____

_____

Mars

B. Use decimal models to find 1.71 ÷ 0.57. Describe your method.

_____

_____

_____

_____

_____

_____

So, the pull of gravity on Neptune is _____ times greater than the pull of gravity on Mars.

C. An object that weighs 2.34 pounds on Earth will weigh 0.39 pound on the moon. How many times greater is the pull of gravity on Earth than the pull of gravity on the moon? Use decimal models.

_____

Draw Conclusions

1. **Analyzing** There are 3 groups of 5.7 in 17.1. How can you use this fact to find 17.1 ÷ 5.7? What is the quotient?

   _____

   _____

2. **H.O.T.** **Compare** the division problem you solved on the previous page with the problem 17.1 ÷ 5.7 = 3. What patterns do you see?

   _____

   _____

3. **Predict** the quotient 171 ÷ 57. _____

4. **Describe** what happens to the quotient of a division problem when you multiply the dividend and divisor by the same power of 10.

   _____

Make Connections

You can use a model or use patterns to help you divide a decimal by a decimal.

STEP 1

Use decimal models to find 1.25 ÷ 0.25. _____

STEP 2

Multiply the dividend and divisor of 1.25 ÷ 0.25 by 10 and divide.

12.5 ÷ _____ = 5

STEP 3

Multiply the dividend and divisor of 1.25 ÷ 0.25 by 100 and divide.

_____ ÷ _____ = _____

So, 1.25 ÷ 0.25 = _____.

If you multiply the dividend and divisor by the same power of 10, how is the quotient affected?

_____

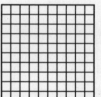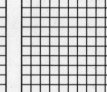

$$0.25\overline{)1.25}$$

> **Math Talk** Explain how to use decimal models to find 6.5 ÷ 1.3.

Name _____

Share and Show   . . . .

Identify the dividend, divisor, and quotient shown by the model.

1.

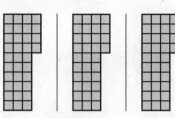

dividend: _____

divisor: _____

quotient: _____

2.

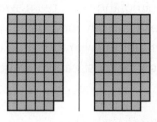

dividend: _____

divisor: _____

quotient: _____

Use a model to find the quotient.

3. $9.3 \div 3.1 =$ _____

4. $7.5 \div 1.5 =$ _____

5. $2.1 \div 0.7 =$ _____

✓ 6. $0.52 \div 0.13 =$ _____

7. $4.14 \div 1.38 =$ _____

8. $4.04 \div 1.01 =$ _____

9. $3 \div 1.5 =$ _____

10. $2.8 \div 0.7 =$ _____

11. $0.78 \div 0.26 =$ _____

12. $4.5 \div 0.9 =$ _____

13. $2 \div 0.4 =$ _____

14. $7.8 \div 1.3 =$ _____

Use the model to find the missing value.

✓ 15. $2.64 \div$ _____ $= 2$

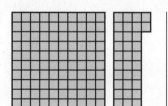

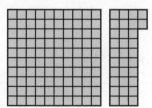

16. _____ $\div 0.27 = 4$

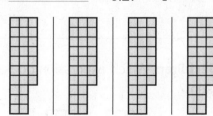

17. **Write Math** ▸ Carla knows that $1.74 \div 0.29 = 6$. Explain how she can find the quotient $174 \div 29$ using mental math.

_____

_____

_____

Problem Solving  REAL WORLD

18. The captain of the swim team swam a distance of 1.92 miles each day for 2 days. He challenged each team member to swim the same distance as he swam. How far must each member swim?

_____

19. Sakura swam the distance in 4 days. How far did she swim each day? Use models to solve.

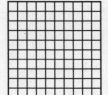 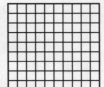 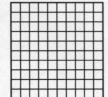 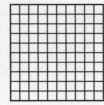

_____

20. **Write Math** ▶ **What's the Question?** The answer is 0.64 mile per day.

_____

_____

_____

21. ⭐ **Test Prep** Which expression does the model represent?

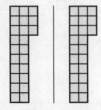

Ⓐ 0.32 ÷ 3   **Ⓒ** 0.46 ÷ 0.23

Ⓑ 0.23 ÷ 2   **Ⓓ** 0.23 ÷ 0.46

FOR MORE PRACTICE:
Standards Practice Book, pp. P33–P34

Name _____

Divide with Decimals

Essential Question How do you divide whole numbers and decimals by decimals?

CONNECT Find each quotient to discover a pattern.

$4 \div 2 =$ _____

$40 \div 20 =$ _____

$400 \div 200 =$ _____

When you multiply both the dividend and the divisor by the same

power of _____, the quotient is the _____. You can use this fact to help you divide decimals.

UNLOCK the Problem REAL WORLD

Tami is training for a triathlon. In a triathlon, athletes compete in three events: swimming, cycling, and running. She cycled 66.5 miles in 3.5 hours. If she cycled at a constant speed, how far did she cycle in 1 hour?

> **Remember**
> Compatible numbers are pairs of numbers that are easy to compute mentally.

 Divide 66.5 ÷ 3.5.

Estimate using compatible numbers.

$60 \div 3 =$ _____

STEP 1

Make the divisor a whole number by multiplying the divisor and dividend by 10.

Think: $3.5 \times 10 = 35$ $66.5 \times 10 = 665$

STEP 2

Divide.

$3.5 \overline{)66.5}$

$35 \overline{)665}$

So, Tami cycled _____ in 1 hour.

- **Explain** whether your answer is reasonable.

_____

🔑 Example 1 Divide 17.25 ÷ 5.75. Check.

STEP 1

Make the divisor a whole number by multiplying the divisor and dividend by _____.

$5.75\overline{)17.25}$

5.75 × _____ = _____

17.25 × _____ = _____

STEP 2

Divide.

$575\overline{)1,725}$

STEP 3

Check.

So, 17.25 ÷ 5.75 = _____.

Sometimes, you may need to add a zero to the right of the dividend so that you can move the decimal point.

🔑 Example 2 Divide 37.8 ÷ 0.14.

STEP 1

Make the divisor a whole number by multiplying the divisor and dividend by _____.

$0.14\overline{)37.80}$

_____ × _____ = _____

_____ × _____ = _____

 ERROR Alert

Be careful to move the decimal point in the dividend the same number of places that you moved the decimal point in the divisor.

STEP 2

Divide.

$14\overline{)3,780}$

So, 37.8 ÷ 0.14 = _____.

Math Talk Explain how to check the quotient.

Name _____

Share and Show ....

1. Find the quotient.

Think: Make the divisor a whole number by

multiplying the divisor and dividend by _____.

$$14.8\overline{)99.456}$$

Estimate. Then find the quotient.

2. $10.80 ÷ $1.35

3. 26.4 ÷ 1.76

4. $8.7\overline{)53.07}$

Math Talk Explain how you know how many places to move the decimal point in the divisor and the dividend.

On Your Own ....

Estimate. Then find the quotient.

5. 75 ÷ 12.5

6. 544.6 ÷ 1.75

7. $2.7\overline{)22.41}$

Practice: Copy and Solve Find the quotient.

8. 2.64 ÷ 0.2

9. 1.43 ÷ 1.1

10. $0.3\overline{)3.15}$

11. $0.78\overline{)0.234}$

Algebra Evaluate the expression.

12. 36.4 + (9.2 − 4.9 ÷ 7)

13. 4^2 ÷ 2.5 − 3.2 × 0.043

14. 142 ÷ (42 − 6.5) × 3.9

Amoebas

Amoebas are tiny one-celled organisms. Their flexible outer membranes enable them to constantly change the shape of their bodies. Amoebas can range in size from 0.01 mm to 5 mm in length. You can study amoebas by using a microscope or by studying photographic enlargements of them.

Jacob has a photograph of an amoeba that has been enlarged 1,000 times. The length of the amoeba in the photo is 60 mm. What is the actual length of the amoeba?

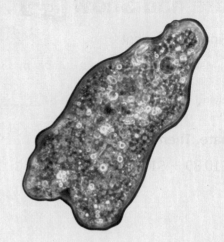

Divide 60 ÷ 1,000 by looking for a pattern.

60 ÷ 1 = 60

60 ÷ 10 = 6.0   The decimal point moves _____ place to the left.

60 ÷ 100 = _____   The decimal point moves _____ places to the left.

60 ÷ 1,000 = _____   The decimal point moves _____ places to the left.

So, the actual length of the amoeba is _____ mm.

15. **Explain** the pattern.

_____

_____

16. Jacob has a photograph of *Amoeba proteus* that has been enlarged 100 times. In the photo, the amoeba appears to have a length of 70 mm. What is its actual length? Explain your reasoning.

_____

_____

17. *Pelomyxa palustris* is the largest amoeba found in pond water. Some specimens are as large as 4.9 mm in length. How long would this amoeba appear in a photograph enlarged 1,000 times? Justify your answer.

_____

_____

Solve a Simpler Problem · Estimate with Decimals

Essential Question How can you use estimation with decimals to make a problem simpler?

UNLOCK the Problem REAL WORLD

In February 2007, tropical cyclone Gamede struck the island of La Réunion in the Indian Ocean. For 3 days, rain fell at a rate of 36.3 centimeters every 6.6 hours, a world record. At that rate, how much rain fell in 9.75 hours?

Estimate by rounding to whole numbers and solve a simpler problem.

Rain fell at a rate of about 35 cm every 7 hours. How much rain fell in 10 hours?

Read the Problem	Solve the Problem
What do I need to find? I need to find the amount of rain that fell in _____ hours.	• First find how much rain fell in 1 hour. $35 \div 7 =$ _____
What information do I need to use? I need to use the amount of rain that fell in _____ hours.	• Then find how much rain fell in 10 hours. _____ $\times 10 =$ _____
How will I use the information? First I will _____ the total rainfall by hours to find how much rain fell in 1 hour. Then I will _____ the amount of rain that fell in 1 hour by _____ to find how much rain fell in _____ hours.	

So, _____ centimeters of rain fell in 10 hours.

1. **Reflect** Use the original numbers and the steps from the simpler problem to find how much rain fell in 9.75 hours.

_____

_____

🔒 Try Another Problem

Justine drove 153.5 miles in 2.5 hours. At that rate, how far can she drive in 5.55 hours?

Estimate by rounding to whole numbers and solve a simpler problem.

Justine drove about _____ miles in 3 hours. How

far can she drive in _____ hours?

Read the Problem

What do I need to find?

What information do I need to use?

How will I use the information?

Solve the Problem

> **Math Talk** Explain how the strategy of solving a simpler problem helped you solve the problem.

So, in 6 hours, Justine can drive _____ miles.

2. **Reflect** Use the original numbers and the steps from the simpler problem to find how far Justine can drive in 5.55 hours.

_____

_____

3. How could you use the fact that 5.5 hours is about twice 2.5 hours to estimate how far Justine could drive in 5.5 hours?

_____

_____

Name _____

Share and Show MATH BOARD ....

UNLOCK the Problem *Tips*
√ Circle the question.
√ Underline important facts.

☑ **1.** Carlos bought 3 sweaters on sale for a total of $86.85. Nicole bought 2 sweaters at the same price per sweater. How much did she pay for her purchases?

First, round to whole numbers and solve a simpler problem.

Estimated cost per sweater: _____

Estimated total cost of 2 sweaters: _____

Next, find the exact solution.

_____

So, Nicole paid _____ for the sweaters.

SHOW YOUR WORK

2. **H.O.T.** **What if** the price Carlos paid had included $4.50 in sales tax? How much would Nicole have paid for her purchases if her total cost included $3.00 in sales tax?

_____

☑ **3.** Autumn worked 28.5 hours at a rate of $7.80 per hour. April earned the same total amount that Autumn earned by working only 22.8 hours. How much did April earn per hour?

_____

4. Desmond is driving to visit his grandmother. At the beginning of the drive, the odometer on Desmond's car read 18,577.6 miles. At the end of the drive, the odometer read 19,019.8 miles. Desmond's total travel time was 8.25 hours. What was his average rate of speed for the journey?

_____

5. Ashley can line one edge of her patio with bricks measuring 25.2 centimeters on a side or with tiles measuring 32.4 centimeters on a side. If it takes 45 bricks to line the patio, how many tiles does it take?

_____

On Your Own . . . .

6. Harlan is training to run a marathon. One day he ran 13.3 miles in 1.75 hours. The following day he ran at the same average rate of speed but for only 0.85 hour. How far did he run?

_____

7. Nan checked a novel out of the library. Each of the first 2 days that she had the book she read 47 pages. Each of the next 3 days she read 38 pages. After reading for 5 days, she was 119 pages from the end. How many pages did the book have?

_____

8. ⚡H.O.T. Using 2 horizontal lines and 2 vertical lines, you can make a 9-square tic-tac-toe pattern. How many squares will there be in a pattern made from 8 horizontal and 8 vertical lines?

_____

9. ⟩ Write Math ▶ Nolan is 3 times as old as his son. The sum of Nolan's age and his son's age is 68. **Explain** how you could find Nolan's age.

_____

_____

_____

_____

10. ⭐ **Test Prep** You can travel from Oakdale to Sycamore in 1.5 hours if you average 40.5 miles per hour. What speed must you travel in order to complete the journey in only 1.2 hours?

   Ⓐ 40.2 miles per hour   Ⓒ 48.6 miles per hour

   Ⓑ 40.8 miles per hour   Ⓓ 50.625 miles per hour

**Choose a
STRATEGY**

Work Backward
Solve a Simpler Problem
Choose an Operation
Use a Model
Use a Formula
Draw a Diagram

····· SHOW YOUR WORK ┊····

Name _____

✓ Chapter 2 Review/Test

▶ Concepts and Skills

1. Divide 12.344 ÷ 4. Explain how to check your answer. (pp. 63–66)

   _____

   _____

2. Divide 78.3 ÷ 2.9. Explain how to use compatible numbers
   to estimate the quotient and decide if your answer is
   reasonable. (pp. 71–74)

   _____

   _____

Estimate. Then find the sum or difference. (pp. 49–52)

3. 7.6 + 3.2 + 22.8	4. 452.3 − 74.06	5. 520.85
		  − 93.807
			6. 54
			   0.7
			 + 11.23

Estimate. Then find the product. (pp. 57–60)

7. 375.1 × 0.9	8. 0.7 × 0.3	9. $32.21 × 7	10. 9.23 × 0.79

Estimate. Then find the quotient. (pp. 63–66, 71–74)

11. 278.53 ÷ 7	12. 42)3.276	13. 9.2)619.16	14. 1.5 ÷ 0.03

Fill in the bubble to show your answer.

15. The distance from Bisbee to Ferndale is 1,065.9 miles. A TV tower between Bisbee and Ferndale is 75.4 miles from Bisbee. How far is the tower from Ferndale? (pp. 49–52)

  (A) 311.9 miles

  (B) 990.5 miles

  (C) 1,090.5 miles

  (D) 1,141.3 miles

16. The distance around the outside of Cedar Park is 0.8 mile. Joanie ran 0.25 of the distance during her lunch break. How far did she run? (pp. 53–56)

  (A) 0.2 mile

  (B) 0.25 mile

  (C) 1.05 miles

  (D) 2 miles

17. What is the cost of 6.5 pounds of trail mix selling for $2.98 per pound? (pp. 57–60)

  (A) $18.37

  (B) $19.27

  (C) $19.37

  (D) $32.78

18. Lana paid $36.72 for 4 CDs. What was the average cost of each CD? (pp. 63–66)

  (A) $9.18

  (B) $9.28

  (C) $12.24

  (D) $148.88

19. Mr. DeLuca had $568.34 in a bank account. How much money did he have left in his bank account after he used his debit card two times, each time for $27.50? (pp. 49–52)

  (A) $513.34   (C) $540.84

  (B) $523.34   (D) $595.84

Fill in the bubble to show your answer.

20. Zoe earned $28.38 working for 3.3 hours. How much did she earn per hour? (pp. 71–74)

Ⓐ $8.30

Ⓑ $8.33

Ⓒ $8.56

Ⓓ $8.60

21. A one-celled organism measures 32 millimeters in length in a photograph. If the photo has been enlarged by a factor of 100, what is the actual length of the organism? (pp. 71–74)

Ⓐ   0.32 millimeter

Ⓑ   3.2 millimeters

Ⓒ   320 millimeters

Ⓓ 3,200 millimeters

22. You can buy 5 T-shirts at Baxter's for the same price that you can buy 4 T-shirts at Bixby's. If Bixby's sells T-shirts for $11.80, how much do they cost at Baxter's? (pp. 75–78)

Ⓐ $9.44

Ⓑ $10.80

Ⓒ $11.55

Ⓓ $14.75

23. The mens' world record for the high jump is 2.45 meters. A puma can jump about 1.9 times as high. What is the height a puma can jump? (pp. 57–60)

Ⓐ 4.5 meters

Ⓑ 4.555 meters

Ⓒ 4.565 meters

Ⓓ 4.655 meters

▶ Short Answer

24. Is the product 0.53×1.95 greater than or less than 1.95? Explain how you can tell without multiplying. (pp. 57–60)

_____

_____

_____

25. To estimate the quotient $98.3 \div 52.6$, Brady used compatible numbers: $100 \div 5 = 20$. Is his estimate reasonable? Explain.
(pp. 71–74)

_____

_____

_____

▶ Performance Task

26. The Hawk Mountain Sanctuary in eastern Pennsylvania is one of the best sites in the United States to watch the fall migration of predatory birds. One of the hiking trails that loops around the sanctuary is 5.25 miles long.

Ⓐ If a group of hikers completes the trail in 3.5 hours in September, what is their average rate per hour?

_____

_____

Ⓑ If the hikers walk 0.25 mile per hour faster in October, how long will it take them to finish the hike?

_____

_____

Ⓒ The hikers complete the 5.25-mile trail in 4.2 hours in November and a 6.5-mile trail in 5 hours. Is their rate faster on the 5.25-mile trail or the 6.5-mile trail? Explain.

_____

_____

Decimals and Fractions

Show What You Know

Check your understanding of important skills.

Name _____

▶ **Compare and Order Whole Numbers** Write <, >, or =.

1. 327 ◯ 370

2. 662,117 ◯ 662,117

3. 7,821 ◯ 7,283

▶ **Model Fractions** Write a fraction that names the shaded part.

4.

5.

6.

_____ | _____ | _____

▶ **Add and Subtract Like Fractions** Write the sum or difference in simplest form.

7. $\frac{1}{8} + \frac{3}{8}$

8. $\frac{15}{16} - \frac{3}{16}$

9. $\frac{6}{7} + \frac{3}{7}$

10. $\frac{5}{9} - \frac{2}{9}$

Esmeralda is trying to find the music that mysteriously disappeared from her mom's MP3 player. If she can figure out the time for each missing song, she can match the times to the song titles on her mom's computer. Be a Math Detective and help Esmeralda find her mom's missing music. Here are some clues: Song 2 is $1\frac{3}{6}$ minutes shorter than Song 1. Song 2 plus Song 3 is 2 minutes longer than Song 1.

Playlist	
Song	Time (min)
Song 1	$3\frac{5}{6}$
Song 2	
Song 3	

Vocabulary Builder

▶ **Visualize It** ••

Complete the flow map using review words.

Add Fractions

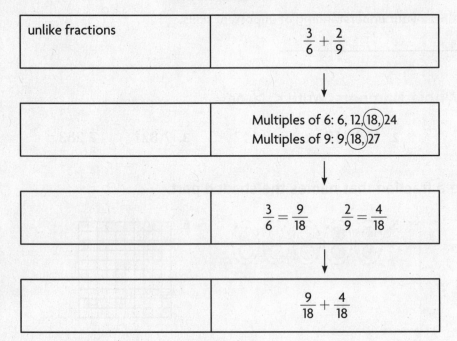

| unlike fractions | $\frac{3}{6} + \frac{2}{9}$ |

↓

| | Multiples of 6: 6, 12, ⃝18, 24
Multiples of 9: 9, ⃝18, 27 |

↓

| | $\frac{3}{6} = \frac{9}{18}$ $\frac{2}{9} = \frac{4}{18}$ |

↓

| | $\frac{9}{18} + \frac{4}{18}$ |

▶ **Understand Vocabulary** ••••••••••••••••••••••••••••••••••••••

Complete the sentences using the preview words.

1. A _____ is a number represented by a
whole number that is not zero and a fraction.

2. Fractions with different denominators are

_____ .

3. The _____ is the least common
multiple of two or more denominators.

4. A _____ is a decimal representation of
a number that has a repeating pattern that continues endlessly.

5. A _____ is a decimal representation of
a number that eventually ends.

GO
Online

• eStudent Edition • Multimedia eGlossary

Name _____

Fractions and Decimals

Essential Question How do you convert between fractions and decimals?

CONNECT You can use place value to write a decimal as a fraction or a mixed number. A **mixed number** is a number represented by a whole number greater than zero and a fraction, such as $1\frac{1}{2}$.

Place Value

Ones	Tenths	Hundredths	Thousandths
1	2	3	4

 UNLOCK the Problem REAL WORLD

The African pygmy hedgehog is a popular pet in North America. The average African pygmy hedgehog weighs between 0.5 lb and 1.25 lb. How can these weights be written as fractions or mixed numbers?

- How can you find the greatest common factor (GCF) of two numbers?

_____

_____

_____

 Write 0.5 as a fraction and 1.25 as a mixed number in simplest form.

A 0.5

0.5 is five _____.

$0.5 = \dfrac{5}{}$

Use division and the

GCF, _____, to write the fraction in simplest form.

$\dfrac{5}{} = \dfrac{5 \div }{ \div } = \dfrac{}{}$

B 1.25

1.25 is one and

_____.

$1.25 = 1\dfrac{}{}$

Use division and the GCF,

_____, to write the fraction in simplest form.

$1\dfrac{}{} = \dfrac{ \div }{ \div } = 1\dfrac{}{}$

So, the average African pygmy hedgehog weighs between

_____ lb and _____ lb.

Math Talk Explain how you can use place value to write 0.05 and 0.005 as fractions in simplest form.

Terminating and Repeating Decimals You can use division to write a fraction or a mixed number as a decimal.

 Example Write the mixed number or fraction as a decimal. Tell whether the decimal terminates or repeats.

A $6\frac{3}{8}$

A **terminating decimal** eventually ends.

STEP 1

Use division to rename the fraction part as a decimal.

The quotient has _____ decimal places.

_____

STEP 2

Add the whole number to the decimal.

$6 +$ _____ = _____

So, $6\frac{3}{8} =$ _____. The decimal form of $6\frac{3}{8}$ is a _____ decimal.

$$8\overline{)3.000}$$

$$\underline{}$$

$$\underline{}$$

$$\underline{}$$

$$0$$

> **Math Talk** Explain why zeros were placed after the decimal point in the dividend.

B $\frac{5}{11}$

A **repeating decimal** has one or more digits that repeat endlessly.

STEP 1

Use division to rename the fraction as a decimal.

_____ repeats in the quotient.

_____

STEP 2

Write the repeating decimal.

$\frac{5}{11} = 0.454545...$ $\frac{5}{11} = 0.\overline{45}$

So, $\frac{5}{11} =$ _____ or _____ .

The decimal form of $\frac{5}{11}$ is a _____ decimal.

$$
\begin{array}{r}
0.45 \\
11\overline{)5.0000} \\
-44 \\
\hline
60 \\
-55 \\
\hline
 \\
 \\
5
\end{array}
$$

> **Math Idea**
> To write a repeating decimal, show the pattern and then three dots, or draw a bar over the repeating digits.

Name _____

Share and Show

Write as a fraction or as a mixed number in simplest form.

1. $95.5 = 95\dfrac{5}{\boxed{}} = \boxed{}$

2. 0.6

✓ 3. 5.75

Write as a decimal. Tell whether the decimal terminates or repeats.

4. $\dfrac{7}{8}$

✓ 5. $\dfrac{2}{3}$

6. $\dfrac{3}{25}$

Math Talk Explain how you know a decimal is repeating.

On Your Own

Write as a fraction or as a mixed number in simplest form.

7. 0.27

8. 0.055

9. 2.45

Write as a decimal. Tell whether the decimal terminates or repeats.

10. $\dfrac{1}{6}$

11. $3\dfrac{1}{5}$

12. $2\dfrac{11}{20}$

Identify a decimal and a fraction in simplest form for the point.

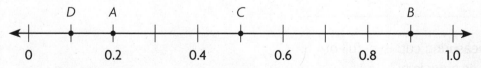

13. Point A

14. Point B

15. Point C

16. Point D

Problem Solving · REAL WORLD

Use the table for 17–19.

Ozark Trail Hiking Club		
Hiker	**June**	**July**
Maria	2.95	$2\frac{5}{8}$
Devin	3.25	$3\frac{1}{8}$
Kelsey	3.15	$2\frac{7}{8}$
Zoey	2.85	$3\frac{3}{8}$

17. Members of the Ozark Trail Hiking Club hiked a steep section of the trail in June and July. The table shows the distances club members hiked in miles. Write Maria's July distance as a decimal.

_____

18. Write Kelsey's June hiking distance as a fraction in simplest form.

_____

19. How much farther did Zoey hike in July than in June? **Explain** how you found your answer.

_____

_____

20. **H.O.T.** **What's the Error?** Tabitha's hiking distance in July was $2\frac{1}{6}$ miles. She wrote the distance as $2.\overline{16}$. What error did she make?

_____

_____

_____

21. **Write Math** ▶ Write $\frac{4}{9}$, $\frac{5}{9}$, and $\frac{6}{9}$ as decimals. What pattern do you see? Use the pattern to predict the decimal form of $\frac{7}{9}$ and $\frac{8}{9}$.

_____

_____

_____

22. ⭐ **Test Prep** Winona's measuring cup is $\frac{5}{18}$ full of water. What is this amount as a decimal?

(A) 0.27

(B) $0.2\overline{7}$

(C) 0.28

(D) $0.\overline{28}$

Name _____

Compare and Order Fractions and Decimals

Essential Question How do you compare and order fractions and decimals?

To compare fractions with the same denominators, compare the numerators. To compare fractions with the same numerators, compare the denominators.

Same Denominators

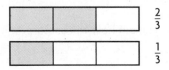 $\dfrac{2}{3}$

$\dfrac{1}{3}$

Two of three equal parts is greater than one of three equal parts.

So, $\dfrac{2}{3} > \dfrac{1}{3}$.

Same Numerators

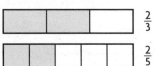 $\dfrac{2}{3}$

$\dfrac{2}{5}$

Two of three equal parts is greater than two of five equal parts.

So, $\dfrac{2}{3} > \dfrac{2}{5}$.

🔑 UNLOCK the Problem › REAL WORLD

Three new flowering dogwood trees were planted in a park in Springfield, Missouri. The trees were $6\frac{1}{2}$ ft, $5\frac{2}{3}$ ft, and $5\frac{5}{8}$ ft tall. Order the plant heights from least to greatest.

To compare and order fractions with unlike denominators, write equivalent fractions with common denominators.

> **Remember**
> • Equivalent fractions are fractions that name the same amount or part.
> • A common denominator is a denominator that is the same in two or more fractions.

 Order $6\frac{1}{2}$, $5\frac{2}{3}$, and $5\frac{5}{8}$ from least to greatest.

STEP 1

Compare the whole numbers first.

$6\frac{1}{2}$ $5\frac{2}{3}$ $5\frac{5}{8}$

5 ◯ 6

STEP 2

If the whole numbers are the same, compare the fractions.

Use common denominators to write equivalent fractions.

$5\dfrac{2 \times 8}{3 \times 8} = 5\underline{}$ $5\dfrac{5 \times }{8 \times } = 5\underline{}$

Think: _____ is a multiple of 3 and 8,

so _____ is a common denominator.

STEP 3

Compare the numerators.

Order the fractions from least to greatest.

$5\underline{} < 5\underline{} < 6\frac{1}{2}$

So, from least to greatest, the order is _____ ft, _____ ft, _____ ft.

Math Talk Explain how you could compare $3\frac{3}{4}$ and $3\frac{3}{7}$.

Fractions and Decimals You can compare fractions and decimals.

🔑 One Way Compare to $\frac{1}{2}$.

Compare 0.92 and $\frac{2}{7}$. Write <, >, or =.

STEP 1 Compare 0.92 to $\frac{1}{2}$.

0.92 ◯ $\frac{1}{2}$

STEP 2 Compare $\frac{2}{7}$ to $\frac{1}{2}$.

$\frac{2}{7}$ ◯ $\frac{1}{2}$

So, 0.92 ◯ $\frac{2}{7}$.

Math Talk Explain how to compare $\frac{2}{7}$ to $\frac{1}{2}$.

🔑 Another Way Rewrite the fraction as a decimal.

Compare 0.8 and $\frac{3}{4}$. Write <, >, or =.

STEP 1 Write $\frac{3}{4}$ as a decimal.

$4\overline{)3.00}$

$-\underline{}$

$-\underline{}$

0

$\frac{3}{4} =$ _____

STEP 2 Use <, >, or = to compare the decimals.

0.80 ◯ _____

So, 0.8 ◯ $\frac{3}{4}$.

You can use a number line to order fractions and decimals.

🔑 Example Use a number line to order 0.95, $\frac{3}{10}$, $\frac{1}{4}$, and 0.45 from least to greatest.

STEP 1 Write each fraction as a decimal.

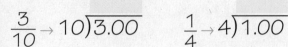

$\frac{3}{10} \rightarrow 10\overline{)3.00}$ $\qquad$ $\frac{1}{4} \rightarrow 4\overline{)1.00}$

Math Idea
- Numbers read from left to right on a number line are in order from least to greatest.
- Numbers read from right to left are in order from greatest to least.

STEP 2 Locate each decimal on a number line.

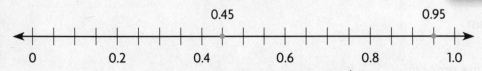

So, from least to greatest, the order is _____, _____, _____, _____.

© Houghton Mifflin Harcourt Publishing Company

Name _____

Share and Show

Order from least to greatest.

1. $3\frac{3}{6}$, $3\frac{5}{8}$, $2\frac{9}{10}$

Think: Compare the whole numbers first.

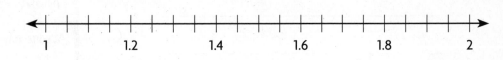

$3\frac{3 \times}{6 \times}\rule{1cm}{0.4pt} = 3\rule{1cm}{0.4pt}$ $\qquad$ $3\frac{5 \times}{8 \times}\rule{1cm}{0.4pt} = 3\rule{1cm}{0.4pt}$ $\qquad$ _____, _____, _____

Write <, >, or =.

✓ 2. $0.8 \bigcirc \frac{4}{12}$ | **3.** $0.22 \bigcirc \frac{1}{4}$ | **4.** $\frac{1}{20} \bigcirc 0.06$

Use a number line to order from least to greatest.

✓ 5. $1\frac{4}{5}$, 1.25, $1\frac{1}{10}$

```
←——|——|——|——|——|——|——|——|——|——|——|——|——|——|——|——|——|——|——|——|——→
    1        1.2        1.4        1.6        1.8         2
```

_____

Math Talk Explain how to compare $\frac{3}{5}$ and 0.37 by comparing to $\frac{1}{2}$.

On Your Own

Order from least to greatest.

6. $1\frac{3}{4}$, $\frac{5}{7}$, $1\frac{3}{5}$

7. 0.6, $\frac{2}{3}$, 0.66

8. $\frac{1}{2}$, $\frac{2}{5}$, $\frac{7}{15}$

Write <, >, or =.

9. $\frac{7}{15} \bigcirc \frac{7}{10}$ | **10.** $\frac{1}{8} \bigcirc 0.125$ | **11.** $7\frac{1}{3} \bigcirc 6\frac{2}{3}$

Order from greatest to least.

12. $5\frac{1}{2}$, 5.05, $5\frac{5}{9}$

13. $\frac{37}{10}$, $3\frac{2}{5}$, $3\frac{1}{4}$

14. $\frac{5}{7}$, $\frac{5}{6}$, $\frac{5}{12}$

Problem Solving  REAL WORLD

Use the table for 15–19.

15. In one week, Altoona, PA, and Bethlehem, PA, received snowfall every day, Monday through Friday. On which days did Altoona receive more snowfall than Bethlehem?

_____

16. **H.O.T.** **What if** Altoona received an additional 0.3 inch of snow on Thursday? How would the total amount of snow in Altoona compare to the amount received in Bethlehem that day?

_____

_____

17. **Explain** two ways you could compare the snowfall amounts in Altoona and Bethlehem on Monday.

_____

_____

_____

18. **Explain** how you could compare the snowfall amounts in Altoona on Thursday and Friday.

_____

_____

_____

19. The snowfall amounts recorded in inches in Reading, PA, on Monday through Friday during the same week were $2\frac{2}{5}$, $3\frac{1}{8}$, $2\frac{4}{5}$, $4\frac{2}{3}$, and $2\frac{7}{10}$. List the three cities in order of amount of snowfall received on Wednesday from least to greatest.

Ⓐ Reading, Altoona, Bethlehem

Ⓑ Bethlehem, Reading, Altoona

Ⓒ Bethlehem, Altoona, Reading

Ⓓ Reading, Bethlehem, Altoona

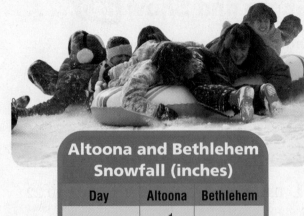

Altoona and Bethlehem Snowfall (inches)

Day	Altoona	Bethlehem
Monday	$2\frac{1}{4}$	2.6
Tuesday	$3\frac{1}{4}$	3.2
Wednesday	$2\frac{5}{8}$	2.5
Thursday	$4\frac{3}{5}$	4.8
Friday	$4\frac{3}{4}$	2.7

SHOW YOUR WORK

FOR MORE PRACTICE:
Standards Practice Book, pp. P45–P46

Add and Subtract Fractions

Essential Question How do you add and subtract fractions with unlike denominators?

Unlike fractions are fractions with different denominators. To add or subtract unlike fractions, write equivalent fractions using a common denominator or the **least common denominator (LCD)**. The LCD is the least common multiple (LCM) of two or more denominators.

🔑 UNLOCK the Problem · REAL WORLD

The roadrunner of the American Southwest has a tail nearly as long as its body. What is the total length of a roadrunner with a body measuring $\frac{5}{6}$ feet and a tail measuring $\frac{5}{9}$ feet?

- How do you know to add to solve the problem?

  _____

- Estimate fraction sums and differences using the closest benchmark: 0, $\frac{1}{2}$, or 1.

🔑 Add $\frac{5}{6} + \frac{5}{9}$.

STEP 1

Use benchmarks to estimate the sum.

| $\frac{5}{6}$ is close to _____. | $\frac{5}{9}$ is close to _____. | Estimate. _____ + _____ = _____ |

_____

STEP 2

Write equivalent fractions using a common denominator.

Think: I can use any common multiple of 6 and 9 for my common denominator.

$$\frac{5}{6} = \frac{5 \times 6}{6 \times 6} = \frac{30}{36} \qquad \frac{5}{9} = \frac{5 \times \boxed{}}{9 \times \boxed{}} = \frac{\boxed{}}{36}$$

_____

STEP 3

Add the numerators. Write the sum over the common denominator.

$$\frac{30}{36} + \frac{\boxed{}}{36} = \frac{\boxed{}}{\boxed{}}$$

_____

STEP 4

Use the GCF to write the sum in simplest form.

$$\frac{50 \div 2}{36 \div 2} = \frac{\boxed{}}{\boxed{}} = 1\frac{\boxed{}}{\boxed{}}$$

Remember

To rename a fraction greater than 1 as a mixed number, divide the numerator by the denominator.

Use the remainder as the numerator and the divisor as the denominator.

$$\frac{13}{5} = 2 \text{ r}3 = 2\frac{3}{5}$$

Compare your answer to your estimate. Since the estimate is _____, the answer is reasonable.

So, the total length of the roadrunner is _____ feet.

Example 1 Use the LCD to find $\frac{7}{12} - \frac{1}{3}$.

STEP 1

Write an equivalent fraction using the LCD.

$$\frac{7}{12} = \frac{7}{12}$$

$$-\frac{1}{3} = \frac{1 \times}{3 \times} = -\frac{}{}$$

 ERROR Alert

Make sure you multiply both the numerator and the denominator by the same factor to find an equivalent fraction.

STEP 2

Subtract the numerators.

$$\frac{7}{12} = \frac{7}{12}$$

$$-\frac{1}{3} = -\frac{}{}$$

$$\frac{}{} = \frac{}{}$$

Keep the common denominator.

Use the GCF to write the difference in simplest form.

So, $\frac{7}{12} - \frac{1}{3} =$ _____.

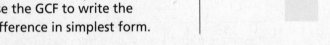 **Example 2** Evaluate $\frac{2}{3} + h$ for $h = \frac{2}{5}$.

STEP 1

Replace h with $\frac{2}{5}$.

$$\frac{2}{3} + \frac{2}{5}$$

STEP 2

Write equivalent fractions using the LCD.

$$\frac{2}{3} = \frac{2 \times}{3 \times} = \frac{}{}$$

$$+ \frac{2}{5} = \frac{2 \times}{5 \times} = + \frac{}{}$$

STEP 3

Add the numerators.

$$\frac{2}{3} = \frac{}{}$$

$$+ \frac{2}{5} = + \frac{}{}$$

$$\frac{}{}$$

Write the sum as a fraction or as a mixed number.

$$\frac{}{} \text{ or } \boxed{}$$

So, $\frac{2}{3} + h$ for $h = \frac{2}{5}$ is _____ or _____.

Math Talk Describe an advantage of using the LCD as a common denominator rather than using a common denominator that is not the LCD.

Name _____

Share and Show

Estimate. Then write the sum or difference in simplest form.

1. $\frac{2}{3} + \frac{1}{12}$

   Estimate.

   _____ + _____ = _____

   Write an equivalent fraction. Then add.

   $\frac{}{} + \frac{1}{12} = \frac{}{}$

   Write the sum in simplest form.

   $\frac{}{} = \frac{}{}$

2. $\frac{11}{18} - \frac{3}{18}$

3. $\frac{4}{15} + \frac{2}{5}$

4. $\frac{5}{6} - \frac{5}{12}$

Evaluate for the given value of the variable.

5. $\frac{7}{16} + y$ for $y = \frac{3}{4}$

6. $\frac{2}{3} - n$ for $n = \frac{1}{6}$

7. $p + \frac{1}{2}$ for $p = \frac{3}{8}$

Math Talk Explain how to find $\frac{1}{8} + \frac{5}{6}$.

On Your Own

Estimate. Then write the sum or difference in simplest form.

8. $\frac{7}{9} + \frac{1}{2}$

9. $\frac{4}{5} - \frac{1}{15}$

10. $\frac{3}{8} - \frac{1}{10}$

Practice: Copy and Solve Evaluate for the given value of the variable.

11. $c - \frac{1}{4}$ for $c = \frac{2}{3}$

12. $\frac{11}{20} + w$ for $w = \frac{9}{10}$

H.O.T. Find the sum or difference. Write <, >, or =.

13. $\frac{2}{3} - \frac{1}{4} \bigcirc \frac{6}{10} + \frac{4}{15}$

14. $\frac{1}{2} + \frac{1}{3} \bigcirc \frac{4}{5} - \frac{2}{5}$

15. $\frac{2}{3} + \frac{1}{5} \bigcirc \frac{5}{8} - \frac{1}{4}$

© Houghton Mifflin Harcourt Publishing Company

Problem Solving......................................

 What's the Error?

16. Andre estimated the sum $\frac{5}{6} + \frac{3}{4}$. Then he added the fractions and simplified the sum.

Look at how Andre solved the problem. Find his error.

Estimate. $1 + 1 = 2$

Solution:

$$\frac{5}{6} = \frac{5 \times 2}{6 \times 2} = \frac{10}{12}$$

$$+ \frac{3}{4} = \frac{3 \times 2}{4 \times 3} = + \frac{6}{12}$$

$$= \frac{16}{12} = 1\frac{4}{12} = 1\frac{1}{3}$$

Correct the error. Estimate the sum. Then add the fractions and simplify.

So, $\frac{5}{6} + \frac{3}{4} =$ _____.

• Describe the error that Andre made.

_____

_____

_____

• **Explain** how Andre's estimate might help him see which answer is reasonable.

_____

_____

• **Explain** another method Andre could use to find his error.

_____

_____

FOR MORE PRACTICE:
Standards Practice Book, pp. P47–P48

Name _____

Add and Subtract Mixed Numbers

Essential Question How do you add and subtract mixed numbers?

 UNLOCK the Problem REAL WORLD

Jared's baseball team played a doubleheader. During the first game, players ate $2\frac{3}{8}$ lb of peanuts. During the second game, players ate $1\frac{5}{6}$ lb of peanuts. How many pounds of peanuts did the players eat during both games?

🔑 **Add $2\frac{3}{8} + 1\frac{5}{6}$.**

Estimate. _____ + _____ = _____

- How do you know to add to solve the problem?

  _____

  _____

- Estimate fraction sums and differences using the closest benchmark: 0, $\frac{1}{2}$, or 1.

STEP 1

Write equivalent fractions using the LCD.

$$2\frac{3}{8} = 2\frac{3 \times \boxed{}}{8 \times \boxed{}} = 2\frac{\boxed{}}{\boxed{}}$$

$$+ 1\frac{5}{6} = 1\frac{5 \times \boxed{}}{6 \times \boxed{}} = + 1\frac{\boxed{}}{\boxed{}}$$

STEP 2

Add the fractions.

Add the whole numbers.

$$2\frac{3}{8} = 2\frac{\boxed{}}{\boxed{}}$$

$$+ 1\frac{5}{6} = + 1\frac{\boxed{}}{\boxed{}}$$

STEP 3

Rename the fraction greater than 1 as a mixed number.

$$3\frac{\boxed{}}{24} = 3 + 1 + \frac{\boxed{}}{24} = 4\frac{\boxed{}}{24}$$

Compare your answer to your estimate. Since the estimate

is _____, the answer is reasonable.

So, players ate _____ lb of peanuts.

Math Talk **Explain** how to rename a fraction greater than 1 as a mixed number.

🔑 Example 1 Use the LCD to find $5\frac{5}{6} - 3\frac{1}{5}$.

Estimate. _____ − _____ = _____

STEP 1

Write equivalent fractions using the LCD.

$$5\frac{5}{6} = 5\frac{5 \times}{6 \times} = 5\underline{}$$

$$-3\frac{1}{5} = 3\frac{1 \times}{5 \times} = -3\underline{}$$

STEP 2

Subtract the fractions.

Subtract the whole numbers.

$$5\frac{5}{6} = 5\underline{}$$

$$-3\frac{1}{5} = -3\underline{}$$

$$2\underline{}$$

Compare your answer to your estimate. Since the estimate is _____, the

answer is _____. So, $5\frac{5}{6} - 3\frac{1}{5} = $ _____.

🔑 Example 2

It is a $7\frac{7}{8}$ mile hike to Johnson Lake in Yosemite National Park. Craig hiked $3\frac{1}{2}$ miles before lunch and $2\frac{1}{4}$ miles after lunch. How much farther does he have to hike?

STEP 1	**STEP 2**	**STEP 3**
Write the expression.	Add to find Craig's total distance so far.	Subtract to find how far he has to go.
$7\frac{7}{8} - \left(3\frac{1}{2} + 2\frac{1}{4}\right)$	$3\frac{1}{2} = 3\frac{}{4}$ $+2\frac{1}{4} = +2\frac{1}{4}$ $\overline{\frac{}{4}}$	$7\frac{7}{8} = 7\frac{7}{8}$ $-\frac{}{4} = -5\frac{}{8}$ $\overline{2\frac{}{8}}$

So, Craig has _____ miles farther to hike.

Math Talk Explain why you needed to use both addition and subtraction to solve the problem.

Name _____

Share and Show

Estimate. Then write the sum or difference in simplest form.

1. $8\frac{7}{8} - 2\frac{1}{8}$

Estimate.

_____ − _____ = _____

Subtract the fractions. Subtract the whole numbers.

$8\frac{7}{8}$
$- 2\frac{1}{8}$
_____

2. $3\frac{7}{8} + 3\frac{1}{2}$

3. $8\frac{1}{3} - 1\frac{2}{15}$

4. $4\frac{1}{6} + 3\frac{1}{4} - 2\frac{1}{3}$

Math Talk **Explain** whether the actual answer for $4\frac{3}{8} - 2\frac{1}{5}$ will be more or less than the estimate, $2\frac{1}{2}$.

On Your Own

Practice: Copy and Solve **Estimate. Then write the sum or difference in simplest form.**

5. $16\frac{3}{4} - 5\frac{1}{3}$

6. $30\frac{5}{6} - 21\frac{2}{3}$

7. $25\frac{7}{18} + 15\frac{1}{6}$

8. $5\frac{7}{12} + 2\frac{2}{3}$

9. $4\frac{1}{2} + 3\frac{4}{5}$

10. $12\frac{2}{3} + 6\frac{3}{4}$

11. $7\frac{5}{6} - 4\frac{1}{5}$

12. $8\frac{3}{8} + 2\frac{1}{3}$

13. $4\frac{7}{10} - 1\frac{2}{5}$

14. $4\frac{1}{2} + 7\frac{1}{6} - 2\frac{1}{3}$

15. $2\frac{3}{4} + \left(5\frac{7}{8} - 1\frac{1}{2}\right)$

H.O.T. **Algebra** **Find the unknown number. Identify which property of addition you used.**

16. $5\frac{1}{2} +$ _____ $= 3\frac{1}{4} + 5\frac{1}{2}$

17. $1\frac{1}{6} + \left(1\frac{1}{5} + 1\frac{1}{4}\right) = \left(1\frac{1}{6} +$ _____$\right) + 1\frac{1}{4}$

18. The table shows the maximum speed in miles per hour of 5 roller coasters. How much faster is the fastest roller coaster than the slowest roller coaster?

(A) $16\frac{2}{15}$ miles per hour

(B) 16 miles per hour

(C) $15\frac{9}{15}$ miles per hour

(D) $145\frac{3}{5}$ miles per hour

a. What do you need to find?

_____

_____

b. How can you use the table to help you solve the problem?

_____

_____

Roller Coaster Speeds	
Roller Coaster	**Maximum Speed (mi per hr)**
Silver Star	$78\frac{9}{10}$
Stealth	$79\frac{1}{2}$
Beast	$64\frac{4}{5}$
Thunder Dolphin	$80\frac{2}{3}$
Zaturn	$80\frac{4}{5}$

c. Complete the sentences.

The fastest roller coaster goes _____ miles per hour. The slowest roller coaster goes _____

miles per hour. The fastest roller coaster goes _____ miles per hour faster than the slowest roller coaster.

Fill in the bubble for the correct answer choice above.

Use the above table for 19–20.

19. How much faster is the Zaturn roller coaster than the Stealth?

(A) $1\frac{3}{10}$ miles per hour

(B) $1\frac{6}{10}$ miles per hour

(C) $2\frac{1}{2}$ miles per hour

(D) $2\frac{3}{5}$ miles per hour

20. Which 2 roller coasters have the least difference in maximum speed?

(A) Silver Star and Stealth

(B) Stealth and Thunder Dolphin

(C) Thunder Dolphin and Zaturn

(D) Beast and Zaturn

Name _____

☑ Mid-Chapter Checkpoint

▶ ## Vocabulary

Choose the best term from the box.

1. The least common multiple of two or more denominators

   is the _____. (p. 93)

2. A _____ is a decimal representation of a

   number that has a repeating pattern that continues endlessly. (p. 86)

3. A number represented by a whole number that is not zero and

   a fraction is a _____. (p. 85)

▶ ## Concepts and Skills

Write as a decimal. Tell whether the decimal terminates or repeats. (pp. 85–88)

4. $\frac{7}{12}$

5. $8\frac{39}{40}$

6. $1\frac{4}{9}$

7. $\frac{19}{25}$

_____ | _____ | _____ | _____

Order from least to greatest. (pp. 89–92)

8. $\frac{4}{5}$, $\frac{3}{4}$, 0.88

9. 0.65, 0.59, $\frac{3}{5}$

10. $1\frac{1}{4}$, $1\frac{2}{3}$, $\frac{11}{12}$

11. 0.9, $\frac{8}{9}$, 0.86

_____ | _____ | _____ | _____

Estimate. Then write the sum or difference in simplest form. (pp. 93–96, 97–100)

12. $\frac{3}{7} + \frac{1}{2}$

13. $16\frac{3}{4} - 5\frac{1}{3}$

14. $\frac{7}{8} - \frac{1}{6}$

15. $4\frac{1}{2} + 3\frac{4}{5}$

_____ | _____ | _____ | _____

Fill in the bubble to show your answer.

16. Following the Baltimore Running Festival in 2009, volunteers collected and recycled 3.75 tons of trash. How can you write 3.75 as a mixed number in simplest form? (pp. 85–88)

    Ⓐ $3\frac{1}{2}$

    Ⓑ $3\frac{2}{3}$

    Ⓒ $3\frac{3}{4}$

    Ⓓ $\frac{15}{4}$

17. Four students took an exam. The fraction of the total possible points that each received is given. Which student had the highest score? (pp. 89–92)

    Ⓐ Monica, $\frac{22}{25}$

    Ⓑ Lily, $\frac{17}{20}$

    Ⓒ Nikki, $\frac{4}{5}$

    Ⓓ Sydney, $\frac{3}{4}$

18. $\frac{9}{10}$ of the human body is made up of oxygen, carbon, and hydrogen. If $\frac{3}{5}$ of the body is made up of oxygen and $\frac{1}{10}$ is hydrogen, what fraction of the human body is made up of carbon? (pp. 93–96)

    Ⓐ $\frac{1}{10}$ Ⓒ $\frac{7}{10}$

    Ⓑ $\frac{1}{5}$ Ⓓ $\frac{4}{5}$

19. Donovan jumped $18\frac{3}{4}$ feet in the long jump, $1\frac{3}{8}$ feet farther than his previous best. What was the length of his previous longest jump? (pp. 97–100)

    Ⓐ $16\frac{3}{8}$ feet   Ⓒ $17\frac{7}{16}$ feet

    Ⓑ $17\frac{3}{8}$ feet   Ⓓ $18\frac{3}{8}$ feet

20. A marathon runner had a goal to run $20\frac{3}{4}$ miles during the first week of training. On Sunday she ran $8\frac{1}{2}$ miles. On Tuesday she ran $6\frac{1}{8}$ miles. How many more miles did she need to run that week to meet her goal? (pp. 97–100)

    Ⓐ $6\frac{1}{8}$ miles   Ⓒ $12\frac{1}{4}$ miles

    Ⓑ $6\frac{1}{4}$ miles   Ⓓ $14\frac{5}{8}$ miles

Name _____

Subtract Fractions with Renaming

Essential Question How do you subtract mixed numbers with unlike denominators by renaming?

UNLOCK the Problem · REAL · WORLD

A total solar eclipse occurs when the moon passes between the sun and the Earth, causing the sky to go dark. The length of darkness during a 1999 total solar eclipse was $2\frac{1}{3}$ minutes. The length for one in 2003 was $1\frac{5}{6}$ minutes. How much longer was the eclipse in 1999?

🔑 **Use the LCD to find $2\frac{1}{3} - 1\frac{5}{6}$.**

Estimate. _____ − _____ = _____

STEP 1	
Use the LCD to write equivalent fractions.	$2\frac{1}{3} = 2\frac{1 \times }{3 \times } = 2\frac{}{}$ $-1\frac{5}{6} = -1\frac{5}{6}$

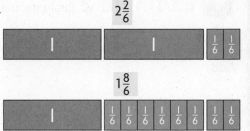

STEP 2	
$\frac{5}{6}$ is greater than $\frac{2}{6}$, so rename $2\frac{2}{6}$.	$2\frac{2}{6} = 1 + \frac{6}{6} + \frac{2}{6} = 1\frac{8}{6}$

STEP 3	
Subtract fractions using the renamed fraction. Subtract whole numbers. Write the difference in simplest form.	$2\frac{1}{3} = 1\frac{}{}$ $-1\frac{5}{6} = -1\frac{5}{6}$ $\frac{}{} = \frac{}{}$

So, the solar eclipse in 1999 was _____ longer.

Math Talk **Explain** whether your answer is reasonable.

Chapter 3 103

 **Example 1** Use the LCD to find $7 - 2\frac{4}{5}$.

Estimate. _____ − _____ = _____

STEP 1

Rename the whole number.

Think: I am subtracting fifths, so I will rename 7 as 6 + 1 or $6\frac{\quad}{5}$.

$$7 = 6\frac{\quad}{5}$$
$$-2\frac{4}{5} = -2\frac{4}{5}$$

STEP 2

Subtract the fractions.

Subtract the whole numbers.

$$7 = 6\frac{\quad}{5}$$
$$-2\frac{4}{5} = -2\frac{4}{5}$$
$$\overline{}\frac{\quad}{\quad}$$

Compare your answer to your estimate. Since the estimate is _____, the answer is reasonable. So, $7 - 2\frac{4}{5} =$ _____.

 Example 2 Evaluate the expression $5\frac{1}{9} + 4\frac{4}{9} - 3\frac{8}{9}$.

STEP 1

Add.

$$5\frac{1}{9}$$
$$+4\frac{4}{9}$$
$$\overline{9\frac{\quad}{\quad}}$$

STEP 2

Subtract.

$\frac{8}{9} > \frac{\quad}{9}$, so rename $9\frac{\quad}{9}$.

Think: $8 + 1 + \frac{\quad}{9}$

$$9\frac{\quad}{9} = 8 + \frac{\quad}{9} + \frac{\quad}{9} = 8\frac{\quad}{9}$$
$$-3\frac{8}{9} \qquad\qquad\qquad = -3\frac{8}{9}$$
$$\qquad\qquad\qquad\qquad \frac{\quad}{\quad} = \frac{\quad}{\quad}$$

So, $5\frac{1}{9} + 4\frac{4}{9} - 3\frac{8}{9} =$ _____.

Name _____

Share and Show

Estimate. Then write the difference in simplest form.

1. $4\frac{3}{8} - 2\frac{5}{8}$

Estimate.

_____ – _____ = _____

Rename $4\frac{3}{8}$ and subtract.

$$4\frac{3}{8} = 3\frac{}{8}$$
$$-2\frac{5}{8} = -2\frac{5}{8}$$

2. $1\frac{3}{4} - \frac{5}{6}$

✓ **3.** $12\frac{1}{9} - 7\frac{1}{6}$

✓ **4.** $6 - 2\frac{3}{7}$

Evaluate the expression. Write the answer in simplest form.

5. $5\frac{3}{8} + 3\frac{1}{8} - 5\frac{7}{8}$

6. $3\frac{1}{4} - 2\frac{3}{4} + 4\frac{5}{6}$

Math Talk Explain how you know when to rename a mixed number.

On Your Own

Practice: Copy and Solve Estimate. Then write the difference in simplest form.

7. $2\frac{1}{5} - 1\frac{4}{5}$

8. $3\frac{2}{3} - 1\frac{11}{12}$

9. $4\frac{1}{4} - 2\frac{1}{3}$

10. $9\frac{1}{6} - 2\frac{3}{4}$

11. $8\frac{1}{6} - 2\frac{2}{3}$

12. $6 - 3\frac{1}{2}$

13. $7\frac{5}{9} - 2\frac{5}{6}$

14. $4 - 3\frac{7}{8}$

Algebra Evaluate for the given value of the variable.

15. $5\frac{3}{5} + h - 2\frac{2}{5}$ for $h = 1\frac{2}{5}$

16. $2\frac{5}{6} - 1\frac{8}{9} + y$ for $y = \frac{2}{3}$

Problem Solving REAL WORLD

Use the table for 17–20.

Rock Climbing Walls	
Company	**Wall Height (ft)**
Adventure Land	$27\frac{2}{3}$
Rock-a-Wall	$30\frac{1}{4}$
Climbing Nation	32
Scale-a-Wall	$27\frac{1}{2}$

17. What is the difference in wall heights at Adventure Land and Rock-a-Wall?

_____

18. Which company's rock wall height is $2\frac{3}{4}$ ft shorter than Rock-a-Wall's?

_____

SHOW YOUR WORK

19. **Pose a Problem** Look back at Problem 18. Write a similar subtraction problem that involves Climbing Nation. Then solve your problem.

_____

_____

_____

_____

20. **H.O.T.** During a speed climbing competition, Claudio climbed the climbing walls at Adventure Land, Rock-a-Wall, and Scale-a-Wall in $5\frac{5}{6}$ min. Find the total height that he climbed.

_____

21. ⭐ **Test Prep** Jessica studied $6\frac{1}{4}$ hours for a history test and $5\frac{3}{4}$ hours for a math test. How much longer did she study for the history test than for the math test?

(A) $\frac{1}{3}$ hour   (C) $1\frac{1}{12}$ hours

(B) $\frac{1}{2}$ hour   (D) $1\frac{1}{2}$ hours

FOR MORE PRACTICE:
Standards Practice Book, pp. P51–P52

Choose an Operation

Practice Addition and Subtraction

Essential Question How can breaking a multistep problem into single steps help you find the solution?

> ## 🔑 UNLOCK the Problem REAL WORLD

The Diaz family is cross-country skiing the Big Tree trails, which have a total length of 4 miles. Yesterday, they skied the $\frac{7}{10}$ mile Oak Trail. Today, they skied the $\frac{3}{5}$ mile Pine Trail. If they plan to ski all of the Big Tree trails, how many more miles do they have left to ski?

Use the graphic organizer to help you solve the problem.

Read the Problem	Solve the Problem
What do I need to find? I need to find the distance _____.	• Use benchmarks to estimate the solution. Distance skied _____ + _____ = _____ mi Distance remaining _____ − _____ = _____ mi
What information do I need to use? I need to use the distance _____ _____ and the total distance _____.	• Solve. Distance skied Distance remaining $\dfrac{7}{10} = \dfrac{7}{10}$ $4\quad = \quad 3\dfrac{}{10}$ $+\dfrac{3}{5} = +\dfrac{}{10}$ $-1\dfrac{3}{10} = -1\dfrac{3}{10}$ $\quad\ \ = \dfrac{13}{10}$ $\quad\ \ = 1\dfrac{}{10}$
How will I use the information? First I can _____ to find the number of miles they have already skied. Then I can _____ that sum from _____.	Is the answer reasonable? _____

So, the family has _____ miles left to ski.

1. Describe the steps you used to solve the problem.

_____

_____

Try Another Problem

As part of their study of Native American basket weaving, Lia's class is making wicker baskets. Lia starts with a 36 in. strip of wicker. She cuts an $11\frac{5}{8}$ in. piece and a $7\frac{3}{4}$ in. piece from the strip. Does she have enough wicker left over to cut two $6\frac{1}{2}$ in. pieces?

Read the Problem	**Solve the Problem**
What do I need to find?	
What information do I need to use?	
How will I use the information?	

Does Lia have enough wicker left over to cut two $6\frac{1}{2}$ in. pieces? _____

2. **Explain** how you can work backward to check your solution.

_____

_____

_____

3. **Explain** how you know your answer is reasonable.

_____

_____

Share and Show MATH BOARD

✓ **1.** Caitlin has $4\frac{3}{4}$ lb of oven-fire clay. She uses $1\frac{1}{10}$ lb to make a cup, and another 2 lb to make a jar. How many pounds are left?

First, estimate the answer.

_____ lb

Next, find the exact answer.

weight used to make cup and jar:

_____ lb

weight remaining:

_____ lb

So, _____ pounds of clay remain.

2. **H.O.T.** **What if** Caitlin had used more than 2 lb of clay to make a jar? Would the amount remaining have been more or less than your answer to Problem 1?

_____

✓ **3.** A pet store donated 50 lb of food for adult dogs, puppies, and cats to an animal shelter. $19\frac{3}{4}$ lb was adult dog food and $18\frac{7}{8}$ lb was puppy food. How many pounds of cat food did the pet store donate?

_____

4. After spending $\frac{1}{6}$ of her weekly allowance on dog toys and $\frac{1}{3}$ on dog food, Thelma has $9.50 left. What is her weekly allowance?

Think: What fraction of her allowance did Thelma spend?

_____

SHOW YOUR WORK

On Your Own

5. Martin is making a model of a Native American canoe. He has $5\frac{1}{2}$ ft of wood. He uses $2\frac{3}{4}$ ft for the hull and $1\frac{1}{4}$ ft for the paddles and struts. How much wood does he have left?

_____

6. **H.O.T.** What fraction of the wood that Martin began with did he use making the hull?

_____

7. Beth's summer vacation lasted 87 days. At the beginning of her vacation, she spent 3 weeks at soccer camp, 5 days at her grandmother's house, and 13 days visiting Glacier National Park with her parents. How many vacation days remained?

_____

8. **Write Math** ➤ You can buy 2 DVDs for the same price you would pay for 3 CDs selling for $13.20 apiece. **Explain** how you could find the price of 1 DVD.

_____

_____

_____

_____

9. ⭐ **Test Prep** Between 8 A.M. and 5 P.M., Bret spent $5\frac{3}{4}$ hours in class and $1\frac{1}{2}$ hours at band practice. How much time did he spend on other activities?

(A) $\frac{3}{4}$ hour

(B) $1\frac{1}{4}$ hours

(C) $1\frac{1}{2}$ hours

(D) $1\frac{3}{4}$ hours

Choose a
STRATEGY

Work Backward
Solve a Simpler Problem
Choose an Operation
Use a Model
Use a Formula
Draw a Diagram

SHOW YOUR WORK

Name _____

▶ **Vocabulary**

Choose the best term from the box.

Vocabulary
repeating decimal
terminating decimal
unlike fractions

1. A _____ is a decimal representation of a number that eventually ends. (p. 86)

2. Fractions with different denominators are

_____. (p. 93)

▶ **Concepts and Skills**

Write as a decimal. Tell whether the decimal terminates or repeats. (pp. 85–88)

3. $2\frac{3}{20}$

4. $6\frac{7}{9}$

5. $3\frac{5}{6}$

6. $1\frac{1}{8}$

Order from least to greatest. (pp. 89–92)

7. $\frac{3}{10}$, 0.19, $\frac{1}{5}$

8. $1\frac{1}{4}$, 1.22, $1\frac{1}{5}$

9. 4.75, $4\frac{5}{8}$, $3\frac{8}{9}$

10. $\frac{5}{6}$, $\frac{3}{4}$, 0.78

Estimate. Then write the sum or difference in simplest form. (pp. 97–100, 103–106)

11. $12\frac{1}{5} - 7\frac{1}{3}$

12. $5\frac{1}{6} - 4\frac{2}{5}$

13. $3\frac{3}{8} - 2\frac{1}{2}$

14. $9\frac{7}{20} + 5\frac{1}{4}$

Fill in the bubble to show your answer.

15. One twenty-fifth of the students at Westside Middle School were absent yesterday. How can you write $\frac{1}{25}$ as a decimal? (pp. 85–88)

Ⓐ 0.025

Ⓑ 0.04

Ⓒ 0.25

Ⓓ 0.4

16. The table gives the heights of 4 trees. Which tree is tallest? (pp. 89–92)

Type of Tree	Height (feet)
Sycamore	$15\frac{2}{3}$
Oak	$14\frac{3}{4}$
Maple	$15\frac{3}{4}$
Birch	15.72

Ⓐ oak

Ⓑ sycamore

Ⓒ maple

Ⓓ birch

17. A punch recipe calls for $\frac{3}{4}$ quart of cherry juice and $\frac{5}{8}$ quart of ginger ale. How much total liquid does the recipe call for? (pp. 93–96)

Ⓐ $1\frac{1}{4}$ quarts   Ⓒ $1\frac{7}{16}$ quarts

Ⓑ $1\frac{3}{8}$ quarts   Ⓓ $1\frac{1}{2}$ quarts

18. Melody is making apple carrot muffins. The recipe calls for $\frac{3}{4}$ cup of buttermilk. Melody has $\frac{1}{8}$ cup of buttermilk. How much more buttermilk does Melody need to make the muffins? (pp. 93–96)

Ⓐ $\frac{1}{4}$ cup   Ⓒ $\frac{5}{8}$ cup

Ⓑ $\frac{1}{2}$ cup   Ⓓ $\frac{7}{8}$ cup

Fill in the bubble to show your answer.

19. Becca adopted two dogs at the animal shelter. One weighed $19\frac{3}{16}$ pounds and the other weighed $15\frac{7}{8}$ pounds. What was the combined weight of the two dogs? (pp. 97–100)

Ⓐ $34\frac{1}{16}$ pounds

Ⓑ $35\frac{1}{16}$ pounds

Ⓒ $35\frac{1}{8}$ pounds

Ⓓ $35\frac{3}{16}$ pounds

20. Raynard plans to study for his history exam for 3 hours. So far he has studied $1\frac{3}{4}$ hours. How much longer does he plan to study? (pp. 103–106)

Ⓐ $\frac{1}{6}$ hour

Ⓑ $\frac{5}{6}$ hour

Ⓒ $1\frac{1}{4}$ hours

Ⓓ $1\frac{5}{6}$ hours

21. Vince receives 4 weeks of vacation each year. So far he has spent $1\frac{2}{5}$ weeks on a bicycle trip and $1\frac{4}{5}$ weeks at the seashore. How much vacation time does he have left? (pp. 107–110)

Ⓐ $\frac{4}{5}$ week

Ⓑ $1\frac{1}{5}$ weeks

Ⓒ $1\frac{2}{5}$ weeks

Ⓓ $1\frac{4}{5}$ weeks

22. A figure skater likes to listen to music while he trains. He only has 12 more minutes of memory on his MP3 player. If he downloads one song that is $3\frac{1}{10}$ minutes long and another that is $2\frac{3}{5}$ minutes long, how many minutes of memory will he have left? (pp. 107–110)

Ⓐ $5\frac{7}{10}$ minutes   Ⓒ 7 minutes

Ⓑ $6\frac{3}{10}$ minutes   Ⓓ $8\frac{9}{10}$ minutes

23. John's backpack weighs 5.65 pounds. Ray's backpack weighs $5\frac{5}{8}$ pounds. Whose backpack weighs more? Explain. (pp. 89–92)

_____

_____

_____

24. Rose cut lengths of $3\frac{1}{6}$ feet and $4\frac{3}{8}$ feet from a rope measuring $11\frac{3}{4}$ feet in length. Find the length of rope that remained. (pp. 107–110)

_____

▶ **Performance Task**

25. Jorge has $27\frac{1}{4}$ inches of wicker to make a basket handle using three pieces of wicker.

Ⓐ The first piece must be $9\frac{3}{4}$ inches long and the second piece must be $\frac{1}{2}$ inch longer than the first piece. How long is the second piece?

_____

Ⓑ The third piece must be $9\frac{1}{2}$ inches shorter than the sum of the lengths of the first and second pieces. How long is the third piece?

_____

Ⓒ Does Jorge have enough wicker to make the basket handle? Explain.

_____

_____

Ⓓ Jorge thinks that he needs $32\frac{1}{2}$ inches more wicker to make 2 basket handles. Is he correct? Explain.

_____

_____

_____

Multiplying and Dividing Fractions

Show What You Know

Check your understanding of important skills.

Name _____

▶ **Estimate Products** Estimate the product.

1. $18 \times 42 =$ _____

2. $73 \times 312 =$ _____

3. $23 \times 348 =$ _____

4. $29 \times 138 =$ _____

▶ **Benchmark Fractions and Mixed Numbers** Write whether the fraction is closest to 0, $\frac{1}{2}$ or 1.

5. $\frac{3}{5}$ _____

6. $\frac{6}{7}$ _____

7. $\frac{1}{6}$ _____

8. $\frac{1}{3}$ _____

▶ **Understand Fractions** Draw a model to show the fraction.

9. $\frac{4}{7}$

10. $\frac{1}{6}$

11. $\frac{2}{3}$

MATH DETECTIVE
WITH
CARMEN
SANDIEGO ™

Cyndi bought an extra large pizza, cut into 12 pieces, for today's meeting of the Mystery Club. She ate $\frac{1}{6}$ of the pizza yesterday afternoon. Her brother ate $\frac{1}{5}$ of what was left last night. Cyndi knows that she needs 8 pieces of pizza for the club meeting. Be a math detective and help Cyndi figure out if she has enough pizza left for the meeting.

Vocabulary Builder

▶ **Visualize It**

Complete the Bubble Map using review words.

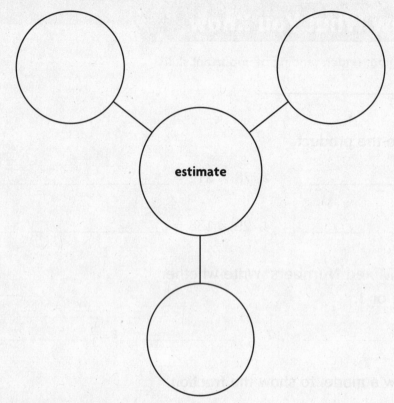

Review Words

✓ benchmark
✓ compatible numbers
✓ dividend
✓ divisor
  fractions
  mixed numbers
  product
✓ quotient
✓ simplest form
  reasonable

Preview Words

✓ multiplicative inverse
✓ reciprocal

▶ **Understand Vocabulary**

Complete the sentences using the checked words.

1. _____ are numbers that are easy to compute with mentally.

2. One of two numbers whose product is 1 is a

   _____ or a _____.

3. A _____ is a reference point that is used for estimating fractions.

4. When the numerator and denominator of a fraction have only

   1 as a common factor, the fraction is in _____.

5. In a division problem, the _____ is the number

   you are dividing, the _____ is the number you

   are dividing by, and the _____ is the number
   that results from dividing.

GO Online • eStudent Edition • Multimedia eGlossary

Model Fraction Multiplication

Essential Question How can you use a model to multiply fractions?

Investigate

Materials ■ fraction circles, color pencils

A Four girls each ate $\frac{1}{6}$ of a pizza. What fraction of the pizza did they eat?

Multiply $4 \times \frac{1}{6}$.

Think: $4 \times \frac{1}{6}$ means _____ groups

of _____ of a pizza.

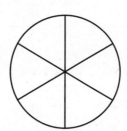

- Use fraction circle pieces to model $4 \times \frac{1}{6}$ and draw your model.

- Write $4 \times \frac{1}{6}$ as repeated addition. $\frac{1}{6} + \frac{1}{6} + \frac{1}{6} + \frac{1}{6} = \underline{\quad}$

$4 \times \frac{1}{6} =$ _____ , so the girls ate _____ of the pizza.

B $\frac{1}{2}$ of a pizza is left over from yesterday. If Zubin eats $\frac{1}{3}$ of the leftover pizza today, what fraction of the original pizza will he eat?

Multiply $\frac{1}{3} \times \frac{1}{2}$.

Think: $\frac{1}{3} \times \frac{1}{2}$ means $\frac{1}{3}$ of a group

of _____ of a pizza.

- Use fraction circle pieces to

  model 1 of _____ equal parts of $\frac{1}{2}$ and draw your model.

- How much of a whole pizza is that one part?

  _____ of _____ equal parts or _____ of the pizza.

$\frac{1}{3} \times \frac{1}{2} =$ _____ , so Zubin will eat _____ of the original pizza.

Draw Conclusions

1. Is the product of $4 \times \frac{1}{6}$ greater than or less than 4? **Explain**.

   _____

   _____

2. **H.O.T.** **Compare** multiplying a whole number by a fraction with multiplying a whole number by another whole number.

   _____

   _____

   _____

Make Connections

You can use rectangles to multiply fractions.

Timothy and his brother ate lasagna for dinner. $\frac{3}{8}$ of the pan of lasagna was left over. The next day, Timothy's sister ate $\frac{1}{2}$ of the leftover lasagna. What fraction of the original lasagna did Timothy's sister eat?

Multiply $\frac{1}{2} \times \frac{3}{8}$.

Think: $\frac{1}{2} \times \frac{3}{8}$ means _____ of a group of _____ of the lasagna.

STEP 1 Shade the rectangle to show the ——

of the pan of lasagna that is left over.

_____

STEP 2 Double-shade —— of $\frac{3}{8}$.

_____

STEP 3 Divide the remaining eighths into two parts so that all of the parts are equal.

What fraction of the lasagna is represented by the

double-shaded region? _____

$\frac{1}{2} \times \frac{3}{8} =$ _____ , so Timothy's sister ate _____ of the lasagna.

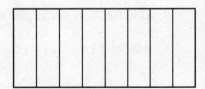

Math Talk Explain why you shade $\frac{3}{8}$ first when you model $\frac{1}{2} \times \frac{3}{8}$.

Name _____

Share and Show

Use the model to find the product.

1. $\frac{1}{4}$ of a pizza was left over. Maddy ate $\frac{1}{2}$ of the leftover pizza. What fraction of the pizza did Maddy eat?

   $\frac{1}{2} \times \frac{1}{4}$

   Think: $\frac{1}{2}$ of a group of $\frac{1}{4}$ of a pizza.

   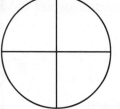

   _____

2. Three people each ate $\frac{1}{8}$ of a pizza. How much pizza did they eat?

   $3 \times \frac{1}{8}$

   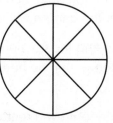

   _____

 3. $\frac{2}{3} \times \frac{3}{4}$

   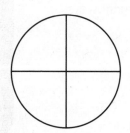

   _____

4. $\frac{3}{4} \times \frac{1}{4}$

   _____

5. $\frac{1}{3} \times \frac{5}{6}$

   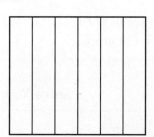

   _____

6. $\frac{1}{6} \times \frac{3}{4}$

   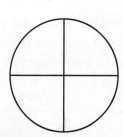

   _____

Math Talk Explain how to use a rectangle to multiply $\frac{1}{3} \times \frac{2}{3}$.

Write the multiplication problem shown by the model.

7.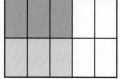

   _____

8.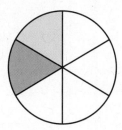

   _____

 9.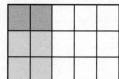

   _____

10. **Pose a Problem** Write and solve a word problem for the expression $\frac{1}{3} \times \frac{2}{3}$.

_____

_____

Problem Solving  REAL WORLD

Pose a Problem

11. Mario's family is planting a vegetable garden. They want to plant flowers in $\frac{1}{4}$ of the garden to attract beneficial insects. Mario is working on a plan for the garden. He wants to know what fraction of the garden will be sunflowers if $\frac{1}{2}$ of the flowers are sunflowers.

To find the fraction of the garden that will be sunflowers, Mario knows that he needs to find $\frac{1}{2}$ of $\frac{1}{4}$ of the garden so he wrote the expression $\frac{1}{2} \times \frac{1}{4}$.

Mario drew a rectangle, divided it into 4 equal parts, and shaded one of the parts to show $\frac{1}{4}$ of the garden. Then he double-shaded $\frac{1}{2}$ of $\frac{1}{4}$ to show the part that will be sunflowers.

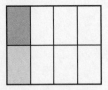

So, $\frac{1}{8}$ of the garden will be sunflowers.

Root vegetables will be planted in part of the garden and some of the root vegetables will be carrots. Write a new problem using fractions to represent the amount of root vegetables and carrots in the garden.

Pose a Problem	**Solve Your Problem**
_____	
_____	
_____	
_____	
_____	

12. **H.O.T.** Will the part of the garden with sunflowers in the first problem be greater than or less than the part of the garden with vegetables? **Explain.**

_____

_____

FOR MORE PRACTICE:
Standards Practice Book, pp. P59–P60

Name _____

Estimate Products

Essential Question How do you estimate products of fractions and mixed numbers?

 UNLOCK the Problem REAL WORLD

In recent years, biologists have developed "fast" plants that grow at amazing speeds. One such plant grows an average of $\frac{3}{8}$ in. per day. It flowers just 14 days after planting. Estimate the height of the plant after 14 days.

You can use benchmarks to estimate products of fractions and whole numbers.

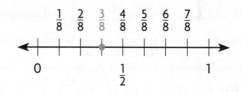

- Will the product be greater than or less than 14 in.? Explain.

_____

- Will the product be greater than or less than $\frac{3}{8}$ in.? Explain.

_____

_____

🔑 **Estimate 14 × $\frac{3}{8}$.**

STEP 1

Choose an appropriate benchmark.

Think: Is $\frac{3}{8}$ closer to 0 or $\frac{1}{2}$? It is closer to _____.

$$\frac{1}{8} \quad \frac{2}{8} \quad \frac{3}{8} \quad \frac{4}{8} \quad \frac{5}{8} \quad \frac{6}{8} \quad \frac{7}{8}$$

$$0 \qquad \frac{1}{2} \qquad 1$$

STEP 2

Rewrite using the benchmark. $14 \times \frac{1}{2}$

STEP 3

Use the Commutative Property so you $14 \times \frac{1}{2} = $ _____ $\times 14$
can take a fraction of a whole number.

STEP 4

Estimate the product.

Think: What is half of 14? $\frac{1}{2} \times 14 = $ _____

So, the plant will be about _____ in. tall after 14 days.

1. **Explain** why it is helpful to use the Commutative Property in Step 3.

_____

_____

🔑 Example 1

Diana wants to put a wallpaper border around her room. She has $2\frac{1}{3}$ rolls of wallpaper border. If each roll is $4\frac{3}{4}$ yd long, about how many yards of wallpaper border does she have?

You can estimate the product of two mixed numbers by choosing whole numbers that are close to the factors.

Estimate $2\frac{1}{3} \times 4\frac{3}{4}$.

STEP 1

Rewrite using whole numbers. _____ × _____

_____

STEP 2

Estimate the product. $2 \times 5 =$ _____

So, Diana has about _____ yd of wallpaper border.

🔑 Example 2 Tell whether the product is less than, greater than, or between the factors.

$\frac{1}{3} \times \frac{3}{8}$

 Think: The product will be _____ $\frac{3}{8}$ because the problem asks for _____ of $\frac{3}{8}$.

$\frac{1}{3} \times \frac{3}{8} = \frac{3}{8} \times \frac{1}{3}$ Use the Commutative Property.

 Think: The product will be _____ $\frac{1}{3}$ because the problem asks for _____ of $\frac{1}{3}$.

The product of $\frac{1}{3} \times \frac{3}{8}$ is _____ $\frac{3}{8}$ and _____ $\frac{1}{3}$.

So, the product of $\frac{1}{3} \times \frac{3}{8}$ is _____ the factors.

2. Helena said that the product of two fractions between 0 and 1 is always less than either fraction. Do you agree? **Explain**.

_____

_____

Name _____

Share and Show

Estimate the product.

1. $32 \times \dfrac{5}{8}$

Rewrite using a benchmark. $32 \times$ _____

Use the Commutative Property.   _____ $\times 32$

Estimate the product.   _____ $\times 32 =$ _____

2. Victor brings 7 bags of pretzels to a party. If each bag weighs $7\dfrac{7}{8}$ ounces, about how many ounces of pretzels will he bring?

_____

3. $3\dfrac{5}{6} \times 5\dfrac{1}{5}$

4. $29\dfrac{7}{9} \times \dfrac{3}{8}$

5. $7\dfrac{9}{10} \times 5\dfrac{7}{8}$

6. $2\dfrac{3}{4} \times 5\dfrac{1}{3}$

Math Talk Explain how to estimate the product of $29\dfrac{7}{9} \times \dfrac{3}{8}$.

On Your Own

Estimate the product.

7. Joe brings 3 jars of pickles to a party. If each jar weighs $1\dfrac{1}{4}$ lb, about how many pounds of pickles will Joe bring?

_____

8. Frank brings $2\dfrac{3}{4}$ bags of popcorn to the party. If one bag weighs 2 lb, about how much popcorn does Frank bring?

_____

9. $9\dfrac{2}{15} \times 4\dfrac{5}{6}$

10. $6\dfrac{1}{5} \times \dfrac{4}{9}$

11. $13 \times \dfrac{7}{8}$

12. $7\dfrac{4}{5} \times 1\dfrac{7}{8}$

13. $6\dfrac{1}{3} \times 2\dfrac{9}{10}$

14. $2\dfrac{1}{4} \times \dfrac{3}{5}$

15. $8\dfrac{1}{5} \times 2\dfrac{9}{10}$

16. $3\dfrac{2}{7} \times 3\dfrac{7}{10}$

Problem Solving · REAL WORLD

Use the table for 17–20.

Fabric Sale				
	Green	**Red**	**Purple**	**Orange**
Yards Available	$4\frac{1}{3}$	$19\frac{1}{2}$	$5\frac{1}{3}$	21

17. Lydia only needs $\frac{3}{8}$ of the green fabric that is available. About how much fabric does she need?

_____

18. Lisa needs $6\frac{3}{4}$ times the amount of purple fabric available and 3 times the amount of green fabric available. About how many yards of fabric does she need?

_____

19. **H.O.T.** About how many pieces of red fabric will Shane get if he divides all the red fabric into $1\frac{7}{8}$ yd lengths?

_____

20. **Write Math** Elaine needs $3\frac{1}{3}$ yd of orange fabric to make one pillow. She estimates that she can buy enough orange fabric to make 7 pillows. Is she correct? Explain.

_____

_____

_____

_____

21. ⭐ **Test Prep** A machine makes an average of $9\frac{7}{8}$ bottles per minute. Which is the best estimate of the number of bottles the machine can make in $4\frac{1}{6}$ minutes?

Ⓐ 36

Ⓑ 40

Ⓒ 45

Ⓓ 50

.... SHOW YOUR WORK ....

FOR MORE PRACTICE:
Standards Practice Book, pp. P61–P62

Name _____

Multiply Fractions

Essential Question How do you multiply fractions?

🔓 UNLOCK the Problem ⟩ REAL WORLD

Sasha still has $\frac{3}{5}$ of a scarf left to knit. If she finishes $\frac{1}{2}$ of the remaining part of the scarf today, how much of the scarf will Sasha knit today?

Multiply $\frac{1}{2} \times \frac{3}{5}$.

- How can you restate this problem using the "groups of objects" meaning of multiplication?

_____

- Will the product be less than, greater than, or between the factors? How do you know?

_____

_____

🔑 One Way Use a model.

Shade the model to show _____ × _____.

$2 \times 5 =$ _____ parts

$1 \times 3 =$ _____ parts are double-shaded.

Think: _____ of _____ parts are double-shaded,

so _____ of the model is double-shaded.

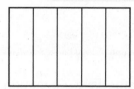

So, $\frac{1}{2} \times \frac{3}{5} =$ _____.

1. **Compare** the numerator and denominator of the product with the numerators and denominators of the factors.

_____

_____

🔑 Another Way Use paper and pencil.

You can multiply fractions without using a model.

$\dfrac{\text{numerator} \times \text{numerator}}{\text{denominator} \times \text{denominator}} = \dfrac{\text{numerator}}{\text{denominator}}$

Multiply the numerators.
Multiply the denominators.

$\dfrac{1}{2} \times \dfrac{3}{5} = \dfrac{1 \times }{2 \times }$

$= \dfrac{}{}$

$\frac{1}{2} \times \frac{3}{5} =$ _____, so Sasha will knit _____ of the scarf today.

🔑 Example 1

Find $4 \times \frac{5}{12}$. Write the product in simplest form.

Estimate. $4 \times$ _____ = _____

Write the whole number as a fraction.

$$4 \times \frac{5}{12} = \frac{4}{\square} \times \frac{5}{12}$$

Multiply the numerators.
Multiply the denominators.

$$= \frac{4 \times \square}{\square \times \square} = \frac{\square}{\square}$$

Write the product as a fraction or a mixed number in simplest form.

$$= \frac{\square \div \square}{12 \div \square} = \frac{\square}{\square} \text{ or } \_\_\_\_$$

Since the estimate is _____, the answer is reasonable.

So, $4 \times \frac{5}{12} =$ _____, or _____.

When a numerator and a denominator have a common factor, you can simplify before you multiply.

🔑 Example 2 Evaluate $c \times \frac{14}{15}$ for $c = \frac{5}{8}$.

Replace c with _____.

$$\frac{5}{8} \times \frac{14}{15}$$

Divide the numerators and denominators by the GCFs.

$$\overset{1}{\underset{}{\frac{\cancel{5}}{\cancel{8}}}} \times \frac{\cancel{14}}{\cancel{15}}_{3}$$

The GCF of 5 and 15 is _____.

The GCF of 8 and 14 is _____.

Multiply the numerators.
Multiply the denominators.

$$\frac{1 \times \square}{\square \times 3} = \frac{\square}{\square}$$

> ⚠️ **ERROR Alert**
>
> Be sure to divide both a numerator and a denominator by a common factor to write a fraction in simplest form.

So, $c \times \frac{14}{15} =$ _____ for $c = \frac{5}{8}$.

2. What if you divided by a common factor other than the GCF before you multiplied? How would that affect your answer?

_____

_____

Name _____

Share and Show . . . .

Find the product. Write it in simplest form.

1. $6 \times \frac{3}{8}$

$\frac{\cancel{6}}{1} \times \frac{3}{\cancel{8}} = \frac{\quad}{\quad}$

or _____

⊘2. $\frac{3}{8} \times \frac{8}{9}$

3. $\frac{2}{3} \times 27$

⊘4. $\frac{5}{12}$ of a pizza is left over. Sam eats $\frac{3}{5}$ of the leftover pizza. What fraction of the pizza does he eat?

Algebra Evaluate for the given value of the variable.

5. $\frac{1}{2} \times c$ for $c = \frac{3}{5}$

6. $t \times \frac{4}{5}$ for $t = \frac{2}{3}$

7. $m \times \frac{5}{8}$ for $m = \frac{1}{3}$

8. $4 \times y$ for $y = \frac{1}{5}$

> **Math Talk** Explain two ways to find the product $\frac{1}{6} \times \frac{2}{3}$ in simplest form.

On Your Own . . . .

Find the product. Write it in simplest form.

9. $2 \times \frac{1}{8}$

10. $\frac{4}{9} \times \frac{4}{5}$

11. $\frac{1}{6} \times \frac{2}{3}$

12. $\frac{1}{7} \times 30$

13. $\frac{5}{6}$ of the pets in the pet show are cats. $\frac{4}{5}$ of the cats are calico cats. What fraction of the pets are calico cats?

14. Five cats each ate $\frac{1}{4}$ cup of food. How much food did they eat altogether?

Algebra Evaluate for the given value of the variable.

15. $\frac{2}{5} \times c$ for $c = \frac{4}{7}$

16. $m \times \frac{4}{21}$ for $m = \frac{7}{8}$

17. $\frac{2}{3} \times t$ for $t = \frac{1}{8}$

18. $y \times \frac{4}{5}$ for $y = 5$

Problem Solving  REAL WORLD

Speedskating is a popular sport in the Winter Olympics. Many young athletes in the U.S. participate in speedskating clubs and camps.

19. At a camp in Green Bay, Wisconsin, $\frac{7}{9}$ of the participants were from Wisconsin. $\frac{3}{5}$ of that group were 12 years old. What fraction of the group was from Wisconsin and 12 years old?

_____

20. **H.O.T.** Maribel wants to skate $1\frac{1}{2}$ miles Monday. If she skates $\frac{9}{10}$ mile Monday morning and $\frac{2}{3}$ of that distance Monday afternoon, will she reach her goal? **Explain**.

_____

_____

_____

SHOW YOUR WORK

21. **Write Math** ▶ $\frac{5}{6}$ of the skaters at the camp one day are beginners. $\frac{1}{3}$ of the beginners are girls. What fraction of the skaters are girls and beginners? **Explain** why your answer is reasonable.

_____

_____

_____

22. ⭐ **Test Prep** Wednesday, Danielle skated $\frac{2}{3}$ of the way around the track in 2 minutes. Her younger brother skated $\frac{3}{4}$ of Danielle's distance in 2 minutes. What fraction of the track did Danielle's brother finish in 2 minutes?

Ⓐ $\frac{1}{3}$ Ⓒ $\frac{5}{7}$

Ⓑ $\frac{1}{2}$ Ⓓ $\frac{3}{4}$

FOR MORE PRACTICE: Standards Practice Book, pp. P63–P64

Name _____

Multiply Mixed Numbers

Essential Question How do you multiply mixed numbers?

 **UNLOCK the Problem** REAL WORLD

One-third of a $1\frac{1}{4}$ acre park has been set aside as a dog park. Find the number of acres that are used as a dog park.

Multiply $\frac{1}{3} \times 1\frac{1}{4}$.

One Way Use a model.

STEP 1 Shade the model to represent the size of the whole park.

Think: The whole park is _____ acres.

$1 = \dfrac{4}{\quad}$ $\qquad$ $1\dfrac{1}{4} = \dfrac{4}{\quad} + \dfrac{1}{4} = \dfrac{\quad}{\quad}$

STEP 2 Double-shade the model to represent the part of the park that is used as a dog park.

Think: The dog park is _____ of the park.

Divide the _____ horizontally into _____.

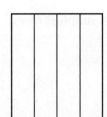

STEP 3 Divide the remaining fourths into three parts so that all of the parts are equal.

Think: $\dfrac{4}{\quad} + \dfrac{1}{\quad} = \dfrac{\quad}{\quad}$

Another Way Rename the mixed number as a fraction.

Estimate $\frac{1}{3} \times 1\frac{1}{4}$. _____ × 1 = _____

Write the mixed number as a fraction greater than 1.

$$\frac{1}{3} \times 1\frac{1}{4} = \frac{1}{3} \times \frac{\quad}{4}$$

Multiply the fractions.

$$= \frac{1 \times \quad}{3 \times 4} = \frac{\quad}{\quad}$$

So, $\frac{1}{3} \times 1\frac{1}{4} =$ _____ acre.

Math Talk Explain why your answer is reasonable.

🔑 Example 1 Rename the whole number.

Multiply $12 \times 2\frac{1}{6}$. Write the product in simplest form.

Estimate. $12 \times$ _____ = _____

Write the whole number and mixed number as fractions.

$$12 \times 2\frac{1}{6} = \frac{}{1} \times \frac{}{6}$$

Simplify the fractions.

$$= \frac{\cancel{12}}{1} \times \frac{13}{\cancel{6}}$$

Multiply the fractions.

$$= \frac{ \times 13}{1 \times } = \underline{}$$

So, $12 \times 2\frac{1}{6} =$ _____.

Math Talk Explain whether the product will be greater than or less than 12.

🔑 Example 2 Use the Distributive Property.

Multiply $16 \times 4\frac{1}{8}$. Write the product in simplest form.

Estimate. $16 \times$ _____ = _____

Rewrite the expression by using the Distributive Property.

$$16 \times 4\frac{1}{8} = 16 \times (\underline{} + \frac{1}{8})$$

Multiply 16 by each number.

$$= (16 \times 4) + (16 \times \underline{})$$

Add.

$$= \underline{} + 2 = \underline{}$$

So, $16 \times 4\frac{1}{8} =$ _____.

Math Talk Explain how you know that your answers to both examples are reasonable.

1. **Explain** why you might choose to use the Distributive Property to solve this problem.

_____

2. When you multiply two factors greater than 1, is the product less than, between, or greater than the two factors? **Explain**.

_____

_____

© Houghton Mifflin Harcourt Publishing Company

Name _____

Share and Show   . . . .

Find the product. Write it in simplest form.

1. $1\frac{2}{3} \times 3\frac{4}{5} = \frac{\boxed{}}{3} \times \frac{\boxed{}}{5}$

   $= \dfrac{\boxed{}}{\rule{1cm}{0.4pt}}$

   $= \rule{1.5cm}{0.4pt}$

2. $\frac{1}{2} \times 1\frac{1}{3}$

_____

Estimate. Then write the product in simplest form.

✓ 3. $1\frac{1}{8} \times 2\frac{1}{3}$

✓ 4. $\frac{3}{4} \times 6\frac{5}{6}$

5. $1\frac{2}{7} \times 1\frac{3}{4}$

6. $\frac{3}{4} \times 1\frac{1}{4}$

_____ _____ _____ _____

Use the Distributive Property to find the product.

7. $16 \times 2\frac{1}{2}$

8. $1\frac{4}{5} \times 15$

_____ _____

> **Math Talk** **Explain** how multiplying a mixed number by a whole number is similar to multiplying two mixed numbers.

On Your Own . . . .

Estimate. Then write the product in simplest form.

9. $\frac{3}{4} \times 1\frac{1}{2}$

10. $4\frac{2}{5} \times 1\frac{1}{2}$

11. $5\frac{1}{3} \times \frac{3}{4}$

12. $2\frac{1}{2} \times 1\frac{1}{5}$

_____ _____ _____ _____

13. $12\frac{3}{4} \times 2\frac{2}{3}$

14. $3 \times 4\frac{1}{2}$

15. $2\frac{3}{8} \times \frac{4}{9}$

16. $1\frac{1}{3} \times 1\frac{1}{4} \times 1\frac{1}{5}$

_____ _____ _____ _____

Use the Distributive Property to find the product.

17. $10 \times 2\frac{3}{5}$

18. $3\frac{3}{4} \times 12$

_____ _____

Connect to Health

Changing Recipes

You can make a lot of recipes more healthful by reducing the amounts of fat, sugar, and salt.

Kelly has a recipe for muffins that calls for $1\frac{1}{2}$ cups of sugar. She wants to use $\frac{1}{2}$ that amount of sugar and more cinnamon and vanilla. How much sugar will she use?

Multiply $\frac{1}{2}$ by $1\frac{1}{2}$ to find what part of the original amount of sugar to use.

Write the mixed number as a fraction greater than 1.

$$\frac{1}{2} \times 1\frac{1}{2} = \frac{1}{2} \times \frac{\boxed{}}{2}$$

Multiply.

$$= \frac{\boxed{}}{\boxed{}}$$

So, Kelly will use _____ cup of sugar.

19. Michelle has a recipe that calls for $2\frac{1}{2}$ cups of vegetable oil. She wants to use $\frac{2}{3}$ that amount of oil and use applesauce to replace the rest. How much vegetable oil will she use?

_____

20. Tony's recipe for soup calls for $1\frac{1}{4}$ teaspoons of salt. He wants to use $\frac{1}{2}$ that amount. How much salt will he use?

_____

21. Jeffrey's recipe for oatmeal muffins calls for $2\frac{1}{4}$ cups of oatmeal and makes one dozen muffins. If he makes $1\frac{1}{2}$ dozen muffins for a club meeting, how much oatmeal will he use?

_____

22. Cara's muffin recipe calls for $1\frac{1}{2}$ cups of flour for the muffins and $\frac{1}{4}$ cup of flour for the topping. If she makes $\frac{1}{2}$ of the original recipe, how much flour will she use altogether?

_____

© Houghton Mifflin Harcourt Publishing Company

132 FOR MORE PRACTICE:
Standards Practice Book, pp. P65–P66

Name _____

✓ Mid-Chapter Checkpoint

▶ Concepts and Skills

1. Is the product of two fractions between 0 and 1 always less than, greater than, or between the factors? Explain. (pp. 125–128)

_____

_____

2. Explain how to estimate the product of $18\frac{1}{8} \times \frac{4}{9}$. (pp. 121–124)

_____

_____

Use the model to find the product. (pp. 117–120)

3. $\frac{3}{5} \times \frac{2}{3}$ 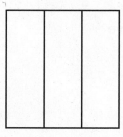 _____

4. $\frac{1}{2} \times \frac{1}{6}$ 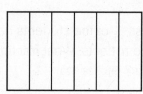 _____

Find the product. Write it in simplest form. (pp. 125–128)

5. $\frac{2}{3} \times \frac{1}{8}$

6. $\frac{4}{5} \times \frac{2}{5}$

7. $12 \times \frac{3}{4}$

8. Mia climbs $\frac{5}{8}$ of the height of the rock wall. Lee climbs $\frac{4}{5}$ of Mia's distance. What fraction of the wall does Lee climb?

Estimate. Then write the product in simplest form. (pp. 121–124, 129–132)

9. $6\frac{2}{3} \times 4\frac{2}{5}$

10. $1\frac{4}{7} \times 3\frac{2}{11}$

11. $2 \times 5\frac{3}{4}$

12. Liam used $3\frac{1}{3}$ tubes of paint for his picture. The paint comes in $3\frac{3}{8}$ oz tubes. How much paint did he use?

13. One-third of the students at Finley High play sports. Two-fifths of the students who play sports are girls. Which expression can you evaluate to find the fraction of all students who are girls that play sports? (pp. 117–120)

(A) $\frac{2}{5} + \frac{1}{3}$

(B) $\frac{2}{5} - \frac{1}{3}$

(C) $\frac{2}{5} \times \frac{1}{3}$

(D) $\frac{2}{5} \div \frac{1}{3}$

14. Beth hiked for $3\frac{7}{8}$ hours at an average rate of $3\frac{1}{4}$ miles per hour. Which is the best estimate of the distance that she hiked? (pp. 121–124)

(A) 9 miles   (C) 12 miles

(B) 10 miles   (D) 16 miles

15. In Zoe's class, $\frac{4}{5}$ of the students have pets. Of the students who have pets, $\frac{1}{8}$ have rodents. What fraction of the students in Zoe's class have rodents? (pp. 125–128)

(A) $\frac{1}{40}$

(B) $\frac{1}{10}$

(C) $\frac{2}{5}$

(D) $\frac{1}{2}$

16. A recipe calls for $2\frac{2}{3}$ cups of flour. Terell wants to make $\frac{3}{4}$ of the recipe. How much flour should he use? (pp. 129–132)

(A) $\frac{1}{2}$ cup   (C) $1\frac{1}{2}$ cups

(B) $\frac{2}{3}$ cup   (D) 2 cups

17. Mia buys 6 bags of peanuts. Each bag weighs $2\frac{1}{4}$ pounds. Which shows the number of pounds of peanuts Mia buys? (pp. 129–132)

(A) $8\frac{1}{4}$ pounds

(B) $12\frac{1}{4}$ pounds

(C) $13\frac{1}{4}$ pounds

(D) $13\frac{1}{2}$ pounds

Name _____

Model Fraction Division

Essential Question How can you use a model to show division of fractions?

CONNECT There are two types of division problems. In one type you find how many or how much in each group, and in the other you find how many groups.

Investigate

Materials ■ fraction bars

A class is working on a community project to clear a path near the lake. They are working in teams on sections of the path.

A. Four students clear a section that is $\frac{2}{3}$ mi long. If each student clears an equal part, what fraction of a mile will each clear?

Divide $\frac{2}{3} \div 4$.

- Use fraction bars to model the division. Draw your model.

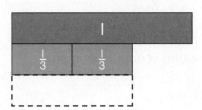

- Which type of division is represented in the problem?

_____

$\frac{2}{3} \div 4 =$ _____, so each student will clear _____ of a mile.

B. Another team clears a section of the path that is $\frac{3}{4}$ mi long. If each student clears $\frac{1}{8}$ of a mile, how many students are on the team?

Divide $\frac{3}{4} \div \frac{1}{8}$.

- Use fraction bars to model the division. Draw your model.

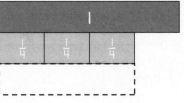

- Which type of division is represented in the problem?

_____

$\frac{3}{4} \div \frac{1}{8} =$ _____, so there are _____ students on the team.

Draw Conclusions

1. In problem A, is the quotient greater than or less than the dividend? **Explain**.

_____

2. ⟨H.O.T.⟩ **Analysis** Suppose a whole number is divided by a fraction between 0 and 1. Is the quotient greater than or less than the dividend? **Explain** and give an example.

_____

Make Connections

You can draw a model to help you solve a fraction division problem.

Jessica is making a recipe that calls for $\frac{3}{4}$ cup of flour. Suppose she only has a $\frac{1}{2}$ cup-size measuring scoop. How many $\frac{1}{2}$ cup scoops of flour does she need?

Divide $\frac{3}{4} \div \frac{1}{2}$.

STEP 1 Draw a model that represents the total amount of flour.

Think: Divide a whole into _____.

Shade _____.

STEP 2 Draw fraction parts that represent the scoops of flour.

Think: Which type of division is represented in the problem?

_____

There is _____ full group of $\frac{1}{2}$ and _____ of a group of $\frac{1}{2}$.

So, there are _____ groups of $\frac{1}{2}$ in $\frac{3}{4}$.

$\frac{3}{4} \div \frac{1}{2} =$ _____, so Jessica will need _____ scoops of flour.

> **Math Talk** Explain how to use a model to divide $\frac{7}{8} \div \frac{1}{4}$.

Name _____

Share and Show

Use the model to find the quotient.

1. $\frac{1}{2} \div 3 =$ _____

Think: $\frac{1}{2}$ is shared among 3 groups.

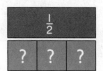

2. $\frac{3}{4} \div \frac{3}{8} =$ _____

Use fraction bars to find the quotient. Then draw the model.

3. $\frac{1}{3} \div 4 =$ _____

4. $\frac{3}{5} \div \frac{3}{10} =$ _____

Draw a model to solve.

5. How many $\frac{1}{4}$ cup servings of raisins are in $\frac{3}{8}$ cup of raisins?

6. How many $\frac{1}{3}$ lb bags of trail mix can Josh make from $\frac{5}{6}$ lb of trail mix?

7. **Write Math** ► **Pose a Problem** Write and solve a problem for $\frac{3}{4} \div 3$ that represents how much in each of 3 groups.

_____

_____

Problem Solving REAL WORLD

The table shows the amount of each material that students in a sewing class need for one purse.

Use the table for 8–11. Use models to solve.

8. Mrs. Brown has $\frac{2}{3}$ yd of denim. How many purses can be made using denim as the main fabric?

_____

9. **H.O.T.** One student brings $\frac{1}{2}$ yd of ribbon. If 3 students receive an equal length of the ribbon, how much ribbon will each student receive? Will each of them have enough ribbon for a purse? **Explain.**

_____

Purse Materials (yd)	
Ribbon	$\frac{1}{4}$
Main fabric	$\frac{1}{6}$
Trim fabric	$\frac{1}{12}$

10. **What's the Error?** There was $\frac{1}{2}$ yd of purple and pink striped fabric. Jessie said she could only make $\frac{1}{24}$ of a purse using that fabric as the trim. Is she correct? **Explain** using what you know about the meanings of multiplication and division.

_____

_____

_____

······· **SHOW YOUR WORK** ·····

11. **Pose a Problem** Use information in the table to write a new problem that represents how many groups of $\frac{1}{4}$ in $\frac{7}{8}$.

_____

_____

12. ⭐ **Test Prep** $\frac{2}{3}$ of the purses made by the class are blue. $\frac{1}{8}$ of the blue purses have red ribbon straps. What fraction of the purses are blue and have red ribbon straps?

Ⓐ $\frac{1}{24}$　　Ⓒ $\frac{1}{6}$

Ⓑ $\frac{1}{12}$　　Ⓓ $5\frac{1}{3}$

Name _____

Estimate Quotients

Essential Question How can you use compatible numbers to estimate quotients?

CONNECT You have used compatible numbers to estimate quotients of whole numbers and decimals. You can also use compatible numbers to estimate quotients of fractions and mixed numbers.

Remember
Compatible numbers are pairs of numbers that are easy to compute mentally.

 UNLOCK the Problem REAL WORLD

Humpback whales have "songs" that they repeat continuously over periods of several hours. Eric is using an underwater microphone to record a $3\frac{5}{6}$ min humpback song. He has $15\frac{3}{4}$ min of battery power left. About how many songs will he be able to record?

- Which operation should you use to solve the problem? Why?

  _____

  _____

- How do you know that the problem calls for an estimate?

  _____

🔑 **Estimate** $15\frac{3}{4} \div 3\frac{5}{6}$ **using compatible numbers.**

Think: What whole numbers close to $15\frac{3}{4}$ and $3\frac{5}{6}$ are easy to divide mentally?

$15\frac{3}{4}$ is close to _____.

$3\frac{5}{6}$ is close to _____.

Rewrite the problem using compatible numbers.

$$15\frac{3}{4} \div 3\frac{5}{6}$$
$$\downarrow \qquad \downarrow$$

Divide.

$$16 \div 4 = \text{_____}$$

So, Eric will be able to record about _____ complete whale songs.

1. To estimate $15\frac{3}{4} \div 3\frac{5}{6}$, Martin used 15 and 3 as compatible numbers. Tina used 15 and 4. Were their choices good ones? **Explain** why or why not.

   _____

   _____

   _____

🔑 Example Estimate using compatible numbers.

Ⓐ $5\frac{2}{3} \div \frac{5}{8}$

Rewrite the problem using compatible numbers.

$$5\frac{2}{3} \qquad \div \qquad \frac{5}{8}$$
$$\downarrow \qquad\qquad \downarrow$$
$$\underline{\hspace{2cm}} \div \underline{\hspace{2cm}}$$

Think: How many halves are there in 6?

$$6 \div \frac{1}{2} = \underline{\hspace{2cm}}$$

So, $5\frac{2}{3} \div \frac{5}{8}$ is about $\underline{\hspace{2cm}}$.

Ⓑ $\frac{7}{8} \div \frac{1}{4}$

Rewrite the problem using compatible numbers.

$$\frac{7}{8} \qquad \div \qquad \frac{1}{4}$$
$$\downarrow \qquad\qquad \downarrow$$
$$\underline{\hspace{2cm}} \div \frac{1}{4}$$

Think: How many fourths are there in 1?

$$1 \div \frac{1}{4} = \underline{\hspace{2cm}}$$

So, $\frac{7}{8} \div \frac{1}{4}$ is about $\underline{\hspace{2cm}}$.

---

2. Will the actual quotient $5\frac{2}{3} \div \frac{5}{8}$ be greater than or less than the estimated quotient? **Explain**.

_____

_____

_____

3. Will the actual quotient $\frac{7}{8} \div \frac{1}{4}$ be greater than or less than the estimated quotient? **Explain**.

_____

_____

_____

4. **Explain** how you would estimate the quotient $14\frac{3}{4} \div 3\frac{9}{10}$ using compatible numbers.

_____

Name _____

Estimate using compatible numbers.

1. $22\frac{4}{5} \div 6\frac{1}{4}$

$\downarrow \qquad \downarrow$

_____ $\div$ _____ $=$ _____

2. $12 \div 3\frac{3}{4}$

✓ **3.** $33\frac{7}{8} \div 5\frac{1}{3}$

✓ **4.** $3\frac{7}{8} \div \frac{5}{9}$

5. $34\frac{7}{12} \div 7\frac{3}{8}$

6. $1\frac{2}{9} \div \frac{1}{6}$

Math Talk Explain how using compatible numbers is different than rounding to estimate $35\frac{1}{2} \div 6\frac{5}{6}$.

On Your Own ....

Estimate using compatible numbers.

7. $\frac{13}{16} \div \frac{9}{10}$

8. $51\frac{5}{6} \div 5\frac{1}{2}$

9. $44\frac{1}{4} \div 11\frac{7}{9}$

10. $5\frac{11}{15} \div \frac{9}{19}$

11. $36\frac{2}{9} \div 2\frac{4}{5}$

12. $71\frac{11}{12} \div 8\frac{3}{4}$

13. $\frac{9}{10} \div \frac{1}{3}$

14. $13\frac{7}{8} \div \frac{1}{2}$

15. $1\frac{1}{6} \div \frac{1}{8}$

H.O.T. **Estimate to compare. Write <, >, or =.**

16. $21\frac{3}{10} \div 2\frac{5}{6}$ ◯ $35\frac{7}{9} \div 3\frac{2}{3}$

17. $29\frac{4}{5} \div 5\frac{1}{6}$ ◯ $27\frac{8}{9} \div 6\frac{5}{8}$

18. $55\frac{5}{6} \div 6\frac{7}{10}$ ◯ $11\frac{5}{7} \times \frac{5}{8}$

Problem Solving REAL WORLD

What's the Error?

19. Megan is making pennants from a piece of butcher paper that is $10\frac{3}{8}$ yards long. Each pennant requires $\frac{3}{8}$ yard of paper. To estimate the number of pennants she could make, Megan estimated the quotient $10\frac{3}{8} \div \frac{3}{8}$.

Look at how Megan solved the problem. Find her error.

Estimate:

$$10\frac{3}{8} \div \frac{3}{8}$$

$$\downarrow \quad \downarrow$$

$$10 \div \frac{1}{2} = 5$$

Correct the error. Estimate the quotient.

So, Megan can make about _____ pennants.

- Describe the error that Megan made.

  _____

- Tell which compatible numbers you used to estimate $10\frac{3}{8} \div \frac{3}{8}$. **Explain** why you chose those numbers.

  _____

  _____

- **What if** Megan wanted to make pennants that each required four times the amount of butcher paper? About how many pennants could she make? **Explain** your answer.

  _____

  _____

FOR MORE PRACTICE:
Standards Practice Book, pp. P69–P70

Name _____

Divide Fractions

Essential Question How do you divide fractions?

UNLOCK the Problem  REAL WORLD

Activity

You can use reciprocals and inverse operations to divide fractions. Two numbers whose product is 1 are **reciprocals** or **multiplicative inverses**.

$\frac{2}{3} \times \frac{3}{2} = 1$ $\frac{2}{3}$ and $\frac{3}{2}$ are reciprocals.

A Use fraction bars to divide $\frac{4}{5} \div \frac{2}{5}$.

Think: How many groups of $\frac{2}{5}$ are in $\frac{4}{5}$?

$$\frac{4}{5} \div \frac{2}{5} = \text{\_\_\_\_\_}$$

B Multiply $\frac{4}{5} \times \frac{5}{2}$.

$$\frac{4}{5} \times \frac{5}{2} = \text{\_\_\_\_\_}$$

• What is the same in both problems?

_____

• The second term in the division problem, _____, and the second term

  in the multiplication problem, _____, are _____.

• Dividing $\frac{4}{5}$ by $\frac{2}{5}$ is the same as multiplying $\frac{4}{5}$ by _____.

Example 1

Toby and his dad are building a doghouse. They need to cut a 3 ft board into $\frac{1}{4}$ ft pieces. How many $\frac{1}{4}$ ft pieces can they cut?

Use reciprocals and inverse operations to divide $3 \div \frac{1}{4}$.

Write the whole number as a fraction.

$$3 \div \frac{1}{4} = \frac{\boxed{}}{1} \div \frac{1}{4}$$

Use the reciprocal of the divisor to write a multiplication problem.

$$= \frac{\boxed{}}{1} \times \frac{\boxed{}}{\boxed{}}$$

Multiply.

$$= \frac{\boxed{}}{1}, \text{ or } \text{\_\_\_\_\_}.$$

So, Toby and his dad can cut _____ $\frac{1}{4}$ ft pieces of the board.

> **Math Idea**
>
> Dividing by a number is the same as multiplying by its reciprocal.

🔑 Example 2 Find the quotient.

A Winnie needs pieces of string for a craft project. How many $\frac{1}{6}$ yd pieces of string can she cut from a piece that is $\frac{2}{3}$ yd long?

Divide $\frac{2}{3} \div \frac{1}{6}$. Check.

Use the reciprocal of the divisor to write a multiplication problem.

$$\frac{2}{3} \div \frac{1}{6} = \frac{2}{3} \times \underline{\hspace{1cm}}$$

> ### Math Idea
> Since multiplication and division are inverse operations, you can use multiplication to check your answer.

Simplify the fractions.

$$= \frac{2}{\cancel{3}} \times \frac{\cancel{6}}{1}$$

Multiply.

$$= \underline{\hspace{1.5cm}}$$

Check your answer.

$$\frac{1}{6} \times \underline{\hspace{1.5cm}} = \underline{\hspace{1.5cm}} = \underline{\hspace{1.5cm}}$$

So, Winnie can cut _____ $\frac{1}{6}$ yd pieces of string.

B Winnie has a piece of string that is $\frac{5}{6}$ yd long. She wants to cut the string into 3 equal pieces. How long will each piece be?

Divide $\frac{5}{6} \div 3$. Check.

Estimate. _____ ÷ 3 = _____

Write the whole number as a fraction.

$$\frac{5}{6} \div 3 = \frac{5}{6} \div \frac{}{1}$$

Use the reciprocal of the divisor to write a multiplication problem.

$$= \frac{5}{6} \times \underline{\hspace{1cm}}$$

Multiply.

$$= \underline{\hspace{1.5cm}}$$

Check your answer.

$$3 \times \underline{\hspace{1.5cm}} = \underline{\hspace{1.5cm}}$$

So, each piece of string will be _____ yd long.

> **Math Talk** **Explain** why your answer is reasonable.

Try This! Find the quotient. Check.

A $4 \div \frac{3}{5}$

B $\frac{2}{3} \div \frac{5}{12}$

144

Name _____

Share and Show

1. Complete: If $1 \div \frac{3}{5} = 1 \times \frac{5}{3}$, then $4 \div \frac{3}{5} = 4 \times$ _____ .

Estimate. Then write the quotient in simplest form.

2. $\frac{3}{4} \div \frac{5}{6}$

3. $3 \div \frac{3}{4}$

4. $\frac{1}{2} \div \frac{3}{4}$

5. $\frac{5}{12} \div 3$

6. Toby cuts a 5 ft board into $\frac{1}{3}$ ft pieces. How many $\frac{1}{3}$ ft pieces can he cut?

7. How many $\frac{1}{12}$ yd pieces of string can Winnie cut from a piece that is $\frac{5}{6}$ yd long?

Math Talk Explain how to find a reasonable estimate for $\frac{11}{12} \div \frac{1}{4}$.

On Your Own

Estimate. Then write the quotient in simplest form.

8. $2 \div \frac{1}{8}$

9. $\frac{3}{4} \div \frac{3}{5}$

10. $\frac{2}{5} \div 5$

11. $4 \div \frac{1}{7}$

12. Marlene has a piece of ribbon that is $\frac{2}{3}$ yd long. She wants to cut the ribbon into 6 equal pieces. How long will each piece be?

13. Soon Yee has $\frac{3}{4}$ lb of orange slices. She puts them in bags that hold $\frac{1}{8}$ lb each. How many bags does she fill?

Evaluate using the order of operations.

14. $\left(\frac{3}{5} + \frac{1}{10}\right) \div 2$

15. $\frac{3}{5} + \frac{1}{10} \div 2$

16. $\frac{3}{5} + 2 \div \frac{1}{10}$

Problem Solving REAL WORLD

Use the table for 17–21.

Tree House Measurements	
Item	**Board Length**
Ladder rung	$\frac{3}{4}$ ft
"Keep Out" sign	$\frac{5}{8}$ yd
Windowsill	$\frac{1}{2}$ yd

17. Kristen wants to cut ladder rungs from a 6 ft board. How many ladder rungs can she cut?

_____

18. **H.O.T.** **Pose a Problem** Look back at Problem 17. Write and solve a new problem by changing the length of the board Kristen is cutting for ladder rungs.

_____

_____

_____

19. Dan paints a design that has 8 equal parts along the entire length of the windowsill. How long is each part of the design?

_____

20. Dan has a board that is $\frac{15}{16}$ yd. How many "Keep Out" signs can he make if the length of the sign is changed to half of the original length?

_____

21. **Write Math** Cade has a 4 yd board. The answer is 8. What's the question?

_____

_____

22. ⭐ **Test Prep** Hal has $\frac{3}{4}$ yard of string. How many $\frac{1}{12}$ yard pieces of string can he cut from $\frac{3}{4}$ yard?

(A) 3

(B) 6

(C) 9

(D) 12

SHOW YOUR WORK

FOR MORE PRACTICE:
Standards Practice Book, pp. P71–P72

Name _____

Divide Mixed Numbers

Essential Question How do you divide mixed numbers?

🔑 UNLOCK the Problem REAL WORLD

🔓 Activity

Materials ■ pattern blocks

Find $1\frac{2}{3} \div \frac{1}{6}$, or the number of sixths in $1\frac{2}{3}$.

- Show $1\frac{2}{3}$ using pattern blocks. Draw your model.

Think: One _____ block represents $\frac{1}{6}$ of the whole.

- Cover $1\frac{2}{3}$ with _____ blocks. Draw your model.

_____ triangle blocks cover $1\frac{2}{3}$. So, there are _____ sixths in $1\frac{2}{3}$.

🔓 Example 1

A box weighing $9\frac{1}{3}$ lb contains robot kits weighing $1\frac{1}{6}$ lb apiece. How many robot kits are in the box?

Divide $9\frac{1}{3} \div 1\frac{1}{6}$.

Write the mixed numbers as fractions.

$$9\frac{1}{3} \div 1\frac{1}{6} = \frac{}{3} \div \frac{}{6}$$

Use the reciprocal of the divisor to write a multiplication problem.

$$= \frac{28}{3} \times \frac{}{}$$

Simplify.

$$= \frac{28}{\cancel{3}} \times \frac{\cancel{6}}{\cancel{7}}$$

Multiply.

$$= \frac{}{}, \text{ or } _____$$

So, there are _____ robot kits in the box.

Math Talk Explain how you would estimate to determine if this answer is reasonable.

🔑 Example 2 Four hikers shared $3\frac{1}{3}$ qt of energy drink equally. How much did each hiker receive?

Divide $3\frac{1}{3} \div 4$. Check.

Estimate. _____ $\div 4 = 1$

Write the mixed number and the whole number as fractions.

$$3\frac{1}{3} \div 4 = \frac{\boxed{}}{3} \div \frac{\boxed{}}{\boxed{}}$$

Use the reciprocal of the divisor to write a multiplication problem.

$$= \frac{10}{3} \times \frac{\boxed{}}{\boxed{}}$$

Simplify.

$$= \frac{10}{3} \times \frac{1}{4}$$

Multiply.

$$= \underline{\quad\quad}$$

Check your answer.

$$4 \times \underline{\quad\quad} = \frac{\boxed{}}{\boxed{}} = \underline{\quad\quad}$$

So, each hiker received _____ qt.

> **Math Talk** Explain why your answer is reasonable using the information in the problem.

1. **Describe** which type of division the example above represents.

_____

_____

2. **Explain** how the model on the previous page shows whether the quotient $1\frac{2}{3} \div \frac{1}{6}$ is greater than or less than the dividend.

_____

_____

3. **H.O.T.** The divisor in a division problem is between 0 and 1. Will the quotient be greater than or less than the dividend? **Explain.**

_____

_____

_____

148

Name _____

Share and Show

Estimate. Then write the quotient in simplest form.

1. $4\frac{1}{3} \div \frac{3}{4} = \dfrac{}{3} \div \frac{3}{4}$

$= \dfrac{13}{3} \times \dfrac{}{}$

$= \dfrac{}{}$, or $5\dfrac{}{9}$

2. Six hikers shared $4\frac{1}{2}$ lb of trail mix. How much trail mix did each hiker receive?

_____

3. $5\frac{2}{3} \div 3$

4. $7\frac{1}{2} \div 2\frac{1}{2}$

_____

Math Talk Explain why you write a mixed number as a fraction before using it as a dividend or divisor.

On Your Own

Estimate. Then write the quotient in simplest form.

5. How many $3\frac{1}{3}$ yd pieces can Amanda get from a $13\frac{1}{3}$ yd ribbon?

6. Samantha cut $6\frac{3}{4}$ yd of yarn into 3 equal pieces. How long was each piece?

_____

7. $5\frac{3}{4} \div 4\frac{1}{2}$

8. $5 \div 1\frac{1}{3}$

9. $6\frac{3}{4} \div 2$

10. $2\frac{2}{9} \div 1\frac{3}{7}$

11. $3\frac{3}{5} \div 2\frac{1}{4}$

12. $1\frac{5}{6} \div 1\frac{2}{9}$

13. $4\frac{1}{4} \div 12\frac{3}{4}$

14. $1\frac{1}{2} \div 1\frac{1}{4}$

Practice: Copy and Solve Evaluate using the order of operations.

15. $1\frac{1}{2} \times 2 \div 1\frac{1}{3}$

16. $1\frac{2}{5} \div 1\frac{13}{15} + \frac{5}{8}$

17. $3\frac{1}{2} - 1\frac{5}{6} \div 1\frac{2}{9}$

UNLOCK the Problem

18. Dina hikes $\frac{1}{2}$ of the easy trail and stops for a break every $3\frac{1}{4}$ miles. How many breaks will she take?

(A) 2

(B) 3

(C) 6

(D) 10

Hiking Trails			
Park	Trail	Length (mi)	Difficulty
Cuyahoga Valley National Park, Ohio	Ohio and Erie Canal Towpath	$19\frac{1}{2}$	easy
	Brandywine Gorge	$1\frac{1}{4}$	moderate
	Buckeye Trail (Jaite to Boston)	$5\frac{3}{5}$	difficult

a. What problem are you asked to solve?

_____

_____

_____

b. How will you use the information in the table to solve the problem?

_____

_____

_____

c. How can you find the distance Dina hikes? How far does she hike?

_____

_____

_____

d. What operation will you use to find how many breaks Dina takes? How many does she take?

_____

e. Fill in the bubble for the correct answer choice above.

19. One weekend Michael hikes the $1\frac{1}{4}$ mile trail twice on Saturday and the $5\frac{3}{5}$ mile trail once on Sunday. How far does he hike that weekend?

(A) $2\frac{1}{2}$ miles

(B) $6\frac{17}{20}$ miles

(C) $8\frac{1}{10}$ miles

(D) $11\frac{1}{5}$ miles

20. Josh makes picture frames from old CD cases by gluing cases side-by-side to a strip of wood. If the length of a CD case is $4\frac{7}{8}$ inches, how many cases can Josh glue to a piece of wood that is $19\frac{1}{2}$ inches long?

(A) 2

(B) $3\frac{1}{2}$

(C) 4

(D) 6

Use a Model · Fraction Operations

Essential Question How can you use a model to solve multistep problems with fractions and mixed numbers?

🔑 UNLOCK the Problem REAL WORLD

Sam had $\frac{3}{4}$ lb of granola. Each day he took $\frac{1}{8}$ lb to school for a snack. If he had $\frac{1}{4}$ lb left over, how many days did Sam take granola to school?

Use the graphic organizer below to help you solve the problem.

Read the Problem

What do I need to find?	What information do I need to use?	How will I use the information?
I need to find _____ _____ _____.	Sam started with _____ lb of granola and took _____ lb each day. He had _____ lb left over.	I will draw a bar model to find how much _____ _____ _____.

Solve the Problem

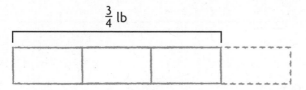

$\frac{3}{4}$ lb

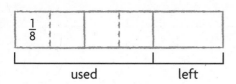

$\frac{1}{8}$

used   left

The model shows that Sam used _____ lb of granola.

_____ groups of $\frac{1}{8}$ are equivalent to $\frac{1}{2}$

so $\frac{1}{2} \div \frac{1}{8} =$ _____ .

So, Sam took granola to school for _____ days.

🔓 Try Another Problem

For a science experiment, Mr. Barrows divides $\frac{2}{3}$ cup salt into small jars, each containing $\frac{1}{12}$ cup. If he has $\frac{1}{6}$ cup of salt left over, how many jars does he fill?

Read the Problem

What do I need to find?	What information do I need to use?	How will I use the information?

Solve the Problem

So, Mr. Barrows fills _____ jars.

1. Write an expression you could use to solve the problem.

_____

2. Suppose that Mr. Barrows starts with $1\frac{2}{3}$ cups of salt. **Explain** how you could find how many jars he fills.

_____

_____

_____

Name _____

Share and Show

? UNLOCK the Problem Tips

- Circle the question.
- Underline important information.
- Check to make sure you answered the question.

1. There is $\frac{4}{5}$ lb of sand in the class science supplies. If one scoop of sand weighs $\frac{1}{20}$ lb, how many scoops of sand can Maria get from the class supplies and still leave $\frac{1}{2}$ lb in the supplies?

First, draw a bar model.

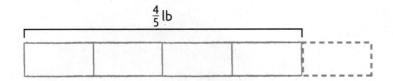

$\frac{4}{5}$ lb

SHOW YOUR WORK

Next, find how much sand Maria gets.

Maria will get $\frac{}{10}$ lb of sand.

Finally, find the number of scoops.

_____ groups of $\frac{1}{20}$ are equivalent to $\frac{}{10}$

so $\frac{}{10} \div \frac{1}{20} =$ _____.

So, Maria will get _____ scoops of sand.

2. **H.O.T.** **What if** Maria leaves $\frac{2}{5}$ lb of sand in the supplies? How many scoops of sand can she get?

_____

3. There are 6 gallons of distilled water in the science supplies. If 10 students each use an equal amount of the distilled water and there is 1 gal left in the supplies, how much will each student get?

_____

On Your Own......................................

Choose a STRATEGY

Work Backward
Solve a Simpler Problem
Choose an Operation
Use a Model
Use a Formula
Draw a Diagram

4. **H.O.T.** The total weight of the fish in a tank of tropical fish at Fish 'n' Fur was $\frac{7}{8}$ lb. Each fish weighed $\frac{1}{64}$ lb. After Eric bought some fish, the total weight of the fish remaining in the tank was $\frac{1}{2}$ lb. How many fish did Eric buy?

_____

5. An adult gerbil at Fish 'n' Fur weighed $\frac{1}{5}$ lb. A young gerbil weighed $\frac{1}{4}$ of that amount. How much did the young gerbil weigh?

_____

6. Fish 'n' Fur had a bin containing $2\frac{1}{2}$ lb of gerbil food. After selling bags of gerbil food that each held $\frac{3}{4}$ lb, $\frac{1}{4}$ lb of food was left in the bin. How many bags of gerbil food were sold?

_____

······· **SHOW YOUR WORK** ·······

7. **Write Math** ▶ Niko bought 2 lb of dog treats. He gave his dog $\frac{3}{5}$ lb of treats one week and $\frac{7}{10}$ lb of treats the next week. To find how much was left, he wrote the expression $2 - \left(\frac{3}{5} + \frac{7}{10}\right)$. Niko subtracted $\frac{3}{5}$ from 2, then added $\frac{7}{10}$ to the sum. Did he get the right answer? **Explain.**

_____

_____

_____

8. ⭐ **Test Prep** Keisha cut $\frac{35}{36}$ yard of fabric into 7 pieces. How long was each piece?

Ⓐ $\frac{1}{8}$ yard

Ⓑ $\frac{5}{36}$ yard

Ⓒ $\frac{1}{7}$ yard

Ⓓ $\frac{7}{36}$ yard

FOR MORE PRACTICE:
Standards Practice Book, pp. P75–P76

Name _____

Choose a Method

Essential Question How can you decide whether to use mental math or paper and pencil to multiply and divide fractions?

🔑 UNLOCK the Problem REAL WORLD

How many $\frac{1}{2}$ cup servings can Ricky pour from a pitcher of juice that holds 6 cups?

Sometimes, you can use mental math to solve fraction problems.

🔓 One Way Use a related multiplication sentence.

Divide $6 \div \frac{1}{2}$.

Use a related multiplication number sentence.

$$6 = \blacksquare \times \frac{1}{2}$$

Use mental math to find the missing factor.

Think: How many halves in 6 wholes?

$$6 = \underline{\quad} \times \frac{1}{2}$$

Use the factor as the quotient in the original division sentence.

$$6 \div \frac{1}{2} = \underline{\quad}$$

So, $6 \div \frac{1}{2} = \underline{\quad}$.

🔓 Another Way Use a common denominator.

Divide $\frac{3}{4} \div \frac{1}{8}$.

Find equivalent fractions using a common denominator.

$$\frac{}{8} \div \frac{1}{8}$$

Think: How many eighths in 1 fourth?
How many eighths in 3 fourths?

Divide mentally.

$$\frac{}{8} \div \frac{1}{8} = \underline{\quad}$$

Think: How many groups of $\frac{1}{8}$?

So, $\frac{3}{4} \div \frac{1}{8} = \underline{\quad}$.

Math Talk Explain why mental math can be used to solve the problems on this page.

🔒 Example

Alyssa makes picture frames using $1\frac{1}{6}$ yd of ribbon for each frame. She has enough ribbon to make $12\frac{3}{4}$ picture frames. What is the least amount of ribbon that Alyssa could have?

Some numbers are not easy to work with mentally, so use paper and pencil.

Multiply $1\frac{1}{6} \times 12\frac{3}{4}$.

Write the mixed numbers as fractions.

$$1\frac{1}{6} \times 12\frac{3}{4} = \frac{\boxed{}}{6} \times \frac{\boxed{}}{4}$$

Multiply.

$$= \frac{\boxed{} \times \boxed{}}{6 \times 4}$$

$$= \frac{\boxed{}}{24}$$

Write the product as a mixed number and simplify.

$$= \underline{\hspace{2cm}}$$

So, Alyssa has at least _____ yd of ribbon.

---

1. **Explain** why mental math would probably not be a good method to use to solve this problem.

   _____

   _____

2. **Give** an example of a division problem involving two different fractions that would be easy to solve using mental math. Explain why it would be easy.

   _____

3. **Explain** how to solve $2\frac{1}{2} \times 8$ using mental math.

   _____

   _____

4. **Explain** how to divide $2\frac{1}{2} \div \frac{1}{4}$ using mental math.

   _____

   _____

Name _____

Share and Show

Solve. Choose mental math or paper and pencil.

1. $5 \div \frac{1}{3}$

$5 =$ _____ $\times \frac{1}{3}$

$5 \div \frac{1}{3} =$ _____

2. $10 \times \frac{7}{15}$

_____

3. $7\frac{1}{2} \div \frac{3}{8}$

_____

Solve. Choose mental math or paper and pencil. Explain which method you used.

4. Melissa has $\frac{6}{7}$ yd of ribbon to decorate hats. If each hat requires $\frac{2}{7}$ yd of ribbon, how many hats can Melissa decorate?

_____

_____

_____

5. Some paint comes in $\frac{5}{6}$ oz tubes. Carol used $4\frac{1}{5}$ tubes of paint to stencil the walls in her room How much paint did she use?

_____

_____

_____

Math Talk Explain when mental math might be an appropriate method to use to solve a problem.

On Your Own

Solve. Choose mental math or paper and pencil.

6. $3\frac{3}{5} \div 1\frac{1}{5}$

_____

7. $3\frac{3}{4} \times \frac{1}{5}$

_____

8. $4\frac{1}{3} \times \frac{7}{16}$

_____

9. $\frac{1}{6} \div \frac{7}{12}$

_____

Solve. Choose mental math or paper and pencil. Explain which method you used.

10. Rai used $4\frac{1}{5}$ qt of paint on her jewelry boxes. If she used $2\frac{1}{3}$ qt of paint on each box, how many boxes did she paint?

_____

_____

_____

11. $\frac{4}{5}$ of the students in one class had pets. $\frac{3}{8}$ of those students had dogs. What fraction of the students had dogs?

_____

_____

_____

Problem Solving 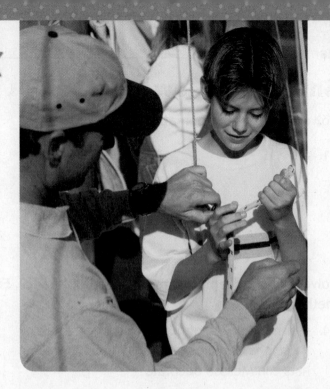 REAL WORLD

12. Nola is learning to tie a square knot. She practiced for $\frac{1}{2}$ hour on Monday. She practiced $1\frac{1}{2}$ times as long on Tuesday. How long did Nola practice on Tuesday?

_____

13. Into how many $\frac{5}{8}$ yd pieces can Carl cut a length of wire that is $6\frac{7}{8}$ yd long?

_____

14. **H.O.T.** Malia makes a pillow and sews 108 buttons onto it. If $\frac{8}{9}$ of the buttons are silver, how many buttons are not silver?

_____

SHOW YOUR WORK

15. Natalie has 30 ft of rope that will be cut into $\frac{5}{6}$ ft pieces. How many $\frac{5}{6}$ ft pieces can she cut from the rope?

_____

16. **Write Math** ➤ A can of green chiles weighs $\frac{1}{4}$ lb. Explain how you can use mental math to find the number of cans of green chiles in a carton weighing 12 lb.

_____

_____

_____

17. ⭐ **Test Prep** Carly volunteered a total of 15 hours at the animal shelter last summer. If she worked for $1\frac{1}{2}$ hours each day, how many days did she volunteer?

Ⓐ 10

Ⓑ 12

Ⓒ 15

Ⓓ $22\frac{1}{2}$

FOR MORE PRACTICE:
Standards Practice Book, pp. P77–P78

Name _____

 Chapter 4 Review/Test

▶ **Vocabulary**

Choose the best term from the box.

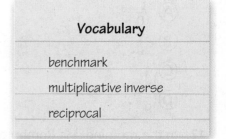

Vocabulary
benchmark
multiplicative inverse
reciprocal

1. A number is a _____ if it is one of two numbers

   whose product is 1. (p.136)

2. Another term for one of two numbers whose product is 1 is

   _____. (p.136)

▶ **Concepts and Skills**

Use the model to find the quotient. (pp. 135–138)

3. $\frac{3}{4} \div 3 =$ _____

4. $\frac{2}{3} \div \frac{1}{6} =$ _____

Find the product or quotient. Write it in simplest form.

(pp. 125–128, 143–146, 155–158)

5. $\frac{7}{8} \div \frac{3}{5}$

6. $\frac{1}{5} \times \frac{1}{4}$

7. Jon has $\frac{3}{4}$ cup of raisins. He puts the raisins into bags, each holding $\frac{1}{8}$ cup. How many bags will Jon use?

_____   _____   _____

Estimate. Then write the product or quotient in simplest form.

(pp. 129–132, 147–150, 155–158)

8. $2\frac{1}{5} \times 3\frac{3}{4}$

9. $3\frac{3}{4} \div 6$

10. Josiah cuts $13\frac{1}{8}$ yd of grape vines into 7 equal pieces to make wreaths. How long is each piece?

_____   _____   _____

Fill in the bubble to show your answer.

11. $\frac{2}{5}$ of the fish in Gary's fish tank are guppies. $\frac{1}{4}$ of the guppies are red. What fraction of the fish in Gary's tank are red guppies?

    (pp. 117–120, 125–128)

    (A) $\frac{1}{10}$

    (B) $\frac{3}{20}$

    (C) $\frac{1}{5}$

    (D) $\frac{2}{9}$

12. In the morning, Mr. Romburg drove $\frac{1}{3}$ of the distance from Appledale to Hardy. In the afternoon, he drove $\frac{1}{3}$ of the remaining distance. What fraction of the total distance from Appledale to Hardy did Mr. Romburg drive in the afternoon? (pp. 117–120, 125–128)

    (A) $\frac{1}{9}$

    (B) $\frac{2}{9}$

    (C) $\frac{1}{3}$

    (D) $\frac{2}{3}$

13. Louis used $\frac{2}{5}$ of a roll of a $22\frac{1}{8}$ foot roll of tape to wrap birthday presents. Which is the best estimate of the amount of tape that he used? (pp. 121–124)

    (A) 6 feet

    (B) 11 feet

    (C) 16 feet

    (D) 22 feet

14. It is $4\frac{3}{8}$ miles from Fran's house to the Civic Center, and $1\frac{3}{5}$ times that far from her house to City Hall. How far is it from her house to City Hall? (pp. 129–132, 155–158)

    (A) $2\frac{5}{8}$ miles

    (B) $4\frac{47}{64}$ miles

    (C) 7 miles

    (D) 8 miles

15. Monty is making punch in a $\frac{7}{8}$ gallon container. How many cups of punch can he make? (1 cup $= \frac{1}{16}$ gallon) (pp. 135–138, 143–146)

    (A) 2 cups   (C) 14 cups

    (B) 7 cups   (D) 16 cups

Fill in the bubble to show your answer.

16. Margie hiked a $17\frac{7}{8}$ mile trail. She stopped every $3\frac{2}{5}$ miles to take a picture. Which is the best estimate of the number of times she stopped? (pp. 139–142)

    (A) 4
    (B) 6
    (C) 7
    (D) 8

17. Sophie has $\frac{3}{4}$ quart of peanut butter. If she divides the peanut butter into containers that hold $\frac{1}{16}$ quart, how many containers can she fill? (pp. 143–146)

    (A) $\frac{3}{32}$
    (B) 3
    (C) 12
    (D) 48

18. Brad and Wes are building a tree house. They cut a $12\frac{1}{2}$ foot piece of wood into 5 equally-sized pieces. How long is each piece of wood? (pp. 147–150)

    (A) $\frac{1}{2}$ foot
    (B) $2\frac{1}{4}$ feet
    (C) $2\frac{1}{2}$ feet
    (D) $12\frac{1}{2}$ feet

19. Sal had a board $\frac{5}{6}$ yard in length. He cut off $\frac{1}{3}$ yard, then cut what remained into pieces each $\frac{1}{6}$ yard long. How many pieces were there? (pp. 151–154)

    (A) 2
    (B) 3
    (C) 4
    (D) 6

20. Ink cartridges weigh $\frac{1}{8}$ pound. The total weight of the cartridges in a box is $4\frac{1}{2}$ pounds. How many cartridges does the box contain? (pp. 147–150, 155–158)

    (A) 18   (C) 36
    (B) 32   (D) 40

▶ Short Answer

21. A bag contained $\frac{3}{4}$ pound of marbles. Each marble weighed $\frac{1}{36}$ pound. After Ashley removed some marbles from the bag, it weighed $\frac{1}{3}$ pound. How many marbles did Ashley remove? (pp. 151–154)

_____

22. Beth had 1 yard of ribbon. She used $\frac{1}{3}$ yard for a project. She wants to divide the rest of the ribbon into $\frac{1}{6}$ yard pieces. How many $\frac{1}{6}$ yard pieces of ribbon can she make? Explain your solution. (pp. 143–146)

_____

_____

_____

▶ Performance Task

23. Brianna makes wooden birdhouses. She needs $\frac{3}{8}$ quart of paint for each birdhouse.

A If Brianna has $\frac{3}{4}$ quart paint, how many birdhouses can she paint?

_____

B Brianna wants to paint 3 birdhouses half red and half yellow. How much red paint will she need?

_____

C Brianna has $5\frac{1}{4}$ quarts of paint. How much will she have left after she paints 5 birdhouses?

_____

D Brianna has $\frac{7}{8}$ quart of red paint left. Will she have enough to paint 4 birdhouses half red and half yellow? Explain.

_____

_____

E Brianna wants to paint 20 birdhouses to sell at a crafts fair. Estimate the amount of paint she will need. Explain your answer.

_____

Ratio, Proportional Reasoning, and Percent

Focal POINT Number and Operations: Connecting ratio and rate to multiplication and division

The St. Louis Cardinals, based in St. Louis, Missouri, were founded in 1882.

Meet Me in St. Louis

Baseball teams, like the St. Louis Cardinals, record information about each player on the team. These statistics are used to describe a player's performance.

Project

You will begin to learn about the Big Idea when you work on this project.

Batting averages are usually recorded as a decimal to the thousandths place. The table shows the batting averages of three baseball players who received the Most Valuable Player award while playing for the St. Louis Cardinals. Write each batting average as a decimal to the thousandths place and as a percent. Then list the players in order from the highest batting average to the lowest batting average.

Important Facts

Player Name	Batting Average
Albert Pujols (2008)	$\frac{187}{524}$
Stan Musial (1948)	$\frac{230}{611}$
Rogers Hornsby (1925)	$\frac{203}{504}$

Stan Musial also won the Most Valuable Player award in 1946 when he had a batting average of 36.5% and in 1943 when he had a batting average of $\frac{220}{611}$. In which year (1943, 1946, or 1948) did Musial have the highest batting average?

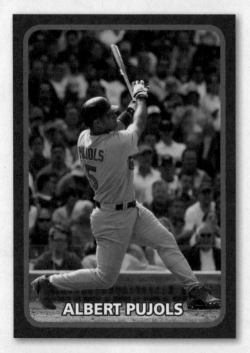

ALBERT PUJOLS

Completed by _____

Ratios, Rates, and Percents

Show What You Know

Check your understanding of important skills.

Name _____

▶ **Multiply or Divide to Find Equivalent Fractions** Multiply or divide to find two equivalent fractions for the given fraction.

1. $\frac{1}{2}$

2. $\frac{5}{6}$

3. $\frac{12}{18}$

_____ _____ _____

▶ **Write Decimals as Fractions** Write each decimal as a fraction in simplest form.

4. 0.05

5. 0.43

6. 0.12

7. 0.7

_____ _____ _____ _____

▶ **Compare Numbers** Compare. Write < or >.

8. 0.66 ◯ 0.60

9. 3.39 ◯ 3.43

10. 2.54 ◯ 2.546

11. 0.29 ◯ $\frac{1}{4}$

12. $\frac{3}{8}$ ◯ 0.38

13. $\frac{1}{7}$ ◯ $\frac{1}{9}$

14. $\frac{2}{5}$ ◯ $\frac{4}{5}$

15. $\frac{1}{3}$ ◯ $\frac{2}{9}$

The student council should have 1 representative for every 25 students. Be a Math Detective and determine which of these situations fits the description. Explain your answer.

a. 5 representatives for 100 students

b. 10 representatives for 250 students

c. 15 representatives for 300 students

Vocabulary Builder

▶ **Visualize It** ••

Complete the bubble map with review words that are related to fractions.

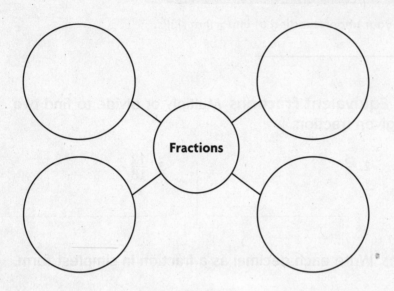

Review Words

denominator

equivalent fraction

factor

formula

numerator

pattern

simplify

variable

Preview Words

equivalent ratios

percent

proportion

rate

ratio

unit rate

▶ **Understand Vocabulary** •••••••••••••••••••••••••••••••••••••

Complete the sentences using the preview words.

1. A comparison of one number to another by division is a

   _____.

2. _____ name the same comparison.

3. A ratio that compares quantities with different units is a

   _____.

4. A _____ is a rate that compares a quantity
   to 1 unit.

5. A _____ is a statement that two ratios are equal.

6. A _____ is a ratio that compares a number
   to 100.

166   **GO**
           Online   • eStudent Edition • Multimedia eGlossary

Name _____

Ratios

Essential Question How can you write ratios and find equivalent ratios?

UNLOCK the Problem REAL WORLD

During the 2009 Great Backyard Bird Count, there were 30 bald eagles spotted in Arizona, 498 bald eagles spotted in Missouri, and 160 bald eagles spotted in Pennsylvania.

You can compare the number of bald eagles seen in these states using ratios. A **ratio** is a comparison of two quantities by division. There are three ways to write the ratio of bald eagles spotted in Arizona to those spotted in Pennsylvania.

Using words	As a fraction	With a colon
30 to 160	$\frac{30}{160}$	30:160

Ratios can be written to compare a part to a part, a part to a whole, or a whole to a part.

🔑 **Write each ratio using words, as a fraction, and with a colon.**

Ⓐ **Arizona bald eagles to Missouri bald eagles**

_____ to _____ | ⎯⎯⎯⎯ | _____ : _____   Part to part

Ⓑ **Pennsylvania bald eagles to total bald eagles in the three states**

_____ to _____ | ⎯⎯⎯⎯ | _____ : _____   Part to whole

Ⓒ **Total bald eagles in the three states to Missouri bald eagles**

_____ to _____ | ⎯⎯⎯⎯ | _____ : _____   Whole to part

Chapter 5 167

Equivalent ratios Equivalent ratios are ratios that name the same comparison. You can find equivalent ratios by multiplying or dividing both quantities in a ratio by the same number.

🔓 One Way Multiply or divide by a form of one.

Write two equivalent ratios for $\frac{6}{8}$.

A Multiply by a form of one.

Multiply the numerator and denominator by the same number.

$$\frac{6 \cdot \boxed{}}{8 \cdot \boxed{}} = \underline{}$$

B Divide by a form of one.

Divide the numerator and denominator by the same number.

$$\frac{6 \div \boxed{}}{8 \div \boxed{}} = \frac{\boxed{}}{\boxed{}}$$

So, $\frac{6}{8}$, _____, and _____ are equivalent ratios.

🔓 Another Way Use a table.

Jessa made fruit punch by mixing 2 pints of orange juice with 5 pints of pineapple juice. To make more punch, she needs to mix orange juice and pineapple juice in the same ratio. Write three equivalent ratios for $\frac{2}{5}$.

	Original ratio	2 · 2 ↓	2 · 3 ↓	2 · ☐ ↓
Orange juice (pints)	2	☐	☐	8
Pineapple juice (pints)	5	☐	15	☐
		↑ 5 · 2	↑ 5 · ☐	↑ 5 · 4

So, $\frac{2}{5}$, _____, _____, and _____ are equivalent ratios.

Math Talk Explain how ratios are similar to fractions. Explain how they are different.

Name _____

1. Write the ratio of the number of red bars to blue stars.

_____

Write the ratio in two different ways.

2. 8 to 16

_____

3. $\frac{4}{24}$

_____

4. 1:3

_____

✓ 5. 7 to 9

_____

Write two equivalent ratios.

✓ 6. $\frac{2}{10}$

_____

7.

3		
7		

8.

5		
2		

Math Talk Explain whether the ratios 5:2 and 2:5 are the same or different.

On Your Own

Write each ratio in two different ways.

9. $\frac{16}{40}$

_____

10. 8:12

_____

11. 4 to 11

_____

12. 2:13

_____

Write two equivalent ratios.

13. $\frac{6}{9}$

_____

14.

9		
8		

15.

5		
2		

Determine whether the ratios are equivalent.

16. $\frac{2}{3}$ and $\frac{8}{12}$

_____

17. $\frac{8}{10}$ and $\frac{6}{10}$

_____

18. $\frac{16}{60}$ and $\frac{4}{15}$

_____

19. $\frac{3}{14}$ and $\frac{9}{28}$

_____

Problem Solving · REAL WORLD

Use the diagram of a birdhouse for 20–22.

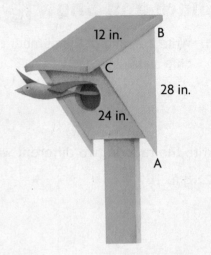

12 in. B
C
28 in.
24 in.
A

20. Write the ratio of *AB* to *BC*. Then write three equivalent ratios.

_____

21. Write the ratio of the shortest side length of triangle *ABC* to the perimeter of the triangle. Then write three equivalent ratios.

_____

22. Write the ratio of the perimeter of triangle *ABC* to the longest side length of the triangle. Then write three equivalent ratios.

_____

· · · · · · **SHOW YOUR WORK** · · · · ·

23. Leandra has three pictures on her dresser. The pictures measure 4 inches wide by 6 inches long, 5 inches wide by 7 inches long, and 8 inches wide by 10 inches long. Which picture(s) have a width to length ratio equivalent to 2:3?

_____

24. ☀ **H.O.T.** **What's the Question?** The ratio of total students in Ms. Murray's class to students in the class who have an older brother is 3 to 1. The answer is 1:2. What is the question?

_____

_____

25. **Write Math** ▶ How are equivalent ratios like equivalent fractions?

_____

_____

_____

26. ⭐ **Test Prep** There are usually 2 boys for every 3 girls in a school drama club. If 21 girls sign up for drama club this year, how many boys would you expect to sign up?

(**A**) 21   (**C**) 14

(**B**) 18   (**D**) 12

FOR MORE PRACTICE:
Standards Practice Book, pp. P83–P84

Name _____

Rates

Essential Question How can you use unit rates to make comparisons?

UNLOCK the Problem — REAL WORLD

The star fruit, or carambola, is the fruit of a tree that is native to Indonesia, India, and Sri Lanka. Slices of the fruit are in the shape of a five-pointed star. Lara paid $9.60 for 16 oz of star fruit. Find the price of 1 ounce of star fruit.

A **rate** is a ratio that compares two quantities that have different units of measure.

When a rate makes a comparison to 1 unit, that rate is called a **unit rate**. You can find a unit rate by dividing the numerator and denominator by the number in the denominator.

- Underline the sentence that tells you what you are trying to find.
- Circle the numbers you need to use to solve the problem.

Write the unit rate for the price of star fruit.

Write a ratio that compares _____

to _____.

Divide the numerator and denominator by

the quantity in the _____.

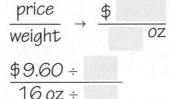

$$\frac{price}{weight} \rightarrow \frac{\$\ \rule{1cm}{0.15mm}}{\rule{1cm}{0.15mm}\ oz}$$

$$\frac{\$9.60 \div \rule{1cm}{0.15mm}}{16\ oz \div \rule{1cm}{0.15mm}}$$

$$\frac{\$\ \rule{1cm}{0.15mm}}{1\ oz}$$

So, the unit rate is _____. The price is _____ per ounce.

Math Talk Explain the difference between a ratio and a rate.

- Explain why the unit rate is equivalent to the original rate.

_____

_____

_____

_____

🔒 Example

A During migration, a hummingbird can fly **210** miles in **7** hours, and a goose can fly **165** miles in **3** hours. Which bird flies at a faster rate?

Write the rate for each bird.

Hummingbird: $\dfrac{\text{miles}}{7\ \text{hours}}$ 　　 Goose: $\dfrac{165\ \text{miles}}{\text{hours}}$

Write the unit rates.

$\dfrac{210\ \text{mi} \div }{7\ \text{hr} \div }$ 　　 $\dfrac{165\ \text{mi} \div }{3\ \text{hr} \div }$

$\dfrac{\text{mi}}{1\ \text{hr}}$ 　　 $\dfrac{\text{mi}}{1\ \text{hr}}$

Compare the unit rates. _____ miles per hour is faster than _____ miles per hour.

So, the _____ flies at a faster rate.

B A 64-ounce bottle of apple juice costs **$5.76**. A 15-ounce bottle of apple juice costs **$1.80**. Which item costs less per ounce?

Write the rate for each bottle.

64-ounce bottle: $\dfrac{}{64\ \text{ounces}}$ 　　 15-ounce bottle: $\dfrac{}{\text{ounces}}$

Write the unit rates.

$\dfrac{ \div }{64\ \text{oz} \div }$ 　　 $\dfrac{\$1.80 \div }{\text{oz} \div }$

$\dfrac{}{1\ \text{oz}}$ 　　 $\dfrac{}{\text{oz}}$

Compare the unit rates. _____ per ounce is less expensive than _____ per ounce.

So, the _____-ounce bottle costs less per ounce.

Try This! At one grocery store, a dozen eggs cost **$1.20**. At another store, $1\frac{1}{2}$ dozen eggs cost **$2.16**. Which is the better buy?

Store 1: 　　　　　　　　　　　 Store 2:

The unit price is lower at Store _____, so a dozen eggs for _____ is the better buy.

Name _____

Share and Show   . . . .

Write the rate as a fraction. Then find the unit rate.

1. Sara drove 72 miles on 4 gallons of gas.

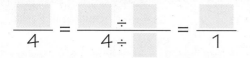

$$\frac{}{4} = \frac{ \div }{4 \div } = \frac{}{1}$$

2. Dean paid $27.00 for 4 movie tickets.

_____

3. Amy and Mai have to read *Bud, Not Buddy* for a class. Amy reads 20 pages in 2 days. Mai reads 35 pages in 3 days. Who reads at a faster rate?

_____

4. An online music store offers 5 downloads for $6.25. Another online music store offers 12 downloads for $17.40. Which store offers the better deal?

_____

> **Math Talk** Explain how to find a unit rate.

On Your Own . . . .

Write the rate as a fraction. Then find the unit rate.

5. A company packed 108 items in 12 boxes.

_____

6. There are 112 students for 14 teachers.

_____

7. Geoff charges $27 for 3 hours of swimming lessons. Anne charges $32 for 4 hours of swimming lessons. Which swimming instructor offers a better deal?

_____

8. One florist made 16 bouquets in 5 hours. A second florist made 40 bouquets in 12 hours. Which florist makes bouquets at a faster rate?

_____

Tell which rate is faster by comparing unit rates.

9. $\frac{160 \text{ mi}}{2 \text{ hr}}$ and $\frac{210 \text{ mi}}{3 \text{ hr}}$

10. $\frac{270 \text{ ft}}{9 \text{ min}}$ and $\frac{180 \text{ ft}}{9 \text{ min}}$

11. $\frac{250 \text{ m}}{10 \text{ s}}$ and $\frac{120 \text{ m}}{4 \text{ s}}$

_____

12. Ryan wants to buy treats for his puppy.
If Ryan wants to buy the treats that cost the
least per pack, which treat should he buy?
Explain.

a. What do you need to find?

_____

_____

Cost of Dog Treats

Name	Cost	Number of Packs
Pup Bites	$5.76	4
Doggie Treats	$7.38	6
Pupster Snacks	$7.86	6
Nutri-Biscuits	$9.44	8

b. Find the price per pack for each treat.
Explain each step.

_____

_____

_____

_____

_____

_____

c. Complete the sentences.
The treat with the highest price per pack is

_____.

The treat with the lowest price per pack is

_____.

Ryan should buy _____

because _____

_____.

13. **Write Math** What information do
you need to consider in order to decide
whether one product is a better deal than
another? When might the lower unit rate not
be the best choice? **Explain**.

_____

_____

_____

_____

_____

14. **Test Prep** A 32-oz box of cereal costs
$3.84. What is the unit rate?

(A) $0.12 for 1 oz

(B) $1.92 for 16 oz

(C) $0.24 for 1 oz

(D) $3.84 for 32 oz

Model Proportions

Essential Question How can you model proportions?

A **proportion** is a statement that shows that two ratios are equivalent.
An example of a proportion is $\frac{1}{2} = \frac{4}{8}$ since $\frac{1}{2}$ and $\frac{4}{8}$ are equivalent ratios.
Two fractions that form a proportion are said to be proportional.

Investigate

Materials ■ two-color counters

Shirin made a rectangular piece of digital art on the computer. Its
dimensions are 12 inches and 18 inches. She prints out a smaller
version of her artwork. The dimensions of the printed art are
whole numbers of inches. The dimensions of the original artwork
and the printed version are proportional.

Use two-color counters to model the proportion.

A. Use red and yellow counters to model the ratio $\frac{12}{18}$.

B. Separate the red and yellow counters into two equal
groups. Write the ratio of the number of red counters
to the number of yellow counters in each group.

_____

C. Separate the counters into smaller equal groups.
How many groups do you have? Write the ratio of
the number of red counters to the number of yellow
counters in each group.

_____

D. Use the ratios you found in B and C to write a proportion.

_____

Draw Conclusions

1. **Explain** how you used counters to find equivalent ratios.

   _____

   _____

2. **Tell** how a single group of five counters representing $\frac{2}{3}$ can be equivalent to $\frac{12}{18}$.

   _____

   _____

3. **H.O.T.** **Application** How can you use counters to find a ratio equivalent to $\frac{3}{5}$ and then write a proportion?

   _____

   _____

   _____

Make Connections

You can determine whether two ratios form a proportion by finding a common denominator. Two ratios form a proportion if the ratios are equivalent.

Determine whether $\frac{3}{4}$ and $\frac{24}{36}$ form a proportion.

Determine a common denominator.

Rewrite the ratios using the _____.

Compare the ratios to determine whether they are

_____.

36 is a multiple of _____, so _____ is the

least common _____.

$$\frac{3 \times \quad}{4 \times \quad} \overset{?}{=} \frac{24}{36}$$

$$\frac{\quad}{36} \overset{?}{=} \frac{24}{36}$$

The ratios _____ equivalent, so they _____ form a proportion.

Math Talk **Tell** whether $\frac{3}{4}$ and $\frac{12}{18}$ form a proportion.

Name _____

Share and Show

Write the ratio shown. Then find an equivalent ratio to write
a proportion.

1.

$$\frac{}{} = \frac{}{}$$

_____

2.

_____

3.

_____

4.

_____

Use common denominators to determine whether the ratios form
a proportion.

5. $\frac{2}{3}$ and $\frac{6}{10}$

_____

6. $\frac{3}{5}$ and $\frac{9}{15}$

_____

7. $\frac{6}{7}$ and $\frac{12}{14}$

_____

8. $\frac{12}{24}$ and $\frac{10}{20}$

_____

9. $\frac{3}{6}$ and $\frac{6}{9}$

_____

10. $\frac{3}{12}$ and $\frac{2}{3}$

_____

11. **Write Math** ▶ Explain how to tell whether the ratios $\frac{8}{10}$ and $\frac{20}{25}$
form a proportion.

_____

_____

Problem Solving · REAL WORLD

Use the table for 12–16.

Carbon

Sulfur

Subatomic Particles of Elements			
Element	Protons	Neutrons	Electrons
Carbon	6	6	6
Chromium	24	28	24
Krypton	36	48	36
Oxygen	8	8	8
Sodium	11	12	11
Sulfur	16	16	16
Titanium	22	26	22
Zinc	30	35	30

Zinc

12. Write the ratio of the number of electrons in carbon to the number of electrons in oxygen. Then find an equivalent ratio to write a proportion.

SHOW YOUR WORK

13. Write the ratio of the number of protons in oxygen to the number of protons in sulfur. Identify two other elements that have an equivalent ratio of protons. Then use the ratios to write a proportion.

14. Write the ratio of the number of protons in chromium to the number of neutrons in chromium. Identify another element that has an equivalent ratio of protons to neutrons. Then use the ratios to write a proportion.

15. **H.O.T.** **Write Math** ▶ The ratio of two elements' protons forms a proportion with the ratio 1 to 6. What are the two elements? Explain.

16. The ratio of one element's electrons to another element's neutrons forms a proportion with the ratio 3 to 2. What are the two elements?

    (A) sulfur to chromium

    (B) chromium to sulfur

    (C) sodium to carbon

    (D) krypton to zinc

FOR MORE PRACTICE:
Standards Practice Book, pp. P87–P88

Name _____

Solve Proportions Using Equivalent Ratios

Essential Question How can you use equivalent ratios to solve proportions?

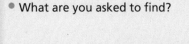 **UNLOCK the Problem** REAL WORLD

In warm weather, the Anderson family likes to spend time on the family's boat. The boat uses 2 gallons of gas to travel 12 miles on the lake. How much gas would the boat use to travel 48 miles?

> • What are you asked to find?
> _____
> _____

 Solve the proportion.

Let g represent the unknown number of gallons. Write a proportion.

$$\frac{\text{gallons}}{\text{miles}} \rightarrow \frac{2}{12} = \frac{g}{48} \leftarrow \frac{\text{gallons}}{\text{miles}}$$

Make a table of equivalent rates.

	Original rate	$2 \cdot 2$ ↓	$2 \cdot$ ☐ ↓	$2 \cdot$ ☐ ↓
Gas used (gallons)	2	☐	6	☐
Distance (miles)	12	24	☐	48
		↑ $12 \cdot$ ☐	↑ $12 \cdot 3$	↑ $12 \cdot$ ☐

The rates $\frac{2}{12}$ and _____ are equivalent rates,

so $\dfrac{2}{12} = \dfrac{☐}{48}$.

$g =$ _____

The boat will use _____ gallons of gas to travel 48 miles.

• **What if** the boat uses 14 gallons of gas? Explain how you can use equivalent rates to find the number of miles the boat travels when it uses 14 gallons of gas.

_____

_____

Chapter 5 179

🔑 Example Solve the proportion.

A $\frac{3}{4} = \frac{n}{20}$

You can use common denominators to write equivalent ratios.

_____ is a multiple of 4, so _____ is a common denominator.

Multiply the _____ and denominator by _____ to write the ratios using a common denominator.

The _____ are the same, so the _____ are equal to each other.

$n =$ _____

$$\frac{3}{4} = \frac{n}{20}$$

$$\frac{3 \times \boxed{}}{4 \times \boxed{}} = \frac{n}{20}$$

$$\frac{\boxed{}}{20} = \frac{n}{20}$$

Check your answer by making a table of equivalent ratios.

Original ratio

| 3 · | 3 · | 3 · | 3 · |

3	6			
4	8			

4 ·   4 ·   4 ·   4 ·

B $\frac{56}{42} = \frac{8}{x}$

Write an equivalent ratio with 8 in the numerator.

Think: Divide 56 by _____ to get 8.

So, divide the denominator by _____ as well.

The _____ are the same, so the _____ are equal to each other.

$x =$ _____

$$\frac{56}{42} = \frac{8}{x}$$

$$\frac{56 \div \boxed{}}{42 \div \boxed{}} = \frac{8}{x}$$

$$\frac{8}{\boxed{}} = \frac{8}{x}$$

Check your answer by making a table of equivalent ratios.

Original ratio

| 8 · | 8 · | 8 · | 8 · | 8 · | 8 · |

8	16					
6	12					

6 ·   6 ·   6 ·   6 ·   6 ·   6 ·

Math Talk Give an example of a proportion. **Explain** how you know that it is a proportion.

Name _____

Share and Show

Solve the proportion.

1. $\dfrac{a}{10} = \dfrac{4}{5}$

$\dfrac{a}{10} = \dfrac{4 \cdot \boxed{}}{5 \cdot \boxed{}}$

$\dfrac{a}{10} = \dfrac{\boxed{}}{10}$

$a = \underline{\hspace{2cm}}$

2. $\dfrac{18}{24} = \dfrac{6}{b}$

$\dfrac{18 \div \boxed{}}{24 \div \boxed{}} = \dfrac{6}{b}$

$\dfrac{6}{\boxed{}} = \dfrac{6}{b}$

$b = \underline{\hspace{2cm}}$

3. $\dfrac{3}{6} = \dfrac{15}{c}$

$c = \underline{\hspace{2cm}}$

4. $\dfrac{d}{5} = \dfrac{8}{10}$

$d = \underline{\hspace{2cm}}$

5. $\dfrac{7}{4} = \dfrac{e}{12}$

$e = \underline{\hspace{2cm}}$

6. $\dfrac{10}{f} = \dfrac{40}{12}$

$f = \underline{\hspace{2cm}}$

Math Talk Explain how to solve a proportion using equivalent ratios.

On Your Own

Solve the proportion.

7. $\dfrac{2}{6} = \dfrac{g}{30}$

$g = \underline{\hspace{2cm}}$

8. $\dfrac{5}{h} = \dfrac{55}{110}$

$h = \underline{\hspace{2cm}}$

9. $\dfrac{3}{9} = \dfrac{9}{j}$

$j = \underline{\hspace{2cm}}$

10. $\dfrac{k}{6} = \dfrac{16}{24}$

$k = \underline{\hspace{2cm}}$

11. $\dfrac{18}{15} = \dfrac{6}{m}$

$m = \underline{\hspace{2cm}}$

12. $\dfrac{n}{16} = \dfrac{4}{8}$

$n = \underline{\hspace{2cm}}$

13. $\dfrac{14}{p} = \dfrac{7}{9}$

$p = \underline{\hspace{2cm}}$

14. $\dfrac{42}{54} = \dfrac{q}{9}$

$q = \underline{\hspace{2cm}}$

Problem Solving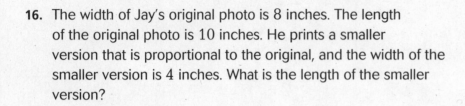

Write and solve a proportion.

15. It takes 8 minutes for Sue to make 2 laps around the go-kart track. How many laps can Sue complete in 24 minutes?

_____

16. The width of Jay's original photo is 8 inches. The length of the original photo is 10 inches. He prints a smaller version that is proportional to the original, and the width of the smaller version is 4 inches. What is the length of the smaller version?

_____

SHOW YOUR WORK

17. Ariel bought 3 raffle tickets for $5. How many tickets could Ariel buy for $15?

_____

18. **H.O.T.** **Reasoning** Is the solution of the proportion $\frac{2}{3} = \frac{n}{18}$ the same as the solution of the proportion $\frac{3}{2} = \frac{18}{n}$? **Explain.**

_____

_____

19. **What's the Error?** Greg used the steps shown to solve a proportion. Describe his error and give the correct solution.

$$\frac{2}{6} = \frac{y}{12}$$

$$\frac{2 \cdot 12}{6 \cdot 12} = \frac{y}{12}$$

$$\frac{24}{72} = \frac{y}{12}$$

$$y = 24$$

_____

_____

_____

20. ⭐ **Test Prep** A speedboat can travel 24 miles on 3 gallons of gas. How many miles could the boat travel on 12 gallons of gas?

(A) 6 miles (C) 72 miles

(B) 33 miles (D) 96 miles

Name _____

Solve Proportions Using Unit Rates

Essential Question How can you use unit rates to solve proportions?

UNLOCK the Problem REAL WORLD

The Champies are traveling from Sierra Vista, Arizona, to San Antonio, Texas. On the first leg of the trip, they drove 390 miles in 6 hours. If they continue driving at the same rate, how many hours will it take them to drive 715 miles?

You can use a proportion to find the number of hours it will take the Champie family to drive 715 miles. You may need to find a unit rate before you can write equivalent ratios.

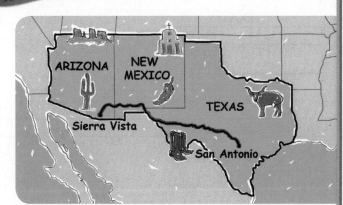

Write and solve a proportion.

Write a proportion.

715 is not a multiple of 390.

Write the known ratio as a unit rate.

$$\begin{array}{l}\text{miles} \rightarrow \\ \text{hours} \rightarrow \end{array} \dfrac{390}{6} = \dfrac{715}{x} \begin{array}{l}\leftarrow \text{miles} \\ \leftarrow \text{hours}\end{array}$$

$$\dfrac{390 \div \boxed{}}{6 \div 6} = \dfrac{715}{x}$$

$$\dfrac{\boxed{}}{1} = \dfrac{715}{x}$$

Write an equivalent rate by multiplying the

_____ and _____ by the same value.

Think: Multiply 65 by _____ to get 715.

So, multiply the denominator by _____ also.

$$\dfrac{65 \cdot \boxed{}}{1 \cdot \boxed{}} = \dfrac{715}{x}$$

The _____ are the same, so the

_____ are equal to each other.

$$\dfrac{\boxed{}}{11} = \dfrac{715}{x}$$

x = _____

So, it will take the Champies _____ hours to drive 715 miles.

Math Talk Explain why you needed to find a unit rate first.

🔑 Example

Kenyon earns $105 for mowing 3 yards. How much would Kenyon earn for mowing 10 yards?

STEP 1 Draw a bar model to represent the situation:

$105

$?

STEP 2 Solve the problem.

The model shows that 3 units represent $105.

You need to find the value represented by _____ units.

Write a unit rate:

1 unit represents $_____.

10 units are equal to 10 times 1 unit,

$$\frac{\$105}{3} = \frac{\$105 \div \boxed{}}{3 \div \boxed{}} = \frac{\$\boxed{}}{1}$$

so 10 units = 10 × $_____.   10 × $_____ = $_____

Kenyon will earn $_____ for mowing 10 yards.

Try This!

Last summer, Kenyon earned $210 for mowing 7 yards. How much did he earn for mowing 5 yards last summer?

STEP 1 Draw a bar model to represent the situation:

STEP 2 Solve the problem.

Name _____

Share and Show

Solve the proportion.

1. $\dfrac{d}{10} = \dfrac{3}{6}$

$\dfrac{d}{10} = \dfrac{3 \div 3}{6 \div \boxed{}}$

$\dfrac{d}{10} = \dfrac{1}{\boxed{}}$

$\dfrac{d}{10} = \dfrac{1 \cdot \boxed{}}{2 \cdot \boxed{}}$

$\dfrac{d}{10} = \dfrac{\boxed{}}{10}$

$d = \underline{\quad\quad}$

2. $\dfrac{8}{6} = \dfrac{20}{n}$

$\dfrac{8 \div 8}{6 \div \boxed{}} = \dfrac{20}{n}$

$\dfrac{1}{\boxed{}} = \dfrac{20}{n}$

$\dfrac{1 \cdot \boxed{}}{0.75 \cdot 20} = \dfrac{20}{n}$

$\dfrac{20}{\boxed{}} = \dfrac{20}{n}$

$n = \underline{\quad\quad}$

Draw a bar model to solve the proportion.

3. $\dfrac{6}{30} = \dfrac{14}{t}$

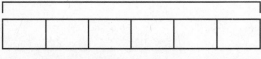

$t = \underline{\quad\quad}$

Math Talk Explain how to solve a proportion using a unit rate.

On Your Own

Solve the proportion.

4. $\dfrac{8}{40} = \dfrac{p}{45}$

$p = \underline{\quad\quad}$

5. $\dfrac{14}{42} = \dfrac{5}{h}$

$h = \underline{\quad\quad}$

6. $\dfrac{2}{r} = \dfrac{8}{56}$

$r = \underline{\quad\quad}$

7. $\dfrac{m}{4} = \dfrac{26}{13}$

$m = \underline{\quad\quad}$

Practice: Copy and Solve Solve the proportion.

8. $\dfrac{4}{32} = \dfrac{9}{q}$

_____

9. $\dfrac{9}{3} = \dfrac{y}{4}$

_____

10. $\dfrac{e}{14} = \dfrac{9}{8}$

_____

11. $\dfrac{3}{z} = \dfrac{2}{1.25}$

_____

Problem Solving

Pose a Problem

13. Josie runs a T-shirt printing company. The table shows the length and width of four sizes of T-shirts. The measurements of each size T-shirt are proportional.

What is the length of an extra-large T-shirt?

Write and solve a proportion:

$$\frac{\text{Length of medium}}{\text{Width of medium}} \rightarrow \frac{30}{20} = \frac{x}{24} \leftarrow \frac{\text{Length of X-large}}{\text{Width of X-large}}$$

$$\frac{30 \div 20}{20 \div 20} = \frac{x}{24} \rightarrow \frac{1.5}{1} = \frac{x}{24} \rightarrow \frac{1.5 \cdot 24}{1 \cdot 24} = \frac{x}{24} \rightarrow \frac{36}{24} = \frac{x}{24}$$

The length of an extra-large T-shirt is 36 inches.

Write a problem that can be solved by using the information in the table and could be solved by writing a proportion.

Adult T-Shirt Sizes

Size	Length (inches)	Width (inches)
Small	27	18
Medium	30	20
Large	y	22
X-large	x	24

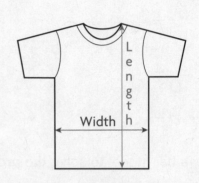

Pose a Problem

Solve Your Problem

- **Describe** how you could draw a bar model to solve your problem.

Name _____

✓ Mid-Chapter Checkpoint

▶ Vocabulary

Choose the best term from the box.

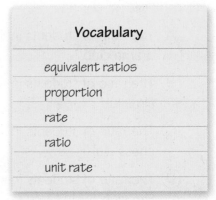

Vocabulary
equivalent ratios
proportion
rate
ratio
unit rate

1. Two ratios that name the same comparison are

   _____. (p. 168)

2. A _____ is a statement that two ratios are
   equivalent. (p. 175)

▶ Concepts and Skills

Write two equivalent ratios. (pp. 167–170)

3. $\frac{2}{7}$

4. $\frac{6}{5}$

5. $\frac{9}{12}$

6. $\frac{18}{6}$

_____ | _____ | _____ | _____

Write the rate as a fraction. Then find the unit rate. (pp. 171–174)

7. Julian played 16 notes in 4 seconds.

8. Brianna types 165 words in 5 minutes.

_____ | _____

Solve the proportion. (pp. 179–186)

9. $\frac{a}{5} = \frac{6}{15}$

10. $\frac{3}{4} = \frac{18}{d}$

11. $\frac{7}{h} = \frac{21}{9}$

12. $\frac{8}{3} = \frac{k}{12}$

$a =$ _____ | $d =$ _____ | $h =$ _____ | $k =$ _____

13. $\frac{15}{f} = \frac{6}{18}$

14. $\frac{n}{9} = \frac{12}{4}$

15. $\frac{48}{16} = \frac{p}{11}$

16. $\frac{9}{36} = \frac{8}{y}$

$f =$ _____ | $n =$ _____ | $p =$ _____ | $y =$ _____

17. There are 36 students in the chess club, 40 students in the drama club, and 24 students in the film club. Which ratio is equivalent to 5:3? (pp. 167–170)

    Ⓐ The ratio of students in the chess club to students in the drama club

    Ⓑ The ratio of students in the chess club to students in the film club

    Ⓒ The ratio of students in the drama club to students in the chess club

    Ⓓ The ratio of students in the drama club to students in the film club

18. A gym offers a 3-month membership for $84, a 4-month membership for $112, a 6-month membership for $144, and a 1-year membership for $300. Which membership is the best deal? (pp. 171–174)

    Ⓐ 3-month membership

    Ⓑ 4-month membership

    Ⓒ 6-month membership

    Ⓓ 1-year membership

19. There are 32 adults and 20 children at a school play. Which of these ratios does not form a proportion with the ratio of adults to children? (pp. 175–178)

    Ⓐ 16 to 10

    Ⓑ 24 to 15

    Ⓒ 48 to 25

    Ⓓ 64 to 40

20. Sonya got 8 out of 10 questions right on a quiz. She got the same score on a quiz that had 20 questions. How many questions did Sonya get right on the second quiz? (pp. 179–186)

    Ⓐ 10

    Ⓑ 16

    Ⓒ 18

    Ⓓ 20

Write Percents as Fractions and Decimals

Essential Question How can you write percents as fractions and decimals?

A **percent** is a ratio that compares a number to 100. Percent (%) means "per hundred." For example, $37\% = \frac{37}{100}$.

You can model percents on a 10-by-10 grid. The large square represents the whole, or 100%. Each small square represents 1%. This grid shows 37% because 37 out of 100 small squares are shaded.

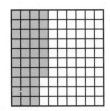

🔑 UNLOCK the Problem REAL WORLD

Carlos eats a banana, an orange, and a blueberry muffin for breakfast. What fraction of the daily value of vitamin C does each item contain?

Vitamin C Content	
Item	**Percent of Daily Value**
Banana	15%
Orange	113%
Blueberry Muffin	0.5%

🔓 **Write each percent as a fraction.**

Ⓐ **Write 15% as a fraction.**

$$15\% = \frac{\boxed{}}{100} = \frac{\boxed{}}{\boxed{}}$$

15% is 15 out of 100.

Write the fraction in simplest form.

So, $15\% = $ _____.

Ⓑ **Write 113% as a fraction.**

$$113\% = \frac{\boxed{}}{100} + \frac{13}{100}$$

$$= \underline{} + \frac{13}{100}$$

113% is 100 out of 100 plus 13 out of 100.

$\frac{100}{100} = 1$

So, $113\% = $ _____.

Write the sum as a mixed number.

Ⓒ **Write 0.5% as a fraction.**

$$0.5\% = \frac{\boxed{}}{100}$$

$$= \frac{0.5 \cdot 10}{100 \cdot 10} = \frac{\boxed{}}{1,000}$$

$$= \frac{1}{\boxed{}}$$

0.5% is 0.5 out of 100.

Multiply the numerator and denominator by 10 to get a whole number in the numerator.

Write the fraction in simplest form.

So, $0.5\% = $ _____.

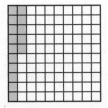

Math Talk Explain how you could shade a 10-by-10 grid to show 0.5%.

🔑 Example

A Write 72% as a decimal.

$$72\% = \frac{\boxed{}}{100}$$

$$= \underline{}$$

So, 72% = _____ .

72% is 72 out of 100.

Use place value to write 72 hundredths as a decimal.

B Write 4% as a decimal.

$$4\% = \frac{\boxed{}}{100}$$

```
        .
100 )4.00
     -0 ↓
      40
      -0 ↓
      400
     -400
        0
```

So, 4% = _____ .

4% is 4 out of 100.

Use long division to divide.

Since the dividend, 4, is less than the divisor, 100, put a 0 in the ones place in the quotient.

Put a decimal point above the decimal point in the dividend.

C Write 25.81% as a decimal.

$$25.81\% = \frac{\boxed{}}{100}$$

$$= \underline{}$$

So, 25.81% = _____ .

25.81% is 25.81 out of 100.

To divide by 100, move the decimal point 2 places to the left: 0.2581

> **Remember**
> When you divide decimal numbers by powers of 10, you move the decimal point one place to the left for each factor of 10.

Share and Show . . . .

Write the percent as a fraction.

1. 80%

$$80\% = \frac{\boxed{}}{100} = \frac{}{\boxed{}}$$

2. 150%

_____

✓ **3.** 0.2%

_____

Write the percent as a decimal.

✓ **4.** 58%

_____

5. 9%

_____

> **Math Talk** Explain how to use estimation to check that your answer is reasonable when you write a percent as a fraction or decimal.

On Your Own ....

Write the percent as a fraction or mixed number.

6. 17%

7. 20%

8. 125%

9. 355%

10. 0.1%

11. 2.5%

Write the percent as a decimal.

12. 89%

13. 30%

14. 2%

15. 122%

16. 3.5%

17. 6.33%

18. About 21.6% of the population of Canada speaks French. Write 21.6% as a decimal.

19. Georgianne completed 60% of her homework assignment. Write the portion of her homework that she still needs to complete as a fraction.

Problem Solving · REAL WORLD

Use the graph for 20 and 21.

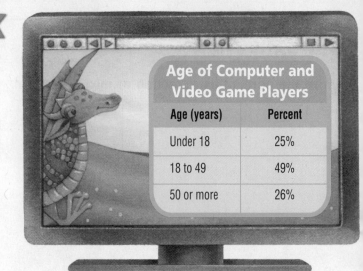

Age of Computer and Video Game Players

Age (years)	Percent
Under 18	25%
18 to 49	49%
50 or more	26%

20. What fraction of computer and video game players are 50 years old or more?

_____

21. What fraction of computer and video game players are 18 years old or more?

_____

22. **H.O.T.** Box A and Box B each contain black tiles and white tiles. They have the same total number of tiles. In Box A, 45% of the tiles are black. In Box B, $\frac{11}{20}$ of the tiles are white. Compare the number of black tiles in the boxes. Explain your reasoning.

_____

_____

_____

_____

SHOW YOUR WORK

23. **What's the Error?** About 8.4% of the students at Jenna's school are in the drama club. Jenna says 0.84 of the students are in the drama club. Is she correct? Explain.

_____

_____

_____

24. ⭐ **Test Prep** A large carrot contains 41% of the daily value of vitamin A. Which is the best estimate of the fraction of the daily value of vitamin A in a large carrot?

Ⓐ $\frac{1}{4}$ Ⓒ $\frac{3}{4}$

Ⓑ $\frac{2}{5}$ Ⓓ $\frac{4}{5}$

FOR MORE PRACTICE:
Standards Practice Book, pp. P93–P94

Name _____

Write Fractions and Decimals as Percents

Essential Question How can you write fractions and decimals as percents?

UNLOCK the Problem · REAL WORLD

During the 2008–2009 season of the National Basketball Association (NBA), the Phoenix Suns won about $\frac{11}{20}$ of their games. The Miami Heat won about 0.524 of their games. Which team was more successful during the season?

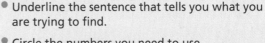

- Underline the sentence that tells you what you are trying to find.
- Circle the numbers you need to use.

To compare the season performances of the Suns and the Heat, it is helpful to write the fraction and the decimal as a percent.

🔑 **Write the fraction or decimal as a percent.**

A $\frac{11}{20}$

Multiply the _____ and

$$\frac{11}{20} = \frac{11 \times \boxed{}}{20 \times \boxed{}}$$

_____ by the same value to write an equivalent fraction with a denominator of 100.

$$= \frac{\boxed{}}{100}$$

A percent is a ratio comparing a number

to _____. Write the ratio

$= $ _____

as a _____.

So, the percent of games won by the Phoenix Suns is _____.

B 0.524

To write a percent as a decimal, divide by _____.

To write a decimal as a percent,

_____ by 100. $0.524 \times 100 = 52.4$

To multiply by 100, move the decimal

point 2 places to the _____. $0.524 = $ _____ %

So, the percent of games won by the Miami Heat is _____.

Because they won a greater percentage of their games, the _____ were more successful during the 2008–2009 season.

CONNECT You can use what you know about fractions, decimals, and percents to write numbers in different forms.

🔑 Example

A **Write 0.7 as a fraction and as a percent.**

0.7 means 7 _____. Write 0.7 as a fraction.

To write as a percent, first write an equivalent fraction with a denominator

of _____.

Write the ratio of _____ to

_____ as a percent.

$0.7 = \dfrac{7}{\quad}$

$= \dfrac{7 \times \quad}{10 \times \quad}$

$= \dfrac{\quad}{100}$

$= \underline{\quad}$

So, 0.7 written as a fraction is _____, and

0.7 written as a percent is _____.

B **Write $\dfrac{3}{40}$ as a decimal and as a percent.**

Since 40 is not a factor of 100, it is more difficult to find an equivalent fraction. Use long division to divide.

Divide 3 by 40.

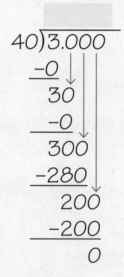

To write a decimal as a percent,

_____ by 100.

Move the decimal point 2 places to the

_____.

$\dfrac{3}{40} = 0.075$

$0.075 = \underline{\qquad}$

So, $\dfrac{3}{40}$ written as a decimal is _____, and

$\dfrac{3}{40}$ written as a percent is _____.

Math Talk Explain why it makes sense that $\dfrac{3}{40}$ is less than 10%.

Name _____

Share and Show ·

Write the fraction or decimal as a percent.

1. $\frac{3}{25}$

$$\frac{3 \times \boxed{}}{25 \times \boxed{}} = \frac{\boxed{}}{100}$$

_____

2. $\frac{3}{10}$

_____

3. 0.717

_____

④ 4. 0.02

_____

Write the number in two other forms (fraction, decimal, or percent).

5. 0.9

_____

6. $\frac{3}{8}$

_____

④ 7. 0.45

_____

8. $\frac{5}{16}$

_____

Math Talk Explain how you know that $\frac{5}{4}$ is greater than 100%.

On Your Own ·

Write the fraction or decimal as a percent.

9. $\frac{7}{50}$

_____

10. $\frac{4}{5}$

_____

11. 0.902

_____

12. 1.25

_____

Write the number in two other forms (fraction, decimal, or percent).

13. 0.01

_____

14. $\frac{13}{40}$

_____

15. $\frac{6}{5}$

_____

16. 0.008

_____

Sand Sculptures

Every year, dozens of teams compete in the U.S. Open Sandcastle Competition. Recent winners have included complex sculptures in the shape of flowers, elephants, and racing cars.

Teams that participate in the contest build their sculptures using a mixture of sand and water. Finding the correct proportions of these ingredients is essential for creating a stable sculpture.

The table shows the recipes that three teams used. Which team used the greatest percent of sand in their recipe?

Convert to percents. Then order from least to greatest.

Team A	$\dfrac{30}{30+10} = \dfrac{30}{40} = 0.75 = $ _____ %
Team B	$\dfrac{19}{20} = \dfrac{19 \times \boxed{}}{20 \times \boxed{}} = \dfrac{\boxed{}}{100} = \boxed{} $ _____ %
Team C	$0.84 = \boxed{}$ _____ %

Sand Sculpture Recipes

Team	Sand	Water
A	30 cups	10 cups
B	$\dfrac{19}{20}$	$\dfrac{1}{20}$
C	0.84	0.16

From least to greatest, the percents are _____.

So, Team _____ used the greatest percent of sand.

Solve.

17. Which team used the greatest percent of water in their recipe?

_____

18. In 2005, scientists discovered that the ideal recipe for sand sculptures contains 88.9% sand. Which team's recipe is closest to the ideal recipe?

_____

19. Team D used a recipe that consists of 20 cups of sand, 2 cups of flour, and 3 cups of water. How does the percent of sand in Team D's recipe compare to that of the other teams?

_____

_____

Name _____

Compare and Order Fractions, Decimals, and Percents

Essential Question How can you compare and order fractions, decimals, and percents?

 UNLOCK the Problem REAL WORLD

According to the Motion Picture Association of America, 4% of all movie advertising is on the Internet and $\frac{1}{10}$ of all movie advertising is in newspapers. Which form of advertising is used more often?

Compare percents.

$\frac{1}{10}$ = [ ]   Write $\frac{1}{10}$ as a percent.

[ ] % < [ ] %   **Think:** 4 out of 100 is less than 10 out of 100.

So, _____ is the type of advertising that is used more often.

 Activity **Equivalent Decimals, Fractions, and Percents**

- The number line shows equivalent decimals, fractions, and percents from 0 to 1.
- Complete the number line by filling in the missing values.

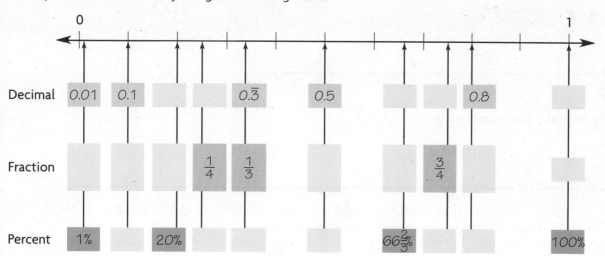

- **Explain** how you could place the value 60% on the number line with its equivalent decimal and fraction.

_____

_____

🔒 Example

The table shows the five most popular music genres according to the Recording Industry Association of America. List the genres in order from most popular to least popular.

Compare and order fractions, decimals, and percents.

Top 5 Music Genres	
Genre	**Portion of Music Sales**
Country	0.12
Pop	9%
R & B	10%
Rap	$\frac{11}{100}$
Rock	$\frac{8}{25}$

STEP 1

Write all of the values as decimals.

Country   The value is already a decimal. 0.12

Pop   9% is _____ out of 100.

Use place value to write

9 _____ as a decimal.

$$9\% = \frac{}{100}$$

$$= \boxed{}$$

R & B   10% is $\frac{10}{\boxed{}}$ or $\frac{1}{10}$. Use place value to

write 1 _____ as a decimal.

$$10\% = \frac{1}{10} = \boxed{}$$

Rap   Use place value to write 11

_____ as a decimal.

$$\frac{11}{100} = \boxed{}$$

Rock   Write an _____ _____ with a denominator of 100.

Use place value to write the fraction as a decimal.

$$\frac{8}{25} = \frac{8 \times }{25 \times } = \frac{}{100}$$

$$= \boxed{}$$

STEP 2

Plot the decimals on a number line.

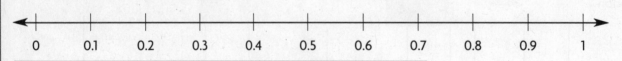

0   0.1   0.2   0.3   0.4   0.5   0.6   0.7   0.8   0.9   1

STEP 3

To list the genres from most popular to least popular, read the values plotted on the number line in order from right to left.

So, the genres from most popular to least popular are:

_____

Math Talk Explain why you read the values plotted on the number line from right to left in this example.

198

Name _____

Share and Show

Compare. Write <, >, or =.

1. 43% ◯ 0.09

$$0.09 = \frac{}{100}$$

Think: 43 out of

100 is _____

than 9 out of 100.

2. $\frac{7}{10}$ ◯ 70%

3. 0.65 ◯ 6.5%

☑ **4.** 30% ◯ $\frac{1}{3}$

Write the values in order from least to greatest.

5. 0.1, $\frac{1}{2}$, 20%

☑ **6.** 25%, $\frac{3}{25}$, 0.2

7. $\frac{2}{3}$, 75%, 0.68

Math Talk Explain how you can compare a fraction and a percent.

On Your Own

Compare. Write <, >, or =.

8. $\frac{7}{20}$ ◯ 30%

9. 120% ◯ 12.0

10. 5% ◯ $\frac{1}{20}$

11. 0.025 ◯ 20%

Write the values in order from least to greatest.

12. 2.5, 25%, $\frac{1}{25}$

13. $\frac{2}{5}$, 32%, 0.05

14. $\frac{57}{100}$, 5.6, $\frac{3}{5}$, 66%

15. 0.1, $\frac{1}{8}$, 12%, 1.2

Problem Solving REAL WORLD

Use the table for 16 and 17.

16. Did a greater portion of overseas visitors to the United States come from Europe or Asia? Explain.

   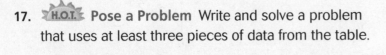

17. **H.O.T. Pose a Problem** Write and solve a problem that uses at least three pieces of data from the table.

   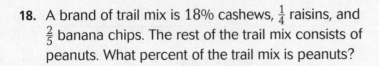

Overseas Visitors to the United States	
Region	**Portion of All Visitors**
Asia	0.25
Caribbean	5%
Central America	0.03
Europe	$\frac{12}{25}$
South America	$\frac{1}{10}$

18. A brand of trail mix is 18% cashews, $\frac{1}{4}$ raisins, and $\frac{2}{5}$ banana chips. The rest of the trail mix consists of peanuts. What percent of the trail mix is peanuts?

   _____

19. **Write Math** ▶ Describe two different methods you could use to determine whether $\frac{7}{8}$ is greater than or less than 85%.

   _____

   _____

   _____

20. ⭐ **Test Prep** One-fourth of a movie's advertising budget is spent on television, 30% of the budget is spent on billboards, and the rest is spent on radio. What is the order of the three types of advertising, from the greatest part of the budget to the least?

   Ⓐ radio, television, billboards

   Ⓑ radio, billboards, television

   Ⓒ billboards, radio, television

   Ⓓ billboards, television, radio

SHOW YOUR WORK

Name _____

Percent of a Number

Essential Question How do you find a percent of a number?

 UNLOCK the Problem REAL WORLD

A typical family of four uses about 400 gallons of water each day, and 30% of this water is for outdoor activities, such as gardening. How many gallons of water does a typical family of four use each day for outdoor activities?

- Will the number of gallons of water for outdoor activities be greater than or less than 200 gallons? Explain.

_____

_____

One Way Use proportional reasoning.

Draw a bar model.

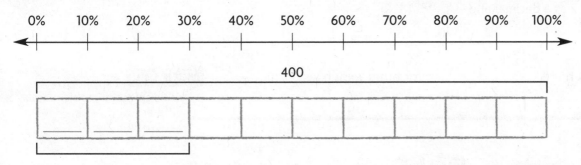

The model shows that 100% represents 400 gallons.

Think: 30% is 3 groups of 10%, so divide the model into 10 equal groups.

Find the value of 10% of 400. $10\% \text{ of } 400 = 400 \times \frac{1}{10} = 400 \div _____ = _____$

Find the value of 30% of 400. $30\% = 3 \times _____ = _____$

Another Way Multiply.

You can find 30% of 400 by multiplying.

Write the percent as a decimal. $30\% = 0.30$

Multiply by the decimal. $0.30 \times 400 = _____$

So, 30% of 400 is _____.

Math Talk How can you find the number of gallons of water used for indoor activities?

Try This! Find 30% of 400 by writing the percent as a fraction and then multiplying.

$30\% = _____$

$_____ \times 400 = _____$

🔑 Example

Charla earns $4,000 per month. She spends 40% of her salary on rent and 15% of her salary on groceries. How much money does Charla have left for other expenses?

STEP 1 Add to find the total percent of Charla's salary that is used for rent and groceries.

40% + _____ % = _____ %

STEP 2 Subtract the total percent from 100% to find the percent that is left for other expenses.

100% − _____ % = 45%

STEP 3 Write the percent from Step 2 as a decimal and multiply.

45% = _____

_____ × 4,000 = _____

So, Charla has $ _____ left for other expenses.

Math Talk Explain how you could solve the problem a different way.

Share and Show . . . .

Find the percent of the number.

0%   25%   50%   75%   100%

1. 25% of 320

   25% = $\frac{1}{4}$, so use _____ equal groups.

   320 × $\frac{1}{4}$ = 320 ÷ _____ = _____

   320

⊘ 2. 80% of 50

_____

3. 175% of 24

_____

4. 60% of 210

_____

⊘ 5. A jar contains 125 marbles. Given that 4% of the marbles are green, 60% of the marbles are blue, and the rest are red, how many red marbles are in the jar?

_____

6. There are 32 students in Mr. Moreno's class and 62.5% of the students are girls. How many boys are in the class?

_____

Math Talk Explain how you could estimate 49.3% of 3,000.

On Your Own ·

Find the percent of the number.

7. 75% of 52

8. 60% of 90

9. 1% of 750

10. 17% of 100

11. 40% of 18

12. 25% of 32.4

13. 110% of 300

14. 0.2% of 6,500

15. A baker made 60 muffins for a cafe. By noon, 45% of the muffins were sold. How many muffins were sold by noon?

16. LaToya wants to leave a 15% tip on a lunch bill of $8.40. How much should she leave for the tip?

17. A school library has 260 DVDs in its collection. Given that 45% of the DVDs are about science and 40% are about history, how many of the DVDs are about other subjects?

18. Mitch planted cabbage, squash, and carrots on his 150-acre farm. He planted half the farm with squash and 22% of the farm with carrots. How many acres did he plant with cabbage?

Compare. Write <, >, or =.

19. 45% of 60 ◯ 60% of 45

20. 10% of 90 ◯ 90% of 100

21. 75% of 8 ◯ 8% of 7.5

22. **H.O.T.** Sarah had 12 free throw attempts during a game and made at least 75% of the free throws. What is the greatest number of free throws Sarah could have missed during the game?

23. One third of the juniors in the Linwood High School Marching Band play the trumpet. The band has 50 members and the table shows what percent of the band members are freshmen, sophomores, juniors, and seniors. How many juniors play the trumpet?

(A) 4   (C) 8

(B) 6   (D) 12

Linwood High School Marching Band

Freshmen	26%
Sophomores	30%
Juniors	24%
Seniors	20%

a. What do you need to find?

_____

_____

b. How can you use the table to help you solve the problem?

_____

_____

_____

c. What operation can you use to find the number of juniors in the band?

_____

d. Show the steps you use to solve the problem.

e. Complete the sentences.

The band has _____ members. There are

_____ juniors in the band. The number of juniors who

play the trumpet is _____.

f. Fill in the bubble for the correct answer choice above.

Use the information in Problem 23 and the above table for 24–25.

24. How many more sophomores than freshmen are in the band?

(A) 1   (C) 4

(B) 2   (D) 6

25. The seniors in the band line up in 2 rows, with the same number of seniors in each row. How many seniors are in each row?

(A) 2   (C) 10

(B) 5   (D) 20

© Houghton Mifflin Harcourt Publishing Company

Use a Model · Percent Problems

Essential Question How can you use a model to solve percent problems?

🔑 UNLOCK the Problem · REAL WORLD

A *discount* is a percent of a price that is subtracted from the price. Find the discount and the final price of the pair of running shoes in the advertisement.

Use the graphic organizer to help you solve the problem.

Regular price is $40.

15% discount this week only.

Read the Problem

What do I need to find?	**What information do I need to use?**	**How will I use the information?**
Write what you need to find.	Write the important information.	What strategy can you use?
_____		_____
_____	_____	_____
_____	_____	_____
_____	_____	_____

Solve the Problem

Draw a bar model.

```
                    100%
        ┌─────────────────────────────┐
Regular │           $40               │
Price   └─────────────────────────────┘

        ┌──────────────────────┐    ┌──────┐
Final   │                      │    │$____ │
Price   └──────────────────────┘    └──────┘
                                       15%
```

The model shows that 100% = $40,

so $1\% = \frac{\$40}{100} = \$$ _____.

$15\% = 15 \times \$$ _____ = $ _____

So, the discount is _____. The final price is

$40 − _____ = _____.

• How can you use estimation to show that your answer is reasonable?

_____

🔑 Try Another Problem

Sales tax is a percent of a price that is added to the price. In Lee's town, the sales tax is 8%. She buys a pair of jeans whose price is $23. What is the sales tax and what is the final cost of the jeans?

Read the Problem

What do I need to find?	What information do I need to use?	How will I use the information?

Solve the Problem

So, the sales tax is _____.

The final cost is $23 + _____
= _____.

1. Does your answer make sense? Explain how you know.

_____

_____

2. Suppose the sales tax was 4%. Explain how you could find the amount of tax in this case without solving the problem from the beginning.

_____

_____

Math Talk Compare the model you used to solve this problem with the model on page 205.

206

Name _____

Share and Show [MATH BOARD]

1. A *tip* is a percent of a bill that is added to the total to pay for service. Cole's dinner bill is $15 and he wants to leave an 18% tip. What are the amount of the tip and the final cost of the meal?

SHOW YOUR WORK

   First, draw a bar model.

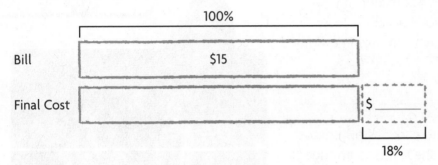

   Next, find 1%.

   $100\% = \$15$, so $1\% = \dfrac{\$15}{100} = \$$ _____

   Then, find 18%, the amount of the tip.

   $18\% = 18 \times \$$ _____ $= \$$ _____

   Finally, add to find the final cost of the meal.

   So, the final cost of the meal is _____.

2. **H.O.T.** **What if** Cole decides to leave a 20% tip? What are the amount of the tip and the final cost of the meal?

   _____

3. Ricardo buys a backpack for $19 and 5 notebooks that cost $3 each. The sales tax in Ricardo's town is 6%. What is the total sales tax and what is the final cost of the items?

   _____

4. **H.O.T.** **Sense or Nonsense** The regular price of a lawn mower is $102.95. It is on sale for 20% off. The clerk says the final price after the discount is $92.66. Estimate the amount of the discount and the final price by rounding the regular price to a whole number. Explain whether the clerk's statement is sense or nonsense.

   _____

   _____

On Your Own

5. Jordan takes 50% of the cherries from a bowl. Then Mei takes 50% of the remaining cherries. Finally, Greg takes 50% of the remaining cherries. There are 3 cherries left. How many cherries were in the bowl before Jordan arrived?

_____

6. Kevin is hiking on a trail that is 4.2 miles long. So far, he has hiked 80% of the total distance. How many more miles does Kevin have to hike in order to complete the trail?

_____

7. H.O.T. An employee at a state park has 53 photos of animals found at the park. She wants to arrange the photos in rows so that every row except the bottom row has the same number of photos. She also wants there to be at least 5 rows. Describe two different ways she can arrange the photos.

_____

_____

8. Write Math ▶ Maya wants to mark a length of 7 inches on a sheet of paper, but she does not have a ruler. She has pieces of wood that are 4 inches, 5 inches, and 6 inches long. Explain how she can use these pieces to mark a length of 7 inches.

_____

_____

_____

9. ⭐ Test Prep Amelia buys a camera whose regular price is $65. She has a coupon for 20% off the regular price. The sales tax in her town is 7%. What is the final cost of the camera?

Ⓐ $13.91 　Ⓒ $52.00

Ⓑ $48.36 　Ⓓ $55.64

Choose a
STRATEGY

Work Backward

Solve a Simpler Problem

Choose an Operation

Use a Model

Use a Formula

Draw a Diagram

SHOW YOUR WORK

Name _____

Chapter 5 Review/Test

▶ Vocabulary

Choose the best term from the box.

Vocabulary
percent
proportion
rate
ratio

1. A _____ compares two quantities by division. (p. 167)

2. A ratio that compares a number to 100 is a _____. (p. 189)

3. A _____ is a ratio that compares two quantities that have different units. (p. 171)

▶ Concepts and Skills

Solve the proportion. (pp. 179–186)

4. $\frac{12}{16} = \frac{b}{4}$

   $b =$ _____

5. $\frac{18}{g} = \frac{6}{7}$

   $g =$ _____

6. $\frac{5}{25} = \frac{13}{j}$

   $j =$ _____

7. $\frac{s}{21} = \frac{27}{9}$

   $s =$ _____

Write the number in two other forms (fraction, decimal, or percent). (pp. 189–196)

8. $\frac{5}{8}$

9. 44%

10. 0.75

11. $\frac{3}{5}$

Write the numbers in order from least to greatest. (pp. 197–200)

12. 45%, $\frac{4}{5}$, 0.4

13. $\frac{7}{8}$, 88%, 0.089

14. 0.125, 14%, $\frac{3}{20}$

15. $\frac{5}{9}$, 50%, 0.052

Find the percent of the number. (pp. 201–204)

16. 35% of 125

17. 6% of 78

18. 20% of 282

19. 23% of 60

20. 98% of 76

21. 1.5% of 400

22. 0.1% of 48

23. 125% of 302

Fill in the bubble to show your answer.

24. An aquarium contains 12 guppies and 16 swordfish. Which ratio is not equivalent to the ratio of guppies to swordfish? (pp. 167–170)

Ⓐ $\frac{3}{4}$

Ⓑ $\frac{6}{8}$

Ⓒ $\frac{8}{10}$

Ⓓ $\frac{24}{32}$

25. A 3-pound bag of almonds costs $16.50, a 5-pound bag of walnuts costs $28.75, and a 4-pound bag of cashews costs $24.80. Which list shows the items in order from the best deal to the worst deal? (pp. 171–174)

Ⓐ cashews, walnuts, almonds

Ⓑ cashews, almonds, walnuts

Ⓒ almonds, cashews, walnuts

Ⓓ almonds, walnuts, cashews

26. The ratio of dahlias to tulips in a flower arrangement is 2 to 5. Which of these could be the number of dahlias and tulips in the arrangement? (pp. 175–178)

Ⓐ 8 dahlias, 25 tulips

Ⓑ 12 dahlias, 30 tulips

Ⓒ 14 dahlias, 17 tulips

Ⓓ 20 dahlias, 40 tulips

27. The ratio of adults to children at a museum is usually 5:2. There are currently 35 adults at the museum. How many children do you expect to be at the museum? (pp. 179–182)

Ⓐ 10

Ⓑ 14

Ⓒ 21

Ⓓ 32

28. Marci bought 4 yards of ribbon for $6. How much should Marci expect to pay for 10 yards of the ribbon? (pp. 183–186)

Ⓐ $12

Ⓑ $15

Ⓒ $18

Ⓓ $24

Fill in the bubble to show your answer.

29. One cup of cooked spinach contains 377% of the recommended daily value of vitamin A. What fraction of the recommended daily value of vitamin A is in one cup of cooked spinach? (pp. 189–192)

   Ⓐ $37\frac{7}{10}$

   Ⓑ $3\frac{77}{100}$

   Ⓒ $3\frac{7}{10}$

   Ⓓ $\frac{377}{1,000}$

30. About $\frac{4}{10}$ of the population has blood type O+. What percent of the population has blood type O+? (pp. 193–196)

   Ⓐ 0.04%

   Ⓑ 0.4%

   Ⓒ 4%

   Ⓓ 40%

31. At a frozen yogurt shop, $\frac{7}{25}$ of sales are chocolate, 0.09 of sales are mocha, 23% of sales are strawberry, and $\frac{2}{5}$ of sales are vanilla. Which flavor is most popular? (pp. 197–200)

   Ⓐ Chocolate

   Ⓑ Mocha

   Ⓒ Strawberry

   Ⓓ Vanilla

32. A magazine has 96 pages. There are advertisements on 75% of the pages. How many of the magazine's pages do not have advertisements? (pp. 201–208)

   Ⓐ 12

   Ⓑ 24

   Ⓒ 71

   Ⓓ 72

33. An electrician has a piece of wire that is 18 feet long. He cuts off 20% of the wire. Then he cuts the remaining piece of wire into 6 equal pieces. What is the length of each piece? (pp. 201–208)

   Ⓐ 0.6 feet

   Ⓑ 2.4 feet

   Ⓒ 3.6 feet

   Ⓓ 14.4 feet

TEST PREP

34. A cat's heart beats 30 times in 12 seconds, an elephant's heart beats 20 times in 40 seconds, and a monkey's heart beats 32 times in 10 seconds. List the animals in order from the fastest heart rate to the slowest heart rate. (pp. 171–174)

_____

35. Alex's bill for lunch is $8. He wants to leave a 15% tip. What should the amount of Alex's tip be? What will the total be for his meal, including tip? Explain. (pp. 205–208)

_____

_____

_____

► **Performance Task**

36. The regular admission fee at a theme park is $22.

A A group of 6 students wants to go to the theme park on Saturday. What is the total amount paid by the 6 students for admission?

_____

B On Wednesdays, the park offers a 15% discount to students. How much money can the group save if they go on Wednesday instead of Saturday?

_____

C What is the total amount the 6 students would pay if they went to the theme park on Wednesday?

_____

D Brandon won't be able to go if the group decides to go to the park on Saturday. Will it cost more for 6 students to go to the park on Wednesday or for 5 students to go on Saturday? Explain.

_____

_____

_____

_____

Chapter 6 Units of Measure

Show What You Know ✓

Check your understanding of important skills

Name _____

▶ **Choose the Appropriate Unit** Circle the more reasonable unit to measure the object.

1. the length of a car
inches or feet

2. the length of a soccer field
meters or kilometers

▶ **Multiply and Divide by 10, 100, and 1,000** Use mental math.

3. 2.51×10

_____

4. 5.3×100

_____

5. $0.71 \times 1,000$

_____

6. $3.25 \div 10$

_____

7. $8.65 \div 100$

_____

8. $56.2 \div 1,000$

_____

▶ **Multiply with Decimals** Find the product.

9. 1.5×7

_____

10. 5.83×6

_____

11. 3.7×0.8

_____

12. 0.27×0.9

_____

MATH DETECTIVE WITH **CARMEN SANDIEGO**™

Steve set his watch at 8:15 A.M. when the school bell rang. When the bell rang again at 11:15 A.M., he noticed that his watch had lost 2 minutes. Be a math detective and find what time Steve's watch will show when the bell rings at 8:15 A.M. tomorrow if his watch continues to lose time at the same rate.

Vocabulary Builder

▶ **Visualize It** ·····································

Sort the review words into the Venn diagram.

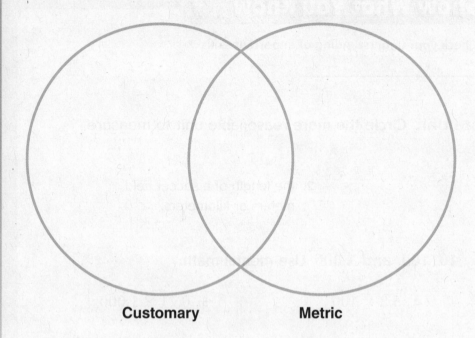

Customary   **Metric**

Review Words

✓ capacity

gallon

gram

length

liter

✓ mass

meter

ounce

pint

pound

quart

ton

✓ weight

Preview Words

✓ accuracy

✓ conversion factor

✓ elapsed time

✓ precision

▶ **Understand Vocabulary** ······················

Complete the sentences by using the checked words.

1. The time that passes from the beginning of an activity to

   the end of the activity is called _____.

2. _____ is the closeness of a given
   measurement to the actual measurement of an object.

3. A rate in which the two quantities are equal, but use different

   units, is called a _____.

4. The _____ of a measurement indicates the
   level of detail in the measurement.

5. _____ is the the amount of matter in an object.

6. _____ is the amount a container can hold.

7. The _____ of an object tells how heavy the
   object is.

GO Online • eStudent Edition • Multimedia eGlossary

Name _____

Elapsed Time

Essential Question How can you find elapsed time across A.M./P.M. and across days?

UNLOCK the Problem REAL WORLD

Streetcars transport passengers along the city streets in Seattle, Washington. Ana got off the streetcar at 8:15 A.M. to go to work. She got back on a streetcar at 5:35 P.M. to return home. How much time elapsed between Ana's streetcar rides?

🔑 The time that passes from the start to the end of an activity is called **elapsed time**. You can use a clock like a number line to count and find elapsed time.

STEP 1

Count the minutes from the start time to the next hour.

8:15 A.M. to 9:00 A.M. _____ minutes

STEP 2

Count the hours.

9:00 A.M. to 5:00 P.M. _____ hours

STEP 3

Count the minutes from 5:00 P.M. to the end time.

5:00 P.M. to 5:35 P.M. _____ minutes

STEP 4

Find the total elapsed time.

_____ minutes + _____ hours + _____ minutes

= 8 hours and _____ minutes   Rename 80 minutes.

= _____ hours and _____ minutes

So, _____ hours and _____ minutes elapsed between Ana's streetcar rides.

Math Talk Explain how to rename 80 minutes using hours and minutes.

Chapter 6 215

Elapsed Time Across Days Recall that one day is equal to 24 hours. You can use this fact to find the elapsed time over multiple days.

🔒 Example

Satvik's grandmother sent him an autographed photo of his favorite football player for his birthday. If the photo was shipped at 8:05 A.M. on Thursday, and spent 33 hours and 25 minutes in transit, when did the photo arrive at Satvik's house?

Use a clock to find the arrival time.

Start time: 8:05 A.M. on Thursday

STEP 1

Count ahead 24 hours.   time: 8:05 A.M.   day: _____

STEP 2

Count ahead 9 hours
to get to 33 hours.   time: _____   day: _____

STEP 3

Count ahead 25 minutes.   time: _____   day: _____

So, the photo arrived at _____ on _____.

Remember
There are 24 hours in a day.

Try This!

Layla's volleyball tournament ended at 9:57 P.M. If the tournament lasted 14 hours and 27 minutes, at what time did it start?

Count back 12 hours.   time: _____

Count back 2 hours
to get to 14 hours.   time: _____

Count back 27 minutes.   time: _____

So, the tournament started at _____.

- A winter storm hit Philadelphia, Pennsylvania at 10:30 P.M. on Monday and lasted 29 hours and 22 minutes. **Explain** how to find the time the storm ended.

_____

_____

216

Name _____

Share and Show

Find the start, elapsed, or end time.

1. Find the elapsed time between 8:17 A.M. and 2:35 P.M.

   8:17 A.M. to 9:00 A.M. _____ minutes

   9:00 A.M. to 2:00 P.M. _____ hours

   2:00 P.M. to 2:35 P.M. _____ minutes

   elapsed time _____

2. start time: _____
   elapsed time: 6 hours 8 minutes
   end time: 3:45 P.M. Tuesday

3. start time: 6:21 P.M. Thursday

   elapsed time: _____
   end time: 7:37 A.M. Friday

4. start time: 8:26 A.M. Monday
   elapsed time: 27 hours 32 minutes

   end time: _____

Math Talk Explain how to find the elapsed time when the start time is A.M. one day and the end time is P.M. the next day.

On Your Own

Find the start, elapsed, or end time.

5. start time: 6:05 A.M. Monday

   elapsed time: _____
   end time: 12:40 P.M. Monday

6. start time: 10:24 A.M. Wednesday
   elapsed time: 2 hours 43 minutes

   end time: _____

7. start time: 7:45 P.M. Friday
   elapsed time: 18 hours 20 minutes

   end time: _____

8. start time: 2:15 P.M. Thursday

   elapsed time: _____
   end time: 2:58 A.M. Friday

9. Trey's family left on a camping trip at 8:26 A.M. on Saturday. The trip lasted 28 hours 37 minutes. When did Trey's family return home?

   _____

10. A heat wave lasting 30 hours 14 minutes ended at 3:28 P.M. on Tuesday. What time did the heat wave start?

    _____

Problem Solving  REAL WORLD

Use the table for 11–14.

11. Mr. Kolluri took a business trip to Orlando and returned the next day. How long was his flight from Boston to Orlando?

_____

12. How long was the flight from Orlando back to Boston?

_____

13. How long was Mr. Kolluri away on his business trip, including flight time?

_____

Flight Itinerary

	Depart	Arrive
From Boston to Orlando	11:30 A.M. Thursday	2:39 P.M. Thursday
From Orlando to Boston	10:56 A.M. Friday	3:16 P.M. Friday

14. **Write Math** ▸ How long was Mr. Kolluri in Orlando? **Explain** how you found your answer.

_____

_____

_____

_____

15. **H.O.T.** Eric went to a movie that started at 11:35 A.M. and ended at 1:42 P.M. His parents saw a movie that ended at 1:51 P.M. If Eric's movie lasted 8 minutes longer, what time did his parents' movie start?

_____

16. ⭐ **Test Prep** Ashley's train left St. Paul, Minnesota, at 7:50 A.M. and arrived in Baton Rouge, Louisiana, at 3:55 P.M. on the same day. How long was Ashley's train ride?

Ⓐ 3 hr 45 min   Ⓒ 8 hr 5 min

Ⓑ 4 hr 5 min   Ⓓ 10 hr 45 min

.... SHOW YOUR WORK ....

FOR MORE PRACTICE:
Standards Practice Book, pp. P107–P108

Name _____

Use a Formula · Convert Temperature

Essential Question How can you use a formula to convert between Celsius and Fahrenheit temperatures?

🔑 UNLOCK the Problem REAL WORLD

CONNECT You can evaluate formulas just as you have evaluated algebraic expressions. The formula $C = \frac{5}{9}(F - 32)$ is used to convert Fahrenheit temperatures to Celsius temperatures.

The metal gallium melts at a temperature of 86°F, which is close to human body temperature. What is the melting point of gallium in degrees Celsius (°C)?

Use the graphic organizer to help you solve the problem.

Read the Problem	Solve the Problem
What do I need to find? I need to find _____ _____ .	Write the formula. _____ Substitute for the variable. $C = \frac{5}{9}($ _____ $- 32)$ Evaluate the formula. $C = $ _____ _____ °C
What information do I need to use? I need to use the melting point of gallium in degrees _____ and the formula _____ .	
How will I use the information? I will substitute _____ for _____ and evaluate the _____ .	

Math Talk Explain how you used a formula to find the answer.

So, gallium melts at a temperature of _____ .

© Houghton Mifflin Harcourt Publishing Company

🔑 Try Another Problem

The formula $F = \frac{9}{5}C + 32$ is used to convert Celsius temperatures to Fahrenheit temperatures. The normal body temperature of a chicken is 42°C. How does that compare with the normal human body temperature of 98.6°F?

Use the graphic organizer to help you solve the problem.

Read the Problem	Solve the Problem
What do I need to find?	
What information do I need to use?	
How will I use the information?	

So, the normal body temperature of a chicken is _____

which is _____ warmer than normal human body temperature.

Math Talk Explain how the strategy of using a formula helped you solve the problem.

- How could you use the formula for converting Fahrenheit to Celsius temperatures to check your answer?

_____

_____

Name _____

Share and Show MATH BOARD

⚓ **UNLOCK the Problem** Tips

√ Use the order of operations to evaluate expressions.

√ Check the reasonableness of your answer.

⓵ **1.** The highest temperature ever recorded in Norfolk, Virginia, was 104°F. What was the maximum temperature in degrees Celsius?

First, choose a formula.

_____

Next, substitute 104 for F.

_____

Finally, evaluate the formula.

_____

So, the maximum temperature in degrees Celsius was _____.

SHOW YOUR WORK

2. **H.O.T.** **What if** Norfolk's maximum temperature had been 9 degrees less on a Fahrenheit scale? How would this change the Celsius temperature?

_____

⓵ **3.** The highest temperature ever recorded in Phoenix, Arizona, was 50°C. Convert this temperature to degrees Fahrenheit.

_____

4. The element magnesium melts at a temperature of 650°C. What is magnesium's melting point in degrees Fahrenheit?

_____

5. Water boils at a temperature of 212°F and freezes at a temperature of 32°F. **Explain** how to use a formula to find the boiling and freezing points of water in degrees Celsius.

_____

_____

_____

On Your Own . . . .

Choose a STRATEGY

Work Backward
Solve a Simpler Problem
Choose an Operation
Use a Model
Use a Formula
Draw a Diagram

6. At the electronics store, Chris spent half of his money on a pair of headphones. At the office supply store, he spent half of his remaining money on recordable CDs. At the bookstore, he spent his remaining $12.75 on a book. How much money did he have to begin with?

_____

7. The formula $r = 206.9 - 0.67n$ gives the recommended maximum heart rate r, in beats per minute, during exercise, for a person n years of age. Would an 18 year old or a 24 year old have a higher recommended maximum heart rate? **Explain**.

_____

_____

_____

8. The formula $d = 16t^2$ gives the distance, in feet, that an object will fall in t seconds. How far will an object fall in 3 seconds?

_____

9. **Write Math** ▶ The product of 6 and a certain number is 9. Which operation would you use to find the number? **Explain** your reasoning. What is the number?

_____

_____

_____

10. ⭐ **Test Prep** The formula for the perimeter of a rectangle is $P = 2l + 2w$. A rectangle has a length of 11 inches and a width of 8 inches. What is the perimeter of the rectangle?

   (A) 6 inches   (C) 30 inches

   (B) 19 inches   (D) 38 inches

. . . . **SHOW YOUR WORK** . . . .

FOR MORE PRACTICE:
Standards Practice Book, pp. P109–P110

Convert Units of Length

Essential Question How can you convert from one unit of length to another?

In the customary measurement system, some of the common units of length are inches, feet, yards, and miles. You can multiply by an appropriate conversion factor to convert between units. A **conversion factor** is a rate in which the two quantities are equal, but use different units.

Customary Units of Length	
1 foot (ft)	= 12 inches (in.)
1 yard (yd)	= 36 inches
1 yard	= 3 feet
1 mile (mi)	= 5,280 feet
1 mile	= 1,760 yards

UNLOCK the Problem  REAL WORLD

In a soccer game, Kyle scored a goal from a corner kick. Kyle was 33 feet from the goal. How many yards from the goal was he?

- How are feet and yards related?

_____

- Use the relationship to write two rates equal to one.

_____

 Convert 33 feet to yards.

Choose a conversion factor. **Think:** I'm converting to yards *from* feet.

1 yard = 3 feet, so use the rate $\frac{1\text{ yd}}{3\text{ ft}}$.

Multiply 33 feet by the conversion factor.

$33\text{ ft} \times \frac{1\text{ yd}}{3\text{ ft}} = \frac{33\text{ ft}}{1} \times \frac{1\text{ yd}}{3\text{ ft}} = (\underline{\hspace{1cm}})\text{ yd}$

So, Kyle was _____ yards from the goal.

 How many inches from the goal was Kyle?

Choose a conversion factor. **Think:** I'm converting to inches *from* feet.

12 inches = 1 foot, so use the rate $\frac{12\text{ in.}}{1\text{ ft}}$.

Multiply 33 ft by the conversion factor.

$33\text{ ft} \times \frac{12\text{ in.}}{1\text{ ft}} = \frac{33\text{ ft}}{1} \times \frac{12\text{ in.}}{1\text{ ft}} = (\underline{\hspace{1cm}})\text{ in.}$

So, Kyle was _____ inches from the goal.

- **Explain** how you know which unit to use in the numerator and which unit to use in the denominator of a conversion factor.

_____

_____

Metric Units You can use a similar process to convert metric units. Metric units are used throughout most of the world. The advantage of using the metric system is that the units are related by powers of ten.

Example A Boeing 777-300 passenger airplane measures 73.9 meters from nose to tail. What is the length of the airplane in centimeters? What is the length in kilometers?

🔑 One Way Use a conversion factor.

73.9 meters = ▢ centimeters

Choose a conversion factor.   100 cm = 1 m, so use the rate $\dfrac{\text{cm}}{\text{m}}$

Multiply 73.9 meters by the conversion factor.

$$\dfrac{73.9\ m}{1} \times \dfrac{\text{cm}}{\text{m}} = \underline{\hspace{2cm}} cm$$

So, 73.9 meters is equal to _____ centimeters.

🔑 Another Way Use powers of 10.

Metric units are related to each other by factors of 10.

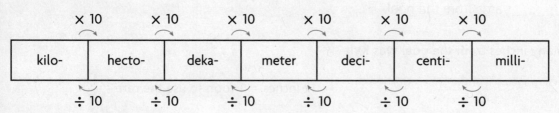

	× 10	× 10	× 10	× 10	× 10	× 10
kilo-	hecto-	deka-	meter	deci-	centi-	milli-
	÷ 10	÷ 10	÷ 10	÷ 10	÷ 10	÷ 10

73.9 meters = ▢ kilometers

Use the chart.

Kilometers are 3 places to the left of meters in the chart. Move the decimal point 3 places to the left. This is the same as dividing by 1,000.

73.9   0.0739

So, 73.9 meters is equal to _____ kilometer.

Math Talk Explain If you convert 285 centimeters to decimeters, will the number of decimeters be greater or less than the number of centimeters?

Name _____

Share and Show ·

Convert to the given unit.

1. 3 miles = [ ] yards

conversion factor: $\dfrac{\text{yd}}{\text{mi}}$

3 miles = $\dfrac{3 \text{ mi}}{1} \times \dfrac{1{,}760 \text{ yd}}{1 \text{ mi}}$ = _____ yd

2. 43 decimeters = _____ hectometer

✓ 3. 9 yards = _____ inches

4. 72 ft = _____ yd

✓ 5. 7,500 mm = _____ dm

> **Math Talk** Explain how to convert from inches to yards and yards to inches.

On Your Own ·

Convert to the given unit.

6. Jason used 9 yards of ribbon while wrapping gifts for a local charity. How many inches of ribbon did he use?

_____

7. The smallest known frog species can reach a maximum length of 12.4 millimeters. What is the maximum length of this frog species in centimeters?

_____

8. A professional football field measures 160 feet wide. What is the width of the field in yards?

_____

9. The height of the Empire State Building measured to the top of the lightning rod is approximately 443.1 meters tall. What is this height in hectometers?

_____

Copy and Solve Compare. Write <, >, or =.

10. 32 feet ◯ 11 yards

11. 537 cm ◯ 5.37 m

12. 75 inches ◯ 6 feet

Problem Solving

What's the Error?

13. The Redwood National Park is home to some of the largest trees in the world. Hyperion is the tallest tree in the park with a height of approximately 379 feet. Tom wants to find the height of the tree in yards.

Tom converted:

$$3 \text{ feet} = 1 \text{ yard}$$

conversion factor: $\frac{3 \text{ ft}}{1 \text{ yd}}$

$$\frac{379 \text{ ft}}{1} \times \frac{3 \text{ ft}}{1 \text{ yd}} = 1{,}137 \text{ yd}$$

Find and describe Tom's error.	**Show how to correctly convert from 379 feet to yards.**

So, 379 feet = _____ yards.

- Explain how you knew Tom's answer was incorrect.

  _____

  _____

  _____

- Stratosphere Giant, located in Humboldt State Park in California, is 4,446 inches tall. **Compare** the heights of Hyperion and Stratosphere Giant.

  _____

  _____

  _____

Name _____

Convert Units of Capacity

Essential Question How can you convert from one unit of capacity to another?

Capacity measures the amount a container can hold when filled. In the customary measurement system, some common units of capacity are fluid ounces, cups, pints, quarts, and gallons. You can convert between units by multiplying the given units by an appropriate conversion factor.

Customary Units of Capacity		
8 fluid ounces (fl oz)	=	1 cup (c)
2 cups	=	1 pint (pt)
2 pints	=	1 quart (qt)
4 cups	=	1 quart
4 quarts	=	1 gallon (gal)

UNLOCK the Problem REAL WORLD

Each dairy cow in the United States produces, on average, 25 quarts of milk per day. How many gallons of milk does a cow produce each day?

• How are quarts and gallons related?

_____

• Why can you multiply a quantity by $\frac{1\ gal}{4\ qt}$ without changing the value of the quantity?

_____

_____

 Convert 25 quarts to gallons.

Choose a conversion factor. **Think:** I'm converting *to* gallons *from* quarts.

1 gallon = 4 quarts, so use the rate $\frac{1\ gal}{4\ qt}$

Multiply 25 qt by the conversion factor.

$$25\ qt \times \frac{1\ gal}{4\ qt} = \frac{25\ qt}{1} \times \frac{1\ gal}{4\ qt} = 6\ \frac{\quad}{4}\ gal$$

When converting to multiple units, the fractional part can be renamed using the smaller unit.

$$6\ \frac{\quad}{4}\ gal = \underline{\quad}\ gallons,\ \underline{\quad}\ quart$$

So, a cow produces _____ gallons, _____ quart of milk each day.

 How many pints of milk does a cow produce each day?

Choose a conversion factor. **Think:** I'm converting *to* pints *from* quarts.

2 pints = 1 quart, so use the rate $\frac{\boxed{}\ pt}{\boxed{}\ qt}$

Multiply 25 qt by the conversion factor.

$$25\ qt \times \frac{\boxed{}\ pt}{\boxed{}\ qt} = \frac{25\ qt}{1} \times \frac{\boxed{}\ pt}{\boxed{}\ qt} = \underline{\quad}\ pt$$

So, a cow produces _____ pints of milk each day.

Metric Units You can use a similar process to convert metric units of capacity. Just like metric units of length, metric units of capacity are related by powers of ten.

Metric Units of Capacity
1,000 milliliters (mL) = 1 liter (L)
100 centiliters (cL) = 1 liter
10 deciliters (dL) = 1 liter
1 dekaliter (daL) = 10 liters
1 hectoliter (hL) = 100 liters
1 kiloliter (kL) = 1,000 liters

Example A piece of Native American pottery has a capacity of 1.7 liters. What is the capacity of the pot in dekaliters? What is the capacity in milliliters?

One Way Use a conversion factor.

1.7 liters = ▢ dekaliters

Choose a conversion factor.   1 dekaliter = 10 liters, so use the rate

$$\frac{\boxed{}\ daL}{\boxed{}\ L}.$$

Multiply 1.7 L by the conversion factor.

$$\frac{1.7\ L}{1} \times \frac{\boxed{}\ daL}{\boxed{}\ L} = \boxed{}\ daL$$

So, 1.7 liters is equivalent to _____ dekaliters.

Another Way Use powers of 10.

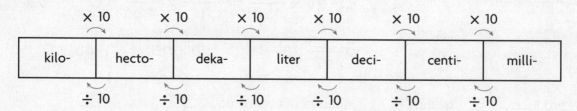

× 10	× 10	× 10	× 10	× 10	× 10
kilo-	hecto-	deka-	liter	deci-	centi-	milli-
÷ 10	÷ 10	÷ 10	÷ 10	÷ 10	÷ 10

1.7 liters = ▢ milliliters

Use the chart.

Milliliters are 3 places to the right of liters. So, move the decimal point 3 places to the right.   1.7   1700.

So, 1.7 liters is equal to _____ milliliters.

> **Math Talk**   Explain why you cannot convert between units in the customary system by moving the decimal point left or right.

• **Describe** how you would convert kiloliters to milliliters.

Name _____

Share and Show . . . .

Convert to the given unit.

1. 5 quarts = [ ] cups

   conversion factor: $\dfrac{\quad c}{\quad qt}$

   5 quarts = $\dfrac{5 \text{ qt}}{1} \times \dfrac{4 \text{ c}}{1 \text{ qt}}$ = _____ c

2. 6.7 liters = _____ hectoliters

✓ 3. 5.3 kL = _____ L   ✓ 4. 36 qt = _____ gal   5. 5,000 mL = _____ cL

Math Talk Compare the customary and metric systems. In which system is it easier to convert from one unit to another?

On Your Own . . . .

Convert to the given unit.

6. Julie drinks 8 cups of water a day. How many quarts of water does she drink a day?

7. Sam squeezed 237 milliliters of juice from 4 oranges. How many liters of juice did Sam squeeze?

8. Anthony filled a bottle with 3.78 liters of water. How many deciliters of water are in the bottle?

9. It takes 41 gallons of water for an average washing machine to wash a load of laundry. How many quarts of water does it take to wash one load?

Copy and Solve Compare. Write <, >, or =.

10. 700,000 L ◯ 70 kL   11. 6 gal ◯ 30 qt   12. 54 kL ◯ 540,000 dL

13. 10 pt ◯ 5 qt   14. 500 mL ◯ 50 L   15. 14 c ◯ 4 qt

16. Jeffrey is loading cases of bottled water onto a freight elevator. Each case holds 24 one-pint bottles. The maximum weight that the elevator can carry is 1,000 pounds. If 1 gallon of water weighs 8.35 pounds, what is the maximum number of full cases Jeffrey can load onto the elevator?

Ⓐ 39 cases

Ⓑ 39.9 cases

Ⓒ 40 cases

Ⓓ 119 cases

a. What do you need to find?

_____

_____

_____

b. How do you know that the answer cannot be choice B?

_____

_____

c. How can you find the weight of 1 case of bottled water? What is the weight?

_____

_____

_____

_____

d. How can you find the number of cases that Jeffrey can load onto the elevator?

_____

_____

_____

_____

_____

e. Fill in the bubble for the correct answer choice above.

17. Each day, a dripping faucet dripped 1 gallon, 1 quart, 1 pint, and 1 cup of water. How many total cups of water did the faucet drip in one day?

Ⓐ 23 cups

Ⓑ 30 cups

Ⓒ 45 cups

Ⓓ 52 cups

18. A warehouse holds 100 barrels in storage. Each barrel has a capacity of 50 liters. If all the barrels are filled with water, how many kiloliters (kL) of water will they hold?

Ⓐ   5 kL

Ⓑ   50 kL

Ⓒ   5,000 kL

Ⓓ 5,000,000 kL

FOR MORE PRACTICE:
Standards Practice Book, pp. P113–P114

Name _____

✓ Mid-Chapter Checkpoint

▶ Vocabulary

Choose the best term from the box.

1. A _____ is a rate in which the two quantities are equal, but use different units. (p. 223)

2. _____ is the time that passes from the beginning of an activity to the end of the activity. (p. 215)

▶ Concepts and Skills

Find the start, elapsed, or end time. (pp. 215–218)

3. Savanna ended her hike at 5:28 P.M., 6 hours 40 minutes after she started. What time did she start?

_____

4. Mr. Gregg left his house at 8:14 A.M. and drove until 3:05 P.M. How long did his drive last?

_____

Use the formula to solve. (pp. 219–222)

5. The element bromine boils at a temperature of 59°F. What is the boiling point in degrees Celsius?
Use the formula $C = \frac{5}{9}(F - 32)$.

_____

6. In one day, Millvale registered a low temperature of 10°C and a high temperature of 30°C. What was the difference between the low and high temperatures in degrees Fahrenheit?
Use the formula $F = \frac{9}{5}C + 32$.

_____

Convert to the given unit. (pp. 223–226, 227–230)

7. 34.2 mm = _____ cm

8. 42 in. = _____ ft

9. 1.4 km = _____ hm

10. 4 gal = _____ qt

11. 53 dL = _____ daL

12. 28 c = _____ pt

Fill in the bubble to show your answer.

13. Chandan's bus ride started at 7:30 A.M. and lasted 13 hours 15 minutes. What time did the ride end? (pp. 215–218)

(A) 8:45 P.M.

(B) 8:30 P.M.

(C) 8:45 A.M.

(D) 7:15 A.M.

14. In the chemistry lab, Nolan heated a liquid to a temperature of 185°F. What was the temperature of the liquid in degrees Celsius? Use the formula $C = \frac{5}{9}(F - 32)$. (pp. 219–222)

(A) 73°F

(B) 85°F

(C) 153°F

(D) 275.4°F

15. Ben's living room is a rectangle measuring 10 yards by 168 inches. By how many feet does the length of the room exceed the width? (pp. 223–226)

(A) 9 feet

(B) 12 feet

(C) 16 feet

(D) 21 feet

16. Jessie served 13 pints of orange juice at her party. How many quarts of orange juice did she serve? (pp. 227–230)

(A) 1 quart 5 pints

(B) 3 quartst 1 pint

(C) 6 quarts 1 pint

(D) 12 quarts 1 pint

17. The baseball game ended at 12:19 A.M., 3 hours and 15 minutes after it started. What time did the game start? (pp. 215–218)

(A) 8:04 P.M.

(B) 9:04 P.M.

(C) 9:34 P.M.

(D) 10:04 P.M.

Name _____

Convert Units of Weight and Mass

Essential Question How can you convert from one unit of weight or mass to another?

In the customary measurement system, the amount of matter in an object is called the weight of the object. Common units of weight include ounces, pounds, and tons.

> **Customary Units of Weight**
>
> 1 pound (lb) = 16 ounces (oz)
> 1 ton (T) = 2,000 pounds

 UNLOCK the Problem REAL WORLD

The largest pearl ever found weighed 226 ounces. What was the pearl's weight in pounds?

- How are ounces and pounds related?

  _____

- Will you expect the number of pounds to be greater than 226 or less than 226? Explain.

  _____

Convert 226 ounces to pounds.

Choose a conversion factor.
Think: I'm converting *to* pounds *from* ounces.

1 lb = 16 oz, so use the rate $\dfrac{\boxed{}\ \text{lb}}{\boxed{}\ \text{oz}}$

Multiply 226 ounces by the conversion factor.

$$226\,oz \times \frac{1\ lb}{16\ oz} = \frac{226\ \cancel{oz}}{1} \times \frac{1\ lb}{16\ \cancel{oz}} = \frac{\boxed{}}{16}\ lb$$

Think: When converting to multiple units, the remainder is the smaller unit.

$$\frac{\boxed{}}{16}\ lb = \underline{}\ lb,\ \underline{}\ oz$$

So, the largest pearl weighed _____ pounds, _____ ounces

 The largest emerald ever found weighed 38 pounds. What was its weight in ounces?

Choose a conversion factor.
Think: I'm converting *to* ounces *from* pounds.

16 oz = 1 lb, so use the rate $\dfrac{\boxed{}\ \text{oz}}{\boxed{}\ \text{lb}}$

Multiply 38 lb by the conversion factor.

$$38\ lb \times \frac{16\ oz}{1\ lb} = \frac{38\ \cancel{lb}}{1} \times \frac{16\ oz}{1\ \cancel{lb}} = \underline{}\ oz$$

So, the emerald weighed _____ ounces.

1. Explain how you could convert the emerald's weight to tons.

_____

_____

Metric Units In the metric system, the amount of matter in an object is called the mass.

Example Corinne caught a rainbow trout with a mass of 2,570 grams. What was the mass of the trout in centigrams? What was the mass in kilograms?

 One Way Use a conversion factor.

2,570 grams to centigrams

Choose a conversion factor.   100 cg = 1 g, so use the rate $\dfrac{\text{cg}}{\text{g}}$

Multiply 2,570 g by the conversion factor. $\dfrac{2{,}570\ \text{g}}{1} \times \dfrac{100\ \text{cg}}{1\ \text{g}} = \underline{\hspace{2cm}}$ cg

So, the trout's mass was _____ centigrams.

 Another Way Use powers of 10.

Recall that metric units are related to each other by factors of 10.

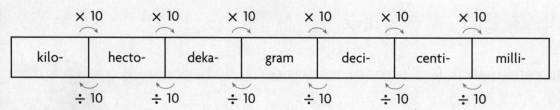

| kilo- | hecto- | deka- | gram | deci- | centi- | milli- |

2,570 grams to kilograms

Use the chart.

Kilograms are 3 places to the left of grams. Move the decimal point 3 places to the left.

2570.   2.570

So, 2,570 grams = _____ kilograms.

> **Math Talk** Compare objects with masses of 1 dg and 1 dag. Which is heavier? Explain.

2. Suppose 2 hoots = 4 floops. Which is heavier, a hoot or a floop? Explain.

_____

_____

Name _____

Share and Show

Convert to the given unit.

1. 9 pounds = [ ] ounces

conversion factor: $\dfrac{\quad}{\quad} \dfrac{oz}{lb}$

9 pounds = 9 lb × $\dfrac{16\ oz}{1\ lb}$ × _____ oz

2. 3.77 grams = _____ dekagram

3. Amanda's netbook weighs 56 ounces. How many pounds does it weigh?

_____

4. A honeybee can carry a 40 mg load of nectar to the hive. How many grams of nectar can a honeybee carry?

_____

Math Talk Compare metric units of capacity and mass. How are they alike? How are they different?

On Your Own

Convert to the given unit.

5. 4 lb = _____ oz

6. 7.13 g = _____ cg

7. 3 T = _____ lb

8. The mass of a standard hockey puck must be at least 156 grams. What is the minimum mass in kilograms?

_____

9. The African Goliath frog can reach weights up to 7 pounds. How many ounces can the Goliath frog weigh?

_____

Copy and Solve Compare. Write <, >, or =.

10. 250 lb ◯ 0.25 T

11. 65.3 hg ◯ 653 dag

12. 5 T ◯ 5,000 lb

13. **H.O.T.** Masses of precious stones are measured in carats, where 1 carat = 200 milligrams. What is the mass of a 50-dg diamond in carats?

_____

Problem Solving · REAL WORLD

Use the table to solve 14–18.

14. Express the weight range for bowling balls in pounds.

   _____

15. By how many pounds does the maximum allowable weight for a soccer ball exceed the maximum allowable weight for a baseball? Round your answer to the nearest hundredth.

   _____

16. **H.O.T.** A manufacturer produces 3 tons of baseballs per day and packs them in cartons of 24 baseballs. If all of the balls are the minimum allowable weight, how many cartons of balls does the company produce each day?

   _____

17. **Write Math** ▶ **Explain** how you could use mental math to estimate the number of soccer balls it would take to produce a total weight of 1 ton.

   _____

   _____

   _____

   _____

18. ★ **Test Prep** A tennis ball must weigh at least 0.4 times the minimum allowable weight for a baseball. What is a tennis ball's minimum allowable weight?

   (A) 1.25 oz

   (B) 2 oz

   (C) 12.5 oz

   (D) 20 oz

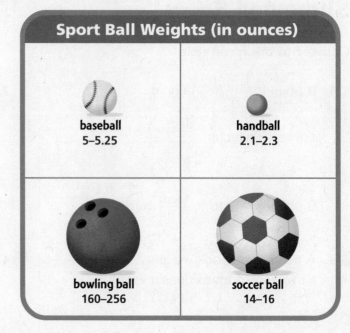

Sport Ball Weights (in ounces)

baseball 5–5.25	handball 2.1–2.3
bowling ball 160–256	soccer ball 14–16

SHOW YOUR WORK

FOR MORE PRACTICE:
Standards Practice Book, pp. P115–P116

Name _____

Precision and Accuracy

Essential Question How can you choose the appropriate level of precision and accuracy for a measurement?

 UNLOCK the Problem REAL WORLD

The **precision** of a measurement indicates the level of detail in the measurement. The smaller the unit of measure, the more precise the measurement is.

Measure the length of the object to the nearest centimeter and to the nearest millimeter.

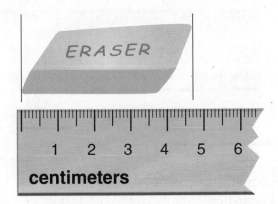

centimeters

> ⚠ **ERROR Alert**
>
> When measuring with a ruler, be sure to line up the end of the object with the tick mark that represents zero on the ruler.

To the nearest centimeter, the line segment is _____ cm long.

To the nearest millimeter, the line segment is _____ mm long.

Math Talk Explain which measurement of the eraser is more precise.

Try This! Measure the length of the pencil to the nearest centimeter and to the nearest millimeter.

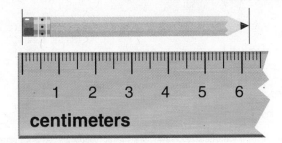

centimeters

_____

1. **Explain** how you could find an even more precise measure for the length of the pencil.

_____

_____

Accuracy All measurements are approximations because a measurement is only as precise as the tool used to measure. **Accuracy** is the closeness of a given measurement to the actual measurement of an object.

🔑 Example 1 Measure the length of the key to the nearest $\frac{1}{4}$ in., $\frac{1}{8}$ in., and $\frac{1}{16}$ in. Explain which measurement is most precise.

nearest $\frac{1}{4}$ in. _____

nearest $\frac{1}{8}$ in. _____

nearest $\frac{1}{16}$ in. _____

_____ is the most precise measurement

because it uses the _____ unit.

inches

Math Talk Explain whether all of the measurements in Example 1 are equally accurate.

When you measure an object, you need to decide which unit has the appropriate levels of precision and accuracy. Using units that result in extremely small or extremely large numbers is usually not appropriate. For example, it is more appropriate to measure the width of a stamp as 18 mm than as 0.000018 km.

🔑 Example 2 Circle the more appropriate unit of measure for each item.

the weight of a cement block
ounce or (pound)

the capacity of a bathtub
milliliter or liter

the length of a highway
mile or foot

the mass of a feather
kilogram or gram

2. **H.O.T.** **Describe** the tools and units you would use to measure the volume and weight of the water in an aquarium.

_____

_____

Name _____

Share and Show ![MATH BOARD] ·

Measure the length of the object to the given levels of precision.

1.

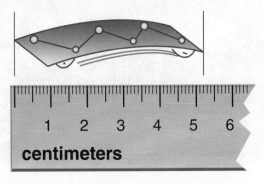

centimeters

nearest centimeter: _____ cm

nearest millimeter: _____ mm

2.

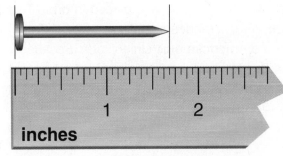

inches

nearest $\frac{1}{8}$ in.: _____ in.

nearest $\frac{1}{16}$ in.: _____ in.

Circle the more precise measurement.

✓**3.** 3 c   or   1 qt   **4.** 7 yd   or   20 ft   **5.** 71 mm   or   7 cm   **6.** 73 in.   or   2 yd

Circle the more appropriate unit of measure for each item.

7. distance around a house
   mile   or   yard

8. capacity of a water pitcher
   kiloliter   or   liter

✓**9.** mass of an apple
   gram   or   milligram

> **Math Talk** Explain how you can tell whether one unit of measure is more precise than another unit of measure.

On Your Own ·

Use your ruler to measure the length of the line segment to the given level of precision.

10. •———————•

nearest millimeter _____

11. •———————•

nearest $\frac{1}{16}$ in. _____

Circle the more precise measurement.

12. 4 pt or 7 c   **13.** 12 m or 1,100 cm   **14.** 50 oz   or   3 lb   **15.** 310 g   or   3 hg

Name an appropriate customary and metric unit for each item.

16. weight or mass of a car

   customary: _____

   metric: _____

17. width of a book

   customary: _____

   metric: _____

18. capacity of a thimble

   customary: _____

   metric: _____

The International Space Station

Construction of the International Space Station began in November 1998. First, the Russian-built Zarya Control Module was placed in orbit. Two weeks later, American astronauts joined Zarya with the American-built Unity Node. Because both Russian and American engineers had made precise measurements, the two components fit together perfectly.

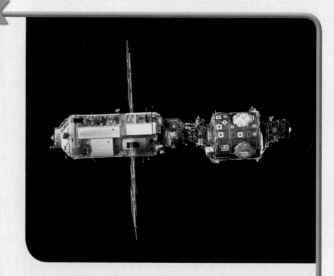

Circle the more precise measurement.

Space Station Component	Measurement
19. Unity Node length	18 ft or 220 in.
20. Zarya weight	42,600 lb or 21 T
21. Zarya solar array length	11 m or 1,070 cm
22. Zarya full fuel tank mass	5,000,000 g or 5,000 kg

Solve. Explain your reasoning.

23. Unity Node has 121 electrical cables. Which is a more appropriatemeasure for the total length of the cables, 6 miles or 381,000 inches? Explain.

_____

_____

_____

24. **H.O.T. Pose a Problem** The maximum altitude of Zarya and Unity Node when they were joined was approximately 390 kilometers. Write a problem similar to Problem 23 involving the maximum altitude.

_____

_____

_____

Name _____

Distance, Rate, and Time

Essential Question How do you solve problems involving rate, time, and distance?

You can solve problems involving distance, rate, and time by using the formulas below. In each formula, *d* represents distance, *r* represents rate, and *t* represents time.

Distance, Rate, and Time Formulas		
To find distance, use $d = rt$	To find rate, use $r = \dfrac{d}{t}$	To find time, use $t = \dfrac{d}{r}$

🔑 UNLOCK the Problem · REAL WORLD

Zachary's class traveled to the Museum of Natural Science for a field trip. To reach the destination, the bus traveled at a rate of 65 miles per hour for 2 hours. What distance did Zachary's class travel?

- What are you asked to find?

  _____

- Which formula should you use?

  _____

🔒 **Use the appropriate formula.**

You need to find a distance, so use $d = rt$. $d = rt$

Substitute 65 for *r*, and 2 for *t*. $d = $ ⬜ × ⬜

Multiply. $d = $ ⬜

So, Zachary's class traveled _____ miles.

---

1. **What if** the bus traveled at a rate of 55 miles per hour for 2.5 hours? How would the distance be affected?

   _____

   _____

   _____

2. **Describe** how to find the distance if you are given the rate and time.

   _____

   _____

🔑 Example Use the appropriate formula.

Formulas
To find distance, use $d = rt$
To find rate, use $r = \dfrac{d}{t}$
To find time, use $t = \dfrac{d}{r}$

Ⓐ Maggie took 45 minutes to walk the length of a trail that is 3,285 yards long. How fast was she walking?

You need to find the rate,
so use the formula $r = \dfrac{d}{t}$.

$$r = \dfrac{d}{t}$$

Substitute 3,285 for d and 45 for t.

$$r = \underline{\quad\quad}$$

Divide.

$$r = \boxed{}$$

So, Maggie was walking at a rate of _____ yards per minute.

Ⓑ Helen drives 221 miles to visit Niagara Falls. She drives at an average speed of 52 miles per hour. How long does the trip take?

You need to find time,
so use the formula $t = \dfrac{d}{r}$.

$$t = \dfrac{d}{r}$$

Substitute 221 for d, and 52 for r.

$$t = \underline{\quad\quad}$$

Divide.

$$t = \boxed{}$$

So, the trip takes _____ hours or _____ hours

and _____ minutes.

---

3. **What if** Helen increases her average speed to 55 miles per hour? How would the time be affected?

_____

_____

_____

4. **Explain** how you know which formula to use.

_____

_____

_____

Name _____

Share and Show . . . .

Choose the appropriate formula. Include the unit in your answer.

1. A jogger runs at a rate of 3 meters per second. How far has she run after 50 seconds?

   Choose a formula: _____

   Replace *r* with _____.

   Replace *t* with _____.

   distance = _____ meters

✓ 2. A car traveled 130 miles in 2 hours. How fast did the car travel?

   _____

✓ 3. A subway car travels at a rate of 32 feet per second. How far does it travel in 16 seconds?

   _____

4. A garden snail travels at a rate of 2.6 feet per minute. At this rate, how long will it take for the snail to travel 65 feet?

   _____

Math Talk Explain what is being measured if the answer is given in feet per second.

On Your Own . . . .

Choose the appropriate formula. Include the unit in your answer.

5. A cyclist travels at a rate of $\frac{1}{4}$ mile per minute. How far will he travel in 32 minutes?

   _____

6. A train travels at a speed of 75 miles per hour. How far does it travel in 3.5 hours?

   _____

7. A pilot flies 441 km in 31.5 minutes. What is the speed of the airplane?

   _____

8. A squirrel can run at a maximum speed of 12 miles per hour. At this rate, how long will it take the squirrel to run 3 miles?

   _____

Copy and Solve.

9. $d = 6.4$ cm

   $r = 2$ cm per sec

   $t = $ ▨

10. $d = 10.4$ yd

    $r = $ ▨

    $t = 4$ min

11. $d = $ ▨

    $r = 12$ km per hr

    $t = 40$ hr

Problem Solving  REAL WORLD

Use the table to solve 12–14.

12. How fast does Ferry A travel in feet per minute?

   _____

13. **Compare** the rates of travel for Ferry B and Ferry C. Which is faster?

   _____

14. Ferry C departs on schedule and travels at an average rate of 2,915 feet per minute. Will it arrive on time? **Explain.**

   _____

Ferry Schedule

	Depart	Arrive	Distance
Ferry A	10:15 A.M.	11:15 A.M.	148,500 ft
Ferry B	10:30 A.M.	11:10 A.M.	141,720 ft
Ferry C	1:30 P.M.	2:25 P.M.	180,730 ft
Ferry D	3:00 P.M.	3:45 P.M.	101,640 ft

15. **H.O.T.** Jeremy and Cynthia leave at the same time and travel 75 miles to an area attraction. Jeremy drives 11 miles in 12 minutes. Cynthia drives 26 miles in 24 minutes. If they continue at the same rates, who will arrive at the attraction first? **Explain.**

   _____

   _____

16. **Sense or Nonsense** Bonnie says that if she drives at an average rate of 40 miles per hour, she can drive 20 miles across town in about 2 hours. Does Bonnie's statement make sense? **Explain.**

   _____

   _____

17. ⭐ **Test Prep** Shane rows for exercise. He rows 18 kilometers at a rate of 9 kilometers per hour. How long does it take Shane to row 18 kilometers?

   Ⓐ $\frac{1}{2}$ hour   Ⓒ 20 hours

   Ⓑ 2 hours   Ⓓ 162 hours

SHOW YOUR WORK

FOR MORE PRACTICE:
Standards Practice Book, pp. P119–P120

Name _____

✓ Chapter 6 Review/Test

▶ Vocabulary

Choose the best term from the box.

1. The _____ of a measurement indicates the level of detail in the measurement. (p. 237)

2. The time that passes from the start of an activity to the end of the activity is called _____. (p. 215)

3. _____ is the closeness of a given measurement to the actual measurement. (p. 238)

▶ Concepts and Skills

Find the start, end, or elapsed time. (pp. 215–218)

4. start time: 8:57 A.M.
   elapsed time: 6 hr 25 min

   end time: _____

5. start time: 9:02 P.M. Monday

   elapsed time: _____
   end time: 6:17 A.M. Tuesday

Convert to the given unit. (pp. 223–226, 227–230, 233–236)

6. 27 yd = _____ ft

7. 3.60 cg = _____ g

8. 68.2 L = _____ dL

9. 4,000 m = _____ km

10. 26 c = _____ qt

11. 8,000 lb = _____ T

Tell which measure is more precise. (pp. 239–242)

12. 15 yd or 46 ft

13. 570 cm or 6 m

14. 17 lb or 270 oz

_____

_____

_____

Use the formula to complete. (pp. 243–246)

15. $d = rt$

   $d =$ ▢

   $r = 6$ cm per sec

   $t = 7$ sec

16. $r = \dfrac{d}{t}$

   $d = 320$ mi

   $r =$ ▢

   $t = 4$ hr

17. $t = \dfrac{d}{r}$

   $d = 72$ m

   $r = 3$ m per sec

   $t =$ ▢

18. The student council meeting began at 11:19 A.M. and ended at 1:15 P.M. How long did the meeting last? (pp. 215–218)

 (A) 56 minutes

 (B) 1 hour and 4 minutes

 (C) 1 hour and 56 minutes

 (D) 2 hours and 4 minutes

19. Jill baked a cake at an oven temperature of 210°C. What was the temperature in degrees Fahrenheit? Use the formula $F = \frac{9}{5}C + 32$.
 (pp. 219–222)

 (A) 178°F

 (B) 346°F

 (C) 378°F

 (D) 410°F

20. Marcy's house is 1,320 feet from the city library. How many miles does she live from the library? (pp. 223–226)

 (A) 0.25 mile

 (B) 0.5 mile

 (C) 0.75 mile

 (D) 3 miles

21. Tina's aquarium has a capacity of 40 gallons of water. She plans to stock her aquarium with 0.25 inches of fish per quart of capacity. Neon tetras are 2 inches in length. How many neon tetras can she have in her aquarium? (pp. 227–230)

 (A) 10 tetras

 (B) 20 tetras

 (C) 40 tetras

 (D) 80 tetras

22. A greyhound ran a distance of 1,200 feet in 30 seconds. Find the greyhound's average rate of speed. (pp. 241–244)

 (A) 25 feet per second

 (B) 36 feet per second

 (C) 40 feet per second

 (D) 400 feet per second

Fill in the bubble to show your answer.

23. Fran's snowmobile weighs 0.3 ton. Mike's weighs 500 pounds.
    What is the difference in the weights of the two vehicles? (pp. 233–236)

    Ⓐ 100 pounds

    Ⓑ 200 pounds

    Ⓒ 250 pounds

    Ⓓ 400 pounds

24. Which shows the length of the line segment to the nearest
    sixteenth inch? (pp. 237–240)

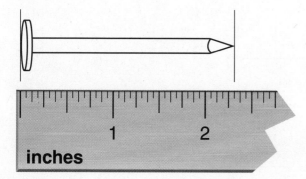

    Ⓐ $2\frac{3}{16}$ inches

    Ⓑ $2\frac{5}{16}$ inches

    Ⓒ $3\frac{1}{16}$ inches

    Ⓓ $3\frac{11}{16}$ inches

25. Eric competed in the 400-meter run. His average rate of speed
    was 5 meters per second. How long did it take Eric to finish
    the race? (pp. 241–244)

    Ⓐ   8 seconds

    Ⓑ   80 seconds

    Ⓒ 125 seconds

    Ⓓ 200 seconds

26. Kevin bought 6 hectograms of cheese selling for $9 per kilogram.
    What was the total cost? (pp. 233–236)

    Ⓐ $0.54

    Ⓑ $4.50

    Ⓒ $5.40

    Ⓓ $54.00

▶ **Short Answer**

27. Which has the greater capacity, a container that holds 50 hectoliters or a container that holds 10 kiloliters? Explain. (pp. 227–230)

_____

_____

_____

28. Explain how you can find the distance that a runner ran if you know the runner's average rate of speed and the total time it took the runner to run the distance. (pp. 241–244)

_____

29. Name an appropriate customary unit and metric unit for measuring the weight or mass of a refrigerator. (pp. 237–240)

_____

▶ **Performance Task**

30. Carina left at 8:15 A.M. on Saturday to visit her parents.

Ⓐ Carina drove 55 miles per hour for 4.5 hours to reach her parents' house. How far did she drive?

_____

Ⓑ What time did Carina arrive at her parents' house?

_____

Ⓒ Before returning home, Carina put 72 quarts of gasoline in her car. How many gallons of gasoline did she put in her car?

_____

Ⓓ Carina needs to be back home by 6:30 P.M. on Sunday. If she leaves for home at 1:23 P.M. driving at an average rate of 45 miles an hour, will she make it home on time? Explain.

_____

_____

Collect, Organize, and Analyze Data

Show What You Know

Check your understanding of important skills

Name _____

▶ **Mean** Find the mean of each set of data.

1. 5, 9, 13, 16, 20 _____

2. 36, 40, 28, 56 _____

▶ **Read Bar Graphs** Use the bar graph to answer the questions.

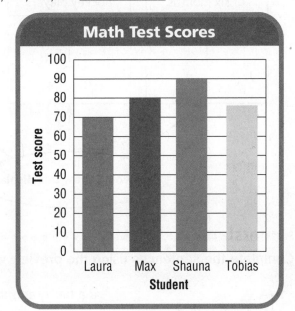

3. Who has the highest test score?

_____

4. Who has a score between 70 and 80?

_____

5. What is the difference between the highest and lowest scores?

_____

▶ **Relate Decimals and Percents** Write each percent as a decimal.

6. 70% _____

7. 25% _____

8. 5% _____

Kayla scored a 110 in the first game she bowled, but she can't remember her score from the second. The average of the two scores is 116. Be a math detective and help her figure out what her second score was.

_____

Vocabulary Builder

▶ **Visualize It**......................................

Sort the review words into the chart.

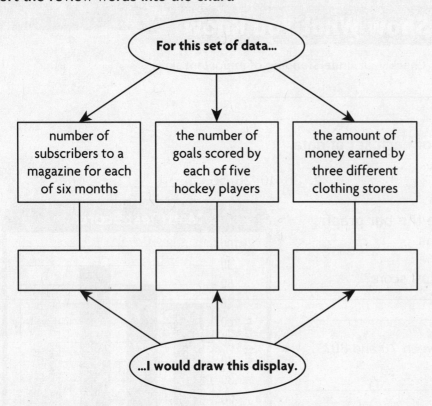

Review Words

bar graph

frequency table

line graph

Preview Words

circle graph

histogram

mode

sample

stem-and-leaf plot

survey

▶ **Understand Vocabulary** ●

Complete the sentences using the preview words.

1. A _____ is a bar graph that shows the
   frequency of data in specific intervals.

2. You can conduct a _____ to find out
   information about a group.

3. A _____ shows a data set as parts of a whole.

4. A _____ organizes a data set by splitting up the
   digits in each item.

5. Gathering data about a small part of a larger population is called

   taking a _____.

6. The item(s) that occurs most often in a data set is called the

   _____ of the data.

GO
Online
• eStudent Edition • Multimedia eGlossary

Name _____

Make and Analyze Graphs

Essential Question How can you display and analyze data in double bar graphs and double line graphs?

A bar graph is a useful way to display data grouped in categories. A **double bar graph** helps compare two sets of data.

 UNLOCK the Problem REAL WORLD

Vanessa organized the CDs in her home by type and by who owns them, as shown in the table. For which type of music is there the greatest difference in the number of CDs Vanessa owns and the number of CDs her parents own?

Number of CDs in Vanessa's Family

	Rock	Country	Pop	Jazz	Classical
Vanessa	12	14	9	3	4
Parents	6	2	5	7	5

🔑 **Make a double bar graph.**

STEP 1

Choose an appropriate scale. Numbers vary from

_____ to _____, so use a vertical scale from 0 to 16.

STEP 2

Draw bars of equal width. Use the data to determine the lengths of the bars. Use different colors to show different sets of data.

STEP 3

Include a title, labels for the axes, and a key that identifies the data sets.

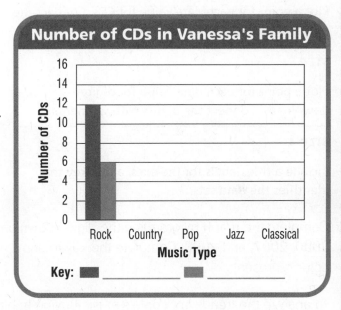

Complete the _____ to show what each color represents. Complete the graph by drawing the bars for the remaining four categories.

To find the type of music for which there is the greatest difference in the number of CDs Vanessa owns and the number of CDs her parents own, compare the lengths of the bars for each category.

The type of music for which there is the greatest difference in the number of CDs Vanessa owns and the number of CDs her parents own is _____.

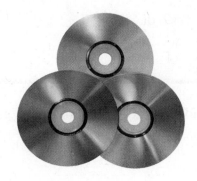

Double Line Graphs A **double line graph** uses line segments to help you compare two sets of data that change over time.

Example

The table from the Recording Industry Association of America shows the format in which people have bought music over several years. How have people's music-buying habits changed over time?

Format of Music Sales					
	2004	2005	2006	2007	2008
Full-Length CD	90%	87%	86%	83%	78%
Digital Download	1%	6%	7%	11%	13%

Make a double line graph.

STEP 1

Choose an appropriate scale. Percents vary from 1% to 90%, so use a vertical scale from 0% to 100%.

STEP 2

Plot a point for each data value for CDs. Connect the points with straight line segments.

STEP 3

Plot a point for each data value for digital downloads. Connect the points with segments.

STEP 4

Include a title, labels for the axes, and a key that identifies the data sets.

Complete the graph by graphing the digital download data for 2006, 2007, and 2008. Complete the key to show what each color represents.

To analyze the trends in people's music-buying habits, compare the path of the blue line to the path of the red line as you move from left to right.

So, sales of _____ are declining, while

sales of _____ are increasing.

> **! ERROR Alert**
>
> When you analyze a line graph, be sure to read the key carefully. Then use your finger to trace the appropriate line for each set of data.

- **Explain** how the double line graph is different from the double bar graph.

_____

_____

Name _____

Share and Show . . . .

For 1–3, use the table.

Sources of Support for Orchestras (in millions)			
	Income from Concerts	Private Contributions	Government Grants
10 Years Ago	$470	$350	$70
This Season	$530	$580	$50

☑ 1. Complete the double bar graph using the data in the table.

☑ 2. Describe how sources of financial support for orchestras have changed over the last 10 years.

_____

_____

_____

_____

3. **H.O.T.** If concert income increases by the same amount in the next 10 years as it increased in the last 10 years, will it reach $600 million? Explain.

_____

_____

_____

_____

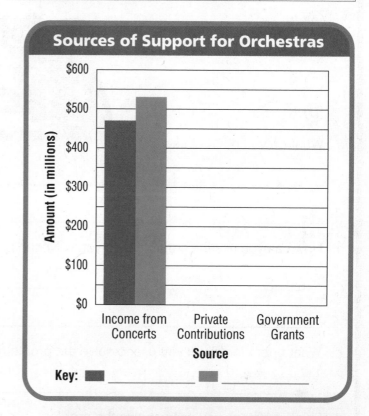

On Your Own . . . .

For 4–5, use the table.

Types of Music Sold (percent of total)				
	2002	2004	2006	2008
Rock	25	24	34	32
Rap/Hip-Hop	14	12	11	11

4. Make a double line graph using the data in the table.

5. In which year was there the greatest difference between the percent of rock music sales and the percent of rap/hip-hop music sales? How do you know?

_____

_____

_____

Types of Music Sold

Percent: 35, 30, 25, 20, 15, 10, 5, 0

Year: 2002, 2004, 2006, 2008

Key: _____ _____

UNLOCK the Problem

6. The graph shows the number of girls and boys in the sixth grade choir over a 4-year period. During this period, how many more girls than boys participated in the choir?

   Ⓐ 3

   Ⓑ 4

   Ⓒ 5

   Ⓓ 6

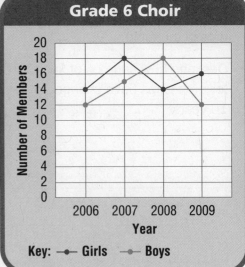

Grade 6 Choir

Number of Members / Year

Key: —•— Girls —•— Boys

a. What do you need to find?

_____

_____

b. How can you use the graph to help you solve the problem?

_____

_____

c. What operation(s) will you use to solve the problem?

_____

d. Show the steps you use to solve the problem.

e. Complete the sentences.

   The choir had a total of _____ girls.

   The choir had a total of _____ boys.

   The difference in the number of girls and the

   number of boys is _____.

f. Fill in the bubble for the correct answer choice above.

Use the above graph for 7–8.

7. In which year was the number of boys closest to the number of girls?

   Ⓐ 2006   Ⓒ 2008

   Ⓑ 2007   Ⓓ 2009

8. How many more boys were in the choir in 2007 than in 2006?

   Ⓐ 1   Ⓒ 4

   Ⓑ 3   Ⓓ 6

Name _____

Circle Graphs

Essential Question How can you display and analyze data in circle graphs?

A **circle graph** shows a data set as parts of a whole. Each category of the data is shown by a wedge of the circle. The wedges are called *sectors*. The size of each sector lets you compare the size of the categories.

The entire circle represents 100% of the data. The percents given for each sector should add up to 100%.

🔑 UNLOCK the Problem REAL WORLD

The circle graph shows how 80 campers at a summer camp participated in three different sports. How many campers participated in tennis?

 Find the number of campers who participated in tennis.

The circle graph says that 15% of campers chose tennis. Find 15% of 80 campers.

15% = _____ Write the percent as a decimal.

_____ × 80 = _____ Multiply the decimal and the total number of campers.

So, _____ campers chose tennis.

Activites Chosen for Summer Camp

Tennis 15%

Basketball 25%

Soccer 60%

Try This! How many campers chose soccer?

_____ % = _____

_____ × 80 = _____

So, _____ campers chose soccer.

- **Explain** how to find the number of campers who chose basketball without using a percent. Then find the number.

_____

_____

🔒 Activity • Make a Circle Graph

Materials • protractor, straightedge

The organizers of a summer camp asked campers to vote for which sport the camp should add next year. The results are shown in the table. Make a circle graph of the results.

Sport	Percent of Votes
Flag football	25%
Volleyball	45%
Lacrosse	30%

1. Convert each percent to a decimal.

   Flag football: 25% = _____

   Volleyball: 45% = _____

   Lacrosse: 30% = _____

2. Multiply each decimal by 360° to find the measure of the central angle for each sector.

   Flag football: _____ × 360° = _____

   Volleyball: _____ × 360° = _____

   Lacrosse: _____ × 360° = _____

3. Use the center of the circle as a vertex, and use a protractor to draw angles with the first two measures you calculated in Step 2.

4. Label each sector of the graph with the corresponding sport and percent.

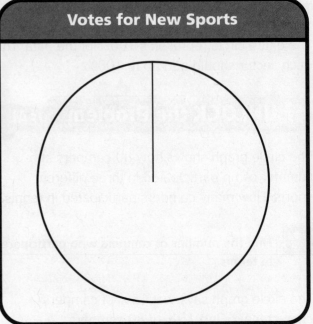

Votes for New Sports

 ERROR Alert

After drawing the first two angles, use your protractor to measure the remaining angle. Make sure that its measure matches your calculation.

Share and Show . . . .

Use the graph for Exercises 1–3.

1. What is the most common way of getting to school?

   _____

2. How many times more people walk than bicycle?

   _____

☑ 3. The graph represents 200 students. How many students ride their bicycles to school?

   _____

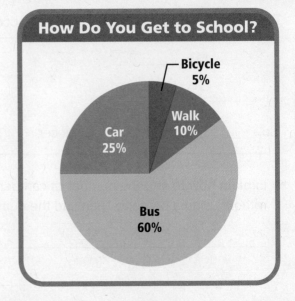

How Do You Get to School?

Bicycle 5%
Walk 10%
Car 25%
Bus 60%

256

Name _____

Share and Show   . . . .

✓ **4.** In a recent election for class president,
Connor received 10% of the vote, Daphne
received 40% of the vote, and Isaiah received
50% of the vote. Find the central angle for
each candidate and draw a circle graph.

Connor: _____

Daphne: _____

Isaiah: _____

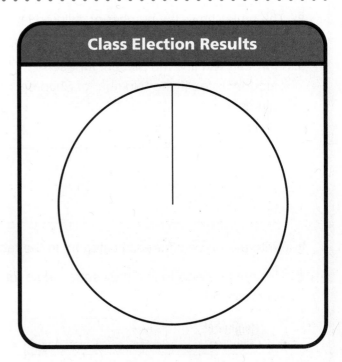

Math Talk Explain how to find the
measure of the central angle for a
sector in a circle graph.

On Your Own . . . .

5. A local middle school asked 75 parents if they
thought the school should require uniforms for
students. The results are shown in the circle
graph. How many parents were opposed to
uniforms?

_____

6. How many more parents support uniforms than
those who oppose them?

_____

7. **H.O.T.** In a follow up to the survey in
Exercise 5, 50% of the parents who originally
said "Yes" said they would change their vote to
"No" if the uniforms had to be special ordered.
How many parents would change their vote?

_____

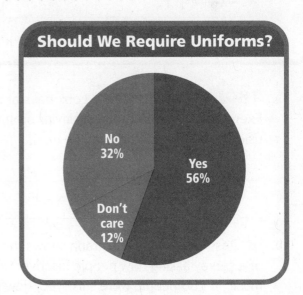

8. The table shows the number of children in 60 households. Draw a circle graph of the data.

Number of Children	Number of Households
No children	9
1 child	18
2 children	24
3 or more children	9

a. How can you find the percent for each category listed in the "Number of Children" column?

_____

_____

_____

b. Write the percent for each category in the table.

c. Use the percents to find the central angle for each category.

Number of Children	Percent	Central Angle
0		
1		
2		
3 or more		

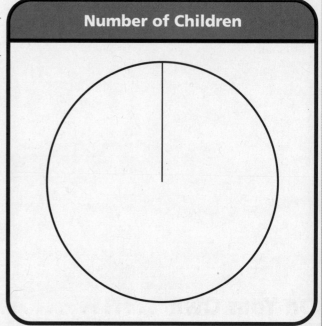

Number of Children

d. Use your results to draw the circle graph.

9. **H.O.T.** **Pose a Problem** Look back at Exercise 3. Write and solve a similar problem using a different category of the data.

_____

_____

10. ⭐ **Test Prep** The circle graph shows the result of a survey asking how people discover new music. If 180 people were surveyed, how many answered "Web"?

Ⓐ 18   Ⓒ 45

Ⓑ 36   Ⓓ 180

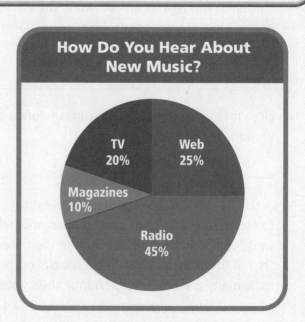

How Do You Hear About New Music?

TV 20%
Web 25%
Magazines 10%
Radio 45%

Mean, Median, Mode, and Range

Essential Question How can you describe a set of data using mean, median, mode, and range?

UNLOCK the Problem ⟩ REAL ⟩ WORLD

Kara is entering a paper airplane in a competition. In one of the categories in the competition, the plane that stays in the air for the longest time wins. The times for Kara's test flights are 5.8 s, 2.9 s, 6.7 s, 1.6 s, 2.9 s, and 4.7 s. What are the mean, median, mode and range of the data?

What unit of time is "s"? _____

How many flight times are given?

_____

 Find the mean, median, mode, and range of the data.

The *mean* is the sum of the data items divided by the number of data items.

$$\text{Mean} = \frac{5.8 + 2.9 + 6.7 + 1.6 + 2.9 + 4.7}{\boxed{}} = \frac{\boxed{}}{} = \boxed{}$$

The *median* is the middle value when the data are written in order. If the number of data items is even, the median is the mean of the two middle values.

Order the values from lowest to highest.

1.6, 2.9, 2.9, 4.7, 5.8, 6.7

Find the mean of the two middle values.

$$\frac{\boxed{} + \boxed{}}{\boxed{}} = \frac{\boxed{}}{} = \boxed{}$$

The *mode* is the data value or values that occur most often.

_____ occurs twice, and all the other values occur once.

_____ is the mode.

The *range* is the difference between the lowest data value and the highest data value.

Range = _____ − _____ = _____

Try This! In 2009, an engineer named Takuo Toda set a world record for flight time for a paper airplane. His plane flew for 27.9 s. If Toda's time was included in Kara's set of times, what would the range be?

_____

Math Talk Explain how the mean would change if you include Toda's time in Kara's data set.

🔑 Example

Thomas is writing an article for the school paper about the paper airplane competition. In the distance category, Kara's airplanes flew 17 ft, 16 ft, 18 ft, 15 ft, and 2 ft. Should Thomas use the mean, median, or mode to best describe Kara's results? Explain your reasoning.

Find the mean, median, and mode and compare them.

Mean = $\dfrac{\rule{1.5cm}{0.2pt} + \rule{1cm}{0.2pt} + \rule{1cm}{0.2pt} + \rule{1cm}{0.2pt} + \rule{1cm}{0.2pt}}{\rule{2cm}{0.2pt}}$

= $\dfrac{\rule{1cm}{0.2pt}}{\rule{1cm}{0.2pt}}$ = $\rule{1.5cm}{0.2pt}$

Order the data from lowest to highest to find the median.

_____ , _____ , _____ , _____ , _____

Median = _____

The data set has no repeated values, so there is no _____ .

The mean is _____ than 4 of the 5 values, so it is not a

good description of the data. The _____ is closer to most

of the values, so it is the best way to describe Kara's results.

> **Remember**
>
> If all of the values in a set of data occur only once, then the data set has no mode.

- **Explain** why the two modes may be a better description than the mean or median of the data set 2, 2, 2, 2, 7, 7, 7, 7.

  _____

  _____

  _____

Share and Show

1. Terrence records the number of e-mails he receives per day. During one week, he receives 7, 3, 10, 5, 5, 6, and 6 e-mails. What are the mean, median, mode, and range of the data?

   Mean = _____   Mode(s) = _____

   Median = _____   Range = _____

Name _____

Share and Show [MATH BOARD]

2. Julie goes to several grocery stores and researches the price of a 12 oz. bottle of juice. Find the mean, median, mode, and range of the prices shown.

Juice Prices		
$0.95	$1.09	$0.99
$1.25	$0.99	$1.99

Mean = _____ Mode(s) = _____ Median = _____ Range = _____

3. Does the mean, median, or mode(s) from Exercise 2 best describe Julie's data? Explain your reasoning.

_____

_____

_____

> **Math Talk** Explain how to find the median of a set of data with an even number of values.

On Your Own

4. T.J. is training for the 200-meter dash event for his school's track team. Find the mean, median, mode, and range of the times shown in the table.

T.J.'s Times		
22.3 s	22.4 s	23.3 s
24.5 s	22.5 s	

Mean = _____ Mode(s) = _____ Median = _____ Range = _____

5. Tobias is researching prices for a new pair of jeans. The prices at seven differnet stores are shown. Does the mean, median, or mode best describe the set of prices? Calculate each value and explain your reasoning.

Jeans Prices	
$18.99	$17.99
$19.99	$17.99
$17.99	$17.00
$10.99	

_____

_____

_____

_____

Problem Solving REAL WORLD

6. **H.O.T.** Laura's Lunch Stop provides the number of calories for each of five lunch specials, shown in the menu. The restaurant wants to advertise the mean or median number of Calories of their special, but they also want to make their lunch menu seem as low-Calorie as they can. Which measure should they use? Explain your reasoning.

_____

_____

_____

· Laura's Lunch Stop ·

Beef and Cheddar: 750 Cal

Turkey and Bacon: 850 Cal

Turkey and Mozzarella: 700 Cal

Caesar Salad: 650 Cal

Greek Salad: 450 Cal

SHOW YOUR WORK

7. In the last six months, Sonia's family used 456, 398, 655, 508, 1,186, and 625 minutes on their cell phone plan. To save money, Sonia's family wants to keep their mean cell phone usage below 600 minutes per month. Did they meet their goal? If not, by how many minutes did they go over?

_____

_____

8. **What's the Error?** Jeremy scored 85, 90, 72, 88, and 92 on his last 5 math tests. The mean of his scores is 85.4. Jeremy scores a 95 on the last test and calculates the mean of his six scores by adding 85.4 and 95 and dividing the sum by 2 to get 90.2. Find the correct mean of Jeremy's scores and explain his error.

_____

_____

_____

9. ⭐ **Test Prep** The school office records the number of days each student is sick. The sick day counts for 10 students are 2, 3, 5, 2, 0, 1, 1, 2, 4, and 1. What is the mode(s) of the data?

(A) 1

(C) 2.1

(B) 0 and 2

(D) 1 and 2

Name _____

Line Plots and Frequency Tables

Essential Question How can you use line plots and frequency tables to organize data?

A **line plot** is a number line with marks that show the frequency of data. A line plot helps you see where data cluster.

🔑 UNLOCK the Problem › REAL WORLD ‹

Hannah is training for a walkathon. The table shows the number of miles she walks each day. She has one day left in her training. How many miles is she most likely to walk on the last day?

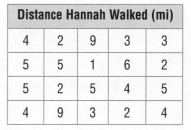

Distance Hannah Walked (mi)

4	2	9	3	3
5	5	1	6	2
5	2	5	4	5
4	9	3	2	4

 Make a line plot.

STEP 1

Draw a number line with an appropriate scale.

Numbers vary from _____ to _____, so use a scale from 0 to 10.

_____

STEP 2

For each piece of data, plot an X above the number that corresponds to the number of miles Hannah walked.

Complete the line plot by making the correct number of X's above the numbers 5 through 10.

The number of miles that Hannah is most likely to walk is the mode of the data. On a line plot, the mode is the value that has

_____.

So, the number of miles Hannah is most likely to

walk on the last day of her training is _____.

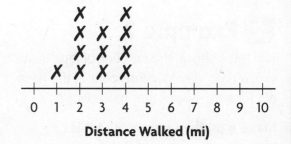

Distance Walked (mi)

Remember

The mode of a set of data is the value or values that occur most often.

- **Explain** why a line plot is useful for solving this problem.

_____

_____

A **frequency table** shows the number of times each piece of data or group of data occurs. A **relative frequency table** shows the percent of time each piece of data or group of data occurs.

🔑 Example 1

Jill kept a record of her workout times. How many of Jill's workouts lasted exactly 90 minutes?

Make a frequency table.

Jill's Workout Times (minutes)						
30	60	30	90	60	30	60
90	60	120	30	60	90	90
60	120	60	60	60	30	30
120	30	120	60	120	60	120

STEP 1

List the workout times in the first column.

STEP 2

Record the frequency of each time in the Frequency column.

Complete the frequency table.

So, _____ of Jill's workouts lasted exactly 90 minutes.

Jill's Workout Times	
Minutes	Frequency
30	7
60	
90	
120	

🔑 Example 2

The table shows the number of laps Ricardo swam each day. What percent of the days did Ricardo swim 18 or more laps?

Make a relative frequency table.

Ricardo's Lap Swimming				
10	10	15	5	12
12	5	19	3	19
16	14	17	18	13
6	17	16	11	8

STEP 1

Determine equal intervals for the data. List the intervals in the first column.

STEP 2

Count the number of data values in each interval. Record this in the Frequency column.

STEP 3

Divide each frequency by the total number of data values. Write the result as a percent in the Relative Frequency column.

Complete the relative frequency table.

So, Ricardo swam 18 or more laps on _____ of the days.

Ricardo's Lap Swimming		
Number of Laps	Frequency	Relative Frequency
3–7	4	20%
8–12	6	30%
13–17	7	
18–22	3	

There are 20 data values.

$\frac{4}{20} = 0.2 = 20\%$

$\frac{6}{20} = 0.3 = 30\%$

Math Talk Explain how you could find the percent of days on which Ricardo swam 13 or more laps.

© Houghton Mifflin Harcourt Publishing Company

Name _____

Share and Show

For 1–4, use the data at right.

✓ **1.** Complete the line plot.

Daily Distance Lionel Biked (km)				
3	5	12	2	1
8	5	8	6	3
11	8	6	4	10
10	9	6	6	6
5	2	1	2	3

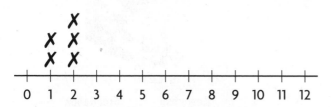

```
            X
    X   X
    X   X
  +--+--+--+--+--+--+--+--+--+--+--+--+--+
  0  1  2  3  4  5  6  7  8  9  10 11 12
```

2. What was the most common distance Lionel biked? How do you know?

_____

3. Make a frequency table. Use the intervals 1–3 km, 4–6 km, 7–9 km, and 10–12 km.

4. Make a relative frequency table. Use the same intervals as in Exercise 3.

On Your Own

Practice: Copy and Solve For 5–9, use the table.

5. Make a line plot of the data.

6. Make a frequency table of the data with 3 intervals.

7. Make a relative frequency table of the data with 3 intervals.

8. **Write Math** ▶ Describe how you decided on the intervals for the frequency table.

Gloria's Daily Sit-Ups				
13	3	14	13	12
12	13	4	15	12
15	13	14	3	11
13	13	12	14	15
11	14	13	15	11

_____

9. **H.O.T.** Could someone use the information in the frequency table to make a line plot? Explain.

_____

10. The manager of a fitness center asked members to rate the fitness center. The results of the survey are shown in the frequency table. What percent of members in the survey rated the center as excellent or good?

Ⓐ 25%   Ⓒ 33%

Ⓑ 30%   Ⓓ 55%

a. What do you need to find?

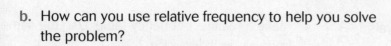

_____

_____

Fitness Center Survey

Response	Frequency
Excellent	18
Good	15
Fair	21
Poor	6

b. How can you use relative frequency to help you solve the problem?

_____

_____

c. Show the steps you use to solve the problem.

d. Complete the sentences.

The percent of members who rated the center

as excellent is _____.

The percent of members who rated the center

as good is _____.

The percent of members who rated the center

as excellent or good is _____.

e. Fill in the bubble for the correct answer choice above.

Use the above table for 11–12.

11. What percent of members in the survey rated the fitness center as fair or poor?

Ⓐ 10%   Ⓒ 35%

Ⓑ 27%   Ⓓ 45%

12. Which response was given by $\frac{1}{4}$ of the members in the survey?

Ⓐ Excellent   Ⓒ Fair

Ⓑ Good   Ⓓ Poor

✓ Mid-Chapter Checkpoint

▶ Vocabulary

Choose the best term from the box.

Vocabulary
circle graph
double line graph
double bar graph

1. A _____ compares two sets of data using

   connected line segments. (p. 252)

2. A graph that displays data as sectors in a circle is called a

   _____ . (p. 255)

▶ Concepts and Skills

3. Find the mean, median, mode, and range of the data set below.
   Then explain which measure(s) best describes the data set.
   (pp. 259–262)

   1.1, 8.9, 8.9, 9.9, 11.4, 12.6

   Mean = _____   Mode(s) = _____

   Median = _____   Range = _____

   _____

   _____

4. Make a double bar graph using the data in the table.
   (pp. 251–254)

Number of Sandwiches Sold at Lunch				
	Turkey	**Chicken**	**Tuna**	**Veggie**
Monday	12	8	7	5
Tuesday	10	14	12	10

TEST PREP

5. The frequency table shows the ages of visitors to a science exhibit for kids. What percent of the visitors are 5 to 8 years old?

(pp. 263–266)

(A) 9%

(B) 18%

(C) 25%

(D) 36%

Visitors to a Science Exhibit	
Age	Frequency
5–8	9
9–12	10
13–16	6

6. The town council took a vote about whether to include more computers with an internet connection in the local library. The circle graph shows the results. If 20 people voted, how many people voted "No"? (pp. 255–258)

(A) 1

(B) 4

(C) 15

(D) 75

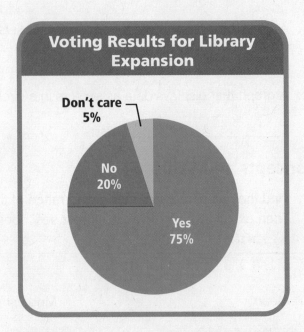

Voting Results for Library Expansion

Don't care 5%

No 20%

Yes 75%

7. According to the double line graph, what was the first year in which the population of Pinewood was greater than Oakville?

(pp. 251–254)

(A) 2006

(B) 2008

(C) 2009

(D) 2010

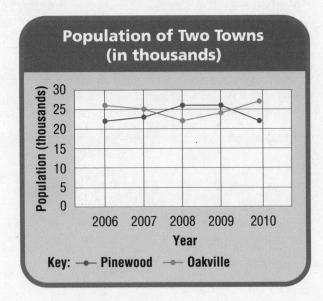

Population of Two Towns (in thousands)

Population (thousands)

2006 2007 2008 2009 2010

Year

Key: —•— Pinewood   —•— Oakville

8. The line plot shows the number of minutes Trevor played a video game each day. What is the mode of the data? (pp. 263–266)

(A) 10 minutes

(B) 18 minutes

(C) 19 minutes

(D) 25 minutes

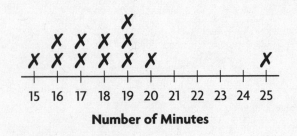

15 16 17 18 19 20 21 22 23 24 25

Number of Minutes

Name _____

Stem-and-Leaf Plots and Histograms

Essential Question How can you use stem-and-leaf plots and histograms to organize data?

A **stem-and-leaf plot** uses place value to organize data. A stem-and-leaf plot is useful when you need to see each item in a data set and the distribution of the data.

 UNLOCK the Problem REAL WORLD

The table shows the ages of winners of the Academy Award for Best Actor from 1991 to 2008. What is the median age of the winners?

Ages of Best Actor Winners					
54	52	37	38	32	45
60	46	40	36	47	29
43	37	38	45	50	48

 Make a stem-and-leaf plot.

STEP 1

Group the data by the tens digits. Then order the data from least to greatest.

29
32, 36, 37, 37, 38, 38
40, 43, 45, 45, 46, 47, 48

_____, _____, _____

_____

STEP 2

Use the tens digits as stems. Use the ones digits as leaves. Write the leaves in increasing order.

Stem	Leaves
2	9
3	2 6 7 7 8 8
4	0 3 5 5 6 7 8
5	
6	

STEP 3

Add a key that tells what the numbers mean.

2|9 = _____

There are 18 data values. The median is the mean of the two middle values. Use the stem-and-leaf plot to find the 9th and 10th values.

$$\frac{ + }{2} = \frac{}{2} = $$

So, the median age of Best Actor winners is _____.

 Remember
The median is the middle value when the data are written in order. If the number of data items is even, the median is the mean of the two middle values.

1. **Explain** how a stem-and-leaf plot makes it easy to find the median.

_____

When there is a large number of data values, it is helpful to group the data into intervals. A **histogram** is a bar graph that shows the frequency of data in intervals. Unlike a bar graph, there are no gaps between the bars in a histogram.

🔒 Example

The table shows the ages of winners of the Academy Award for Best Actress from 1985 to 2008. How many of the winners were under 40 years old?

Ages of Best Actress Winners					
61	21	41	26	80	42
29	33	36	45	49	39
34	26	25	33	35	35
28	30	29	61	32	33

Make a histogram.

STEP 1

Make a frequency table using intervals of 10.

Interval	20–29	30–39	40–49	50–59	60–69	70–79	80–89
Frequency	7	10	4	0	2	0	1

STEP 2

Set up the intervals along the

_____ axis of the graph. Write a scale for the frequencies on

the _____ axis.

STEP 3

Graph the number of winners in each interval.

STEP 4

Give the graph a title and label the axes.

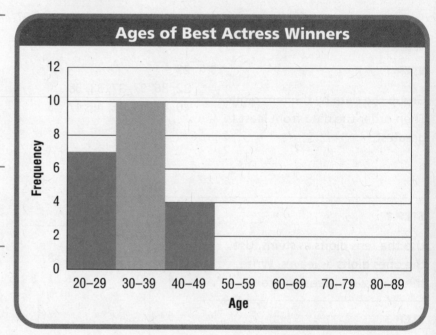

Ages of Best Actress Winners

Complete the histogram by drawing the bars for the intervals 60–69, 70–79, and 80–89.

To find the number of winners who were under 40 years old, add the frequencies for the intervals 20–29 and 30–39.

_____ + _____ = _____

So, _____ of the winners were under 40 years old.

2. **Explain** whether it is possible to find the mode of the data from the histogram.

_____

Name _____

Share and Show

For 1–4, use the data at right.

Ages of People at a Health Club (yr)				
21	25	46	19	33
38	18	22	30	29
26	34	48	22	31

☑ 1. Complete the stem-and-leaf plot.

Stem	Leaves
1	8 9
2	1 2 2 5 6 9
3	_____
4	_____

1|8 = 18

2. Use your stem-and-leaf plot to find the median of the data.

_____

☑ 3. Complete the histogram for the data.

4. Use your histogram to find the number of people at the health club who are 30 or older.

_____

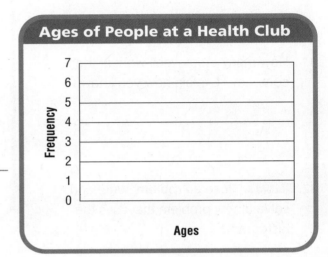

Ages of People at a Health Club

Frequency (y-axis): 0 1 2 3 4 5 6 7

Ages (x-axis)

Math Talk Explain whether you could use the histogram to find the number of people who are 25 or older.

On Your Own

Copy and solve. For 5–9, use the table.

5. Make a stem-and-leaf plot of the data.

6. Use your stem-and-leaf plot to find the median and mode of the data.

7. Make a histogram of the data using the intervals 10–19, 20–29, and 30–39.

8. Make a histogram of the data using the intervals 10–14, 15–19, 20–24, 25–29, 30–34, and 35–39.

9. Explain how using different intervals changed the appearance of your histogram.

_____

_____

Weights of Dogs (lb)				
16	20	15	24	32
33	26	30	15	21
21	12	19	21	37
10	39	21	17	35

Problem Solving 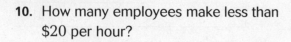 REAL WORLD

The histogram shows the hourly salaries, to the nearest dollar, of the employees at a small company. Use the histogram to solve 10–13.

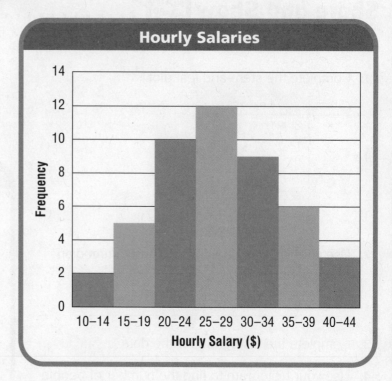

10. How many employees make less than $20 per hour?

_____

11. How many employees work at the company? Explain how you know.

_____

_____

12. H.O.T. **Pose a Problem** Write and solve a new problem that uses the histogram.

_____

_____

13. **Write Math** ▶ Describe the overall shape of the histogram. What does this tell you about the salaries at the company?

_____

_____

14. ★ **Test Prep** The stem-and-leaf plot shows the height, in inches, of some basketball players. What fraction of the players are less than 70 inches tall?

Stem	Leaves
6	9 9
7	0 1 3 6 7 7 7 9
8	0 1

6|9 = 69

Ⓐ $\frac{1}{12}$ Ⓒ $\frac{1}{5}$

Ⓑ $\frac{1}{6}$ Ⓓ $\frac{1}{2}$

Name _____

Draw a Diagram · Choose an Appropriate Graph

Essential Question How do you choose an appropriate display for a set of data?

UNLOCK the Problem REAL WORLD

The table shows the percent of times the World Series was decided in 4, 5, 6, and 7 games. Display the data to show the portion of World Series that were decided in each number of games.

Number of Games in World Series (1999–2008)	
Number of Games	Percent of World Series
4	40%
5	30%
6	10%
7	20%

<table>
<tr><th>Read the Problem</th><th>Solve the Problem</th></tr>
<tr><td>

What do I need to find?

I need to find a way to display the data to show

_____

_____

</td><td>

Find the appropriate angle measure for each percent and then draw the graph.

40% of 360° is _____ × 360° = _____

30% of 360° is _____ × 360° = _____

10% of 360° is _____ × 360° = _____

20% of 360° is _____ × 360° = _____

</td></tr>
<tr><td>

What information do I need to use?

I will use the _____ that are given for each number of games.

</td><td></td></tr>
<tr><td>

How will I use the information?

I will make a _____ graph to show the percent of World Series that were decided by each number of games.

Math Talk Explain why a circle graph is a good choice for this data.

</td><td></td></tr>
</table>

🔒 Try Another Problem

The table shows the attendance for the Pittsburgh Pirates'
last 25 home games of the 2009 baseball season. Display
the data using an appropriate graph.

Attendance at 25 Pittsburgh Pirates Games (in thousands)				
12	13	23	33	21
17	17	24	15	27
19	15	18	11	26
20	24	13	16	16
16	19	36	27	17

Read the Problem	Solve the Problem
What do I need to find?	
What information do I need to use?	
How will I use the information?	

- Justify the type of graph you chose.

_____

_____

_____

Math Talk Describe another way
you could have displayed the
attendance data.

Name _____

Share and Show

UNLOCK the Problem **Tips**

√ Underline important facts.
√ Organize the information.
√ Choose a strategy.
√ Check to make sure you answered the question.

1. The table shows the number of doubles by 11 players on the Detroit Tigers in 2009. Make a graph that displays the individual data values.

Number of Doubles by Detroit Tigers Players										
23	34	31	21	16	11	23	24	11	10	13

First, write the data in order from least to greatest.

_____

Next, set up a stem-and-leaf plot with the stems 1, 2, and 3, as shown.

Then, fill in the leaves to complete the stem-and-leaf plot.

Finally, add a key to the stem-and-leaf plot.

Stem	Leaves
1	_____
2	_____
3	_____

_____

2. **H.O.T.** **What if** you wanted to make a graph to display the doubles data, but did not need to see the individual data values? What type of graph could you make in this case?

_____

3. The table shows the number of home runs hit by Derek Jeter of the New York Yankees. On a separate sheet of paper, make a graph to display the data. Then explain why you chose this type of graph.

_____

_____

Home Runs by Derek Jeter	
Year	Home Runs
2005	19
2006	14
2007	12
2008	11
2009	18

For 4–6, name the best graph to display the data.

4. A school board determines how the school sports budget will be divided among baseball, basketball, and soccer.

_____

5. the number of wins and losses for 5 volleyball teams

_____

6. the height, in inches, of every player in the WNBA

_____

On Your Own.....................

7. **H.O.T.** A recipe for punch calls for apple juice and cranberry juice. The ratio of apple juice to cranberry juice is 3:2. Tyrone wants to make at least 20 cups of punch, but no more than 30 cups of punch. Describe two different ways he can use apple juice and cranberry juice to make the punch.

_____

_____

_____

Choose a STRATEGY

Work Backward

Solve a Simpler Problem

Choose an Operation

Use a Model

Use a Formula

Draw a Diagram

8. The Golden Gate Bridge is 2.7 kilometers long. Grace walks across the bridge taking photos. She takes a photo at the beginning and end of the bridge, and every 0.3 km along the way. How many photos does she take altogether?

_____

9. **Write Math** ▶ In a bookcase, $\frac{1}{5}$ of the books are mysteries and $\frac{1}{3}$ of the mysteries are by Agatha Christie. Given that there are 4 books by Agatha Christie, explain how to find the total number of books in the bookcase.

_____

_____

_____

SHOW YOUR WORK

10. A softball game featured 9 players on each team. At the end of the game, each player on the winning team shook hands with each player on the losing team. How many handshakes were there?

_____

11. ⭐ **Test Prep** A table shows the percent of baseball players who bat right handed, the percent who bat left handed, and the percent who are switch hitters. Which type of graph is best for displaying the data?

(A) circle graph

(B) histogram

(C) line graph

(D) stem-and-leaf plot

FOR MORE PRACTICE:
Standards Practice Book, pp. P135–P136

Name _____

Samples and Surveys

Essential Question How can you learn about a population by taking a sample?

A **survey** is a method of gathering information about a group. Surveys are usually made up of questions or other items that require responses. You can survey a population, which is the entire group of individuals or objects. If the population is large, you can survey a part of the population, called a **sample**.

UNLOCK the Problem REAL WORLD

Ron surveys students at his school about their favorite pizza toppings. He surveys the first 25 students to walk into school on Monday morning. What sampling method does he use?

> • Underline the sentence that tells you what you are trying to find.

 Identify the sampling method.

A **sampling method** is a way to choose a sample of a population. The table summarizes some sampling methods.

Sampling Method	Definition	Example
Random Sampling	Every individual or object has an equal chance of being chosen for the survey.	Assign a number to every student in the school. Then use a computer to randomly select numbers.
Convenience Sampling	Individuals or objects that are easily available are chosen for the survey.	Choose a convenient location, such as the library, and survey students as they enter.
Systematic Sampling	Choose a random individual or object as the starting point of a pattern and then use a pattern to choose additional individuals or objects.	Randomly choose a name from a list of all students and then choose every 10th name after that.

Describe how Ron chooses the sample for his survey.

_____

So, Ron uses _____ sampling.

Try This!

Meg takes a similar survey. She chooses one name at random from a list of all students at the school. Then she chooses every 15th name after that. What sampling method does she use?

_____

A sample contains **bias** (or is a *biased sample*) if it does not represent the population fairly.

For example, if you want to survey students at your school about favorite television shows, a sample containing only girls might be a biased sample. Girls' opinions about television shows may be different from those of boys, so the sample may not represent the entire population.

🔒 Example

Malia surveys employees at an office to find out how they travel to and from work. She surveys 20 employees as they leave the office at 4:45 P.M. Determine whether the sample may be biased.

Employees who leave the office at 4:45 may all be on their way to catch a train. The way they travel to and from work may not be representative of everyone at the office.

So, Malia's sample is _____.

Math Talk Describe another reason why Malia's sample could be biased.

- How could Malia choose a sample that is not biased?

_____

_____

Try This! Determine whether the sample may be biased. Explain.

A	Diego wants to know what sports are most popular in his town. He surveys 40 people at a baseball game.

_____

_____

_____

_____

B	A doctor randomly chooses 50 people from the phone book and surveys them to find out if they take vitamins.

_____

_____

_____

_____

Name _____

Share and Show MATH BOARD ·····················

Identify the sampling method.

1. Brianna randomly chooses 20 names from a database of all students at her school.

   Every student has an equal chance of being chosen. So, Brianna's sample

   is a _____.

2. Jorge randomly chooses one name from a phone list of all employees at his company. Then he chooses every 10th name after that.

   _____

Determine whether the sample may be biased. Explain.

3. A quality-control manager wants to know how many of the light bulbs that a factory produces might be defective. She randomly chooses and tests 30 light bulbs produced at the factory.

   _____

   _____

4. Ray wants to know how many books people in his town read each month. He surveys 50 people at a local library.

   _____

   _____

Math Talk Describe why someone might use a convenience sample rather than a random sample.

On Your Own ·····················

Identify the sampling method.

5. Mitchell stands at the exit of a train station and surveys 25 commuters as they leave the station.

   _____

6. Marie wants to survey owners of pet stores in her city. She chooses the name of a pet store from the phone book. Then she chooses every 3rd pet store after that.

   _____

Determine whether the sample may be biased. Explain.

7. Lashonda wants to know the favorite type of music of teens in her town. She surveys 10 students sitting near her at lunch.

   _____

   _____

8. A caterer randomly chooses 20 names from a list of clients and surveys them to see if they are satisfied with his service.

   _____

   _____

The U.S. Census

The U.S. Census is a count of every person living in the United States. Once every ten years, people across the country participate in the census by filling out survey forms. In addition to counting the number of people in the country, the census gathers data on everything from pet ownership to museum attendance.

According to the latest census data, the average American eats 10.2 pounds of oranges per year.

A food researcher surveyed two samples of Americans. The table shows how many pounds of oranges the participants in the survey ate in one year.

Use the census data for Exercises 9–11.

Consumption of Oranges (pounds)	
Sample A	Sample B
12	16
20	8
9	14
4	12
10	11
11	10
10	9
15	18
4	20
10	18

9. Find the mean for each sample.

   Sample A _____ = _____

   Sample B _____ = _____

10. The researcher chose one of the samples by phoning 10 randomly chosen Americans. Which sample do you think was selected this way? Explain.

    _____

    _____

11. The researcher chose one of the samples by choosing 10 customers as they left a health-food store. Which sample do you think was selected this way? Explain.

    _____

    _____

12. According to the census, the average American drinks 27.6 gallons of bottled water per year. How do you think the average number of gallons of bottled water marathon runners drink would compare to the census data? Why?

    _____

    _____

Investigate: Take a Survey

Essential Question How can you design and take a survey?

Investigate

Materials ▪ compass, protractor, straightedge

How many pets does a "typical" student at your school have? Take a survey, and then use what you have learned about collecting and analyzing data to draw conclusions.

A. Explain how you can choose a sample of students at your school that is representative of the entire population.

_____

_____

B. Survey a sample of at least 20 students. Record each student's response on a separate recording sheet.

C. Organize the data in the frequency table.

Pet Survey	
Number of Pets	**Frequency**
0	
1	
2	
3	
4 or more	

Draw Conclusions . . . .

1. **H.O.T.** Find the mean, median, and mode of your data. Which of these best describes the data set? Why?

_____

_____

2. **Explain** what types of graphs are appropriate for displaying the data.

_____

_____

Make Connections ....

You can make graphs to display the data from your survey.

A. In the space below, make one type of graph to display your data.

B. In the space below, make a different type of graph to display your data.

> **Math Talk** Explain how you decide on the right type of graph to display data.

1. **Compare** your graphs by describing what each graph is good for.

   _____

   _____

2. Based on your survey results and your graphs, how many pets does a typical student at your school have? Explain.

   _____

   _____

Name _____

Share and Show

Use the table for 1–4.

1. Ben and Tonya survey a random sample of 20 students at their school. They ask each student how many pets he or she has. The table shows the data they collect. Find the mean, median, and mode of the data.

Number of Pets				
0	0	1	0	0
1	0	1	1	1
16	0	0	22	1
0	1	0	1	0

_____

2. Describe how the mean, median, and mode for Ben and Tonya's data compare to the mean, median, and mode for your data.

_____

_____

3. In the space below, make two different graphs to display Ben and Tonya's data.

4. **Write Math** ▶ Compare the graphs for Ben and Tonya's data to the graphs you made for your data.

_____

_____

_____

Math Talk Explain what wold happen to the mean if 16 and 22 were not include in the data set.

Problem Solving  REAL WORLD

Lee and Taylor want to find out how many hours per week a typical student at their school spends online. They survey 20 students in the school's computer lab. The table shows their data. Use the data to solve 5–9.

5. **Explain** why the sample might be biased.

   _____

   _____

   _____

Hours Spent Online Each Week				
18	24	8	10	11
12	14	24	35	31
28	4	22	6	22
18	17	4	30	22

6. Find the mean, median, and mode of the data.

   _____

7. 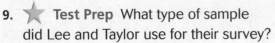 **H.O.T.** How do you think the mean for the entire school might compare to the mean for the sample? Why?

   _____

   _____

   _____

   _____

8. **H.O.T.** **Sense or Nonsense?** Lee and Taylor made graphs for the data as shown. Which graph makes sense? Which graph is nonsense? Explain.

   _____

   _____

   _____

Lee's Graph

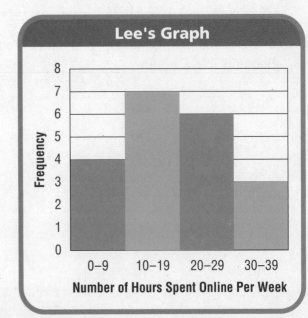

Taylor's Graph

9. ⭐ **Test Prep** What type of sample did Lee and Taylor use for their survey?

   Ⓐ Convenience sampling

   Ⓑ Random sampling

   Ⓒ Systematic sampling

   Ⓓ Unbiased sampling

FOR MORE PRACTICE:
Standards Practice Book, pp. P139–P140

Name _____

 Chapter 7 Review/Test

▶ **Vocabulary**

Choose the best term from the box.

Vocabulary
convenience sample
histogram
random sample

1. A bar graph that shows the frequency of data in intervals is

   called a _____. (p. 270)

2. A _____ is made up of subjects that
   are nearby or easy to access. (p. 277)

▶ **Concepts and Skills**

3. The stem-and-leaf plot shows the times, in minutes,
   it took students to complete a science test. What is the
   median of the data? (pp. 269–272)

   Median = _____

Stem	Leaves
1	5 8 8 9
2	2 2 4 4 4 5 6 8
3	0 0 2 2 4 7 7
4	1 5 5

1|5 = 15

4. The table shows the time, in minutes, that it took
   25 students to complete a 3-mile hike. Make a
   histogram for the data. (pp. 269–272)

Time to Complete Hike (min)				
50	74	55	64	65
90	45	68	60	48
65	90	55	47	94
62	69	60	94	62
65	62	72	69	48

GO Online
Assessment Options
Chapter Test

5. The prices for a 3-pound bag of apples at 5 different grocery stores are $2.99, $1.99, $3.99, $2.50, and $3.25. What is the median price? (pp. 259–262)

(A) $2.99

(C) $3.25

(B) $3.00

(D) $3.99

6. A survey asked what kind of community middle school students would most like to live in. The circle graph shows the results. If 50 people were surveyed, how many said "City"? (pp. 255–258)

(A) 8

(C) 15

(B) 13

(D) 30

7. Robyn collects data on the populations of St. Louis and Kansas City in 1970, 1980, 1990, 2000, and 2010. Which type of graph is best for displaying the data? (pp. 273–276)

(A) circle graph

(B) stem-and-leaf plot

(C) histogram

(D) double line graph

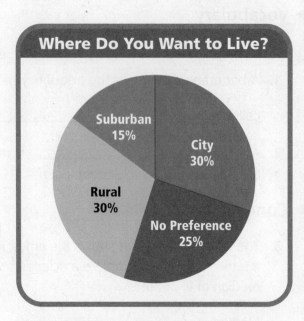

Where Do You Want to Live?

Suburban 15%

City 30%

Rural 30%

No Preference 25%

8. Which flavor of frozen yogurt had the greatest increase in sales from Saturday to Sunday? (pp. 251–254)

(A) cherry

(C) chocolate

(B) vanilla

(D) peach

9. Luis surveys 10 students about the number of hours they spend doing homework on a typical day. The table shows his data. Which is a true statement about his survey results? (pp. 281–284)

Frozen Yogurt Sales

Saturday / Sunday

Number Sold / Flavor: Chocolate, Vanilla, Cherry, Peach

Number of Hours Spent Doing Homework				
1	2	1	2	2
2	1	3	4	3

(A) The mode and the mean are equal.

(B) The mean is greater than the mode.

(C) The median is greater than the mean.

(D) The range is 4.

10. Lorena wants to survey the residents of an apartment building to find out if they think new elevators are needed. She surveys the first 15 people she sees in the lobby of the building. Which sampling method does she use? (pp. 277–280)

(A) convenience sampling

(B) random sampling

(C) systematic sampling

(D) unbiased sampling

11. The frequency table shows the number of frozen yogurts sold during one summer afternoon. What percent of the yogurts were chocolate flavored? (pp. 263–266)

(A) 10%   (C) 32%

(B) 28%   (D) 40%

Sales of Frozen Yogurt	
Flavor	Frequency
Vanilla	7
Chocolate	10
Twist	8

12. Sasha surveys students from her homeroom about the number of siblings each student has. The results are 1, 0, 2, 2, 3, 0, 1, 1, 4, and 5. What is the mode(s) of the data? (pp. 259–262)

(A) 1.5   (C) 1

(B) 0 and 2   (D) 1 and 2

13. Students in Ms. Chu's class rode a roller coaster called the Viper during a class trip to an amusement park. The line plot shows the number of minutes each student waited in line for the ride. What is the range of the data? (pp. 263–266)

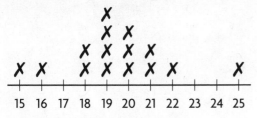

Number of Minutes

(A) 10 min   (C) 19 min

(B) 15 min   (D) 25 min

14. Which of the following sets of data is best displayed in a circle graph? (pp. 273–276)

(A) the weight of 25 quartz crystals

(B) Jake's bowling score in 7 games he played last week

(C) the percent of apple, peach, and cherry fruit chews in a case

(D) Marissa's height, in inches, on January 1 of each year

15. Althea wants to survey 25 students at her school about their favorite types of music. Which sampling method should she use so that her results are likely to be representative of the population? (pp. 277–280)

_____

16. In the 2008 Presidential election, Barack Obama got 53% of the popular vote, John McCain got 46%, and Ralph Nader got 0.6%. If you presented this data in a circle graph, what would be the measure of the central angle for McCain's sector? (pp. 255–258)

_____

▶ **Performance Task**

17. The table gives the number of frozen yogurts sold each day at a cafeteria.

Number of Frozen Yogurts Sold Each Day				
20	24	13	34	39
38	10	38	13	25
21	35	20	27	42
45	16	38	18	25

Ⓐ Make a stem-and-leaf plot of the data.

Ⓑ Make a histogram of the data. Use the intervals 10–19, 20–29, etc.

Ⓒ Sasha says that the mode of a set of data is always in the range represented by the highest bar in a histogram of the data. Use your answers from parts a and b to explain Sasha's error.

_____

_____

Probability

Show What You Know

Check your understanding of important skills.

Name _____

▶ **More Likely, Less Likely, Equally Likely**

1. A bag contains 3 red marbles, 6 yellow marbles, and 1 green marble. You reach into the bag and pull out a marble without looking. Are you more likely to pull a yellow marble or a green marble out of the bag? _____

▶ **Equivalent Fractions** Write an equivalent fraction.

2. $\frac{3}{8}$ _____

3. $\frac{2}{5}$ _____

4. $\frac{10}{12}$ _____

5. $\frac{6}{9}$ _____

▶ **Fractions, Decimals, and Percents** Write each fraction as a decimal and a percent.

6. $\frac{7}{10}$ _____ ; _____

7. $\frac{4}{5}$ _____ ; _____

8. $\frac{5}{8}$ _____ ; _____

9. $\frac{7}{100}$ _____ ; _____

MATH DETECTIVE

WITH

CARMEN SANDIEGO™

Sasha and Jay are playing a game with a number cube. Sasha gets a point each time a 1 or 2 is rolled, and Jay gets a point each time an odd number is rolled. Sasha says the game is unfair because Jay is more likely to win. Is she correct? Be a math detective and compare the chances of Sasha getting a point and Jay getting a point.

Vocabulary Builder

▶ **Visualize It** ●

Sort the review words into the chart.

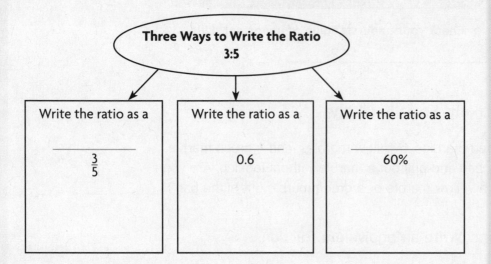

Review Words

decimal

fraction

integer

percent

Preview Words

complement

experiment

experimental
　probability

outcome

sample space

theoretical
　probability

▶ **Understand Vocabulary** ●

Complete the sentences using the preview words.

1. An activity that involves chance, like flipping a coin, is called a(n)

   _____.

2. A possible result of an experiment is a(n)

   _____.

3. The _____ of an experiment is a list of all
   possible outcomes.

4. You can calculate the _____ of an event
   by finding the ratio of the number of favorable outcomes to the
   number of all outcomes in the sample space.

5. All of the ways an event can not happen are called the

   _____ of an event.

GO
Online ● eStudent Edition ● Multimedia eGlossary

Experimental Probability

Essential Question How can you calculate the experimental probability of an event?

An **experiment** is an activity involving chance where the restuls are observed or measured, such as spinning a spinner. A possible result of an experiment is an **outcome**. The **sample space** of an experiment is the set of all possible outcomes.

An **event** is a set of outcomes. The **probability** of an event measures the likelihood that the event will occur. Probabilities range from 0 (the event is impossible) to 1 (the event is certain).

The **experimental probability** of an event is the ratio of the number of times the event occurs to the total number of trials of the experiment.

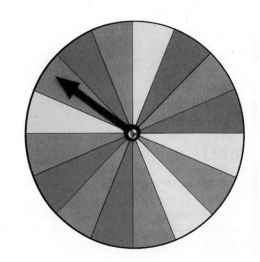

Experimental Probability

$$P(\text{event}) = \frac{\text{number of times that the event occurs}}{\text{total number of trials}}$$

impossible   unlikely   likely   certain

0, or 0% $\frac{1}{2}$, 0.5, or 50%   1, or 100%

🔑 UNLOCK the Problem REAL WORLD

A spinner has 16 sections that are either red, orange, yellow, or green. Cara spins the pointer 20 times and records her results in the table. Write each probability as a fraction, decimal, and percent. What color is the most likely result of a spin?

● Underline the sentence that tells you what you are trying to find.

Color	Red	Orange	Yellow	Green
Frequency	2	11	4	3

🔑 **Write each probability as a fraction, decimal, and percent.**

$P(\text{red}) = \frac{2}{20} = \frac{1}{10}$ or 0.1 or 10%

$P(\text{orange}) = \frac{11}{20}$ or _____ or _____

$P(\text{yellow}) = \frac{\boxed{}}{20} = \frac{1}{\boxed{}}$ or _____ or _____

$P(\text{green}) = \frac{\boxed{}}{\boxed{}}$ or _____ or _____

So, _____ is the most likely result of a spin because this color has the greatest experimental probability.

Math Talk Explain how you compared the experimental probabilities.

🔑 Example

Amirah and Scott each roll a number cube at the same time, and then they record the sum. The table shows their results.

Sum	2	3	4	5	6	7	8	9	10	11	12
Frequency	1	3	3	7	7	8	6	7	5	1	2

Find the experimental probability and write it as a percent.

Ⓐ The sum is 5.

STEP 1

Find the total number of trials.

Add the frequencies.

$1 + 3 + 3 + 7 + 7 + 8 + 6 + 7 + 5 + 1 + 2 =$ _____

STEP 2

Find the experimental probability.

The experimental probability is the ratio of the number of times the event occurs to the total number of trials. Write the fraction as a percent.

$P(\text{sum is 5}) = \dfrac{\quad}{\quad} =$ _____

So, the experimental probability that the sum is 5 is _____.

Ⓑ The sum is 8 or 9.

> **Math Talk** Explain why you add the frequencies for 8 and 9.

STEP 1

Find the total number of times the event occurs.

Add the frequencies for a sum of 8 and a sum of 9.

_____ + _____ = _____

STEP 2

Find the experimental probability.

The experimental probability is the ratio of the number of times the event occurs to the total number of trials. Write the fraction as a percent.

$P(\text{sum is 8 or 9}) = \dfrac{\quad}{\quad} =$ _____

So, the experimental probability that the sum is 8 or 9 is _____.

- **Explain** how you could find the experimental probability that the sum is less than 6.

_____

_____

Name _____

Share and Show

Dylan randomly selects a marble from a bag and replaces it. He repeats this and records his results in the table. Use the table to find the experimental probability. Write the probability as a fraction, decimal, and percent.

Color	Red	Blue	Green
Frequency	12	20	8

1. *P*(red)

$= \dfrac{}{40} = \dfrac{}{}$

$= = $ _____

2. *P*(blue)

_____

3. *P*(green)

_____

A bag contains cards with the letters M, A, T, and H. Jill randomly chooses and replaces a card several times. Use the results in the table to find the experimental probability. Write the probability as a percent.

Letter	M	A	T	H
Frequency	2	6	8	4

4. *P*(M or H)

5. *P*(consonant)

Math Talk Describe a situation for which the experimental probability of an event is 0.

_____ | _____

On Your Own

A spinner has sections labeled A, B, C, D, E, and F. Alberto spins the pointer and records the results in the table. Use the table for 6–7.

Letter	Frequency
A	12
B	6
C	15
D	9
E	15
F	3

6. What is the experimental probability of spinning a D? _____

7. H.O.T. (Write Math) ► Alberto and Susanna play a game with the spinner. When the spinner lands on A or C, Alberto wins a point. When the spinner lands on E or F, Susanna wins a point. Who do you think will win more points? Why?

_____

_____

_____

Genetics

Genetics is the study of heredity in living organisms. The "father of genetics" is Gregor Mendel (1822–1884). Mendel performed experiments with thousands of pea plants to learn how traits, such as color and shape, are passed from one generation to the next.

A scientist crosses hundreds of pairs of pink snapdragons. She records the color of the resulting offspring in the table. About how many times more likely are pink snapdragons than red or white?

Estimate the experimental probability of each color.

The total number of trials of the experiment is $98 + 105 + 199 = 402$.

Round the total number of trials to _____.

Red   Round the number of red snapdragons to 100.

$$P(\text{red}) \approx \frac{100}{400} = \frac{1}{4} \text{ or } 0.25 \text{ or } 25\%$$

White $P(\text{white}) \approx \underline{\hspace{1cm}} = \underline{\hspace{1cm}}$ or _____ or _____

Pink $P(\text{pink}) \approx \underline{\hspace{1cm}} = \underline{\hspace{1cm}}$ or _____ or _____

So, _____ snapdragons appear to be twice as likely as _____ or

_____ snapdragons.

Snapdragon Experiment	
Color	**Frequency**
Red	98
White	105
Pink	199

A scientist crosses pairs of pea plants that have yellow seeds. He records the color of the seeds of the resulting offspring. The table shows the data. Use the table for 9–10.

9. Estimate the experimental probabilities of yellow seeds and green seeds.

_____

_____

10. About how many times more likely are yellow seeds than green seeds? Explain.

_____

_____

Pea Plant Experiment	
Seed Color	**Frequency**
Yellow	75
Green	26

294

FOR MORE PRACTICE:
Standards Practice Book, pp. P145–P146

Name _____

Theoretical Probability

Essential Question How can you calculate the theoretical probability of an event?

CONNECT You have seen that finding an experimental probability requires that you do multiple trials of an experiment. How can you find the probability of an event without doing an experiment?

🔑 UNLOCK the Problem REAL WORLD

Raul and Candace roll a number cube 120 times and keep track of the results. The table shows their results.

Number	1	2	3	4	5	6
Frequency	20	18	21	20	21	20

- How will you find the experimental probabilities?
  _____

🔑 **Calculate the experimental probabilities for each outcome. Write the probability as a fraction.**

Remember that $P(\text{event}) = \dfrac{\text{number of times the event occurs}}{\text{total number of trials}}$.

$P(1) = \dfrac{20}{120} = \dfrac{1}{6}$

$P(2) = \dfrac{18}{120} = \dfrac{\square}{20}$

$P(3) = \dfrac{\square}{120} = \dfrac{\square}{\square}$

$P(4) = \dfrac{\square}{120} = \dfrac{\square}{\square}$

$P(5) = \dfrac{\square}{\square} = \dfrac{\square}{\square}$

$P(6) = \dfrac{\square}{\square} = \dfrac{\square}{\square}$

So, _____ of the experimental probabilities are equal to _____.
The other experimental probabilities are close to this value.

- When you roll a number cube, how many possible outcomes are there? **Explain** how this is related to the experimental probabilities you found.

  _____

  _____

  _____

  _____

The **theoretical probability** of an event is the ratio of the number of ways the event can occur to the total number of equally likely outcomes.

> **Theoretical Probability**
>
> $$P(\text{event}) = \frac{\text{number of ways the event can occur}}{\text{total number of equally likely outcomes}}$$

🔑 Example 1

All of the sections in the spinner at right are equal in size. Terrell spins the pointer. Find the probability and write it as a fraction, decimal, and percent.

A $P(4)$

$$P(4) = \frac{\text{number of ways 4 can occur}}{\text{total number of equally likely outcomes}}$$

There is only _____ way to land on a 4.

$$= \underline{}, \text{ or } \underline{\hspace{3cm}} \text{ or } \underline{\hspace{3cm}} \%$$

There are _____ equally likely outcomes.

B $P(\text{odd})$

$$P(\text{odd}) = \frac{\text{number of ways an odd number can occur}}{\text{total number of equally likely outcomes}}$$

There are _____ odd numbers on the spinner.

$$= \underline{} = \underline{}, \text{ or } \underline{\hspace{3cm}} \text{ or } \underline{} \%$$

There are _____ equally likely outcomes.

The **complement of an event** is all the ways the event can NOT occur. The sum of the probabilities of complementary events is 1. That is, $P(A) + P(\text{not } A) = 1$. So, $P(\text{not } A) = 1 - P(A)$.

🔑 Example 2

For the spinner in Example 1, find the probability that the pointer does not land on 4.

> **Math Idea**
>
> The complement of an event A is usually written not A or $\sim A$.

$P(\text{not } 4) = 1 - P(4)$ Use the complement of landing on 4.

$= 1 - \underline{}$ Substitute $P(4)$.

$= \underline{}$ Subtract.

So, the probability that the pointer does not land on 4 is _____.

> **Math Talk** Describe another way you could calculate $P(\text{not } 4)$.

Name _____

Share and Show

Kate has a set of **10 cards, numbered 1 through 10**. She chooses a card at random. Find the probability and write it as a fraction, decimal, and percent.

1. $P(7) = \dfrac{\text{number of ways a 7 can occur}}{\text{total number of equally likely outcomes}} = \dfrac{}{10}$

_____

2. $P(2 \text{ or } 3)$

✓ 3. $P(\text{greater than 4})$

4. $P(\text{less than 3})$

✓ 5. $P(\text{not } 5)$

6. $P(\text{not odd})$

> **Math Talk** Explain how to find the probability of the complement of an event.

On Your Own

Jason chooses a marble at random from the bag. Find the probability and write it as a fraction.

7. $P(\text{green})$

8. $P(\text{blue})$

9. $P(\text{green or yellow})$

10. $P(\text{not red})$

11. **What's the Error?** A student is asked to find the probability of rolling a 2 on a number cube. He writes $P(2) = \frac{2}{6} = \frac{1}{3}$. Explain the student's error and give the correct probability.

_____

_____

UNLOCK the Problem REAL WORLD

12. Midori and Paul are playing a carnival game. Each player chooses a plastic coin from a bin without looking and replaces it before the next player takes their turn. The coins are shown at right. If Midori draws a red coin that has an even number on it, she wins a prize. If Paul draws a blue coin that has an odd number, he wins a prize. Is this game fair? In other words, are both players equally likely to win? Explain your reasoning.

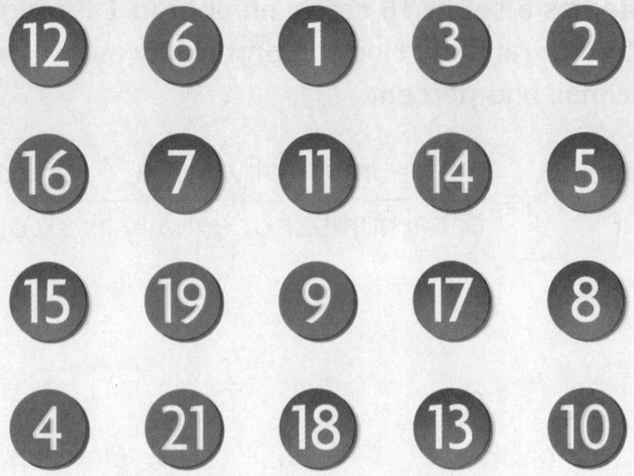

12
6
1
3
2
16
7
11
14
5
15
19
9
17
8
4
21
18
13
10

a. What does the problem ask you to determine?

b. What do you need to calculate to find the answer?

c. Show the steps you used to do the calculations you described in **b**.

d. Write your final answer and explanation.

Use the above table for 13–14.

13. **Test Prep** What is the probability that Midori draws a red coin that has 15 on it?

Ⓐ 0
Ⓑ $\frac{1}{20}$
Ⓒ $\frac{3}{10}$
Ⓓ $\frac{7}{10}$

14. **Test Prep** What is the probability that Paul draws a blue coin that has a multiple of 5 on it?

Ⓐ 0
Ⓑ $\frac{1}{20}$
Ⓒ $\frac{1}{10}$
Ⓓ $\frac{1}{2}$

FOR MORE PRACTICE:
Standards Practice Book, pp. P147–P148

Name _____

✓ Mid-Chapter Checkpoint

► Vocabulary

Choose the best term from the box.

1. All of the possible outcomes for an experiment is called the

   _____ of the experiment. (p. 291)

2. An _____ is a possible result of an experiment.
   (p. 291)

3. The ratio of the number of times an event occurs to the total

   number of trials in an experiment is the _____
   of the event. (p. 291)

► Concepts and Skills

Henry picks a marble from a bag without looking and replaces it. He gets the results shown in the table. Find the experimental probability of the event. Write the probability as a fraction, decimal, and percent. (pp. 291–294)

Color	Frequency
Yellow	3
Black	6
Orange	9
Red	12

4. *P*(red) _____

5. *P*(orange) _____

6. *P*(yellow or black) _____

Shelia spins the pointer for the spinner shown. All of the sections are equal in size. Write the probability for the event as a fraction, decimal, and percent. (pp. 295–298)

7. *P*(2) _____

8. *P*(1) _____

9. *P*(even number) _____

10. A bag contains 4 black marbles, 5 gray marbles, and 16 white marbles. Kimiko chooses a marble without looking. What is the probability that she chooses a marble that is NOT gray? Write the answer as a decimal. (pp. 295–298)

    _____

Fill in the bubble for the correct answer choice.

11. A bag contains 3 white tiles, 8 black tiles, and 9 gray tiles. Eddie chooses a tile from the bag without looking. What is the probability that he chooses a black tile? (pp. 295–298)

(A) $\frac{1}{8}$ (C) $\frac{3}{4}$

(B) $\frac{2}{5}$ (D) $\frac{4}{5}$

12. Vanessa picks a marble from a bag without looking and replaces it. In 60 picks, she gets 15 red marbles, 12 yellow marbles, and 33 orange marbles. What is the experimental probability of picking an orange marble? (pp. 291–294)

(A) 0.18   (C) 0.33

(B) 0.25   (D) 0.55

13. Kurt rolls a number cube many times. His results are shown in the table. What is the experimental probability of rolling a 2 or 3? (pp. 291–294)

Number	1	2	3	4	5	6
Frequency	7	8	10	8	9	8

(A) 9%   (C) 36%

(B) 16%   (D) 68%

14. Kai reaches into a case of fruit chews and picks one at random. He notes the flavor and replaces it in the case. After 40 picks, he finds that he has chosen 12 apricot chews, 16 cherry chews, and 12 peach chews. What is the experimental probability that a fruit chew is a peach chew? (pp. 291–294)

(A) 30%   (C) 0.4

(B) $\frac{3}{7}$ (D) 50%

15. Paula rolls a number cube. Which of the following probabilities is greatest? (pp. 295–298)

(A) P(not 6)   (C) P(less than 5)

(B) P(6)   (D) P(odd)

16. Terry rolls a number cube. Which of the following is equal to $\frac{1}{3}$? (pp. 295–298)

(A) P(even)   (C) $1 - P$(less than 3)

(B) P(less than 3)   (D) $1 - P$(odd)

Name _____

Compare Experimental and Theoretical Probability

Essential Question How can you use an experiment to compare experimental and theoretical probability?

Investigate

Materials ■ standard deck of 52 cards

You can use a deck of cards to compare experimental and theoretical probability.

A. One student in the group should shuffle the deck. Then the student should choose one card from the deck. Put a tally mark in the table below to record the suit of the card (club, heart, spade, or diamond). Replace the card in the deck.

Suit	Club	Heart	Spade	Diamond
Frequency				

B. Pass the deck to the next student. Repeat the process of choosing a card, recording its suit in the table, and replacing the card.

C. Continue until 5 cards have been chosen.

D. Based on your table, what is the experimental probability of choosing a club? Write the answer as a decimal.

_____

E. Now find the theoretical probability of choosing a club.

$$P(\text{club}) = \frac{\text{number of ways a club can occur}}{\text{total number of equally likely outcomes}}$$

The deck contains _____ clubs.

$P(\text{club}) = \dfrac{}{}$

There are _____ cards in the deck.

Simplify the fraction. $= \dfrac{}{}$

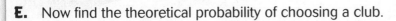

Write the fraction as a decimal. $= $ _____

So, the theoretical probability of choosing a club is _____.

Draw Conclusions

1. **Compare** the experimental probability of choosing a club to the theoretical probability of choosing a club.

_____

_____

2. **H.O.T.** **Make a Conjecture** How do you think the experimental and theoretical probabilities will compare if you did more trials?

_____

_____

Make Connections

You can do more trials of the experiment with a deck of cards to see how the experimental probability changes.

STEP 1

Do 35 more trials of the experiment from the previous page. Record the suit of each card in the table below.

Suit	Club	Heart	Spade	Diamond
Frequency				

STEP 2

Recalculate the experimental probability of choosing a club. Use the data from all 40 of your trials (that is, combine the data from the table on the previous page with the data from the table on this page). Write the answer as a decimal.

_____

_____

STEP 3

Analyze your results. Explain how the experimental probability of choosing a club changes as you add more trials to the experiment.

_____

_____

_____

_____

Math Talk Explain what you think would happen to the experimental probability if you did 1,000 trials.

302

Name _____

Share and Show

•••

1. Conduct an experiment with a number cube. Roll the cube 10 times.
   Use the table to record the results of these rolls.

Number	1	2	3	4	5	6
Frequency						

Based on your results, find the experimental probability of rolling a 4.
Explain how the experimental probability compares to the theoretical
probability.

_____

_____

Do 50 more trials of the experiment. Record the results below.

Number	1	2	3	4	5	6
Frequency						

Recalculate the experimental probability of rolling a 4 using all 60 of
your trials. Explain how the experimental probability compares to the
theoretical probability now.

_____

_____

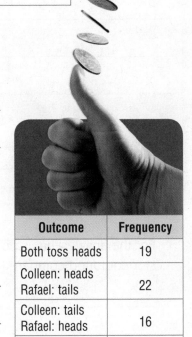

2. Colleen and Rafael each flip a coin at the same time and record their
   results in the table. Find the experimental probability that Colleen's
   coin comes up tails and Rafael's coin comes up heads. Compare this
   with the theoretical probability, which is 25%.

Outcome	Frequency
Both toss heads	19
Colleen: heads Rafael: tails	22
Colleen: tails Rafael: heads	16
Both toss tails	23

_____

_____

3. **Write Math** ▶ Describe what happens to the experimental
   probability of an event as you do more and more trials of the
   experiment.

_____

_____

Problem Solving...

H.O.T. Sense or Nonsense?

4. Deronda and Adam were asked to find the theoretical probability of choosing a red marble from the bag at right. The two papers show their answers. Whose answer makes sense? Whose answer is nonsense? **Explain** your reasoning.

Deronda's Answer

I looked in the bag and counted the marbles.

There are 10 marbles altogether and 4 of the marbles are red.

The theoretical probability of choosing a red marble is:

$P(\text{red}) = \dfrac{\text{number of ways to choose red}}{\text{total number of equally likely outcomes}}$
$= \dfrac{4}{10}$ or $\dfrac{2}{5}$.

Adam's Answer

I did 80 trials of an experiment in which I chose a marble at random, recorded the color, and replaced the marble.

In these trials, I chose a red marble 30 times.

Because I did so many trials, the experimental probability will be equal to the theoretical probability.

So, $P(\text{red}) = \dfrac{30}{80}$ or $\dfrac{3}{8}$.

• For the answer that is nonsense, how does the probability that the student found compare to the correct theoretical probability?

_____

_____

• Is it ever possible for the experimental probability of an event to equal the theoretical probability? Explain.

_____

_____

Name _____

Make Predictions

Essential Question How can you use probability to make predictions?

🔑 UNLOCK the Problem · REAL WORLD

A company manufactures mp3 players. In a random sample of 20 mp3 players, 3 are found to be defective. Predict the number of defective mp3 players in a shipment of 800 mp3 players.

- Underline the sentence that tells you what you need to do to solve the problem.
- Circle the numbers you need to use to solve the problem.

🔑 **Set up a proportion that uses the theoretical probability.**

STEP 1

Find the probability that an mp3 player is defective.

$$P(\text{defective}) = \dfrac{}{}$$

In the random sample, there are _____ ways to choose a defective mp3 player.

There are _____ mp3 players in the sample.

STEP 2

Set up and solve a proportion.

$$\dfrac{\text{defective}}{\text{total}} \rightarrow \dfrac{3}{20} = \dfrac{x}{800} \leftarrow \dfrac{\text{defective}}{\text{total}}$$

Write a proportion. Let x be the number of defective mp3 players in the shipment.

$$\dfrac{3 \times }{20 \times } = \dfrac{x}{800}$$

Multiply the _____ and

denominator by _____ to write the ratios with a common denominator.

$$\dfrac{}{800} = \dfrac{x}{800}$$

The _____ are the same,

so the _____ are equal to each other.

$x = $ _____

So, you can predict that there are _____ defective mp3 players in the shipment.

🔑 Example

The graph shows the number of siblings of 300 randomly selected students from Woodruff Elementary School. There are 1,800 total students at the school.

Predict the number of students at the school who have no siblings.

STEP 1

Find the probability that a student has no siblings.

Number of Siblings

2 siblings 75 · No siblings 45 · 3 or more siblings 75 · 1 sibling 105

$P(\text{no siblings}) = \frac{45}{300}$

$$\frac{45}{300} = \frac{\boxed{}}{100} = \underline{\hspace{1cm}}\%$$

In the random sample, there are _____ students who have no siblings.

There are _____ students in the sample.

Write the probability as a percent.

STEP 2

Find the number of students at the school who have no siblings.

_____% = _____

_____ × 1,800 = _____

Write the percent as a _____.

Multiply.

So, you can predict that about _____ students at the school have no siblings.

Try This! Use a different method.

Show how to solve the above problem by setting up and solving a proportion, as on page 305.

Math Talk Describe two methods of using probabilities to make predictions.

Name _____

Share and Show

1. The manager of a grocery store inspects a shipment of eggs. She checks a random sample of 50 eggs and finds that 3 are cracked. Predict the number of eggs that are cracked in the shipment of 5,000 eggs.

   $P(\text{cracked}) = \dfrac{3}{50}$

   $$\dfrac{3}{50} = \dfrac{x}{\boxed{}}$$

   $$\dfrac{3 \times \boxed{}}{50 \times \boxed{}} = \dfrac{x}{\boxed{}}$$

   $x =$ _____

   So, you can predict there are _____ cracked eggs in the shipment.

2. A library has 750 DVDs in its collection. Sandra looks through a sample of 25 DVDs and finds that 8 of them are comedies. Predict the number of DVDs in the collection that are comedies.

   _____

3. A cafeteria sells three flavors of yogurt. The probability that a randomly chosen container of yogurt is cherry yogurt is 24%. The cafeteria's dairy case contains 150 containers of yogurt. Predict the number of containers of cherry yogurt in the case.

   Math Talk Explain how you decide whether to use a proportion or a percent to solve a prediction problem.

   _____

On Your Own

Trevor surveys 50 randomly chosen students at Sanchez School about their favorite type of book. There are 750 students at the school. Predict the number of students at the school who prefer each type of book.

4. mystery

5. biography

6. science fiction

Book Survey	
Type of Book	Number of Students
Mystery	20
Science fiction	13
History	10
Biography	7

Problem Solving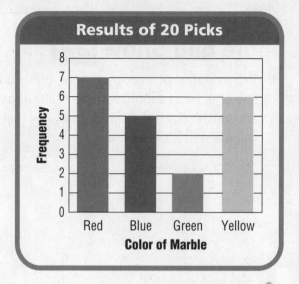

Results of 20 Picks

A jar contains red, blue, green, and yellow marbles. Alma chooses a marble at random, notes the color, and replaces the marble in the jar. She does this 20 times. The bar graph shows her results. Use the graph to solve 7–9.

7. Suppose the jar contains 400 marbles. Predict the number of red marbles in the jar.

   _____

8. Suppose there are 500 marbles in the jar. Predict the number of marbles in the jar that are NOT blue.

   _____

· · · · · · · SHOW YOUR WORK · · · ·

9. **H.O.T.** **What's the Error?** Kade is asked to predict the number of green marbles in the jar if the jar contains a total of 120 marbles. Kade says the probability that a marble is green is 0.2. Since 0.2 × 120 = 24, there are 24 green marbles in the jar. Explain Kade's error and give the correct prediction.

   _____

   _____

10. **Write Math** ▶ Describe how you can use a sample and probability to predict the number of bruised apples in a large crate that contains 1,000 apples.

    _____

    _____

    _____

11. ⭐ **Test Prep** A survey of 25 randomly chosen sixth graders found that 15 of them ordered a hot lunch. Which is the best prediction of the number of students who ordered a hot lunch in the entire sixth grade, given that there are 525 sixth graders?

    Ⓐ 280   Ⓒ 350

    Ⓑ 315   Ⓓ 875

FOR MORE PRACTICE:
Standards Practice Book, pp. P151–P152

Name _____

Draw a Diagram · Counting Methods

Essential Question How can you use tree diagrams to find all possible outcomes of an experiment?

🔑 UNLOCK the Problem REAL WORLD

A board game uses the spinner shown. Brendan spins the pointer two times in a row. How many different outcomes are there for the pair of spins?

Read the Problem

What do I need to find?	**What information do I need to use?**	**How will I use the information?**
The number of different _____ there are when Brendan spins the pointer _____	The spinner has _____ equal sections. The possible outcomes of a single spin are _____	I will use the strategy _____ to show all possible pairs of outcomes.

Solve the Problem

Make a **tree diagram**. A tree diagram is a way of displaying all of the possible outcomes of an experiment.

First write all the possible outcomes of the first spin. Then, draw "branches" to pair each outcome of the first spin with possible outcomes of the second spin. Complete the tree diagram.

| Red | Blue | Yellow | Green |

Red Blue Yellow Green

Count the branches at the bottom of the tree diagram to find the total number of outcomes for the pair of spins.

So, there are _____ different outcomes for the pair of spins.

Try Another Problem

A deli sells pre-made sandwiches. The sandwiches consist of one type of bread, one type of meat, and one type of cheese, as shown at right. Savannah grabs a sandwich at random. What is the probability that she chooses ham and cheddar on wheat?

Sandwich Menu

Breads	White Wheat
Meats	Ham Turkey Chicken
Cheeses	Jack Cheddar

Read the Problem

What do I need to find?	What information do I need to use?	How will I use the information?

Solve the Problem

Counting the branches at the bottom of the tree diagram shows that

there are _____ possible sandwiches. There is _____ way to choose ham and cheddar on wheat.

So, the probability that Savannah chooses ham and cheddar on

wheat is _____.

- **Explain** how you can justify your answer by solving the problem a different way.

_____

_____

Math Talk Describe a different sandwich that has the same probability as ham and cheddar on wheat.

Name _____

Share and Show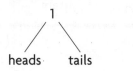

 UNLOCK the Problem *Tips*

✓ Underline important facts.
✓ Choose a strategy.
✓ Be sure to include all the possibilities in a tree diagram.

1. Jamir rolls a number cube and then flips a coin. How many different outcomes are there?

   First, draw a tree diagram. Complete the tree diagram below.

   1   2   3   4   5   6

   heads   tails

   Next, count the number of branches at the bottom of the tree diagram. This gives the total number of outcomes.

   So, there are _____ different outcomes.

2. **H.O.T.** **What if** Jamir rolls a number cube, but then spins the pointer on a spinner with 3 equal sections labeled A, B, and C? Are there more or fewer outcomes in this case? Explain.

   _____

   _____

3. Warren is buying a t-shirt. The shirts are available in red, blue, or black. Each shirt is available in small, medium, or large. Each shirt can have long sleeves or short sleeves. How many choices does Warren have?

   _____

4. Luisa has a spinner with 3 equal sections that are red, orange, and purple. She spins the pointer twice. What is the probability that the pointer lands on red both times?

   _____

5. At Alyssa's school, music practice rooms are labeled with a number from 1 to 4 followed by a letter from A to D. Alyssa is assigned a room randomly. What is the probability that Alyssa's room is labeled 1A?

   _____

On Your Own . . . .

6. A store has four managers. They take turns going out for a 45-minute lunch break. Susan goes first, followed by Arturo, then Mari, and then Jeff. Jeff plans to finish his lunch break at 2:00 PM. At what time should Susan leave for her lunch break?

_____

7. **H.O.T.** **Pose a Problem** A board game includes a spinner with 5 equal sections that are labeled 1 through 5. Write a problem based on the spinner that can be solved using a tree diagram. Then solve the problem.

_____

_____

_____

8. A restaurant seats large groups of diners by placing tables together in a row. One table can seat 4 diners, 2 tables can seat 6 diners, 3 tables can seat 8 diners, and 4 tables can seat 10 diners. How many diners can be seated when 9 of the tables are placed together?

_____

9. **Write Math** ▶ As a workout outfit, Chandra can choose a yellow, red, or blue t-shirt and blue or orange shorts. She also has red, gray, and white socks. How many different outfits can Chandra make if she does not want to wear two items that are the same color? Describe the steps you used to solve the problem.

_____

_____

_____

10. ⭐ **Test Prep** Brett flips a coin 3 times. What is the probability that the coin lands heads up all 3 times?

Ⓐ $\frac{1}{8}$ 　　　 Ⓒ $\frac{1}{4}$

Ⓑ $\frac{1}{6}$ 　　　 Ⓓ $\frac{1}{3}$

Choose a STRATEGY

Work Backward
Solve a Simpler Problem
Choose an Operation
Use a Model
Use a Formula
Draw a Diagram

SHOW YOUR WORK

FOR MORE PRACTICE:
Standards Practice Book, pp. P153–P154

Name _____

 Chapter 8 Review/Test

Vocabulary

Choose the best term from the box.

1. Rolling a number cube is an example of an

   _____. (p. 291)

2. A _____ is a way of organizing and
   counting all of the possible outcomes of an experiment. (p. 309)

3. Probability calculated by finding the ratio of the the number of
   ways an event can occur to the total number of possible

   outcomes is called _____. (p. 295)

Concepts and Skills

4. A pizza shop offers a lunch special. Customers can choose a
   thick-crust pizza or a thin-crust pizza. They can also choose
   one of the following pizza toppings: sausage, mushrooms, or
   pepperoni. The special comes with iced tea or apple juice. How
   many different lunch specials are there? Use a tree diagram to
   find the answer. (pp. 309–312)

   Number of specials = _____

5. A bag contains 5 tiles with the letters A, E, I, O, and U on them.
   Max chooses a tile without looking, notes the letter, and replaces
   the tile. He does this 30 times and finds that he chose a tile with
   the letter E on 9 of the picks. What are the experimental and
   theoretical probabilities of drawing an E? Write the answers as
   fractions, decimals, and percents. (pp. 301–304)

   Experimental probability = _____

   Theoretical probability = _____

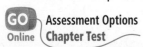

Fill in the bubble for the correct answer choice.

6. A factory produces car batteries. In a random sample of 60 batteries, 4 are found to be defective. The factory produces 1,200 batteries per day. Which is the best prediction of the number of defective batteries in one day's production? (pp. 305–308)

Ⓐ 15   Ⓒ 64

Ⓑ 20   Ⓓ 80

7. DeShawn rolls a number cube multiple times. His results are shown in the table. What is the experimental probability of rolling a 5 or 6? (pp. 291–294)

Number	1	2	3	4	5	6
Frequency	5	3	2	3	3	4

Ⓐ 7%   Ⓒ 35%

Ⓑ 15%   Ⓓ 45%

8. Danielle spins the spinner shown at right. What is the probability that the pointer does NOT land on 2? (pp. 295–298)

Ⓐ $\frac{1}{8}$ Ⓒ $\frac{3}{4}$

Ⓑ $\frac{3}{8}$ Ⓓ $\frac{7}{8}$

9. Benjamin flipped a coin 50 times. The coin landed heads up 20 times and tails up 30 times. Which is a true statement about the experimental probability that the coin lands heads up? (pp. 301–304)

Ⓐ It is less than the theoretical probability.

Ⓑ It is equal to the theoretical probability.

Ⓒ It is less than 20%.

Ⓓ It is greater than 50%.

10. A softball team's jerseys are available in white and gray. The team's pants are available in blue and black. The team's caps are available in red, blue, and black. How many different uniforms can a player make by choosing one jersey, one pair of pants, and one cap? (pp. 309–312)

Ⓐ 7

Ⓑ 8

Ⓒ 12

Ⓓ 32

TEST PREP

11. There are 12 girls and 18 boys in Ms. Ortega's class. She chooses a student at random to serve as class president. What is the probability that she chooses a girl? (pp. 295–298)

(A) 40%   (C) 66%

(B) 60%   (D) 75%

12. A spinner has 5 equal sections that are numbered 1 through 5. The results of 40 spins are shown in the table. For which number is the experimental probability equal to the theoretical probability? (pp. 301–304)

Number	1	2	3	4	5
Frequency	10	8	5	12	5

(A) 1   (C) 3

(B) 2   (D) 4

13. Edward surveyed 40 students at his school about their favorite type of music. Country music was the favorite type of music of 7 of the students. There are 480 students at Edward's school. Which is the best prediction of the number of students at the school who prefer country music? (pp. 305–308)

(A) 12   (C) 84

(B) 47   (D) 280

14. Rosa flips a coin 25 times. The coin lands heads up 12 times and it lands tails up 13 times. What is the experimental probability that the coin lands heads up? (pp. 291–294)

(A) 0.25   (C) 0.5

(B) 0.48   (D) 0.52

15. A cafeteria offers a lunch special in which customers can choose one sandwich, one salad, and one drink, as shown in the table. How many different lunch specials are possible? (pp. 309–312)

(A) 3

(B) 8

(C) 9

(D) 18

Lunch Special	
Sandwiches	Tuna
	Ham
	Veggie
Salads	Caesar
	Green
Drinks	Juice
	Iced Tea
	Milk

16. Blake has a set of 20 cards, numbered 1 through 20. He chooses a card at random. What is the probability that he chooses a card with a prime number? Write the answer as a fraction, decimal, and percent. (pp. 295–298)

_____

17. A doctor finds that 4 of 30 randomly chosen patients take a daily vitamin C supplement. The doctor has 900 patients. Predict the total number of patients that take a daily vitamin C supplement. (pp. 305–308)

_____

▶ Performance Task

18. A booth at a carnival has two spinners. Both spinners have 4 equal sections that are labeled 1, 2, 3, and 4.

Ⓐ Draw a tree diagram to find how many possible outcomes there are for spinning both spinners.

Number of outcomes = _____

Ⓑ For each game, one player spins one pointer, and a second player spins the other. Both players win a prize if the same number comes up on both spinners. What is the probability of both players winning a prize, written as a fraction?

_____

Ⓒ Describe a way to change the rules so that the chance of winning is lower. Tell the probability of winning with your rule.

_____

_____

316

© Houghton Mifflin Harcourt Publishing Company

BIG IDEA 3

Algebra: Expressions, Equations, and Functions

Focal POINT Algebra: Writing, interpreting, and using mathematical expressions and equations

The Columbus Zoo, in Columbus, Ohio, is home to hundreds of different animals, including the Amur tiger.

BIG IDEA Project

This Place is a Zoo!

Planning a zoo is a difficult task. Each animal requires a special environment with different amounts of space and different features.

Project

You will begin to learn about the Big Idea when you work on this project.

You are helping to design a new section of a zoo. The table lists some of the new attractions planned for the zoo. Each attraction includes notes about the type and the amount of space needed for each one.
The zoo owns a rectangle of land that is 100 feet long and 60 feet wide. Find the dimensions of each of the attractions and draw a sketch of the plan for the zoo.

Important Facts

Attraction	Minimum Floor Space (ft²)	Notes
American Alligators	400	rectangular pen with one side at least 24 feet long
Amur Tigers	750	trapezoid-shaped area with one side at least 40 feet long
Howler Monkeys	450	circular cage
Meerkat Village	250	square pen with glass sides
Red Foxes	350	rectangular pen with length twice as long as width
Tropical Aquarium	200	circular aquarium

_____

_____

_____

_____

_____

Completed by _____

Show What You Know

Check your understanding of important skills

Name _____

▶ **Addition Properties** Find the missing number. Tell whether you used the Identity (or Zero) Property, Commutative Property, or Associative Property of Addition.

1. $128 + \underline{\hspace{1cm}} = 128$

_____

2. $(17 + 36) + 14 = 17 + (\underline{\hspace{1cm}} + 14)$

_____

3. $23 + 15 = \underline{\hspace{1cm}} + 23$

_____

4. $9 + (11 + 46) = (9 + \underline{\hspace{1cm}}) + 46$

_____

▶ **Add, Subtract, Multiply, and Divide Whole Numbers** Add, subtract, multiply, or divide.

5.
$$\begin{array}{r} 78 \\ + 47 \\ \hline \end{array}$$

6.
$$\begin{array}{r} 24 \\ \times\ 3 \\ \hline \end{array}$$

7.
$$\begin{array}{r} 315 \\ -\ 69 \\ \hline \end{array}$$

8. $8\overline{)88}$

▶ **Plot Points on a Number Line** Plot and label each point on the number line.

9. A: 4

10. B: 12

11. C: 1

12. D: 7

0 1 2 3 4 5 6 7 8 9 10 11 12

MATH DETECTIVE

WITH

CARMEN SANDIEGO™

This magic square can be filled in with the integers ⁻6, ⁻5, ⁻2, 4, 5, and 8 so that the sum of the integers in each row and each column is 0. Be a Math Detective and fill in the missing numbers by using each of the integers only once.

Vocabulary Builder

▶ **Visualize It** •

Complete the map with review words that are related to the four basic operations. You may use words more than once.

Addition	Subtraction
Multiplication	**Division**

Review Words

addend

Associative Property

Commutative Property

difference

factor

order of operations

product

quotient

sum

Preview Words

absolute value

additive inverse

integers

opposite

▶ **Understand Vocabulary** •

Complete the sentences using the preview words.

1. The _____ are the set of whole numbers and their opposites.

2. The sum of a number and its _____ is zero.

3. The distance of a number from 0 on a number line is the

   number's _____.

Name _____

Understand Integers

Essential Question How do you compare and order integers?

Integers are the set of all whole numbers and their opposites. Two numbers are **opposites** if they are the same distance from 0 on the number line, but on different sides of 0. For example, the integers $^+3$ and $^-3$ are opposites. Zero is its own opposite.

> **Math Idea**
> You do not need to write the + symbol for positive integers, so $^+3$ can also be written as 3.

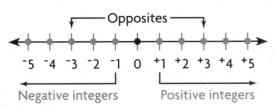

The **absolute value** of a number is its distance from 0 on a number line. The absolute value of $^-3$ is 3. You can write the absolute value of $^-3$ as $|^-3| = 3$.

UNLOCK the Problem — REAL WORLD

The temperature at the start of a 2009 playoff game between the Colorado Rockies and the Philadelphia Phillies was 2°C. During the game, the temperature dropped to $^-4$°C. What are the opposite and absolute value of each temperature?

- **What are you asked to find?**

_____

_____

🔑 **Graph each integer and its opposite on a number line. Then give the absolute value of the integer.**

A 2

The integer 2 is on the _____ side of 0.

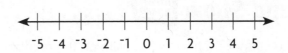

Graph the opposite of 2 at _____.

2 is _____ units from 0 on the number line. So, $|2| =$ _____.

B $^-4$

The integer $^-4$ is on the _____ side of 0.

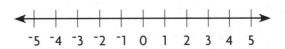

Graph the opposite of $^-4$ at _____.

$^-4$ is _____ units from 0 on the number line. So, $|^-4| =$ _____.

> **Math Talk** Explain how to find all integers with an absolute value of 7.

Comparing and Ordering Integers You can use a number line to help you compare and order integers. On a number line, each number is greater than any number to its left and less than any number to its right.

🔑 Example Compare and order integers.

A Compare the integers ⁻7 and ⁻3. Use <, >, or =.

Graph ⁻7 and ⁻3 on the number line.

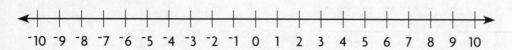

The integer ⁻7 is to the _____ of ⁻3. This means ⁻7 is _____ than ⁻3.

So, ⁻7 ◯ ⁻3.

B Order the integers 4, ⁻5, ⁻8, and 1 from least to greatest.

Graph 4, ⁻5, ⁻8, and 1 on the number line.

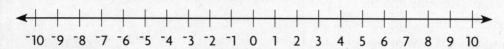

Read the integers you plotted from left (least) to right (greatest).

So, the order from least to greatest is _____.

Math Talk **Explain** whether a positive integer is always greater than a negative integer. **Explain** whether 0 is greater than any negative integer.

Share and Show ·

1. Graph the integer ⁻6 and its opposite on the number line. Then give the absolute value of ⁻6.

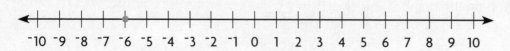

_____

Write the opposite of the integer.

2. ⁻9	3. 4	4. 0	5. ⁻11	6. 34

Name _____

Share and Show

Give the absolute value of the integer.

7. ⁻2 _____ | **8.** 5 _____ | **9.** 0 _____ | **10.** ⁻12 _____ | **11.** 17 _____

Compare. Write <, >, or =.

12. ⁻8 ◯ 5 | **13.** ⁻9 ◯ ⁻2 | **14.** ⁻3 ◯ ⁻5 | **15.** 10 ◯ ⁻13

Order the integers from least to greatest.

16. ⁻9, 2, ⁻4, 1 _____ | **17.** 5, ⁻6, 0, ⁻7 _____ | **18.** 2, ⁻2, 5, ⁻5 _____

Math Talk Explain how to use a number line to order two or more integers.

On Your Own

Compare. Write <, >, or =.

19. ⁻4 ◯ ⁻15 | **20.** 7 ◯ |⁻8| | **21.** |⁻12| ◯ |12| | **22.** |⁻16| ◯ |⁻15|

Order the integers from least to greatest.

23. ⁻7, 0, ⁻9, ⁻10 _____ | **24.** 8, ⁻11, ⁻7, 14 _____ | **25.** 4, ⁻15, 0, ⁻6, 18 _____ | **26.** 4, |5|, |⁻2|, ⁻5 _____

Use the number line to write the letter that represents the integer.

A B C D E F G H I J K L M N O P Q

⁻8   0   8

27. 7 _____ | **28.** ⁻5 _____

29. ⁻2 _____ | **30.** |5| _____

31. ⁻1 _____ | **32.** |⁻1| _____

Write the integer that is 1 more than the given integer.

33. ⁻8 _____ | **34.** 0 _____ | **35.** ⁻1 _____ | **36.** |⁻15| _____

Problem Solving

Use the table for 37–40.

37. Which planet has a greater average surface temperature, Jupiter or Mars? Explain.

_____

38. Neptune, Saturn, and Uranus are the farthest planets from the sun. List these planets in order from the planet with the greatest average surface temperature to the planet with the least average surface temperature.

_____

39. Which planet has an average surface temperature closer to ⁻120°C, Jupiter or Saturn? Explain how you know.

_____

_____

40. **H.O.T. Pose a Problem** Write and solve a new problem that uses the data in the table.

_____

_____

_____

41. **H.O.T.** Write all the integers that have an absolute value less than or equal to 3.

_____

42. **Write Math** ▶ Explain whether ⁻5.2 is an integer.

_____

_____

43. ⭐ **Test Prep** Which set of integers is written in order from least to greatest?

Ⓐ 0, ⁻2, 3, ⁻5   Ⓒ ⁻8, ⁻3, 0, 4

Ⓑ ⁻7, ⁻4, 2, ⁻1   Ⓓ 6, 7, ⁻8, ⁻9

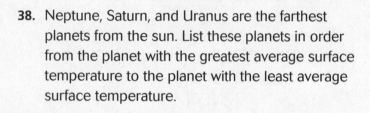

Average Surface Temperature of Planets	
Planet	**Temperature (°C)**
Earth	15
Jupiter	⁻110
Mars	⁻65
Mercury	167
Neptune	⁻200
Saturn	⁻140
Uranus	⁻195
Venus	464

SHOW YOUR WORK

FOR MORE PRACTICE:
Standards Practice Book, pp. P159–P160

Name _____

Integer Addition

Essential Question How can you model addition of integers?

Investigate

Materials ■ two-color counters

During practice, a football team ran pairs of plays. You can add integers to find the overall gain or loss of yards for each pair of plays. Use yellow counters to represent positive numbers and red counters to represent negative numbers.

A. Find the overall gain or loss for a gain of 3 yards and a gain of 4 yards. Use yellow counters to represent 3 and 4.

Combine the counters. The combined counters represent the sum $3 + 4$. Write a number sentence to record the sum.

_____

B. Find the overall gain or loss for a loss of 1 yard and a loss of 5 yards. Use red counters to represent $^-1$ and $^-5$.

Combine the counters. The combined counters represent the sum $^-1 + (^-5)$. Write a number sentence to record the sum.

_____

The **additive inverse** of a number is its opposite. The sum of a number and its additive inverse is 0. When you work with counters, a yellow counter $(^+1)$ and a red counter $(^-1)$ make a *zero pair* that can be removed.

C. Find the overall gain or loss for a loss of 6 yards and a gain of 2 yards. Use red counters to represent $^-6$ and yellow counters to represent 2.

Combine the counters. Remove zero pairs. The remaining counters represent the sum $^-6 + 2$. Write a number sentence to record the sum.

_____

Draw Conclusions

1. Two numbers have the same sign. **Explain** what you know about the sign of the sum of those numbers.

   _____

2. **Tell** whether ‾2 + 3 and 3 + (‾2) have the same sum. Explain.

   _____

3. **Explain** why the sum of a number and its additive inverse is 0.

   _____

   _____

4. **H.O.T.** **Synthesis** If you represent a sum with counters and you have more negative counters than positive counters, will the sum be positive or negative? Why?

   _____

Make Connections

You can also use a number line to model integer addition.

A **Find the sum: 7 + (‾8)**

Draw a number line.

Start at 0. Move 7 units to the _____ to show 7.

From 7, move 8 units to the _____ to add ‾8.

This takes you to the sum, _____.

So, 7 + (‾8) = _____.

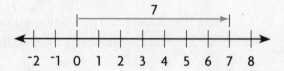

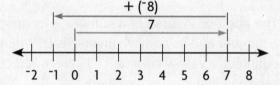

B **Find the sum: ‾4 + 9**

Draw a number line.

Start at 0. Move 4 units to the _____ to show ‾4.

From ‾4, move 9 units to the _____ to add 9.

This takes you to the sum, _____.

So, ‾4 + 9 = _____.

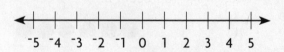

Math Talk Tell when the arrows representing integer addition would both point in the same direction.

326

Name _____

Share and Show

Use the model to find the sum.

☑ **1.** $4 + (^-1)$

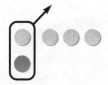

_____

2. $^-5 + 4$

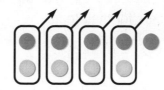

_____

☑ **3.** $^-3 + 5$

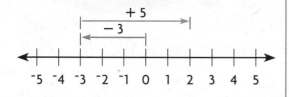

_____

4. $^-2 + (^-5)$

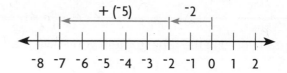

_____

Tell what sum is represented by the model. Then find the sum.

5.

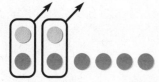

_____

6.

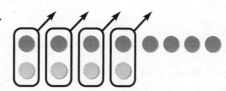

_____

7.

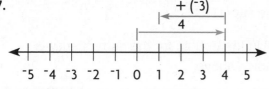

_____

8.

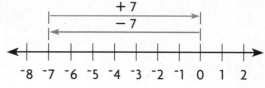

_____

Practice: Copy and Solve Use counters or a number line to find the sum.

9. $^-1 + (^-8)$ | **10.** $8 + 2$ | **11.** $^-6 + 3$ | **12.** $^-5 + 6$

13. **Write Math** ▶ Explain why the sum of 2 and $^-5$ is negative.

_____

_____

UNLOCK the Problem

14. The table shows the scores of four friends in a golf tournament. Keisha and Zack are playing as a team. What is the combined score for their team?

Golf Tournament Scores	
Keisha	$^-5$
Omar	3
Sabrina	$^-4$
Zack	7

   (A) $^-12$ (C) 2

   (B) $^-2$ (D) 12

a. What do you need to find?

   _____

   _____

b. How can you use the table to help you solve the problem?

   _____

   _____

c. What operation can you use to find the combined score for Keisha and Zack?

   _____

d. Draw a model that you can use to help solve the problem.

e. Complete the sentences.

   The combined score for Keisha and Zack

   is the sum of _____ and _____.

   The sum is _____.

f. Fill in the bubble for the correct answer choice above.

Use the table above for 15–16.

15. Omar and Sabrina also play as a team. What is their combined score?

   (A) $^-7$

   (B) $^-1$

   (C) 1

   (D) 7

16. Which of the following pairs of players has the least combined score?

   (A) Keisha and Omar

   (B) Keisha and Sabrina

   (C) Omar and Sabrina

   (D) Omar and Zack

Add Integers

Essential Question How do you add integers?

C̲ONNECT̲ You can use what you learned about adding integers in Lesson 9.2 to develop rules for adding integers.

Adding Integers with the Same Sign

When adding integers with the same sign, add the absolute values of the addends. Use the sign of the addends for the sum.	$2 + 3 = 5$ $^-2 + (^-3) = ^-5$

🔑 UNLOCK the Problem › REAL WORLD

A submarine is 60 meters below the surface of the ocean. After 10 minutes at this location, the submarine descends an additional 75 meters. What is the final location of the submarine?

🔓 **Find the sum of ⁻60 and ⁻75.**

STEP 1

Find the absolute values of the addends.

$|^-60| =$ _____

$|^-75| =$ _____

STEP 2

Add the absolute values of the addends.

$60 + 75 =$ _____

The addends are negative, so the sum is negative.

$^-60 + (^-75) =$ _____

So, the final location of the submarine is an elevation of _____ feet.

> **Math Talk** Explain why you would use the rules for adding integers instead of counters when adding numbers with large absolute values.

Try This! Find the sum.

Ⓐ $15 + 12$

Ⓑ $^-30 + (^-55)$

Adding Integers with Different Signs

When adding integers with different signs, subtract the lesser absolute value from the greater absolute value. Use the sign of the addend with the greater absolute value for the sum.

$$7 + (^-3) = 4$$
$$^-7 + 3 = ^-4$$

UNLOCK the Problem   REAL WORLD

A scuba diver is exploring a sunken ship 50 meters below the surface of the ocean. After exploring the ship, the diver rises 18 meters. What is the final location of the diver?

 Find the sum of ⁻50 and 18.

STEP 1

Find the absolute values of the addends.

|⁻50| = _____

|18| = _____

STEP 2

|18| ◯ |⁻50|, so subtract

|18| from |⁻50|.

_____

STEP 3

The negative number has the greater absolute value, so the

sum is _____.

⁻50 + 18 = _____

So, the diver's final location is an elevation of _____ meters.

- Suppose you model the sum 18 + (⁻50) with counters. Will there be more yellow (positive) or red (negative) counters? What does this tell you about the sum? Why?

_____

_____

Try This! Find the sum.

A 16 + (⁻14)

B ⁻17 + 9

Name _____

Share and Show

Find the sum.

1. ⁻10 + (⁻9)

   |⁻10| = _____ and |⁻9| = _____

   Both addends are negative. Add the absolute values and

   use a _____ sign for the sum. _____

2. 30 + (⁻17)

3. 14 + 20

4. 11 + (⁻19)

5. ⁻21 + 5

6. ⁻12 + (⁻10)

7. ⁻50 + 44

Math Talk Explain whether ⁻20 + 5 is the same sum as 20 + (⁻5).

On Your Own

. . . .

Find the sum.

8. ⁻13 + (⁻13)

9. 40 + (⁻33)

10. ⁻17 + 15

11. ⁻60 + (⁻28)

12. ⁻52 + 80

13. 2 + (⁻23)

Algebra Evaluate the expression.

14. $x + 7$ for $x = ⁻12$

15. ⁻14 + b for $b = ⁻9$

16. $m + (⁻6)$ for $m = 40$

Problem Solving REAL WORLD

Homestake Mine in South Dakota is an underground gold mine. The diagram shows part of the mine. Use the diagram for 17–18.

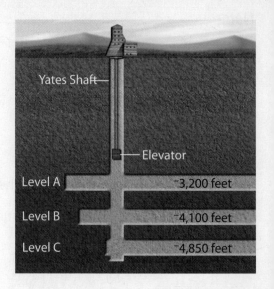

Yates Shaft

Elevator

Level A   ⁻3,200 feet

Level B   ⁻4,100 feet

Level C   ⁻4,850 feet

17. The elevator in Yates Shaft is at Level C. The elevator rises 500 feet. Write a number sentence with integers to find the final location of the elevator.

_____

18. **H.O.T.** Find the average depth of Level A and Level B.

_____

19. **Algebra** Scientists sometimes measure temperature using the Kelvin scale. To convert a temperature c in degrees Celsius to Kelvin, use the expression $c + 273$. Convert ⁻43°C to Kelvin.

_____

20. **H.O.T.** Find a positive integer and a negative integer whose sum is ⁻4.

_____

21. **H.O.T.** Is the sum of ⁻10 and a positive integer greater than or less than ⁻10? **Explain**.

_____

_____

22. **What's the Error?** Marc found that the sum ⁻15 + (⁻15) equals 0. Explain Marc's error and find the correct sum.

_____

_____

23. ⭐ **Test Prep** Serena deposited $42 in her checking account and she wrote a check for $62. Which integer represents the total change in her account balance in dollars?

(A) ⁻104   (C) 20

(B) ⁻20   (D) 104

SHOW YOUR WORK

Integer Subtraction

Essential Question How can you model subtraction of integers?

Investigate

Materials ■ two-color counters

You can use counters to find the difference of two integers.

A. Find $^-3 - (^-1)$.

Use red counters to represent $^-3$. Take away 1 red counter.

$^-3 - (^-1) =$ _____

B. Find $5 - (^-3)$.

Use yellow counters to represent 5.

You need to take away 3 red counters. Add zero pairs until there are 3 red counters that can be taken away.

Now take away 3 red counters.

$5 - (^-3) =$ _____

C. Find $3 - 7$.

Use yellow counters to represent 3.

You need to take away 7 yellow counters. Add zero pairs until there are 7 yellow counters that can be taken away.

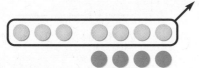

Now take away 7 yellow counters.

$3 - 7 =$ _____

Draw Conclusions

1. **Explain** why you can add zero pairs without changing the value of an expression.

_____

_____

2. **Tell** how many zero pairs you need to add to 3 yellow counters to model $3 - (^-4)$.

_____

3. **H.O.T.** **Analysis** When you represent $^-3 - (^-1)$ with counters, you model $^-3$ with red counters and then remove 1 red counter. Why does it make sense that the result is greater than $^-3$?

_____

_____

Make Connections

You can also use a number line to model integer subtraction. Move left on a number line to subtract a positive integer. Move right on a number line to subtract a negative integer.

A **Find the difference:** $^-1 - 5$

Draw a number line.

Start at 0. Move 1 unit to the _____ to show $^-1$.

From $^-1$, move 5 units to the _____ to subtract 5.

This takes you to the difference, _____.

So, $^-1 - 5 =$ _____.

A number line from $^-8$ to 2.

B **Find the difference:** $4 - (^-3)$

Draw a number line.

Start at 0. Move 4 units to the _____ to show 4.

To subtract a negative number, move _____ on the

number line. So move 3 units to the _____ to subtract $^-3$.

This takes you to the difference, _____.

So, $4 - (^-3) =$ _____.

A number line from $^-2$ to 8.

Math Talk Explain how to model $5 - (^-2)$ on a number line.

334

© Houghton Mifflin Harcourt Publishing Company

Name _____

Share and Show · · · · · · · · · · · · · · · · ·

Use the model to find the difference.

1. ⁻4 − (⁻2)

2. 3 − (⁻3)

3. ⁻3 − 4

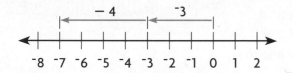

4. 2 − 7

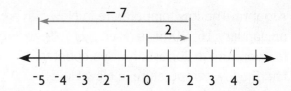

Circle the problem that is represented by the model.

5.

⁻6 − ⁻4 = ⁻2   ⁻6 − 4 = ⁻10

6.

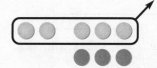

5 − (⁻3) = 8   2 − 5 = ⁻3

7.

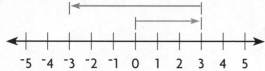

3 − 6 = ⁻3   ⁻3 − 3 = 0

8.

⁻2 − 5 = ⁻7   0 − 2 = ⁻2

Practice: Copy and Solve Use counters or a number line to find the difference.

9. ⁻1 − 8

10. ⁻5 − (⁻5)

11. 4 − 9

12. ⁻3 − (⁻9)

13. 2 − (⁻7)

14. 0 − (⁻1)

15. ⁻5 − 0

16. ⁻4 − 7

Problem Solving  REAL WORLD

On January 16, 2009, a cold wave moved across the United States. The thermometer shows the low temperature for the day in several cities. Use the thermometer for 17–19.

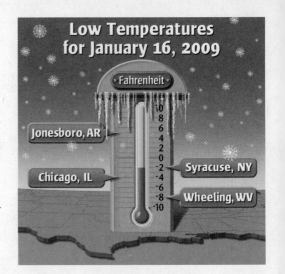

17. Use counters or a number line to find how much greater the low temperature was in Syracuse compared to Chicago?

_____

18. Write a number sentence with integers to find the range of the temperatures shown in the table.

_____

19. **Algebra** The low temperature in New Haven, Connecticut, on January 16, 2009, is given by $j - 9$, where j is the low temperature in Jonesboro. Use counters or a number line to find the low temperature in New Haven.

_____

20. 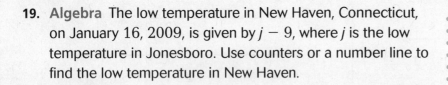 Write a difference that is modeled by the number line. Then write a sum that is modeled by the number line. What can you conclude about the difference and the sum?

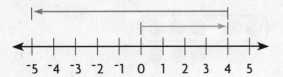

_____

_____

21. **Write Math** ▶ Is it possible for the difference of two negative numbers to be positive? If it is possible, give an example. If it is not possible, explain why it is not possible.

_____

22. ⭐ **Test Prep** A pelican dives from a height of 8 meters above the surface of the ocean to catch a fish below the surface at ⁻3 meters. What is the vertical distance the pelican dives?

Ⓐ 5 meters   Ⓒ 11 meters

Ⓑ 8 meters   Ⓓ 14 meters

SHOW YOUR WORK

Subtract Integers

Essential Question How do you subtract integers?

CONNECT You have used counters to model addition and subtraction of integers. Look at the models for $3 - 6$ and $3 + (^-6)$.

$3 - 6$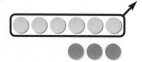

$3 + (^-6)$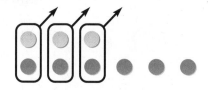

Since both $3 - 6$ and $3 + (^-6)$ are equal to $^-3$, $3 - 6 = 3 + (^-6)$.

> ### Subtracting Integers
>
> To find the difference of two integers, add the opposite (additive inverse) of the integer you are subtracting.
>
> $^-4 - 6 = ^-4 + (^-6) = ^-10$
>
> $3 - (^-5) = 3 + 5 = 8$

UNLOCK the Problem REAL WORLD

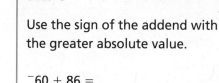

Death Valley National Park in California has the lowest elevations in the Western Hemisphere. The elevation at Furnace Creek is $^-60$ meters. The elevation at Badwater is $^-86$ meters. How much greater is the elevation at Furnace Creek than at Badwater?

 Find the difference of $^-60$ and $^-86$.

STEP 1

Add the opposite of the integer that is being subtracted.

$^-60 - (^-86) =$ _____

STEP 2

Follow the rules for adding integers.

$|^-60| =$ _____

$|86| =$ _____

$86 - 60 =$ _____

STEP 3

Use the sign of the addend with the greater absolute value.

$^-60 + 86 =$ _____

So, the elevation of Furnace Creek is _____ meters greater than the elevation of Badwater.

Math Talk Explain why it makes sense that subtracting a negative number is equivalent to adding a positive number.

🔑 Example

A Evaluate $x - (^-10)$ for $x = ^-18$.

STEP 1

Substitute the value of x in the expression.

$x - (^-10) = $ _____ $- (^-10)$

STEP 2

Write the difference as a sum.

$^-18 - (^-10) = $ _____

STEP 3

Add. Use the sign of the addend with the greater absolute value.

$-18 + 10 = $ _____

So, the value of the expression is _____ when $x = ^-18$.

B Evaluate $^-16 - m$ for $m = 5$.

STEP 1

Substitute the value of m in the expression.

$^-16 - m = ^-16 - $ _____

STEP 2

Write the difference as a sum.

_____ $= $ _____

STEP 3

Add. Both addends are negative, so the sum is negative.

_____ $= $ _____

So, the value of the expression is _____ when $m = 5$.

Share and Show

Find the difference.

1. $^-12 - (^-5)$

   Write the difference as a sum:

   $^-12 - (^-5) = ^-12 + $ _____

   Add: $^-12 + 5 = $ _____

2. $15 - (^-5)$

   _____

☑ 3. $^-2 - (^-16)$

   _____

4. $6 - (^-6)$

   _____

5. $^-20 - 4$

   _____

6. $14 - 25$

   _____

7. $^-4 - 9$

   _____

8. $^-3 - (^-13)$

   _____

Name _____

Share and Show

Evaluate the expression.

9. $15 - c$ for $c = 25$

10. $^-3 - t$ for $t = ^-9$

11. $y - 8$ for $y = ^-12$

12. $b - (^-1)$ for $b = ^-9$

13. $^-11 - n$ for $n = 16$

14. $d - 7$ for $d = 0$

Math Talk Describe two different ways to find the difference $10 - 18$.

On Your Own

Find the difference.

15. $16 - (^-9)$

16. $40 - 75$

17. $-12 - (^-18)$

18. $-20 - (^-20)$

19. $9 - (^-15)$

20. $0 - (^-14)$

Algebra **Evaluate the expression.**

21. $x - (^-20)$ for $x = ^-10$

22. $^-12 - c$ for $c = ^-8$

23. $n - 15$ for $n = ^-15$

24. The highest elevation in Death Valley National Park is 11,049 feet. The lowest elevation is $^-282$ feet. What is the difference between the highest elevation and lowest elevation?

_____

25. The low point of the Java Trench in the Indian Ocean is $^-7,455$ meters. The low point of the Tonga Trench in the Pacific Ocean is 3,427 meters lower. What is the depth of the Tonga Trench?

_____

Windchill

On a cold winter day, the air feels colder on your skin when the wind is blowing. *Windchill* is the temperature that the outside temperature feels like due to the wind. The windchill temperature is always less than or equal to the actual outdoor temperature.

The table shows the windchill temperature for given outside temperatures and wind speeds.

Suppose the outside temperature is 10°F and the wind speed is 20 mi/hr. Find the change in the windchill if the wind speed increases to 40 mi/hr.

Windchill Temperatures				
	Outside Temperature			
	⁻10°F	0°F	10°F	20°F
15 mi/hr	⁻32°F	⁻19°F	⁻7°F	6°F
20 mi/hr	⁻35°F	⁻22°F	⁻9°F	4°F
25 mi/hr	⁻37°F	⁻24°F	⁻11°F	3°F
30 mi/hr	⁻39°F	⁻26°F	⁻12°F	1°F
35 mi/hr	⁻41°F	⁻27°F	⁻14°F	0°F
40 mi/hr	⁻43°F	⁻29°F	⁻15°F	⁻1°F

(Left label: **Wind Speed**)

Find the difference of the windchills.

STEP 1

Use the table to find the windchill for an outside temperature of 10°F and a wind speed of 20 mi/hr.

The windchill is ⁻9°F.

STEP 2

Use the table to find the windchill for an outside temperature of 10°F and a wind speed of 40 mi/hr.

The windchill is _____°F.

STEP 3

Find the difference.

⁻9 − (⁻15) = _____ = _____

So, the change in the windchill is _____.

Solve.

26. The outside temperature is 20°F and the wind speed is 40 mi/hr. How much greater is the outside temperature than the windchill?

_____

27. The outside temperature at noon and at midnight is 0°F. Find the change in the windchill if the wind speed increases from 15 mi/hr at noon to 35 mi/hr at midnight.

_____

FOR MORE PRACTICE:
Standards Practice Book, pp. P167–P168

Name _____

✓ Mid-Chapter Checkpoint

▶ Vocabulary

Choose the best term from the box.

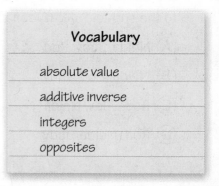

Vocabulary
absolute value
additive inverse
integers
opposites

1. The _____ of a number is the distance of the number from 0 on a number line. (p. 321)

2. The set of whole numbers and their opposites is the set of

   _____. (p. 321)

▶ Concepts and Skills

Order the numbers from least to greatest. (pp. 321–324)

3. $^-4, |^-2|, 1, 5$

4. $7, ^-1, |3|, 0$

5. $|^-5|, ^-4, |^-3|, 2$

6. $^-6, |^-4|, |^-7|, 1$

Find the sum. (pp. 325–332)

7. $^-4 + 1$

8. $9 + (^-2)$

9. $^-3 + (^-5)$

10. $2 + (^-8)$

11. $^-17 + (^-21)$

12. $11 + (^-34)$

13. $24 + (^-7)$

14. $^-23 + 9$

Find the difference. (pp. 333–340)

15. $^-3 - 9$

16. $9 - (^-5)$

17. $^-4 - (^-1)$

18. $7 - 8$

19. $^-24 - (^-24)$

20. $15 - 29$

21. $0 - (^-33)$

22. $^-19 - 1$

Fill in the bubble to show your answer.

23. Judy is scuba diving at ⁻7 meters, Nelda is scuba diving at ⁻9 meters, and Rod is scuba diving at ⁻3 meters. Which list shows the divers in order from the deepest diver to the diver who is closest to the surface? (pp. 321–324)

Ⓐ Nelda, Judy, Rod

Ⓑ Nelda, Rod, Judy

Ⓒ Rod, Judy, Nelda

Ⓓ Rod, Nelda, Judy

24. A football team gains 8 yards on their first play. They lose 12 yards on the next play. Which integer represents the team's overall gain or loss on the two plays? (pp. 325–332)

Ⓐ ⁻20   Ⓒ 4

Ⓑ ⁻4   Ⓓ 20

25. Which of the following sums is closest to zero? (pp. 325–332)

Ⓐ ⁻20 + 6

Ⓑ ⁻6 + 20

Ⓒ ⁻6 + (⁻6)

Ⓓ ⁻20 + (⁻20)

26. Mei is playing a board game. She currently has 3 points. She draws a card that says, "Lose 8 points." What is Mei's score after drawing the card? (pp. 333–340)

Ⓐ ⁻11 points

Ⓑ ⁻8 points

Ⓒ ⁻5 points

Ⓓ ⁻3 points

27. The temperature inside a freezer is ⁻5°C. Over the course of the day, the temperature drops 15°C. What is the final temperature inside the freezer? (pp. 333–340)

Ⓐ ⁻20°C

Ⓑ ⁻15°C

Ⓒ ⁻10°C

Ⓓ 10°C

342

Name _____

Integer Multiplication

Essential Question How can you model multiplication of integers?

Investigate

Materials ■ two-color counters

Rick and Kayla are scuba diving to explore coral reefs. They reach the reefs by making several descents of equal length. You can use counters or number lines to model their dives.

A. Rick dives to a coral reef in 4 equal descents of ⁻3 meters each. To find the reef's location, find 4 × ⁻3.

4 × ⁻3 means 4 groups of ⁻3.

Use red counters to represent 4 groups of ⁻3. The total number of counters is the product.

You can also represent 4 × ⁻3 on a number line.

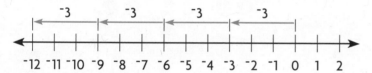

4 × (⁻3) = _____

B. Kayla dives to a coral reef in descents of ⁻2 meters each, and she makes 5 descents. To find the reef's location, find ⁻2 × 5.

By the Commutative Property, ⁻2 × 5 = 5 × ⁻2

Use red counters to represent 5 groups of ⁻2. The total number of counters is the product.

Show how to represent 5 × ⁻2 on the number line below.

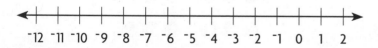

⁻2 × 5 = _____

Draw Conclusions...

1. **Describe** how the counter model for $4 \times {}^-3$ is similar to the number-line model for $4 \times {}^-3$.

   _____

   _____

2. 🔆**H.O.T.** **Analysis** What do you notice about the sign of the product when you multiply a positive integer and a negative integer?

   _____

   _____

Make Connections...

You can also use what you know about opposites to help you model multiplication of integers.

Ⓐ **Find the product: ${}^-3 \times 2$**

Think of ${}^-3 \times 2$ as ${}^-(3 \times 2)$, which is the opposite of 3 groups of 2.

First use counters to show 3 groups of 2.

To show the opposite of 3 groups of 2, flip all the counters over.

The counters represent the product, _____.

So, ${}^-3 \times 2 =$ _____.

Ⓑ **Find the product: ${}^-4 \times {}^-3$**

Think of ${}^-4 \times {}^-3$ as ${}^-(4 \times {}^-3)$, which is the opposite

of _____.

First use counters to show _____.

To show the opposite of _____, flip all the counters over.

The counters represent the product, _____.

So, ${}^-4 \times ({}^-3) =$ _____.

Math Talk Describe how you could show the opposite of 3 groups of 2 on a number line.

Name _____

Share and Show

Use the model to find the product.

1. $3 \times (^-2)$

_____

2. $^-5 \times 2$

_____

3. $2 \times (^-6)$

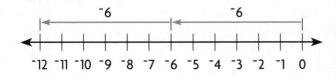

_____

4. $4 \times (^-2)$

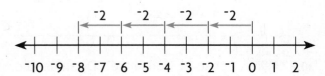

_____

Tell what product is represented by the model. Then find the product.

5.

_____

6.

_____

7.

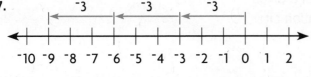

_____

8.

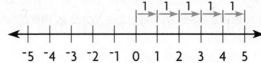

_____

Use counters or a number line to find the product.

9. $4 \times (^-1)$

_____

10. $^-5 \times 3$

_____

11. $7 \times (^-2)$

_____

12. $^-3 \times 1$

_____

13. $^-2 \times (^-3)$

_____

14. $^-3 \times (^-3)$

_____

15. $^-4 \times (^-1)$

_____

16. $^-2 \times (^-5)$

_____

17. **Write Math** ▸ **Explain** why the product $^-3 \times (^-2)$ is positive.

_____

_____

Problem Solving REAL WORLD

Many glaciers around the world are shrinking. This is called *glacier retreat*. The table shows the rate of retreat for four glaciers in Asia. Use the table for 18–19.

18. Write a number sentence with integers to find the number of feet the Milam glacier retreats in 3 months.

_____

19. Over a 6-month period, by how many more feet does the Pindari glacier retreat than the Kolhani glacier?

_____

Rate of Retreat for Glaciers in Asia

Glacier	Rate (feet per month)
Kolhani	⁻4
Machoi	⁻2
Milam	⁻3
Pindari	⁻6

20. **H.O.T.** **Sense or Nonsense?** Dylan used counters to model the product ⁻4 × (⁻2) as shown. From the model, he determined that the product is ⁻8. Explain whether Dylan's answer makes sense.

SHOW YOUR WORK

_____

_____

21. **Algebra** The expression ⁻5m gives the location of a diver in meters after *m* minutes. What is the diver's location after 4 minutes?

_____

22. **Write Math** ▶ Explain how you could use counters to model the product 0 × (⁻4). Then explain how to find the product.

_____

_____

23. ⭐ **Test Prep** An elevator starts at the lobby of a building and descends into the basement. The elevator's height changes by ⁻6 meters each second. What is the change in the elevator's height after 3 seconds?

(A) ⁻3 meters   (C) ⁻9 meters

(B) ⁻6 meters   (D) ⁻18 meters

Multiply Integers

Essential Question How can you multiply integers?

UNLOCK the Problem REAL WORLD

Lydia played in two golf tournaments, and averaged a score of ⁻3 for each of the 6 rounds she played. What was Lydia's combined score for the two tournaments?

Complete the pattern to find the product.

A 6 × (⁻3)

Study the pattern.

As the second factor decreases by 1, the

product _____

by _____.

Use this rule to complete the pattern.

6 × 3 = 18

6 × 2 = 12

6 × 1 = 6

6 × 0 = 0

6 × (⁻1) = ⁻6

6 × (⁻2) = ⬜

6 × (⁻3) = ⬜

So, Lydia's combined score was 6 × (⁻3) = _____.

You can also use patterns to find the product of two negative integers.

B ⁻6 × (⁻3)

Study the pattern.

As the second factor decreases by 1, the

product _____

by _____.

Use this rule to complete the pattern.

⁻6 × 3 = ⁻18

⁻6 × 2 = ⁻12

⁻6 × 1 = ⁻6

⁻6 × 0 = 0

⁻6 × (⁻1) = ⬜

⁻6 × (⁻2) = ⬜

⁻6 × (⁻3) = ⬜

So, ⁻6 × (⁻3) = _____.

Math Talk **Describe** what you notice about the product of two integers with the same sign. **Describe** what you notice about the product of two integers with different signs.

Multiplying Integers

The product of two integers with the same sign is positive.	$^-7 \times (^-2) = 14$
The product of two integers with different signs is negative.	$3 \times (^-4) = ^-12$
The product of any integer and 0 is 0.	$^-5 \times 0 = 0$

🔑 Example

Math Idea

Multiplication can be written with the symbol $\times$ or the symbol $\bullet$ between the factors, or by placing the factors next to each other without a space. The expression $5y$ means 5 times y.

A Evaluate $5y$ for $y = ^-10$.

STEP 1

Substitute the value of y in the expression.

When $y = ^-10$, $5y = 5 \times$ ▢

STEP 2

Find the product. The signs of the integers are different, so the product is _____.

$5 \times$ ▢ $=$ _____

So, the value of the expression is _____ when $y = ^-10$.

B Evaluate ^-3p for $p = ^-12$.

STEP 1

Substitute the value of p in the expression.

When $p = ^-12$, $^-3p = ^-3 \times$ ▢

STEP 2

Find the product. The signs of the integers are the same, so the product is _____.

$^-3 \times$ ▢ $=$ _____

So, the value of the expression is _____ when $p = ^-12$.

Share and Show ·

Find the product.

1. $^-8 \times (^-5)$

   The integers have the same sign, so the

   product is _____.

   Multiply: $^-8 \times (^-5) =$ _____

2. $6 \times (^-4)$

   _____

✓ 3. $^-7 \times 6$

4. $^-10 \times (^-3)$

5. $0 \times (^-8)$

_____   _____   _____

Name _____

Share and Show

Algebra Evaluate the expression.

6. ⁻3x for x = 15

7. ⁻8k for k = ⁻4

8. 7m for m = ⁻1

_____

_____

_____

9. 5c for c = ⁻8

10. ⁻11y for y = 0

Math Talk Explain how to determine the sign of the product when you multiply two integers.

_____

_____

On Your Own

Find the product.

11. ⁻9 × (⁻10)

12. 20 × (⁻3)

13. ⁻14 × 5

_____

_____

_____

14. ⁻8 × (⁻8)

15. ⁻17 × 0

16. ⁻32 × (⁻10)

_____

_____

_____

Algebra Evaluate the expression.

17. 12y for y = ⁻20

18. ⁻6g for g = ⁻15

19. ⁻9n for n = ⁻11

_____

_____

_____

Algebra Use mental math to find the value of the variable.

20. 4c = ⁻12

21. ⁻6m = ⁻12

22. 5x = ⁻15

c = _____

m = _____

x = _____

23. ⁻4y = ⁻16

24. 2z = ⁻20

25. ⁻4b = 24

y = _____

z = _____

b = _____

Problem Solving · REAL WORLD

The graph shows the depths of some shipwrecks in Florida. Use the graph for 26–29.

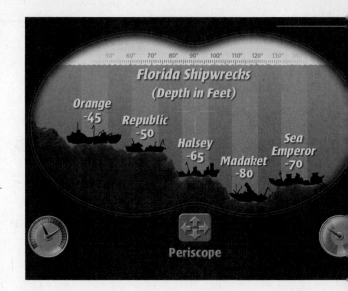

26. The *Jim Atria* is located 3 times deeper than the *Orange*. What is the location of the *Jim Atria*?

_____

27. Delia goes scuba diving to explore the *Madaket*. She begins by diving in 5 equal descents of ⁻14 feet each. How many more feet does she have to descend in order to reach the *Madaket*?

_____

28. The *Lancing*, which is a shipwreck off the coast of North Carolina, is twice as deep as the *Madaket*. How much deeper is the *Lancing* than the *Republic*?

_____

29. H.O.T. **Pose a Problem** Write and solve a new problem that uses multiplication and the data in the graph.

_____

_____

_____

30. Write Math ▶ Explain how you can use reasoning about opposites to show that the product ⁻20 × (⁻5) is positive.

_____

_____

31. ⭐ **Test Prep** At the end of a game show, Lee's score is ⁻80. Eduardo's score is 4 times Lee's score. What is Eduardo's score?

(**A**) ⁻320   (**C**) 20

(**B**) ⁻20   (**D**) 320

······· SHOW YOUR WORK ·······

Name _____

Divide Integers

Essential Question How can you divide integers?

CONNECT Dividing by a number is the inverse of multiplying by that number, so the rules for dividing integers are similar to the rules for multiplying integers.

Dividing Integers	
The quotient of two integers with the same sign is positive.	$^-36 \div (^-9) = 4$
The quotient of two integers with different signs is negative.	$40 \div (^-5) = ^-8$
Zero divided by any integer is 0. Division by 0 is not defined.	$0 \div 12 = 0$

UNLOCK the Problem REAL WORLD

The table shows the monthly profit or loss for David's dog-walking business. What is the average monthly profit or loss?

Monthly Profit or Loss						
Month	Nov	Dec	Jan	Feb	Mar	Apr
Profit or Loss ($)	$^-12$	$^-10$	$^-5$	7	$^-9$	5

> **Remember**
> The average, or mean, of a set of data values is the sum of the values divided by the number of values.

Find the sum of the data values.
$^-12 + (^-10) + (^-5) + 7 + (^-9) + 5 = ^-24$

Divide by the number of data values.
$^-24 \div 6 = \boxed{}$

 **Find the quotient:** $^-24 \div 6$

The integers have different signs, so the
$^-24 \div 6 = \boxed{}$

quotient is _____.

Check your answer.

Use a related multiplication problem. If the product of your answer and 6 is $^-24$, then your answer is correct.
$\boxed{} \times 6 = ^-24$

So, since the quotient is _____, there is an average

monthly loss of _____.

> **Math Talk** Describe how you could use counters to model the quotient $^-24 \div 6$.

Try This! Find the quotient.

A 18 ÷ (⁻3)

_____

B ⁻50 ÷ (⁻10)

_____

 Example

A Evaluate $m ÷ (⁻2)$ for $m = 20$.

STEP 1

Substitute the value of m in the expression.

When $m = 20$,

$m ÷ (⁻2) =$ _____ $÷ (⁻2)$

STEP 2

Divide. The signs of the integers are different, so the quotient is

_____.

☐ $÷ (⁻2) =$ _____

So, the value of the expression is _____ when $m = 20$.

B Evaluate $\dfrac{⁻42}{y}$ for $y = ⁻6$.

STEP 1

Substitute the value of y in the expression.

When $y = ⁻6$,

$\dfrac{⁻42}{y} = \dfrac{⁻42}{\boxed{}}$

STEP 2

Divide. The signs of the integers are the same, so the quotient is

_____.

$\dfrac{⁻42}{\boxed{}} =$ _____

So, the value of the expression is _____ when $y = ⁻6$.

Share and Show ●

Find the quotient.

1. $16 ÷ (⁻2)$

    The integers have different signs,

    so the quotient is _____.

    Divide: $16 ÷ (⁻2) =$ _____

2. $⁻40 ÷ (⁻8)$

    _____

✓3. $⁻22 ÷ 11$

4. $0 ÷ (⁻6)$

5. $⁻35 ÷ (⁻5)$

_____

_____

_____

Name _____

Share and Show

Algebra Evaluate the expression.

6. $n \div 6$ for $n = {}^-48$

7. ${}^-28 \div x$ for $x = {}^-4$

8. $c \div ({}^-12)$ for $c = {}^-36$

_____

9. $t \div ({}^-7)$ for $t = 49$

10. ${}^-25 \div z$ for $z = 25$

_____

Math Talk Explain how you can use multiplication to check your answer when you find a quotient.

On Your Own

Find the quotient.

11. ${}^-65 \div 5$

12. ${}^-81 \div ({}^-3)$

13. $144 \div ({}^-12)$

_____

14. $\dfrac{{}^-23}{{}^-23}$

15. $\dfrac{0}{{}^-18}$

16. $\dfrac{{}^-75}{3}$

_____

Algebra Evaluate the expression.

17. $y \div 20$ for $y = {}^-100$

18. $24 \div x$ for $x = {}^-8$

19. $n \div ({}^-15)$ for $n = 225$

_____

20. Write a number sentence to describe the quotient that is modeled by the counters.

_____

21. H.O.T. The quotient ${}^-5 \div 2$ can be written as ${}^-2$ r ${}^-1$. Model the division problem ${}^-10 \div 7$. Use your model to write the quotient of ${}^-10 \div 7$ with a remainder.

_____

Problem Solving REAL WORLD

With more than 6,000 known caves, Missouri is nicknamed the Cave State. The table shows the lowest point of some caves in Missouri. Use the table for 22–24.

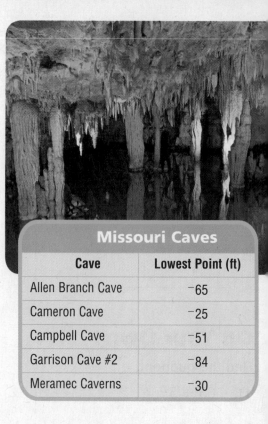

22. Ryan begins at sea level and descends to the lowest point of Allen Branch Cave. He makes several equal changes in elevation, each of ⁻13 feet. Write a number sentence to find how many elevation changes Ryan makes.

_____

23. What is the average elevation of the lowest point for the five caves in the table?

_____

Missouri Caves

Cave	Lowest Point (ft)
Allen Branch Cave	⁻65
Cameron Cave	⁻25
Campbell Cave	⁻51
Garrison Cave #2	⁻84
Meramec Caverns	⁻30

24. What is the elevation of the lowest point of Campbell Cave in yards? Explain how you found your answer.

_____

SHOW YOUR WORK

25. **H.O.T.** Is the quotient of two negative integers greater than or less than the integers? **Explain** how you know.

_____

_____

_____

26. **Write Math** ▶ **Explain** how you can find the quotient ⁻32 ÷ (⁻8) by solving a multiplication problem.

_____

_____

27. ⭐ **Test Prep** In the past week, Eryka made several deposits and withdrawals in her checking account. She recorded these changes as ⁻$30, ⁺$14, ⁺$65, and ⁻$57. What was the average change in Eryka's account?

Ⓐ ⁻$8   Ⓒ ⁺$26.50

Ⓑ ⁻$2   Ⓓ ⁺$41.50

Draw a Diagram · Integers

Essential Question How can you use a diagram to solve integer problems?

🔑 UNLOCK the Problem REAL WORLD

Underwater robots explore the ocean without disturbing marine life. An underwater robot descended 16 meters from its original position. Then it rose, going up in 3 increments of 4 meters each. Its final position was 12 meters below sea level. What was the robot's original position?

Read the Problem	Solve the Problem
What do I need to find? I need to find the _____ _____ .	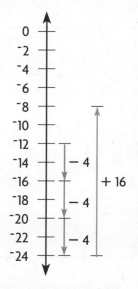

What do I need to find?

I need to find the _____

_____ .

What information do I need to use?

The robot went down _____, then it went up

_____, up _____, and up _____ .

It ended _____ .

How will I use the information?

What strategy can you use?

_____

_____

Draw a diagram. Make a vertical number line to show the robot's motion.

Start at the robot's final position. Work backward to find the robot's starting position.

From ⁻12, go down 4 three times. Then go up 16.

The robot's original position is given by the expression

_____ ,

which equals _____ .

So, the robot's original position was _____ below sea level.

1. How can you check your answer to the problem?

_____

_____

2. What if? The robot rose in 5 increments of 4 meters each. What would the robot's original position have been in this case?

_____

🔑 Try Another Problem

Andrew wrote 4 checks for $8 each. Then he deposited $10 into his checking account. The final balance in his checking account was ⁻$2. What was the starting balance in the account?

Read the Problem

What do I need to find?	What information do I need to use?	How will I use the information?

Solve the Problem

So, the starting balance in Andrew's account was _____ .

3. **Explain** how you could solve the problem using a different strategy.

_____

_____

4. Suppose Andrew wrote the same checks and made the same deposit, but the final balance was ⁻$4. **Explain** how you could find the starting balance in this case.

_____

_____

Math Talk Describe another type of problem you could solve by drawing a number line.

Name _____

Share and Show [MATH BOARD]

UNLOCK the Problem
- ✓ Circle the question.
- ✓ Underline important facts.
- ✓ Choose a strategy.
- ✓ Make sure your answer is reasonable.

1. On a winter afternoon, the temperature dropped 3°F every hour for 4 hours. Then the temperature rose 5°F. The final temperature was ⁻2°F. What was the starting temperature?

   First, draw a number line. A vertical number line works well for temperatures because a vertical number line

   resembles a _____.

   Next, start at the final temperature and work backward.

   The final temperature was _____.

   Then, move down by _____.

   This brings you to _____.

   Finally, go up by _____ four times.

   This brings you to _____.

   So, the starting temperature was _____.

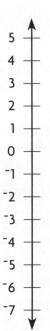

2. **H.O.T.** **What if** the temperature had dropped 4°F every hour for 4 hours, but everything else remained the same? What would the starting temperature have been in this case? **Explain.**

   _____

   _____

3. Charmaine begins hiking and climbs 50 feet. On the next part of her hike, she descends 100 feet every hour for 3 hours. At the end of her hike, she is at an elevation of ⁻50 feet. What was her starting elevation?

   _____

4. A scuba diver makes 5 equal descents of 3 meters each. Then he rises 10 meters. Finally, he rises another 2 meters. His final location is ⁻9 meters. What was the diver's starting location?

   _____

SHOW YOUR WORK

On Your Own......

5. Tom has a case of granola bars. He gives half the granola bars to his sister and then gives 4 granola bars to a friend. He gives half of what is left to his cousin. This leaves Tom with 4 granola bars. How many granola bars were in the case?

_____

6. **H.O.T.** A bag contains red, blue, and green marbles. There are more than 10 marbles in the bag. The probability of randomly choosing a red marble is $\frac{1}{5}$. The probability of randomly choosing a blue marble is $\frac{2}{5}$. How many marbles of each color might there be?

_____

7. **Write Math** ➤ Ms. Montoya's class celebrates the 100th day of the school year with a party. The school year begins on a Tuesday, and Ms. Montoya includes holidays and weekends when counting up to the 100th day. On what day of the week will the class have its party? Explain.

_____

_____

_____

8. A model train is set up on a circular track. There are 6 model telephone poles evenly spaced around the track. It takes the train 8 seconds to go from the first pole to the third pole. How long does it take the train to go completely around the track one time?

_____

9. ⭐ **Test Prep** A cave explorer makes 2 equal descents of 6 meters each. Then she rises 10 meters. Her final location is ⁻7 meters. What was her starting location?

(A) ⁻29 meters   (C) ⁻9 meters

(B) ⁻17 meters   (D) ⁻5 meters

358 FOR MORE PRACTICE: Standards Practice Book, pp. P175–P176

· · · · · · · **SHOW YOUR WORK** · · · ·

Name _____

Operations with Integers

Essential Question How can you solve problems involving combinations
of operations with integers?

CONNECT You learned about the order of operations, a rule for evaluating
expressions. Follow the order of operations to evaluate expressions that
involve combinations of integer operations.

? UNLOCK the Problem REAL WORLD

The table shows the annual change in the
population of elk at a wildlife preserve over a
7-year period. Tell whether the overall change in
the elk population was an increase or decrease
and by how much the population changed.

Year	2004	2005	2006	2007	2008	2009	2010
Change	$^+5$	$^+5$	$^-3$	$^-3$	$^-3$	$^-3$	$^+7$

The overall change is the sum of the annual
changes. The sum of the annual changes may be
written as $2 \times 5 + 4 \times (^-3) + 7$.

  Evaluate the expression: $2 \times 5 + 4 \times (^-3) + 7$

First, _____ from left to right. $2 \times 5 + 4 \times (^-3) + 7$

Next, _____ from left to right. $10 + (^-12) + 7$

                                                     $^-2 + 7$

                                                     5

So, the overall change in the population was a(n)

_____ of _____ elk.

Remember
The order of operations is:
Parentheses
Exponents
Multiplication/Division
Addition/Subtraction

---

1. **Explain** why you need the order of operations to evaluate an
   expression like $2 \times 5 + 4 \times (^-3) + 7$.

   _____

2. **Show** how you could add parentheses to the expression
   $2 \times 5 + 4 \times (^-3) + 7$ to change its value.

   _____

Try This! Evaluate the expression.

Ⓐ $^-3 - (^-8) \times ^-14$

Ⓑ $[9 + (^-5)]^2 + 6$

Properties You can use the Commutative and Associative Properties of addition and multiplication, as well as the Distributive Property, to help you evaluate expressions.

🔑 Example

Use the Commutative, Associative, and/or Distributive Properties to help evaluate the expression.

Ⓐ $17 + [9 + (^-17)]$

Use the _____ Property of Addition to change the order of the addends in parentheses.	$17 + [9 + (^-17)]$ $17 + (^-17 + 9)$
Use the _____ Property of Addition to change the grouping.	$[17 + (^-17)] + 9$
	_____ $+ 9$
Add.	_____

> **Remember**
> Square brackets are another type of grouping symbol.

So, the value of the expression is _____.

Ⓑ $^-6 \times 31$

Write 31 as the sum of a multiple of 10 and a one-digit number.	$^-6 \times 31$ $^-6 \times (30 + 1)$
Use the _____ Property.	$^-6 \times 30 + (^-6) \times 1$
Multiply.	_____ $+$ _____
Add.	_____

So, the value of the expression is _____.

Math Talk **Explain** why using the Distributive Property makes it easier to find the product $^-6 \times 31$.

360

Name _____

Share and Show

Evaluate the expression.

1. $^-12 \div 6 - 3$

= _____ − 3

= _____ + _____

_____

2. $(^-22 + 6) \div 4^2$

_____

3. $6 \times (^-55 \div 5) + 8^2$

_____

Use the Commutative, Associative, and/or Distributive Properties to help evaluate the expression.

4. $^-23 + (18 + 23)$

_____

5. $^-9 \times 52$

_____

Math Talk Explain whether it is possible to use the Commutative and Associative Properties to help you evaluate $^-6 - (13 - 6)$.

On Your Own

Evaluate the expression.

6. $(^-13 - 7) \div (3 + 1)$

_____

7. $8 + (^-10 \times 4)$

_____

8. $6^2 - 3 \times (^-7)$

_____

Use the Commutative, Associative, and/or Distributive Properties to help evaluate the expression.

9. $5 \times (29 \times {}^-2)$

_____

10. $^-7 \times 103$

_____

11. $37 + (^-16 + {}^-37)$

_____

Compare. Write <, >, or =.

12. $[5 - (^-7)] \times 8 \bigcirc [6 + (^-3)] \times 9$

13. $^-24 \div [1 - (^-7)] \bigcirc 18 \div (^-6)$

14. $2 + 7 \times (^-1) \bigcirc {}^-3 + 3 \div (^-1)$

15. $6 \times (^-4 + 9) \bigcirc 9 \times [11 + (^-8)]$

16. During one week, the daily change, in dollars, of a checking account balance was $^-15$, $^-15$, $^-15$, 12, 12, 12, and $^-8$. Write and evaluate an expression to find the overall change for the week.

_____

Problem Solving  REAL WORLD

Pose a Problem

17. Kendra adjusts the settings on a freezer to change the temperature inside the freezer. For the first 5 hours, the temperature drops by 4°F per hour. For the next 3 hours, the temperature drops by 2°F per hour. Tell whether the overall change in temperature inside the freezer is an increase or decrease and by how much the temperature changes.

Write an expression for the overall change in the temperature.

$$5 \times (^-4) + 3 \times (^-2)$$

Multiply.

= _____ + _____

Add.

= _____

So, the overall change in the temperature

is a _____ of _____.

Write a new problem that is similar to the problem above.
Try to make your problem more difficult.

Pose a problem.	**Solve your problem.**
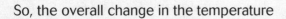	

- **Explain** how you made your problem more difficult than the given problem.

_____

- **Describe** any properties or rules you used to solve your problem.

_____

Name _____

✓ Chapter 9 Review/Test

▶ Vocabulary

Choose the best term from the box.

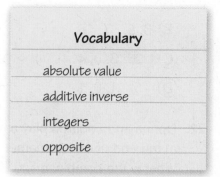

Vocabulary
absolute value
additive inverse
integers
opposite

1. The sum of a number and its _____ is zero. (p. 321, 325)

2. The _____ are the set of whole numbers and their opposites. (p. 321)

▶ Concepts and Skills

Compare. Write <, >, or =. (pp. 321–324)

3. ⁻16 ◯ 0

4. |⁻26| ◯ 26

5. |⁻31| ◯ ⁻41

6. ⁻2 ◯ ⁻22

Add or subtract. (pp. 325–340)

7. 16 + (⁻4)

8. ⁻11 − 5

9. ⁻8 + (⁻15)

10. 5 − 17

Multiply or divide. (pp. 343–354)

11. ⁻6 × (⁻8)

12. ⁻12 ÷ 3

13. 5 × (⁻7)

14. ⁻48 ÷ (⁻12)

Evaluate the expression. (pp. 359–362)

15. ⁻10 + [7 − (⁻3)]

16. [6 − (⁻4)] × 5

17. ⁻12 + (⁻8) ÷ 2

18. ⁻25 × 4 + (⁻50)

19. ⁻6 + (⁻6) ÷ (⁻6)

20. 36 ÷ (⁻9) × (⁻7) + 4

Fill in the bubble to show your answer.

21. Which set of integers is written in order from least to greatest? (pp. 321–324)

    Ⓐ ⁻9, 10, 12, ⁻15

    Ⓑ 3, 5, ⁻7, ⁻8

    Ⓒ ⁻2, ⁻3, 0, 4

    Ⓓ ⁻5, ⁻1, 0, 1

22. Donna and Eduardo play a golf tournament as a team. Donna's score at the end of the tournament is ⁻3, and Eduardo's score is also ⁻3. What is the combined score for their team? (pp. 325–332)

    Ⓐ ⁻6   Ⓒ 0

    Ⓑ ⁻3   Ⓓ 3

23. A diver at sea level descends 35 feet. Then she rises 12 feet. Which number sentence represents this situation? (pp. 325–332)

    Ⓐ 35 + 12 = 47

    Ⓑ 35 + (⁻12) = 23

    Ⓒ ⁻35 + (⁻12) = ⁻47

    Ⓓ ⁻35 + 12 = ⁻23

24. The captain of a boat lowers an anchor from a position 3 feet above the surface of the water to a position 9 feet below the surface of the water. Which number sentence represents the distance the anchor travels? (pp. 333–340)

    Ⓐ 3 − 9 = ⁻6

    Ⓑ ⁻3 − 9 = ⁻12

    Ⓒ 3 − (⁻9) = 12

    Ⓓ 9 − 3 = 6

25. On February 21, 1918, the temperature in Granville, North Dakota, rose from ⁻33°F in the morning to 50°F in late afternoon. What was the increase in temperature? (pp. 333–340)

    Ⓐ ⁻17°F

    Ⓑ 17°F

    Ⓒ 50°F

    Ⓓ 83°F

Fill in the bubble to show your answer.

26. A school of fish usually swims underwater at ⁻3 feet. During a storm, the school of fish swims 4 times deeper than usual. What is the location of the school of fish during the storm? (pp. 343–350)

(A) ⁻34 feet

(B) ⁻12 feet

(C) ⁻9 feet

(D) ⁻7 feet

27. Drew evaluates the expression ⁻10x for a value of x that is a positive integer. Which statement about the value of the expression must be true? (pp. 343–350)

(A) The value is positive.

(B) The value is greater than 10.

(C) The value is negative.

(D) The value is less than ⁻10.

28. Five students' scores in a trivia contest are ⁻34, ⁻18, 8, ⁻12, and 11. What is the average score of the students? (pp. 351–354)

(A) ⁻45   (C) 9

(B) ⁻9   (D) 45

29. Denise withdraws $20 from her bank account. Then she makes 3 deposits of $15 each. The final balance in the account is $35. What was the starting balance in the account? (pp. 355–358)

(A) $5

(B) $10

(C) $55

(D) $60

30. The temperature decreases by 2°C every hour for 8 hours. Then the temperature decreases by 4°C every hour for 3 hours. What is the overall change in the temperature? (pp. 359–362)

(A) ⁻28°C

(B) ⁻2°C

(C) 2°C

(D) 28°C

31. A coral reef is 60 feet below the surface of the ocean. A diver explores the reef and then rises 28 feet. Write a number sentence with integers to find the final location of the diver. (pp. 325–332)

_____

32. Mario wants to use the Distributive Property to make it easier to evaluate ¯4 × 61. Show how he can do this. Then evaluate the resulting expression. (pp. 359–362)

_____

_____

► **Performance Task**

33. At the end of round 1 of a game show, Tyler has ¯40 points, DeShawn has ¯20 points, and Maria has ¯25 points.

A List the contestants in order from the contestant with the greatest score to the contestant with the least score.

_____

_____

B At the end of round 2, Tyler's score has increased by 35 points, and Maria's score is 3 times Tyler's new score. What are Tyler's and Maria's scores at the end of round 2?

_____

_____

C During round 2, Kyla gains 20 points, loses 5 points three times, and gains another 10 points. Her score at the end of round 2 is 15 points. What was her score at the beginning of round 2?

_____

_____

D How many points does DeShawn need to gain in round 2 in order to have the highest score at the end of round 2? Explain.

_____

_____

_____

Algebra: Equations and Functions

Show What You Know

Check your understanding of important skills.

Name _____

▶ **Use a Coordinate Grid** Write the point for the ordered pair on the coordinate grid.

1. (4, 6)

   point _____

2. (8, 4)

   point _____

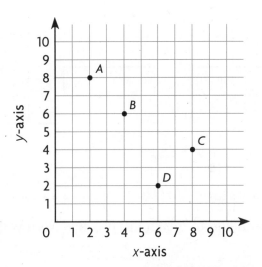

▶ **Missing Factors** Find the missing factor.

3. _____ × 8 = 16   4. _____ × 4 = 32   5. 10 × _____ = 50   6. 9 × _____ = 54

▶ **Solve One-Step Equations** Which of the numbers 3, 4, or 5 is the solution of the equation?

7. $20 + b = 24$ 8. $16 - r = 13$ 9. $6y = 30$ 10. $t \div 4 = 1$

_____   _____   _____   _____

MATH DETECTIVE

WITH

CARMEN SANDIEGO™

Angie finds a treasure map. Be a Math Detective and use the clues to find the location of the treasure. Write the location as an ordered pair.

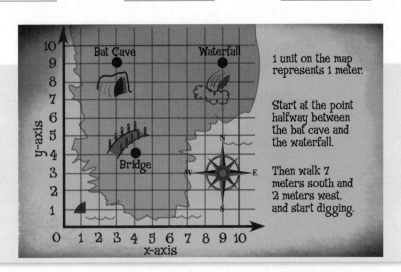

1 unit on the map represents 1 meter.

Start at the point halfway between the bat cave and the waterfall.

Then walk 7 meters south and 2 meters west, and start digging.

Vocabulary Builder

▶ Visualize It

Use the review words to complete the tree diagram.
You may use some words more than once.

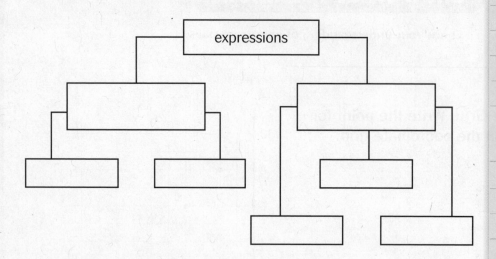

Review Words

algebraic expressions

numbers

numerical expressions

operations

variables

Preview Words

function

inequality

inverse operations

linear equation

origin

sequence

x-coordinate

y-coordinate

▶ Understand Vocabulary

Draw a line to match the preview word with its definition.

Preview Words

1. function

2. inequality

3. inverse operations

4. linear equation

5. sequence

6. *x*-coordinate

7. *y*-coordinate

Definitions

• operations that undo each other

• a list of numbers that often form a pattern

• an input-output relationship that has exactly one output for each input

• a mathematical statement that compares two expressions by using the symbol $<$, $>$, $\leq$, $\geq$, or $\neq$

• the point where the axes in the coordinate plane intersect

• the first number in an ordered pair

• the second number in an ordered pair

• an equation whose solutions form a straight line on the coordinate plane

GO Online • eStudent Edition • Multimedia eGlossary

Name _____

Words and Equations

Essential Question How do you write an equation to represent a situation?

An **equation** is a statement that two mathematical expressions are equal. These are examples of equations:

$$8 + 12 = 20 \qquad 14 = a - 3 \qquad d \div 2 = 7$$

 UNLOCK the Problem REAL WORLD

A circus recently spent $1,650 on new trapezes. The trapezes cost $275 each. Write an equation that could be used to find the number of trapezes *t* that the circus bought.

- Underline the information that you need to write the equation.
- What expression could you use to find the cost of *t* trapezes?

_____

🔑 **Write an equation for the situation.**

Think:

Cost per trapeze	times	number of trapezes	equals	total cost.
↓	↓	↓	↓	↓
_____	×	*t*	=	_____

So, an equation that could be used to find the number of

trapezes *t* is _____.

Try This! Ben is making a recipe for salsa that calls for $3\frac{1}{2}$ cups of tomatoes. He chops 4 tomatoes, which fill $2\frac{1}{4}$ cups. Write an equation that could be used to find how many more cups *c* that Ben needs.

Think:

Cups filled	plus	cups needed	equals	total cups for recipe.
↓	↓	↓	↓	↓
_____	+	_____	=	_____

So, an equation that could be used to find the number of additional

cups *c* is _____.

Math Talk Describe another equation you could use to model the problem.

🔑 Example 1 Write an equation for the word sentence.

Ⓐ Six fewer than a number is 46.33.

Think: Let n represent the unknown number. The phrase "fewer than" indicates

_____.

Six fewer than a number   is   46.33.

↓   ↓   ↓

_____ − _____ = _____

> **! ERROR Alert**
>
> The expression $n - 6$ means
> "6 fewer than n." The expression
> $6 - n$ means "n fewer than 6."

Ⓑ Two-thirds of the cost of the sweater is $18.

Think: Let c represent the _____ of the sweater in dollars. The word "of"

indicates _____.

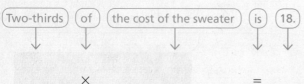

Two-thirds   of   the cost of the sweater   is   18.

↓   ↓   ↓   ↓   ↓

_____ × _____ = _____

🔑 Example 2 Write two word sentences for the equation.

Ⓐ $a + 15 = 24$

• The _____ of a and 15 _____ 24.

• 15 _____ than a _____ 24.

Ⓑ $r \div 0.2 = 40$

• The _____ of r and 0.2 _____ 40.

• r _____ by 0.2 _____ 40.

---

1. **Explain** how you can rewrite the equation $n + 8 = 24$ so that it involves subtraction rather than addition.

_____

_____

2. One student wrote $18 \times d = 54$ for the sentence "The product of 18 and d equals 54." Another student wrote $d \times 18 = 54$ for the same sentence. Are both students correct? **Justify** your answer.

_____

_____

Name _____

Share and Show

1. Write an equation for the word sentence "25 is 13 more than a number."

   What operation does the phrase "more than" indicate? _____

   The equation is _____ = _____ + _____.

Write an equation for the word sentence.

✓ 2. The difference of a number and 2 is $3\frac{1}{3}$.

3. Ten times the number of balloons is 120.

_____

_____

Write a word sentence for the equation.

✓ 4. $x - 0.3 = 1.7$

5. $25 = \frac{1}{4}n$

_____

_____

> **Math Talk** Describe how an equation differs from an expression.

On Your Own

Write an equation for the word sentence.

6. The quotient of a number and 20.7 is 9.

7. 24 less than the number of snakes is 35.

_____

_____

8. $18\frac{1}{2}$ is 75 more than a number.

9. d degrees warmer than 50 degrees is 78 degrees.

_____

_____

Write a word sentence for the equation.

10. $15g = 135$

11. $w \div 3.3 = 0.6$

_____

_____

Problem Solving  REAL WORLD

The distance in miles a car can travel on a certain amount of gas can be found by multiplying the car's fuel efficiency in miles per gallon by the gas used in gallons. Use this information and the table for 12–13.

Fuel Efficiency		
Vehicle	Miles per gallon, city	Miles per gallon, highway
Hybrid SUV	36	31
Minivan	19	26
Sedan	20	28
SUV	22	26

12. Write an equation that could be used to find how many miles a hybrid SUV can travel in the city on 20 gallons of gas.

_____

13. A sedan traveled 504 miles on the highway on a full tank of gas. Write an equation that could be used to find the number of gallons the tank holds.

_____

· · · · · · · SHOW YOUR WORK · · · · ·

14. George Washington was born in 1732. Thomas Jefferson was born 11 years after George Washington. Write an equation that could be used to find the year in which Thomas Jefferson was born.

_____

15. **H.O.T.** A magazine has 110 pages. There are 23 full-page ads and 14 half-page ads. The rest of the magazine consists of articles. Write an equation that can be used to find the number of pages of articles in the magazine.

_____

16. **What's the Error?** Tony is traveling 560 miles to visit his cousins. He travels 313 miles the first day. He says that he can use the equation $m - 313 = 560$ to find the number of miles he has left on his trip. Describe Tony's error.

_____

17. ⭐ **Test Prep** The Vikings scored 7 more points than the Ravens. The Vikings scored 34 points. Which equation could be used to find the number of points p that the Ravens scored?

(A) $p - 7 = 34$ (C) $p + 7 = 34$

(B) $p - 34 = 7$ (D) $p + 34 = 7$

Name _____

Model and Solve Addition Equations

Essential Question How can you use models to solve addition equations?

A **solution of an equation** is a value of a variable that makes an equation true.

$x + 3 = 5$ $x = 2$ is a solution because $2 + 3 = 5$.

You can use algebra tiles to help you find solutions of equations.

Algebra Tiles

x tile   1 tile

Investigate

Materials ▪ MathBoard, algebra tiles

Katheryn has $2. She wants to buy a poster that costs $7. Model and solve the equation $x + 2 = 7$ to find the amount x in dollars that Katheryn needs to save in order to buy the poster.

A. Draw 2 rectangles on your MathBoard to represent the two sides of the equation.

B. Use algebra tiles to model the equation. Model $x + 2$ in the left rectangle, and model 7 in the right rectangle.

C. To solve the equation, get the x tile by itself on one side. If you remove a tile from one side, you can keep the two sides equal by removing the same type of tile from the other side.

- How many 1 tiles do need to remove from each side to

  get the x tile by itself on the left side? _____

- When the x tile is by itself on the left side, how many

  1 tiles are on the right side? _____

D. Write the solution of the equation: $x =$ _____.

So, Katheryn needs to save $ _____ in order to buy the poster.

Math Talk Tell what operation you modeled when you removed tiles.

Draw Conclusions

1. **Describe** how you could use your model to check your solution.

   _____

   _____

   _____

2. Tell how you could use algebra tiles to model the equation $x + 4 = 8$.

   _____

   _____

3. **H.O.T.** **Synthesis** What would you do to solve the equation
   $x + 9 = 12$ without using a model?

   _____

Make Connections

You can solve an equation by drawing a model to represent algebra tiles.

Let a rectangle represent the variable. Let a small square represent 1.

Solve the equation $x + 3 = 7$.

STEP 1

Draw a model of the equation.

STEP 2

Get the variable by itself on one side of the model by doing the same thing to both sides.

Cross out _____ squares on the left side and

_____ squares on the right side.

STEP 3

Draw a model of the solution.

There is 1 rectangle on the left side. There are

_____ squares on the right side.

So, the solution of the equation $x + 3 = 7$ is $x =$ _____.

Math Talk Discuss which approach you prefer to solve equations, using algebra tiles or drawing a model.

© Houghton Mifflin Harcourt Publishing Company

Name _____

Share and Show ·

Model and solve the equation by using algebra tiles.

1. $x + 5 = 7$ _____ | **② 2.** $8 = x + 1$ _____ | **3.** $x + 2 = 5$ _____

4. $x + 6 = 8$ _____ | **5.** $5 + x = 9$ _____ | **6.** $5 = 4 + x$ _____

Solve the equation by drawing a model.

7. $x + 1 = 5$ _____ | **② 8.** $3 + x = 4$ _____

9. $6 = x + 4$ _____ | **10.** $8 = 2 + x$ _____

11. **Write Math** ▶ **Describe** how you would draw a model to solve
the equation $x + 5 = 10$.

_____

_____

_____

_____

Problem Solving  REAL WORLD

12. A movie ticket in the evening costs $9, which is $3 more than in the afternoon. The equation $9 = 3 + c$ can be used to find the cost c in dollars of an afternoon movie ticket. Solve the equation. Then tell what the solution means.

_____

_____

13. The table shows how long several animals have been at a zoo. The giraffe has been at the zoo 4 years longer than the mountain lion. Write and solve an addition equation to find how long the mountain lion has been at the zoo.

Zoo Animals	
Animal	**Time at zoo (years)**
Giraffe	5
Hippopotamus	6
Kangaroo	2
Zebra	9

_____

14. A standard guitar has 6 strings, which is 2 more strings than a violin has. Write and solve an addition equation to find the number of strings a violin has.

· · · · · · **SHOW YOUR WORK**

_____

15. The Maple Leafs beat the Blue Jackets by 3 goals. The Maple Leafs scored 6 goals. Write and solve an addition equation to find the Blue Jackets' score.

_____

16. **H.O.T.** **Sense or Nonsense?** Gabriela is solving the equation $x + 1 = 6$. She says that the solution must be less than 6. Is Gabriela's statement sense or nonsense? Explain.

_____

_____

17. ⭐ **Test Prep** The length of a photo is 3 inches longer than its width. The equation $14 = 3 + w$ can be used to find the photo's width w in inches. What is the width of the photo?

Ⓐ 8 inches

Ⓑ 11 inches

Ⓒ 17 inches

Ⓓ 20 inches

FOR MORE PRACTICE:
Standards Practice Book, pp. P185–P186

Solve Addition and Subtraction Equations

Essential Question How do you solve addition and subtraction equations?

CONNECT To solve an equation, you must get the variable on one side of the equal sign by itself. You have solved equations by using models. You can also solve equations by using Properties of Equality.

Subtraction Property of Equality	$3 + 4 = 7$
If you subtract the same number from both sides of an equation, the two sides will remain equal.	$3 + 4 - 4 = 7 - 4$ $3 + 0 = 3$ $3 = 3$

 UNLOCK the Problem REAL WORLD

The longest distance jumped on a pogo stick is 23 miles. Emilio has jumped 5 miles on a pogo stick. The equation $d + 5 = 23$ can be used to find the remaining distance d in miles he must jump to match the record. Solve the equation, and explain what the solution means.

🔑 **Solve the addition equation.**

To get d by itself, you must undo the addition by 5. Operations that undo each other are called **inverse operations**. Subtracting 5 is the inverse operation of adding 5.

Write the equation. $d + 5 = 23$

Use the Subtraction Property of Equality. $d + 5 - 5 = 23 - \underline{\hspace{1cm}}$

Subtract. $d + 0 = \underline{\hspace{1cm}}$

Use the Identity Property of Addition. $\underline{\hspace{1cm}} = 18$

Check the solution.

Write the equation. $d + 5 = 23$

Replace d with _____. $\underline{\hspace{1cm}} + 5 = 23$

The solution checks. $\underline{\hspace{1cm}} = 23$

So, the solution means that Emilio must jump _____ more miles.

Math Talk Explain how you know what number to subtract from both sides of the equation.

When you solve an equation that involves subtraction, you can use addition to get the variable on one side of the equal sign by itself.

Addition Property of Equality	
If you add the same number to both sides of an equation, the two sides will remain equal.	$7 - 4 = 3$ $7 - 4 + 4 = 3 + 4$ $7 + 0 = 7$ $7 = 7$

 Example

While cooking dinner, Carla pours $\frac{5}{8}$ cup of milk from a carton. This leaves $\frac{7}{8}$ cup of milk in the carton. Write and solve an equation to find how much milk was in the carton when Carla started cooking.

STEP 1 Write an equation.

Let *a* represent the amount of milk in cups in the carton when Carla started cooking.

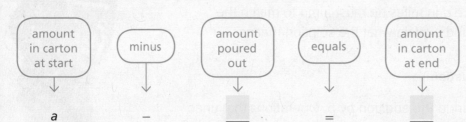

amount in carton at start	minus	amount poured out	equals	amount in carton at end
a	$-$	___	$=$	___

STEP 2 Solve the equation.

Think: $\frac{5}{8}$ is subtracted from *a*, so add $\frac{5}{8}$ to both sides to undo the subtraction.

Write the equation.

$$a - \frac{5}{8} = \frac{7}{8}$$

Use the Addition Property of Equality.

$$a - \frac{5}{8} + \underline{} = \frac{7}{8} + \underline{}$$

Add.

$$a = \underline{}$$

Write the fraction greater than 1 as a mixed number, and simplify.

$$a = \underline{}$$

So, there were _____ cups of milk in the carton when Carla started cooking.

Math Talk Explain how you can check the solution of the equation.

Name _____

Share and Show . . . .

1. Solve the equation $n + 35 = 80$.

$$n + 35 = 80$$

$$n + 35 - 35 = 80 - \underline{\quad\quad}$$ Use the _____ Property of Equality.

$$n = \underline{\quad\quad}$$ Subtract.

Solve the equation, and check the solution.

2. $16 + x = 42$

3. $y + 6.2 = 9.1$

4. $m + \dfrac{3}{10} = \dfrac{7}{10}$

_____

5. $z - \dfrac{1}{3} = 1\dfrac{2}{3}$

6. $12 = x - 24$

7. $25.3 = w - 14.9$

_____

Math Talk Explain how to get the variable by itself on one side of a subtraction equation.

On Your Own . . . .

Practice: Copy and Solve Solve the equation, and check the solution.

8. $y - \dfrac{3}{4} = \dfrac{1}{2}$

9. $75 = n + 12$

10. $m + 16.8 = 40$

11. $w - 36 = 56$

12. $8\dfrac{2}{5} = d + 2\dfrac{2}{5}$

13. $8.7 = r - 1.4$

14. The temperature dropped 8 degrees between 6:00 P.M. and midnight. The temperature at midnight was 26°F. Write and solve an equation to find the temperature at 6:00 P.M.

_____

15. H.O.T. Write an addition equation that has the solution $x = 9$.

_____

16. In July, Kimberly made two deposits into her bank account. She made no withdrawals. At the end of July, her account balance was $120.62. Write and solve an equation to find Kimberly's balance at the beginning of July.

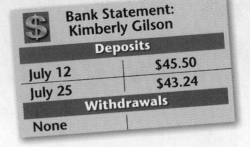

Bank Statement: Kimberly Gilson

Deposits	
July 12	$45.50
July 25	$43.24
Withdrawals	
None	

a. What do you need to find?

_____

_____

b. What information do you need from the bank statement?

_____

_____

c. Write an equation you can use to solve the problem. Explain what the variable represents.

_____

_____

_____

d. Solve the equation. Show your work and describe each step.

e. Write Kimberly's balance at the beginning of July.

_____

17. ⭐ **Test Prep** The equation $h - 120 = 80$ may be used to find the original height h in feet of an elevator before it descended. What was the original height of the elevator?

(A) 40 feet

(B) 100 feet

(C) 160 feet

(D) 200 feet

18. ⭐ **Test Prep** Colin adds $2\frac{3}{4}$ quarts of orange juice to some apple juice to make $4\frac{1}{4}$ quarts of fruit punch. He solves the equation $a + 2\frac{3}{4} = 4\frac{1}{4}$ to find the amount a of apple juice in quarts in the punch. What is the solution of the equation?

(A) $a = \frac{1}{2}$ (C) $a = 2\frac{1}{2}$

(B) $a = 1\frac{1}{2}$ (D) $a = 7$

Name _____

Model and Solve Multiplication Equations

Essential Question How can you use models to solve multiplication equations?

You can use algebra tiles to model and solve equations that involve multiplication.

Algebra Tiles

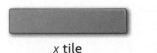

x tile   1 tile

4*x*

To model an expression involving multiplication of a variable, you can use more than one *x* tile. For example, to model the expression 4*x*, you can use four *x* tiles.

Investigate

Materials ■ MathBoard, algebra tiles

Tennis balls are sold in cans of 3 tennis balls each. Anitra needs 15 tennis balls for a tournament. Model and solve the equation $3x = 15$ to find the number of cans *x* that Anitra should buy.

A. Draw 2 rectangles on your MathBoard to represent the two sides of the equation.

B. Use algebra tiles to model the equation. Model 3*x* in the left rectangle, and model 15 in the right rectangle.

C. There are three *x* tiles on the left side of your model. To solve the equation by using the model, you need to find the value of one *x* tile. To do this, divide each side of your model into 3 equal groups.

- When the tiles on each side have been divided into 3 equal groups, how many 1 tiles are in each group on

  the right side? _____

D. Write the solution of the equation: $x = $ _____.

So, Anitra should buy _____ cans of tennis balls.

Math Talk Tell what operation you modeled in Step C.

Draw Conclusions

1. **Explain** how you could use your model to check your solution.

_____

_____

_____

2. **Describe** how you could use algebra tiles to model the equation $6x = 12$.

_____

3. **H.O.T.** **Synthesis** What would you do to solve the equation $5x = 35$ without using a model?

_____

Make Connections

You can also solve multiplication equations by drawing a model to represent algebra tiles. Let a rectangle represent x. Let a square represent 1. Solve the equation $2x = 6$.

STEP 1 Draw a model of the equation.

STEP 2 Find the value of one rectangle.

Divide each side of the model into _____ equal groups.

STEP 3 Draw a model of the solution.

There is 1 rectangle on the left side. There

are _____ squares on the right side.

So, the solution of the equation $2x = 6$ is $x =$ _____.

Math Talk Explain why you divided each side of the model into 2 equal groups.

Name _____

Share and Show

Model and solve the equation by using algebra tiles.

1. $4x = 16$

_____

2. $3x = 12$

_____

3. $4 = 4x$

_____

4. $3x = 9$

_____

5. $2x = 10$

_____

6. $15 = 5x$

_____

Solve the equation by drawing a model.

7. $4x = 8$ _____

8. $3x = 18$ _____

9. $12 = 2x$ _____

10. $2x = 16$ _____

11. **Write Math** ▶ **Explain** the steps you use to solve a multiplication equation with algebra tiles.

_____

_____

_____

_____

Problem Solving REAL WORLD

The bar graph shows the number of countries that competed in the first four modern Olympic Games. Use the bar graph for 12–13.

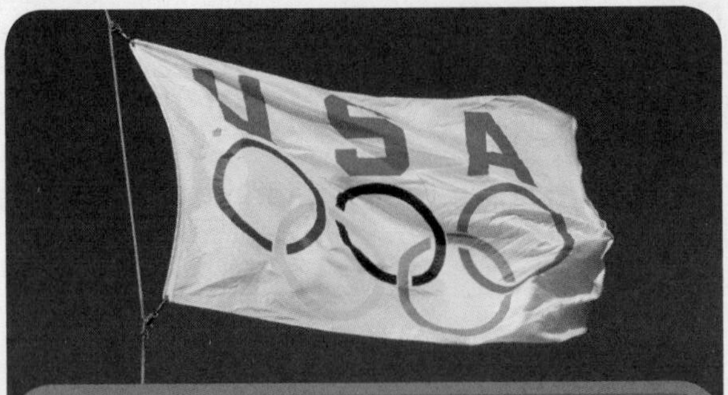

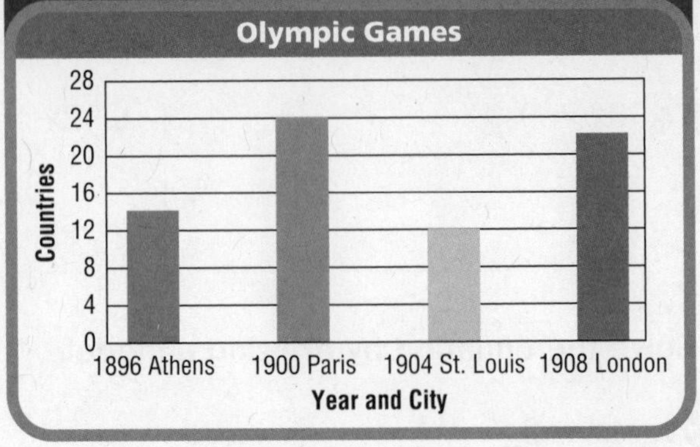

Olympic Games
Countries
28
24
20
16
12
8
4
0
1896 Athens
1900 Paris
1904 St. Louis
1908 London
Year and City

12. Naomi is doing a report about the 1900 Olympic Games. Each page will contain information about 4 of the countries that competed. Write and solve an equation to find the number of pages Naomi will need.

____

13. H.O.T. **Pose a Problem** Use the information in the bar graph to write and solve a problem involving a multiplication equation.

____

____

____

____

____

14. The equation $7s = 21$ can be used to find the number of snakes s in each cage at a zoo. Solve the equation. Then tell what the solution means.

____

15. Write Math ▶ **Explain** how solving an addition equation is similar to solving a multiplication equation.

____

____

____

____

16. ★ **Test Prep** What is the solution of the equation $2x = 8$?

Ⓐ $x = 2$ Ⓒ $x = 8$

Ⓑ $x = 4$ Ⓓ $x = 16$

SHOW YOUR WORK

 FOR MORE PRACTICE: Standards Practice Book, pp. P189–P190

Solve Multiplication and Division Equations

Essential Question How do you solve multiplication and division equations?

CONNECT You can use Properties of Equality and inverse operations to solve multiplication and division equations.

Division Property of Equality	$2 \times 6 = 12$
If you divide both sides of an equation by the same nonzero number, the two sides will remain equal.	$\dfrac{2 \times 6}{2} = \dfrac{12}{2}$
	$1 \times 6 = 6$
	$6 = 6$

 ## UNLOCK the Problem REAL WORLD

Mei ran 14 laps around a track for a total of 4,200 meters. The equation $14d = 4,200$ can be used to find the distance d in meters she ran in each lap. Solve the equation, and explain what the solution means.

Solve a multiplication equation.

To get d by itself, you must undo the multiplication by 14. Dividing by 14 is the inverse operation of multiplying by 14.

Write the equation.

$$14d = 4,200$$

Use the Division Property of Equality.

$$\frac{14d}{\rule{1cm}{0.4pt}} = \frac{4,200}{\rule{1cm}{0.4pt}}$$

Divide.

$$1 \times d = \rule{2cm}{0.4pt}$$

Use the Identity Property of Multiplication.

$$\rule{1.5cm}{0.4pt} = 300$$

Check the solution.

Write the equation. $\hspace{3cm} 14d = 4,200$

Replace d with _____. $\hspace{1cm} 14 \times \rule{2.5cm}{0.4pt} = 4,200$

The solution checks. $\hspace{3cm} \rule{2.5cm}{0.4pt} = 4,200$

So, the solution means that Mei ran _____ meters in each lap.

Math Talk Explain how you know what number to divide both sides of the equation by.

🔐 Example 1 Solve the equation $\frac{2}{3}n = \frac{1}{4}$.

Think: n is multiplied by $\frac{2}{3}$, so divide both sides by $\frac{2}{3}$ to undo the division.

Write the equation.

$$\frac{2}{3}n = \frac{1}{4}$$

Use the _____ Property of Equality.

$$\frac{2}{3}n \div \frac{2}{3} = \frac{1}{4} \div \frac{\square}{\square}$$

To divide by $\frac{2}{3}$, multiply by its reciprocal.

$$\frac{2}{3}n \times \frac{3}{2} = \frac{1}{4} \times \frac{\square}{\square}$$

Multiply.

$$n = \frac{\square}{\square}$$

Multiplication Property of Equality

If you multiply both sides of an equation by the same number, the two sides will remain equal.

$$\frac{12}{4} = 3$$
$$4 \times \frac{12}{4} = 4 \times 3$$
$$1 \times 12 = 12$$
$$12 = 12$$

🔐 Example 2

A biologist divides a water sample equally among 8 test tubes. Each test tube contains 24.5 milliliters of water. Write and solve an equation to find the total volume of the water sample.

STEP 1 Write an equation. Let v represent the total volume in milliliters.

Think: The total volume divided by 8 equals the volume in each test tube.

$$\frac{v}{\square} = \underline{\hspace{2cm}}$$

STEP 2 Solve the equation. v is divided by 8, so multiply both sides by 8 to undo the division.

Write the equation.

$$\frac{v}{8} = 24.5$$

Use the _____ Property of Equality.

$$\underline{\hspace{1cm}} \times \frac{v}{8} = \underline{\hspace{1cm}} \times 24.5$$

Multiply.

$$v = \underline{\hspace{2cm}}$$

So, the total volume of the water sample is _____ milliliters.

Math Talk Explain how you can use the Multiplication Property of Equality to solve Example 1.

Name _____

Share and Show

. . . .

1. Solve the equation $2.5m = 10$.

$$2.5m = 10$$

$$\frac{2.5m}{2.5} = \frac{10}{}$$ Use the _____ Property of Equality.

$$m = \underline{}$$ Divide.

Solve the equation, and check the solution.

2. $3x = 210$

3. $2.8 = 4t$

✓ **4.** $\frac{1}{3}n = 15$

5. $\frac{1}{2}y = \frac{1}{10}$

✓ **6.** $25 = \frac{a}{5}$

7. $1.3 = \frac{c}{4}$

> **Math Talk** **Explain** how to get the variable by itself on one side of a division equation.

On Your Own

. . . .

Practice: Copy and Solve Solve the equation, and check the solution.

8. $150 = 6m$

9. $\frac{4}{5}n = 8$

10. $4 = \frac{p}{15}$

11. $14.7 = \frac{b}{7}$

12. $2t = 18.6$

13. $\frac{1}{4} = \frac{3}{5}s$

14. In a serving of 8 fluid ounces of pomegranate juice, there are 32.8 grams of carbohydrates. Write and solve an equation to find the amount of carbohydrates in each fluid ounce of the juice.

_____

15. Write a division equation that has the solution $x = 16$.

_____

Problem Solving · REAL WORLD

What's the Error?

16. Melinda has a block of clay that weighs 14.4 ounces. She divides
    the clay into 6 equal pieces. To find the weight w in ounces of each
    piece, Melinda solved the equation $6w = 14.4$.

Look at how Melinda solved the equation. Find her error.

Correct the error. Solve the equation, and explain your steps.

This is how Melinda solved the equation:

$$6w = 14.4$$

$$\frac{6w}{6} = 6 \times 14.4$$

$$w = 86.4$$

Melinda concludes that each piece of clay weighs
86.4 ounces.

So, $w =$ _____.

This means each piece of clay weighs _____.

- **Describe** the error that Melinda made.

  _____

  _____

- **Explain** how Melinda could have recognized that her answer was
  not reasonable.

  _____

  _____

  _____

- **Explain** how you know that your solution is correct.

  _____

  _____

FOR MORE PRACTICE:
Standards Practice Book, pp. P191–P192

Name _____

Work Backward · Two-Step Equations

Essential Question How can you solve two-step equations by working backward?

🔑 UNLOCK the Problem · REAL WORLD

Olivia orders 5 sets of beads. She pays $7 for shipping, and the total cost of the order is $52. Solve the equation $5p + 7 = 52$ to find the price p in dollars of each set of beads.

Use the graphic organizer to help you solve the problem.

Read the Problem

What do I need to find?	What information do I need to use?	How will I use the information?
I need to find _____ _____.	I need to solve the equation _____.	I will work backward to get _____ by itself on one side of the equation.

Solve the Problem

The equation uses the operations of multiplication and _____.

By the order of operations, the _____ is done before the addition. To undo the operations, reverse the order of operations.

First undo the _____, and then undo the multiplication.

Write the equation.	$5p + 7 = 52$
To undo the addition, subtract _____ from both sides.	$5p + 7 - 7 = 52 - \underline{}$
Subtract.	$5p = \underline{}$
To undo the multiplication, divide both sides by _____.	$\dfrac{5p}{5} = \dfrac{45}{}$
Divide.	$p = \underline{}$

So, the price of each set of beads is _____.

Math Talk Explain how you know that your answer is correct.

Try Another Problem

A group of friends buys 3 strawberry-banana smoothies. They use the coupon shown for one of the smoothies. The total cost after the coupon is applied is $6.20. Solve the equation $3p - 0.85 = 6.20$ to find the price p in dollars of each smoothie.

Take $0.85 off your next smoothie!

Read the Problem

What do I need to find?	What information do I need to use?	How will I use the information?

Solve the Problem

So, the price of each smoothie is _____.

Math Talk Explain how you can use estimation to check your answer.

- **Explain** how you decided the order in which to undo the operations.

_____

_____

Name _____

Share and Show

Tips
🔑 UNLOCK the Problem
✓ Underline important facts.
✓ Check your answer.

1. The deck of cards for a card game has 64 cards. Andrea deals the same number of cards to each of 4 players. There are 36 cards left over. Solve the equation $4c + 36 = 64$ to find the number of cards c dealt to each player.

   First, decide which operation to undo first. Undo the

   _____ before you undo the _____.

   Next, solve the equation.

   So, _____ cards are dealt to each player.

2. **H.O.T.** What if there were 28 cards left over? How many cards were dealt to each player? Explain.

   _____

   _____

3. Lee started a round on a game show with 65 points. He answered all 5 questions during the round correctly. Lee's score at the end of the round was 105 points. Solve the equation $65 + 5p = 105$ to find the number of points p that are won for each correct answer.

   _____

4. To repair a bike, a bike shop charges a fee of $11, plus $13 for each hour that the mechanic works on the bike. Minh paid $63 to have his bike fixed. Solve the equation $11 + 13h = 63$ to find the number of hours h the mechanic worked on Minh's bike.

   _____

On Your Own..

5. During May, Mr. Dixon deposited $720 into his savings account. He also withdrew $650 to buy a new computer and made two more deposits of $56 each. His account balance at the end of May was $290. What was the balance at the beginning of May?

_____

6. Three friends named Brad, Viktor, and Luis race each other. In how many different orders can the three friends finish?

_____

7. A formula for finding an object's weight m in pounds on Mars when you know its weight e in pounds on Earth is $m = \frac{3}{8}e$. On Earth, an astronaut weighs 130 pounds, and her spacesuit weighs 110 pounds. What would be the combined weight of the astronaut and her spacesuit on Mars?

_____

8. The numbers 7, 37, 179, and 477 contain at least one 7. How many whole numbers from 1 to 500 contain at least one 7?

_____

9. **H.O.T.** **Write Math** ▶ A jar contains only dimes and quarters. There are twice as many dimes as quarters in the jar. Is it possible for the jar to contain exactly $2.50? Why or why not?

_____

_____

_____

10. ⭐ **Test Prep** The membership fee to join a gym is $40. The monthly fee is $20. Ashley pays a total of $120 to the gym. The equation $20m + 40 = 120$ can be used to find the number of months m that Ashley can use the gym. For how many months can Ashley use the gym?

Ⓐ 2 months Ⓒ 6 months

Ⓑ 4 months Ⓓ 8 months.

Choose a STRATEGY

Work Backward
Solve a Simpler Problem
Choose an Operation
Use a Model
Use a Formula
Draw a Diagram

Testing a spacesuit in the Arizona desert

. . . . . **SHOW YOUR WORK** . . . .

Name _____

✓ Mid-Chapter Checkpoint

▶ **Vocabulary**

Choose the best term from the box.

1. A(n) _____ is a statement that two mathematical expressions are equal. (p. 369)

2. Adding 5 and subtracting 5 are _____. (p. 377)

▶ **Concepts and Skills**

Write an equation for the word sentence. (pp. 369–372)

3. The sum of a number and 4.5 is 8.2.

4. Three times the cost is $24.

Solve the equation, and check the solution. (pp. 373–376, 377–380, 381–384, 385–388)

5. $x + 9 = 11$

6. $n - 18 = 40$

7. $a + 2.4 = 7.8$

8. $b - \frac{1}{4} = 3\frac{1}{2}$

9. $3x = 27$

10. $\frac{1}{3}s = \frac{1}{5}$

11. $\frac{t}{4} = 16$

12. $\frac{w}{7} = 0.3$

Fill in the bubble to show your answer.

13. A stadium has a total of 18,000 seats. Of these, 7,500 are field seats, and the rest are grandstand seats. Which equation could be used to find the number of grandstand seats s? (pp. 369–372)

    (A) $s + 7{,}500 = 18{,}000$

    (B) $s - 7{,}500 = 18{,}000$

    (C) $s + 18{,}000 = 7{,}500$

    (D) $s - 18{,}000 = 7{,}500$

14. Aaron wants to buy a bicycle that costs $128. So far, he has saved $56. The equation $a + 56 = 128$ can be used to find the amount a in dollars that Aaron still needs to save. What is the solution of the equation? (pp. 377–380)

    (A) $a = 64$

    (B) $a = 72$

    (C) $a = 132$

    (D) $a = 184$

15. Ms. McNeil buys 2.4 gallons of gasoline. The total cost is $7.56. The equation $2.4p = 7.56$ can be used to find the price p in dollars of one gallon of gasoline. What is the price of one gallon of gasoline?

    (pp. 385–388)

    (A) $1.81

    (B) $2.40

    (C) $3.15

    (D) $5.16

16. A coach orders 6 baseball jerseys from a Web site. The total cost of the order is $98, including $8 for shipping. The equation $6c + 8 = 98$ can be used to find the cost c in dollars of each jersey. How much does each jersey cost? (pp. 389–392)

    (A) $8.33

    (B) $15.00

    (C) $16.33

    (D) $17.00

Patterns and Sequences

Essential Question How can you describe and extend patterns in sequences?

A **sequence** is a list of numbers that may form a pattern. Each number in a sequence is called a **term**.

 UNLOCK the Problem REAL WORLD

The sequence shows the total number of baseball cards in Felipe's collection each week: 4, 12, 20, 28,...

Write a possible rule for the sequence, and then use the rule to find the next 3 terms. What do these terms represent?

Describe and extend the sequence.

Look for a pattern. Compare each term with the next term.

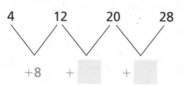

4   12   20   28

+8   +☐   +☐

A rule for the sequence is to add _____ to each term to get the next term.

Use the rule to find the next 3 terms.

$28 + 8 = $ _____

$36 + $ _____ $ = $ _____

$44 + $ _____ $ = $ _____

So, the next 3 terms are _____, _____, and _____, which

represent the number of cards in the 5th, _____, and _____ weeks.

Math Idea

If the terms of a sequence increase, the sequence may involve addition or multiplication of a whole number. If the terms decrease, the sequence may involve subtraction or division of a whole number.

Try This! Write a possible rule for the sequence, and then use the rule to find the missing term.

4.5, 3.9, 3.3, ☐, 2.1, 1.5,...

Look for a pattern. Compare each term with the next term.

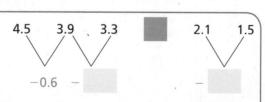

4.5   3.9   3.3   ☐   2.1   1.5

−0.6   −☐   −☐

A rule for the sequence is to subtract _____ from each term to get the next term.

Use the rule to find the missing term. $3.3 - $ _____ $ = $ _____

Math Talk Explain whether it is possible to write a rule for a sequence by looking at only the first two terms.

Sequences and Algebraic Expressions You can use a variable, such as *n*, to represent a term's position in a sequence.

🔑 Example 1 Write an algebraic expression to represent the *n*th term of the sequence 20, 40, 60, 80,.... Then use the expression to find the 10th term of the sequence.

Make a table and look for a pattern between the terms and their positions.

Position of Term	1	2	3	4
Value of Term	20	40	60	80

1×20 2×20 _____ $\times 20$ _____ $\times 20$

Think: You can find the value of each term by multiplying its

position by _____.

To find the *n*th term, multiply *n* by _____, or evaluate the

expression *n* × _____.

Now use the expression to find the 10th term.

Write the expression. $n \times 20$

Replace *n* with 10.   _____ $\times 20$

Multiply.   _____

So, the 10th term of the expression is _____.

Math Talk Explain why it can be useful to describe a sequence with an algebraic expression.

🔑 Example 2 The expression *n* ÷ 2 represents the *n*th term of a sequence. Use the expression to find the first 4 terms of the sequence.

Evaluate the expression *n* ÷ 2 for *n* = 1, 2, 3, and 4.

Write the expression.	$n \div 2$	$n \div 2$	$n \div 2$	$n \div 2$
Replace *n* with the term number.	$1 \div 2$	$2 \div 2$	_____ $\div 2$	_____ $\div 2$
Divide.	$\frac{1}{2}$	_____	_____	_____

So, the first 4 terms of the sequence are $\frac{1}{2}$, _____, _____, and _____.

Name _____

Share and Show

Write a possible rule for the sequence. Then use the rule to find the
next 3 terms.

1. 3, 6, 12, 24,...

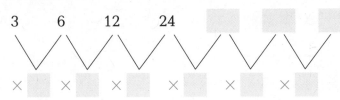

Multiply each term by _____ to get the next term.

✓ **2.** 6, $6\frac{2}{3}$, $7\frac{1}{3}$, 8,...

_____

_____

Write an algebraic expression to represent the *n*th term of the
sequence. Then use the expression to find the given term.

✓ **3.** 4, 5, 6, 7,...; 12th term

_____

4. 0.75, 1.5, 2.25, 3,...; 7th term

_____

5. The expression $n + 10$ represents the *n*th term of a sequence.
Use the expression to find the first 4 terms of the sequence.

_____

Math Talk Describe two different
ways to write a rule for the sequence
3, 1, $\frac{1}{3}$, $\frac{1}{9}$,....

On Your Own

Practice: Copy and Solve Write a possible rule for the sequence.
Then use the rule to find the missing term.

6. 100, 85, 70, ____, 40, 25,...

7. 500, 100, 20, ____, 0.8, 0.16,...

Practice: Copy and Solve Write an algebraic expression to represent
the *n*th term of the sequence. Then use the expression to find the
given term.

8. 97, 98, 99, 100,...; 50th term

9. $\frac{1}{5}$, $\frac{2}{5}$, $\frac{3}{5}$, $\frac{4}{5}$,...; 20th term

10. The expression $3n$ represents the *n*th term of a sequence. Use
the expression to find the first 4 terms of the sequence.

_____

Problem Solving

Caitlyn uses counters to make a sequence of arrays. The figure shows the first three arrays in the sequence. Use the figure for 11–12.

11. **H.O.T.** Write an algebraic expression to represent the number of counters in the *n*th array of the sequence.

_____

12. How many counters does Caitlyn need to make the 12th array in the sequence?

_____

13. The schedule shows the times that a bus is scheduled to stop near Jason's house. Jason misses the 8:32 bus. Based on the sequence shown in the schedule, what time is the next bus scheduled to arrive?

_____

14. A dance troupe practiced for 4 hours in January, 8 hours in February, 12 hours in March, and 16 hours in April. If the pattern continues, how many hours will they practice in September?

_____

SHOW YOUR WORK

15. **Write Math** Does the number 100 appear in the sequence 9, 18, 27, 36, 45,…? **Explain** how you determined your answer.

_____

_____

_____

16. ⭐ **Test Prep** Which could be a rule for the sequence 0.02, 0.2, 2, 20,…?

  Ⓐ Add 0.18 to each term to get the next term.

  Ⓑ Add 1.8 to each term to get the next term.

  Ⓒ Divide each term by 10 to get the next term.

  Ⓓ Multiply each term by 10 to get the next term.

FOR MORE PRACTICE:
Standards Practice Book, pp. P195–P196

Name _____

Functions, Equations, and Tables

Essential Question How can you use equations and tables to represent functions?

A **function** is an input-output relationship that has exactly one output for each input.

Some functions can be represented by an equation with two variables, such as $y = x + 3$. For each input value substituted for x, there is exactly one output value for y.

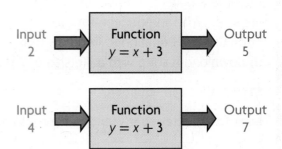

Input 2 → Function $y = x + 3$ → Output 5

Input 4 → Function $y = x + 3$ → Output 7

🔑 UNLOCK the Problem REAL WORLD

A skating rink charges $3.00 for each hour of skating, plus $1.75 to rent skates. Write an equation for the function that gives the total cost y in dollars for skating x hours. Then make a table that shows the cost of skating for 1, 2, 3, and 4 hours.

🔑 **Write an equation for the function, and use the equation to make a table.**

STEP 1 Write an equation.

Think:

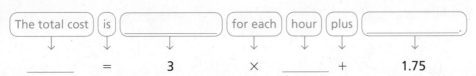

The total cost | is | _____ | for each | hour | plus | _____

_____ = 3 × _____ + 1.75

So, the equation for the function is _____.

STEP 2 Make a table.

Input Time (h), x	Rule $3x + 1.75$	Output Cost ($), y
1	$3 \times 1 + 1.75$	4.75
2		
3		
4		

Replace x with each input value, and then evaluate the function rule to find each output value.

Math Talk Explain how you could use the equation to find the total cost of skating for 6 hours.

© Houghton Mifflin Harcourt Publishing Company

🔒 Example

Jamal downloads songs on his MP3 player. The table shows how the time it takes him to download a song depends on the song's file size. Write an equation for the function shown in the table. Then use the equation to find how many seconds it takes Jamal to download a song with a file size of 7 megabytes.

Download Times	
File Size (MB), x	Time (s), y
4	48
5	60
6	72
7	?
8	96

STEP 1 Write an equation.

Look for a pattern between the file sizes and the download times.

File Size (MB), x	4	5	6	8
Time (s), y	48	60	72	96

Think: You can find each download time by multiplying the file size by _____.

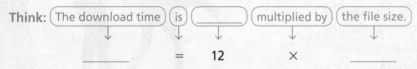

12×4 12×5 $12 \times$ _____ $12 \times$ _____

Think: (The download time) (is) (_____) (multiplied by) (the file size.)

_____ = 12 × _____

So, the equation for the function is _____.

STEP 2 Use the equation to find the download time for a file size of 7 megabytes.

Write the equation. $y = 12x$

Replace x with 7. $y = 12 \times$ _____

Solve for y. $y =$ _____

So, it takes Jamal _____ seconds to download a 7-megabyte song.

1. **Explain** how you can check that your equation for the function is correct.

_____

_____

2. **Describe** a situation in which it would be more useful to represent a function with an equation than with a table of values.

_____

_____

Name _____

Share and Show

Use the equation to complete the table.

1. $y = x + 3$

Input	Rule	Output
x	$x + 3$	y
6	$6 + 3$	
8	$8 + 3$	
10		

2. $y = 2x + 1$

Input	Output
x	y
4	
7	
10	

Write an equation for the function shown in the table. Then find the missing value in the table.

3.

x	1	2	3	4
y	6	12	?	24

_____

4.

x	9	11	13	15
y	4	6	8	?

_____

> **Math Talk** Explain how to write an equation for a function shown by a table of values.

On Your Own

5. It costs $6 to join an online DVD club and $2.50 to rent each DVD. Write an equation for the function that gives the total cost y in dollars for renting x DVDs. Then complete the table.

DVD Club Costs	
DVDs rented, x	Total cost ($), y
3	
4	
5	

_____

Write an equation for the function shown in the table. Then find the missing value in the table.

6.

x	8	9	10	11
y	16	18	?	22

_____

7.

x	10	20	30	40
y	5	10	15	?

_____

Connect to Reading

Cause and Effect

The reading skill *cause and effect* can help you understand how a change in one variable may create a change in another variable.

In karate, a person's skill level is often indicated by the color of his or her belt. At Sara's karate school, students must pass a test to move from one belt level to the next. Each test costs $23. Sara hopes to move up 3 belt levels this year. What effect will this plan have on her karate expenses?

Cause:		Effect:
Sara moves to higher belt levels.	→	Sara's karate expenses go up.

Write an equation for a function that relates the cause and effect. Then use the function to solve the problem.

Let *x* represent the number of belt levels Sara moves up, and let *y* represent the increase in dollars in her karate expenses.

Write the equation for the function. $y = \underline{\hspace{1cm}} \times x$

Sara plans to move up 3 levels, so replace *x* with _____. $y = 23 \times \underline{\hspace{1cm}}$

Solve for *y*. $y = \underline{\hspace{1cm}}$

So, if Sara moves up 3 belt levels this year, her karate expenses will

increase by $_____.

Write an equation for a function that relates the cause and effect. Then use the function to solve the problem.

8. Classes at Tony's karate school cost $29.50 per month. This year he plans to take 2 more months of classes than he did last year. What effect will this change have on Tony's karate expenses?

_____

_____

_____

9. A sporting goods store regularly sells karate uniforms for $35.90 each. The store is putting karate uniforms on sale for 10% off. What effect will the sale have on the price of a karate uniform?

_____

_____

_____

Name _____

Graph on a Coordinate Plane

Essential Question How do you graph points on a coordinate plane?

A **coordinate plane** is a plane formed by a horizontal number line called the **x-axis** that intersects a vertical number line called the **y-axis**. The axes intersect at 0 on both number lines. The point where the axes intersect is the **origin**.

An **ordered pair** is a pair of numbers, such as (3, 2), that can be used to locate a point on the coordinate plane. The first number is the **x-coordinate**; it tells the distance to move left or right from the origin. The second number is the **y-coordinate**; it tells the distance to move up or down from the origin. The ordered pair for the origin is (0, 0).

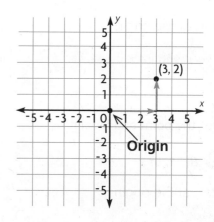

UNLOCK the Problem — REAL WORLD

A screen in a video game shows a coordinate plane. The points P, Q, R, and S represent treasure chests. Write the ordered pair for each treasure chest's location.

• If a point is to the left of the y-axis, is its x-coordinate positive or negative?

_____

 Find the coordinates of each point.

To find the coordinates of point P, start at the origin.

To find the x-coordinate, move right (positive) or left (negative).   Move 2 units to the _____.

To find the y-coordinate, move up (positive) or down (negative).   Move _____ units up.

Point P is located at (⁻2, _____).

Point Q is located at (_____, _____).

Point R is located at (_____, _____).

Point S is located at (_____, _____).

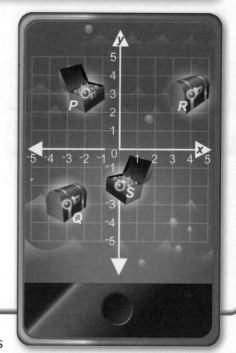

1. **Make a conjecture** about the x-coordinate of any point that lies on the y-axis.

_____

2. **Explain** why (2, 4) represents a different location than (4, 2).

_____

🔑 Example Graph and label the point on the coordinate plane.

Ⓐ A(4, ⁻1)

Start at the origin.

The x-coordinate is positive. Move _____ units to the right.

The y-coordinate is negative. Move 1 unit _____.

Plot the point and label it A.

Ⓑ B(⁻1, 0)

Start at the origin.

The x-coordinate is _____. Move _____ unit to the _____.

The y-coordinate is 0. The point lies on the _____-axis.

Plot the point and label it B.

Ⓒ C(5, 1½)

Start at the origin.

Move _____ units to the _____.

Move _____ units _____.

Plot the point and label it C.

Ⓓ D(2.5, 3.5)

Start at the origin.

Move _____ units to the _____.

Move _____ units _____.

Plot the point and label it D.

> **Math Talk** Describe the location of a point that has a positive x-coordinate and a negative y-coordinate.

Share and Show   ·

1. Write the ordered pair for point J.

   Start at the origin. Move _____ units to the _____

   and _____ units _____.

   The ordered pair is _____.

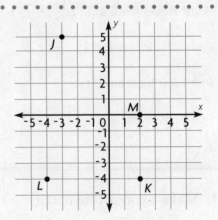

Write the ordered pair for the point.

2. K

✓ 3. L

4. M

404

Name _____

Share and Show 🖊 MATH BOARD ....

Graph and label the point on the coordinate plane.

5. $P(4, 10)$ 6. $Q(^-8, 1)$ 7. $R(0, 6)$

8. $S(^-4, ^-2)$ ✓9. $T(6, ^-8)$ 10. $U(3, 5)$

11. $V(^-2, 0)$ 12. $W(8, 0)$ 13. $X(0, ^-8)$

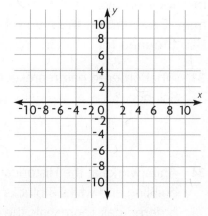

On Your Own ....

Math Talk Explain how graphing $(3, 2)$ is similar to and different from graphing $(3, ^-2)$.

Write the ordered pair for the point. Give approximate coordinates when necessary.

14. A 15. B 16. C

_____   _____   _____

17. D 18. E 19. F

_____   _____   _____

20. G 21. H 22. J

_____   _____   _____

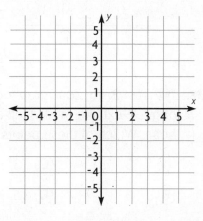

Graph and label the point on the coordinate plane.

23. $M(^-4, 0)$ 24. $N(2, 2)$ 25. $P(^-3, 3)$

26. $Q\left(0, 2\frac{1}{2}\right)$ 27. $R(0.5, 0.5)$ 28. $S\left(^-5, \frac{1}{2}\right)$

29. $T(0, 0)$ 30. $U\left(3\frac{1}{2}, 0\right)$ 31. $V(^-2, ^-4)$

32. A point lies to the left of the y-axis and below the x-axis. What can you conclude about the coordinates of the point?

_____

Problem Solving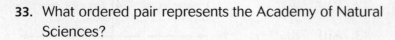

Many of the streets in downtown Philadelphia can be modeled by a coordinate plane, as shown on the map. Each unit on the map represents one block. Use the map for 33–35.

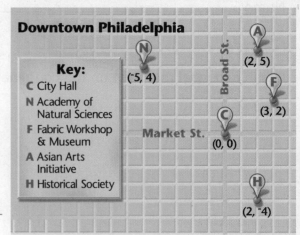

Downtown Philadelphia

Key:
C City Hall
N Academy of Natural Sciences
F Fabric Workshop & Museum
A Asian Arts Initiative
H Historical Society

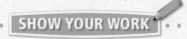

33. What ordered pair represents the Academy of Natural Sciences?

_____

34. Anita works at the Historical Society. She leaves the building and walks 3 blocks north to a restaurant. What ordered pair represents the restaurant?

_____

35. H.O.T. **Pose a Problem** Write and solve a new problem that uses a location on the map of Philadelphia.

_____

_____

_____

36. H.O.T. The points *A*, *B*, *C*, and *D* on a coordinate plane can be connected to form a rectangle. Point *A* is located at (2, 0), point *B* is located at (6, 0), and point *C* is located at (6, 2.5). Write the ordered pair for point *D*.

_____

37. Write Math ▸ **Explain** how you can tell that the line segment connecting two points is vertical without graphing the points.

_____

_____

38. ⭐ **Test Prep** Zena graphed a point by starting at the origin. Next she moved left and then up to plot the point. Which of these points could she have graphed?

(A) ($^-$3, $^-$5)   (C) (3, $^-$5)

(B) ($^-$5, 3)   (D) (5, 3)

. . . . **SHOW YOUR WORK** . . . . . .

FOR MORE PRACTICE:
Standards Practice Book, pp. P199–P200

Graph Functions

Essential Question How do you graph functions?

CONNECT You have learned that tables and equations are two ways to represent functions. You can also represent a function by using a graph.

🔑 UNLOCK the Problem REAL WORLD

A cafeteria has an automatic pancake-making machine. The table shows the relationship between the time in hours and the number of pancakes the machine can make. Graph the function represented by the table.

Pancake Production	
Time (hours)	Pancakes Made
1	200
2	400
3	600
4	800
5	1,000

 Use the table values to graph the function.

STEP 1 Write ordered pairs.

Let *x* represent the time in hours and *y* represent the number of pancakes made. Use each row of the table to write an ordered pair.

(1, 200) (2,_____) (3,_____) (____,_____) (____,_____)

STEP 2 Choose an appropriate scale for each axis of the graph. Label the axes and give the graph a title.

STEP 3 Graph a point for each ordered pair.

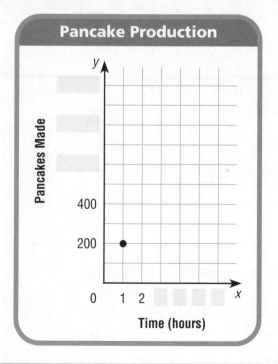

Math Talk Describe any patterns you notice in the set of points you graphed.

🔑 Example Graph the function represented by the table to find the missing value of *y*.

x	y
⁻1	5
0	3
1	?
2	⁻1
3	⁻3

STEP 1 Write ordered pairs.

Use each row of the table to write an ordered pair. Skip the row with the missing *y*-value.

(⁻1, 5)   (0, _____)   (2, _____)   (_____, _____)

STEP 2 Graph a point for each ordered pair on a coordinate plane.

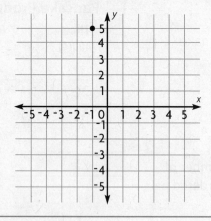

STEP 3 Find the missing *y*-value.

The points on the graph appear to lie on a line. Use a ruler to draw a dashed line through the points.

Use the line to find the *y*-value that corresponds to an *x*-value of 1. Start at the origin, and move 1 unit right. Move up until you reach the line you drew. Then move left to find the *y*-value on the *y*-axis.

So, when *x* has a value of 1, *y* has a value of _____.

1. **Describe** another way you could find the missing value of *y* in the table.

_____

_____

_____

2. **Describe** a situation in which it would be more useful to represent a function with a graph than with a table of values.

_____

_____

Name _____

Share and Show

Graph the function represented by the table.

1.

x	1	2	3	4
y	50	100	150	200

Write ordered pairs.
Then graph.

(1, 50)

(2, _____)

(3, _____)

(_____, _____)

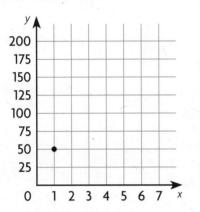

2.

x	20	40	60	80
y	100	200	300	400

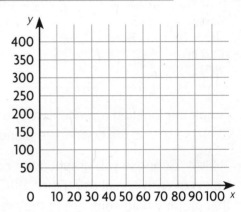

Graph the function represented by the table to find the missing value of y.

3.

x	⁻2	⁻1	0	1	2
y	5	3	1		⁻3

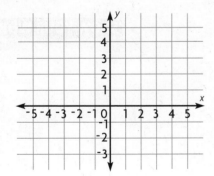

4.

x	⁻4	⁻2	0	2	4
y	⁻1	0	1		3

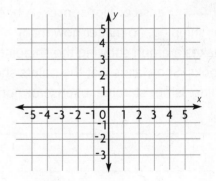

Math Talk Explain how to use a graph to find a missing y-value in a table.

On Your Own

Practice: Copy and Solve Graph the function represented by the table to find the missing value of y.

5.

x	⁻4	⁻2	0	2	4
y	1	0		⁻2	⁻3

6.

x	⁻3	⁻2	0	2	3
y	⁻10	⁻7	⁻1		8

Problem Solving REAL WORLD

The table at the right shows the typical price of a popular brand of corn cereal over time. Use the table for 7–9.

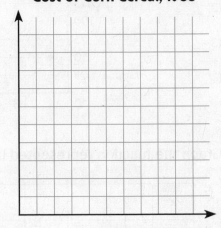

Price of Corn Cereal

Year	Price per box ($)
1968	0.39
1988	1.50
2008	4.50

7. Complete the table below to show the cost of buying 1 to 5 boxes of corn cereal in 1988.

Boxes	1	2	3	4	5
Cost in 1988 ($)	1.50				

8. Graph the function represented by the table you made in Exercise 7. Use the coordinate plane at right.

9. **H.O.T.** Suppose you graphed the cost of buying 1 to 5 boxes of corn cereal using the 2008 price. **Explain** how that graph would compare to the graph you made using the 1988 price.

_____

_____

_____

Cost of Corn Cereal, 1988

Cost ($)

Boxes

10. **H.O.T.** **Sense or Nonsense?** A bookstore charges $4 for shipping, no matter how many books you buy. Irena makes a graph showing the shipping cost for 1 to 5 books. She claims that the points she graphed lie on a line. Is her statement sense or nonsense? Explain.

_____

_____

_____

_____

SHOW YOUR WORK

11. ⭐ **Test Prep** DVDs cost $12 each. Jacob graphs the function that gives the cost *y* in dollars of buying *x* DVDs. Which ordered pair is a point on the graph of the function?

(A) (2, 24)   (C) (12, 1)

(B) (3, 4)   (D) (12, 12)

Name _____

Represent Linear Equations

Essential Question How can you represent linear equations?

The solution of an equation in two variables is an ordered pair that makes the equation true. For example, $(2, 5)$ is a solution of the equation $y = x + 3$ because $5 = 2 + 3$.

A **linear equation** is an equation whose solutions form a straight line on the coordinate plane. Any point on the line is a solution of the equation.

🔑 UNLOCK the Problem REAL WORLD

A blue whale is swimming at an average rate of 3 miles per hour. Write a linear equation for the function that gives the distance y in miles that the whale swims in x hours. Then graph the function.

 Write and graph a linear equation.

STEP 1 Write an equation for the function.

Think: [Distance] [equals] [rate] [multiplied by] [time.]

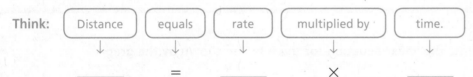

_____ = _____ × _____

STEP 2 Find ordered pairs that are solutions of the equation.

Choose several values of x and find the corresponding values of y.

x	3x	y	Ordered Pair
1	3 × 1	3	(1, 3)
2	3 ×		(2,)
3	3 ×		(,)
4	3 ×		(,)

STEP 3 Graph the function.

Graph the ordered pairs. Draw a line through the points to show all the solutions of the linear equation.

Distance Traveled by Blue Whale

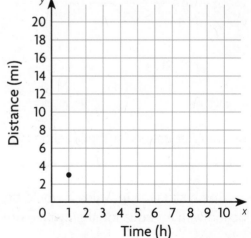

Distance (mi) — y-axis: 2, 4, 6, 8, 10, 12, 14, 16, 18, 20
Time (h) — x-axis: 0, 1, 2, 3, 4, 5, 6, 7, 8, 9, 10

Math Talk **Explain** why the graph does not show negative values of x or y.

🔓 Example 1 Graph the linear equation $y = x + 2$.

STEP 1 Find ordered pairs that are solutions of the equation.

Choose several values of x and find the corresponding values of y.

x	x + 2	y	Ordered Pair
⁻5	⁻5 + 2	⁻3	(⁻5, ⁻3)
⁻2	☐ + 2	☐	(⁻2, ☐)
0	☐ + 2	☐	(☐, ☐)
3	☐ + 2	☐	(☐, ☐)

STEP 2 Graph the equation.

Graph the ordered pairs. Draw a line through the points to show all the solutions of the linear equation.

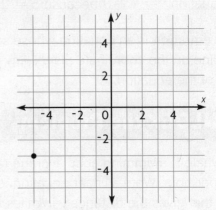

Math Talk **Explain** why the graph in Example 1 includes negative values of x and y.

🔓 Example 2 Write the linear equation for the function shown by the graph.

STEP 1 Use ordered pairs from the graph to complete the table of values below.

STEP 2 Look for a pattern in the table.

Compare each y-value with the corresponding x-value.

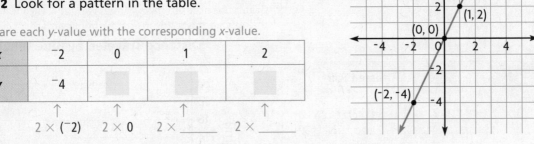

Think: Each y-value is _____ times the corresponding x-value.

So, the linear equation for the function is $y =$ _____.

- **Describe** a situation in which it would be more useful to represent a function with an equation than with a graph.

_____

_____

412

Name _____

Share and Show

Graph the linear equation.

1. $y = x - 2$

Make a table of
values. Then graph.

x	y
⁻2	⁻4
0	
2	
4	

2. $y = ⁻4x$

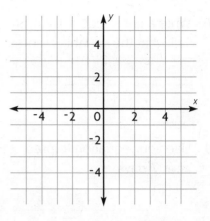

Write the linear equation for the function shown by the graph.

3.

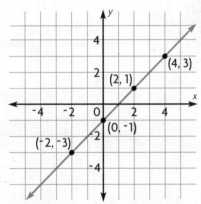

4.

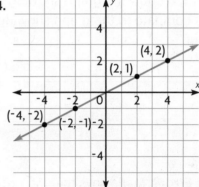

_____

_____

Math Talk Explain how you can tell
whether you have graphed a linear
equation correctly.

On Your Own

Practice: Copy and Solve Graph the linear equation.

5. $y = x + 1$

6. $y = ⁻2x - 1$

7. Write the linear equation for the function
shown by the graph.

_____

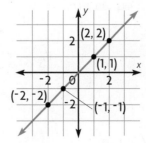

Problem Solving REAL WORLD

**The graph shows the growth of a bamboo plant.
Use the graph for 8–10.**

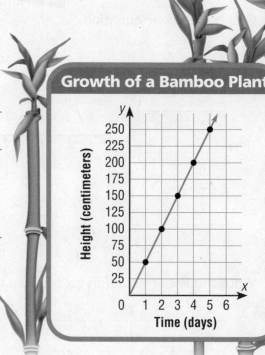

Growth of a Bamboo Plant

8. Write a linear equation for the function shown by the graph.
   Tell what the variables represent.

   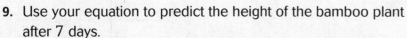

9. Use your equation to predict the height of the bamboo plant
   after 7 days.

   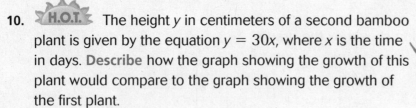

10. **H.O.T.** The height y in centimeters of a second bamboo
    plant is given by the equation $y = 30x$, where x is the time
    in days. **Describe** how the graph showing the growth of this
    plant would compare to the graph showing the growth of
    the first plant.

    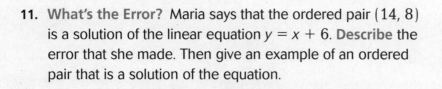

· · · · · **SHOW YOUR WORK** · · ·

11. **What's the Error?** Maria says that the ordered pair (14, 8)
    is a solution of the linear equation $y = x + 6$. **Describe** the
    error that she made. Then give an example of an ordered
    pair that is a solution of the equation.

    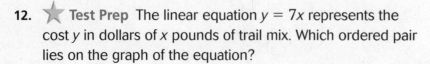

12. ⭐ **Test Prep** The linear equation $y = 7x$ represents the
    cost y in dollars of x pounds of trail mix. Which ordered pair
    lies on the graph of the equation?

    (A) (0, 7)

    (B) (3, 21)

    (C) (4, 11)

    (D) (7, 1)

FOR MORE PRACTICE:
Standards Practice Book, pp. P203–P204

Inequalities

Essential Question How do you solve and graph inequalities?

An **inequality** is a mathematical sentence that compares two expressions using the symbol $<$, $>$, $\leq$, $\geq$, or $\neq$.

A **solution of an inequality** is a value of the variable that makes the inequality true. For example, 3 is a solution of $x > 2$ because $3 > 2$ is a true statement. Inequalities may have more than one solution. You can use a number line to show all of the solutions of an inequality.

$x > 2$

The empty circle at 2 shows that 2 is not a solution. The shading to the right of 2 shows that values greater than 2 are solutions.

UNLOCK the Problem REAL WORLD

The highest temperature ever recorded at the South Pole was 8°F. Write and graph an inequality to show that the temperature t in degrees Fahrenheit at the South Pole is less than or equal to 8°F.

🔑 **Write an inequality and graph its solutions.**

STEP 1 Write an inequality.

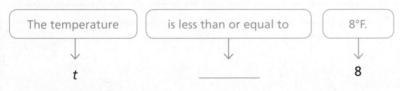

The temperature	is less than or equal to	8°F.
↓	↓	↓
t	_____	8

So, the inequality is _____.

_____

STEP 2 Graph the solutions of the inequality.

Draw a filled-in circle at 8 to show that 8 is a solution. Shade to the left of 8 to show that values less than 8 are also solutions.

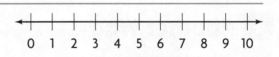

Math Talk Give three values of t that make the inequality true.

Solving inequalities is much like solving equations. To solve an inequality, get the variable on one side by itself by using the Properties of Inequality and inverse operations.

Addition and Subtraction Properties of Inequality	
You can add or subtract the same number on both sides of an inequality, and the inequality will still be true.	$3 + 2 < 8$ $3 + 2 - 2 < 8 - 2$ $3 + 0 < 6$ $3 < 6$

Multiplication and Division Properties of Inequality

You can multiply or divide both sides of an inequality by the same positive number, and the inequality will still be true.

$$2 \times 4 > 6$$
$$\frac{2 \times 4}{2} > \frac{6}{2}$$
$$1 \times 4 > 3$$
$$4 > 3$$

Example Solve and graph the inequality $x + 2 < 6$.

🔑 One Way Use a model.

STEP 1 Draw a model of the inequality.

Let a rectangle represent the variable. Let a square represent 1.

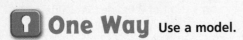

STEP 2 Get the variable by itself on one side of the model by doing the same thing to both sides.

Cross out _____ squares on the left side

and _____ squares on the right side.

STEP 3 Draw a model of the solution.

There is 1 rectangle on the left side. There are

_____ squares on the right side.

So, the solution of the inequality is _____.

🔑 Another Way Use inverse operations.

Write the inequality. $x + 2 < 6$

To undo the addition by 2, subtract _____ from each side. $x + 2 - 2 < 6 - $_____

Subtract. $x < $_____

So, the solution of the inequality is _____.

Graph the solutions of the inequality on the number line.

Draw an empty circle at _____ to show that 4 is not a solution.

Shade to the _____ of _____ to show that values less than 4

are solutions.

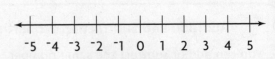

Math Talk Describe the inverse operation you would use to solve $3x < 18$.

Name _____

Share and Show

Write and graph an inequality for the situation.

1. The temperature t is less than 2°C. _____

   Draw an empty circle at _____ to show that 2 is not

   a solution. Shade to the _____ of _____ to show
   that values less than 2 are solutions.

2. The elevation e is greater than or equal to
   5 meters.

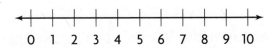

_____

Solve and graph the inequality.

3. $x + 3 < 4$

_____

4. $2s \leq 6$

_____

Math Talk Explain the difference
between $t \leq 4$ and $t < 4$.

On Your Own

Write and graph an inequality for the situation.

5. A passenger's age a is greater than 4 years.

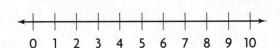

_____

6. The score s is less than or equal to 3.

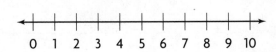

_____

Practice: Copy and Solve Solve and graph the inequality.

7. $n + 5 < 9$

8. $x - 1 \leq 0$

9. $7c > 7$

10. $\dfrac{m}{2} \geq 2$

Problem Solving

Use the table for 11–12.

11. Write an inequality relating the elevation e in meters of any other tunnel to the elevation of the Hitra Tunnel.

_____

12. Write an inequality relating the highest point h in meters of any other bridge to the highest point of the Millau Bridge.

_____

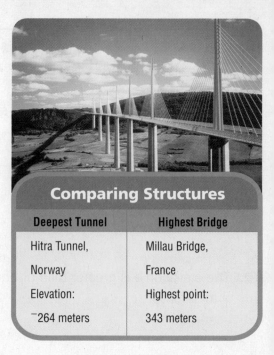

Comparing Structures

Deepest Tunnel	Highest Bridge
Hitra Tunnel, Norway	Millau Bridge, France
Elevation:	Highest point:
$^-264$ meters	343 meters

13. No one under 50 inches tall is allowed to ride a roller coaster. Belinda is 38 inches tall. The inequality $38 + n \geq 50$ can be used to find the number of inches n Belinda must grow to be allowed to ride the roller coaster. Solve the inequality. Explain what the solution means.

_____

SHOW YOUR WORK

14. **H.O.T.** An elephant weighs more than 30 times what a tiger weighs. The elephant weighs 12,000 pounds. Write and solve an inequality to find the possible weight w in pounds of the tiger.

_____

_____

15. **Write Math** ▶ Explain how you know whether to use a filled-in circle or an empty circle when graphing an inequality.

_____

_____

_____

16. ⭐ **Test Prep** The inequality $m + 12 \leq 20$ can be used to find the amount of money m in dollars that Nolan can spend at a circus. What is the greatest amount that Nolan can spend?

(A) $6 (C) $12

(B) $8 (D) $20

Name _____

 # Chapter 10 Review/Test

▶ Vocabulary

Choose the best term from the box.

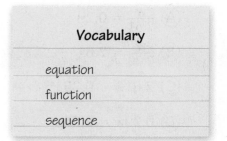

Vocabulary
equation
function
sequence

1. A(n) _____ is a list of numbers that often form a pattern. (p. 395)

2. A(n) _____ is an input-output relationship that has exactly one output for each input. (p. 399)

▶ Concepts and Skills

Solve the equation, and check the solution. (pp. 373–376, 377–380, 385–388)

3. $4 + x = 12$

4. $f - 2.3 = 18.4$

5. $\frac{2}{5}t = 12$

Write a possible rule for the sequence. Then use the rule to find the next 3 terms. (pp. 395–398)

6. 3.3, 4.1, 4.9, 5.7, _____, _____, _____, ...

7. $\frac{1}{8}, \frac{1}{4}, \frac{1}{2}, 1,$ _____, _____, _____, ...

Graph and label the point on the coordinate plane. (pp. 403–406)

8. $A(^-3, 2)$

9. $B(0, ^-4)$

10. $C(2, 1)$

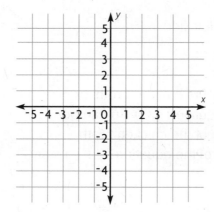

Fill in the bubble to show your answer.

11. One brand of cheddar cheese sells for $0.29 per ounce. Tanya bought a block of the cheese for $2.61. Which equation could be used to determine the weight w of the cheese in ounces? (pp. 369–372)

 (A) $\dfrac{w}{2.61} = 0.29$

 (B) $\dfrac{w}{0.29} = 2.61$

 (C) $2.61w = 0.29$

 (D) $0.29w = 2.61$

12. A helicopter descends 82 meters to an altitude of 45 meters. The equation $a - 82 = 45$ can be used to find the helicopter's starting altitude a in meters. What is the starting altitude of the helicopter? (pp. 377–380)

 (A) 37 meters

 (B) 43 meters

 (C) 127 meters

 (D) 161 meters

13. Alana uses algebra tiles to model the equation $3x = 12$. What should she do next to solve the equation? (pp. 381–384)

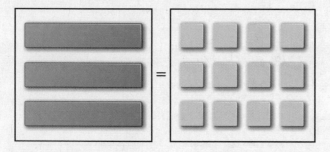

 (A) Divide each side into 3 equal groups.

 (B) Divide each side into 12 equal groups.

 (C) Add 9 more rectangular tiles on the left side.

 (D) Remove 9 square tiles from the right side.

14. A chef has a pot of chicken broth. She pours $\frac{2}{3}$ of the broth, or 36 fluid ounces, into a large bowl. The equation $\frac{2}{3}v = 36$ can be used to find the volume v in fluid ounces of the chicken broth originally in the pot. What is the solution of the equation? (pp. 385–388)

 (A) $v = 24$ (C) $v = 72$

 (B) $v = 54$ (D) $v = 108$

Name _____

Fill in the bubble to show your answer.

15. Kiran has a coupon for $0.65 off the price of one container of orange juice. He buys 5 containers of orange juice for a total of $11.10. The equation $5c - 0.65 = 11.10$ can be used to find the cost c in dollars of each container. How much does each container of orange juice cost? (pp. 389–392)

Ⓐ $1.57

Ⓑ $2.09

Ⓒ $2.22

Ⓓ $2.35

16. The table shows the cost of renting a bicycle. Which equation represents the function shown in the table? (pp. 399–402)

Ⓐ $y = 5x$

Ⓑ $y = 10x$

Ⓒ $y = x + 8$

Ⓓ $y = x + 20$

Bicycle Rental Costs	
Time (hours), x	Cost ($), y
2	10
3	15
4	20
5	25

17. The sequence 9, 10, 11, 12,... represents the number of seats in each of the first few rows of a theater. Which algebraic expression gives the number of seats in the nth row of the theater? (pp. 395–398)

Ⓐ $8n$

Ⓑ $n + 8$

Ⓒ $9n$

Ⓓ $n + 9$

18. The graph shows the distance an elevator travels over time. Which equation represents the function shown in the graph, where x is the time in seconds and y is the distance traveled in feet? (pp. 411–414)

Ⓐ $y = x + 20$

Ⓑ $y = x - 20$

Ⓒ $y = 20x$

Ⓓ $y = \frac{x}{20}$

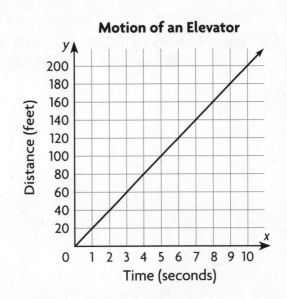

Motion of an Elevator

19. The temperature inside a freezer is always less than 6°F. Write an inequality for the temperature *t* in degrees Fahrenheit inside the freezer. Then graph the inequality. (pp. 415–418)

_____

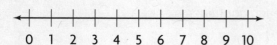

▶ Performance Task

20. The table shows the relationship between the amount Janice earns and the number of hours she babysits.

Janice's Earnings	
Time (hours), *x*	Earnings ($), *y*
1	8
2	16
3	24
4	32
5	40

Ⓐ Graph the function represented by the table.

Janice's Earnings

Ⓑ Write an equation for the function represented by the table.

_____

Ⓒ Janice wants to earn $200 this month. If she babysits for 30 hours, will she be able to make her goal? Explain.

Geometric Figures

Show What You Know ✓

Check your understanding of important skills.

Name _____

▶ **Points, Lines, and Rays** **Identify two of each item in the figure.**

1. points _____

2. line segments _____

3. lines _____

4. rays _____

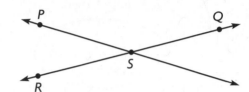

▶ **Name Angles**

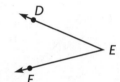

5. Name the angle in three ways. _____

▶ **Identify Polygons** **Name each polygon based on the number of sides.**

6.

7.

8.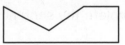

_____ _____ _____

MATH DETECTIVE

WITH

CARMEN SANDIEGO™

Josie's teacher gives her four angles. Angle *A* measures 45°, angle *B* measures 20°, angle *C* measures 40°, and angle *D* measures 120°. Her teacher tells her that three of them can fit together to form a triangle. Be a math detective and find which three angles will form a triangle.

Vocabulary Builder

▶ **Visualize It** •

Sort the review words into the Venn diagram.

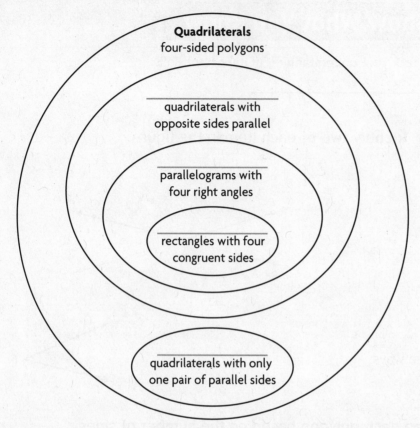

Quadrilaterals
four-sided polygons

_____
quadrilaterals with
opposite sides parallel

_____
parallelograms with
four right angles

_____
rectangles with four
congruent sides

_____
quadrilaterals with only
one pair of parallel sides

▶ **Understand Vocabulary** •

Complete the sentences using the preview words.

1. Angles that are formed by two intersecting lines are called

   _____.

2. _____ are two angles with measures
   that add up to 90°.

3. _____ are angles that share a vertex
   and one side.

4. Angles that are in the same position in two geometric figures are

   _____.

5. Two angles that have measures that add up to 180° are called

   _____.

GO
Online • eStudent Edition • Multimedia eGlossary

© Houghton Mifflin Harcourt Publishing Company

Name _____

Angles

Essential Question How can you measure and classify angles?

Investigate

Materials ■ protractor

An acute angle measures less than 90°. This angle looks like it may be acute, but how can you tell for sure? You can use a protractor to measure the angle and determine if it is acute.

A. Place the protractor on ∠ABC so that the center point of the base of the protractor is on the vertex of the angle, B.

B. Line up the base of the protractor with $\overrightarrow{BC}$.

C. Find where $\overrightarrow{BA}$ intersects the protractor. Read the number on the same scale that reads 0° where $\overrightarrow{BC}$ intersects the protractor.

The measure of ∠ABC is _____.

So, ∠ABC _____ an acute angle.

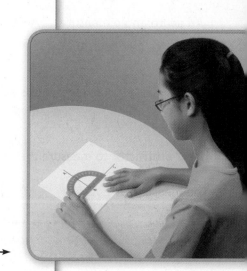

Draw Conclusions ·

1. Explain why an angle that measures 135° is not an acute angle.

_____

2. **H.O.T.** **Analysis** Aaron uses a protractor to measure ∠DEF, as shown. He says that the angle measures 65°. Find the correct measure of the angle and explain Aaron's error.

_____

_____

_____

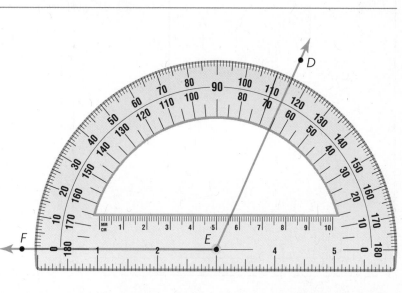

Make Connections ....

Angles can be classified by their measures in one of four ways.

An acute angle measures less than 90°.

A right angle measures exactly 90°.

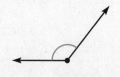

An obtuse angle measures greater than 90° but less than 180°.

A straight angle measures exactly 180°.

Measure ∠RST and classify it as acute, right, obtuse, or straight.

STEP 1

Use a protractor to measure the angle.

The measure of ∠RST is _____.

STEP 2

Use the measure of the angle to classify it.

An angle that measures greater than _____

but less than _____ is _____.

So, ∠RST is _____.

> **Math Talk** Explain how you can use the corner of an index card to decide if an angle is acute, right, or obtuse.

Try This! Measure the angle and classify it as acute, right, obtuse, or straight.

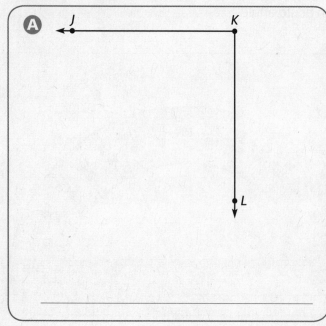

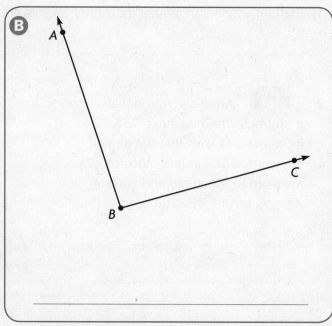

Name _____

Share and Show

Measure the angle and classify it as acute, obtuse, right, or straight.

1.

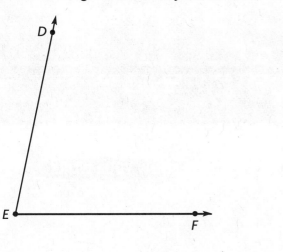

_____

2.

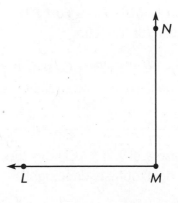

_____

3.

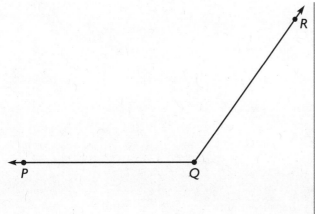

_____

4.

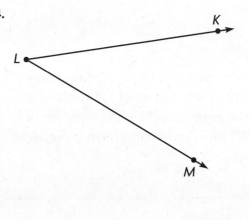

_____

Draw an angle with the given measure on a separate sheet of paper.
Then classify the angle as *acute*, *obtuse*, *right*, or *straight*.

5. 55° _____

6. 135° _____

7. 180° _____

8. 90° _____

9. 60° _____

10. 150° _____

11. **Write Math** ▶ **Describe** the steps for using a protractor to measure an angle.

_____

_____

_____

_____

Problem Solving REAL WORLD

With approximately 450 bridges, Pittsburgh, Pennsylvania, is known as The City of Bridges. The figure shows part of the city's Fort Pitt Bridge. Use the figure for 12–16.

12. What is the measure of ∠*KPM*? Classify the angle as acute, right, obtuse, or straight.

_____

13. What is the measure of ∠*JPK*? Classify the angle as acute, right, obtuse, or straight.

_____

14. **H.O.T.** Name all of the obtuse angles in the figure. What are the measures of these angles?

_____

15. **Algebra** The measure of ∠*LPM* is equal to 3 times the measure of ∠*A*. Write and solve an equation to find the measure of ∠*A*. Tell what the variable in your equation represents.

_____

16. **Write Math** ▶ **What's the Question?** Celia correctly solves a problem about the figure of the Fort Pitt Bridge. Her answer is 180°. What's the question?

_____

_____

17. ⭐ **Test Prep** Which is the best estimate for the measure of ∠*XYZ*?

Ⓐ 60°

Ⓑ 90°

Ⓒ 120°

Ⓓ 170°

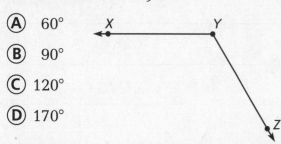

FOR MORE PRACTICE:
Standards Practice Book, pp. P211–P212

Name _____

Angle Relationships

Essential Question How can you use special angle pairs to calculate angle measurements?

Angles sometimes have special relationships with each other. For example, **adjacent angles** are angles that have a common vertex and a common ray, but have no common interior points. In the figure, ∠1 and ∠2 are adjacent angles.

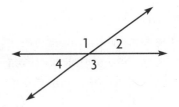

Vertical angles are formed opposite each other when two lines intersect. ∠1 and ∠3 are vertical angles. Note that vertical angles are never adjacent angles.

Vertical angles have the same measure. Angles that have the same measure are **congruent**. Because ∠1 and ∠3 are vertical angles, they are congruent and you can write m∠1 = m∠3.

> **Math Idea**
> The letter "m" indicates the measure of an angle. Read m∠1 as "the measure of angle 1."

UNLOCK the Problem REAL WORLD

Two of the runways at Kansas City International Airport intersect to form the four angles shown in the figure.

Name all of the pairs of congruent angles.

The intersecting runways are redrawn below.

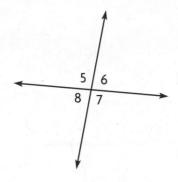

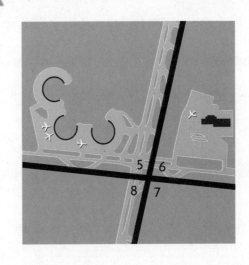

∠5 and ∠7 are opposite each other. This means they are _____ angles.

∠6 and ∠8 are opposite each other. This means they are _____ angles.

Vertical angles are congruent.

So, _____ and _____ are congruent, as are _____ and _____.

- **Explain** what must be true about m∠7 if you know that m∠5 = 95°

_____

Special Angle Pairs When the sum of the measures of two angles equals 90°, the angles are called **complementary angles**. The angles do not need to be adjacent angles in order to be complementary. For example, ∠MNO and ∠PQR are complementary, and each angle is the complement of the other.

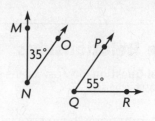

$$35° + 55° = 90°$$

When the sum of the measures of two angles equals 180°, the angles are called **supplementary angles**. You can show that ∠ABC and ∠DEF are supplementary by adding their measures.

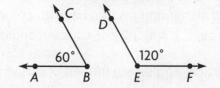

$$60° + 120° = 180°$$

🔒 Example

The figure shows the support beams of a half-pipe skateboard ramp. Find m∠TQG.

∠TQY is a right angle, so it measures _____.

∠TQG and ∠GQY together form ∠TQY, so

they are _____ angles.

m∠TQG + m∠GQY = [ ]   The sum of the measures of complementary angles is _____.

x + [ ] = [ ]   Substitute the measures of the angles.

x + [ ] − [ ] = [ ] − [ ]   Subtract _____ from both sides.

x = [ ]   Simplify.

So, m∠TQG = _____.

Try This! Find m∠ABD.

∠ABC is a straight angle, so it measures _____. ∠ABD and ∠CBD

together form ∠ABC, so they are _____ angles.

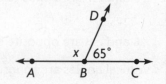

m∠ABD + m∠CBD = [ ]

x + [ ] = [ ]

x + [ ] − [ ] = [ ] − [ ]

x = [ ]

So, m∠ABD = _____.

430

Name _____

Share and Show [MATH BOARD] . . . .

Identify the pairs of congruent angles in the figure.

1.

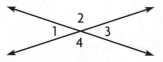

∠1 and ∠3 are opposite each other, so they

are _____.

∠2 and ∠4 are opposite each other, so they

are _____.

Vertical angles are _____.

Congruent pairs: _____

2.

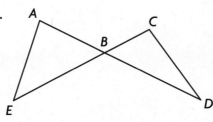

_____

_____

Algebra Find the unknown angle measure.

3.

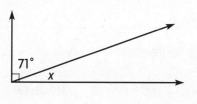

71°

x

_____

4.

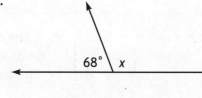

68° x

_____

Math Talk Explain whether it is possible for two angles to be both congruent and complementary.

On Your Own . . . .

Algebra Find the value of x.

5.

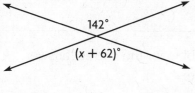

142°

(x + 62)°

_____

6.

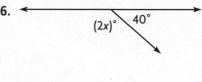

(2x)° 40°

_____

7.

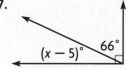

66°

(x − 5)°

_____

8. [Write Math] The figure shows three streets that form a triangular park. A city planner knows that ∠2 and ∠3 are congruent. **Explain** why the city planner can conclude that ∠1 and ∠4 are congruent.

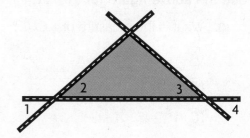

_____

_____

9. What is the measure of ∠DHE?

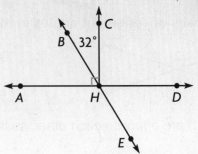

(A) 32°

(B) 42°

(C) 58°

(D) 122°

a. What do you need to find?

_____

b. What information in the figure can help you solve the problem?

_____

c. Describe the steps you will use to solve the problem.

_____

_____

d. Show your work for solving the problem in the space below.

e. Complete the sentences.

The measure of ∠BHA is _____ because

_____.

This means the measure of ∠DHE is _____

because _____

_____

f. Fill in the bubble for the correct answer choice above.

Use the above figure for 10–11.

10. What is the measure of ∠CHE?

(A) 58°

(B) 90°

(C) 122°

(D) 148°

11. Which of these angles is congruent to ∠AHE?

(A) ∠BHC

(B) ∠BHD

(C) ∠CHD

(D) ∠DHE

FOR MORE PRACTICE:
Standards Practice Book, pp. P213–P214

Name _____

Polygons and Congruence

Essential Question How can you tell if two polygons are congruent?

A *polygon* is a closed plane figure formed by line segments that meet only at their endpoints. Each point where two line segments meet is called a *vertex*.

You classify polygons by the number of sides, angles, and vertices.

Triangle	Quadrilateral	Pentagon	Hexagon
3 sides, 3 angles, 3 vertices	4 sides, 4 angles, 4 vertices	5 sides, 5 angles, 5 vertices	6 sides, 6 angles, 6 vertices

Heptagon	Octagon	Nonagon	Decagon
7 sides, 7 angles, 7 vertices	8 sides, 8 angles, 8 vertices	9 sides, 9 angles, 9 vertices	10 sides, 10 angles, 10 vertices

A *regular polygon* is a polygon in which all sides are congruent and all angles are congruent.

regular octagon

8 congruent sides

8 congruent angles

not a regular octagon

Not all sides are congruent.

Not all angles are congruent.

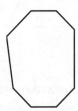

UNLOCK the Problem REAL WORLD

A gazebo is a free-standing, open-sided structure. The figure shows a plan for a gazebo. Describe the polygon.

 Identify the polygon and tell whether it is regular.

The polygon has _____ sides, so it is a _____.

All of the polygon's sides and angles appear to be

_____, so the polygon is a _____.

So, the polygon is a _____.

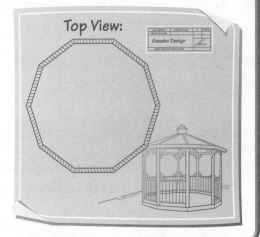

Top View:

Corresponding sides are sides that are in the same position in different figures. **Corresponding angles** are angles that are in the same position in different figures. Two polygons are congruent when all pairs of corresponding sides are congruent and all pairs of corresponding angles are congruent.

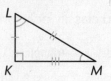

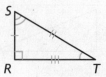

Corresponding Sides	Corresponding Angles
$\overline{KL}$ corresponds to $\overline{RS}$, and $\overline{KL} \cong \overline{RS}$.	∠K corresponds to ∠R, and ∠K ≅ ∠R.
$\overline{LM}$ corresponds to $\overline{ST}$, and $\overline{LM} \cong \overline{ST}$.	∠L corresponds to ∠S, and ∠L ≅ ∠S.
$\overline{MK}$ corresponds to $\overline{TR}$, and $\overline{MK} \cong \overline{TR}$.	∠M corresponds to ∠T, and ∠M ≅ ∠T.

All of the pairs of corresponding sides are congruent and all of the pairs of corresponding angles are congruent. This means ΔKLM is congruent to ΔRST, and you can write the congruence statement ΔKLM ≅ ΔRST.

🔑 Example

Determine whether the polygons are congruent. If the polygons are congruent, write a congruence statement.

A

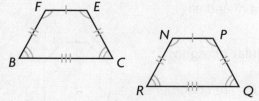

The pairs of corresponding sides are

_____.

The pairs of corresponding angles are

_____.

So, the polygons are _____

and _____.

B

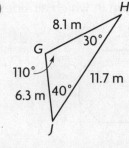

There are three pairs of _____

angles, but there are _____

pairs of congruent sides.

So, the polygons are _____

• **Draw** a figure that has corresponding sides congruent to this figure but is not congruent to the figure.

Name _____

Share and Show

Identify the polygon. Use a ruler and protractor to determine
if it is regular.

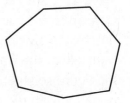

1. The polygon has _____ sides, so it is a _____. The angles

   are _____, so the polygon is _____.

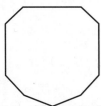

2. _____

   _____

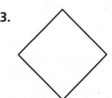

3. _____

   _____

Determine whether the polygons are congruent. If the polygons
are congruent, write a congruence statement.

4.

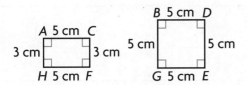

_____

_____

5.

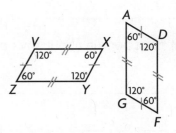

_____

_____

Math Talk Explain whether
you can classify a polygon just
by knowing the number of
vertices it has.

On Your Own

Determine whether the polygons are congruent. If the polygons
are congruent, write a congruence statement.

6.

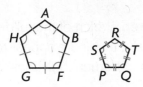

_____

_____

7.

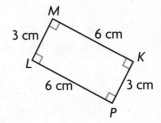

_____

_____

8. Carolyn is designing a stained-glass window. She begins by drawing the figure shown at right. Next, she wants to find a nonagon in the figure so she can fill the interior of the nonagon with red glass. Name one nonagon in the figure.

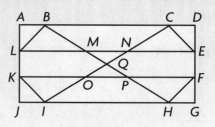

a. What does the problem ask you to do?

_____

b. How will you use the given figure?

_____

c. What must be true about any nonagon?

_____

_____

d. Sketch a nonagon in the space below.

e. Complete the sentence.

A nonagon has _____ sides, _____ angles,

and _____ vertices.

f. Name a nonagon in the above figure.

_____

For 9–10, use the above figure.

9. ⭐ **Test Prep** Which term can be used to describe the polygon *BCNM* in the figure?

(A) triangle

(B) pentagon

(C) regular

(D) not regular

10. ⭐ **Test Prep** Which of the following pairs of polygons in the figure appear to be an example of congruent polygons?

(A) *ABML* and *BCNM*

(B) *MNQ* and *BCQ*

(C) *LMQOK* and *ENQPF*

(D) *KOIJ* and *LNOK*

FOR MORE PRACTICE:
Standards Practice Book, pp. P215–P216

Name _____

Triangles

Essential Question How can you find missing angle measures in triangles?

CONNECT You have already seen that a triangle is a polygon with three sides and three angles. The angles of a triangle have an important property.

If you tear off the corners of a paper triangle and place them together, you will find that they form a straight angle. This suggests that the sum of the measures of the angles in a triangle is 180°.

Angles of a Triangle

The sum of the measures of the angles in a triangle is 180°.

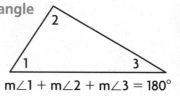

$$m\angle 1 + m\angle 2 + m\angle 3 = 180°$$

🔑 UNLOCK the Problem › REAL WORLD

The towers of the McCallum Hill Center are distinctive features of the skyline in Regina, Canada. Find the missing angle measure in the photo of one of the towers.

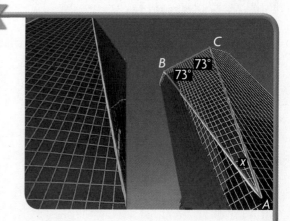

🔑 **Find m∠A.**

The sum of the measures of the angles in a triangle is _____.	$m\angle A + m\angle B + m\angle C = \boxed{}$
Substitute the angle measures.	$x + \boxed{} + \boxed{} = \boxed{}$
Add.	$x + \boxed{} = \boxed{}$
Subtraction Property of Equality	$x + \boxed{} - \boxed{} = \boxed{} - \boxed{}$
Simplify.	$x = \boxed{}$

So, the missing angle measure is _____.

Math Talk Explain why a triangle cannot have two right angles.

Classifying Triangles You can classify a triangle by its sides.

Classify by Sides		
A **scalene triangle** has no congruent sides.	An **isosceles triangle** has at least two congruent sides.	An **equilateral triangle** has three congruent sides.

You can also classify a triangle by its angles.

Classify by Angles		
An **acute triangle** contains only acute angles.	A **right triangle** contains one right angle.	An **obtuse triangle** contains one obtuse angle.

🔑 Example

Find the missing angle measure in the triangle. Then classify the triangle by its angles and by its sides.

First find m∠H.

The sum of the measures of the angles in a

$m\angle H + m\angle J + m\angle K = \boxed{}$

triangle is _____.

Substitute the angle measures.

$x + \boxed{} + \boxed{} = \boxed{}$

Add.

$x + \boxed{} = \boxed{}$

Subtraction Property of Equality

$x + \boxed{} - \boxed{} = \boxed{} - \boxed{}$

Simplify.

$x = \boxed{}$

So, the missing angle measure is _____.

The triangle has one _____ angle, so the

triangle is a _____.

The triangle has two _____ sides, so the

triangle is an _____ triangle. You can say the

triangle is classified as a _____ triangle.

> **Math Talk** Explain what must be true about the angles of a triangle that has three congruent angles.

438

Name _____

Share and Show

Find the missing angle measure.

1.
$$x + 40° + 110° = \boxed{}$$
$$x + \boxed{} = \boxed{}$$
$$x + \boxed{} - \boxed{} = \boxed{} - \boxed{}$$
$$x = \boxed{}$$

(Triangle with vertex A at 40°, vertex C at 110°, and angle x at vertex B)

2.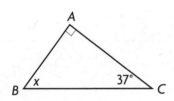

_____

3.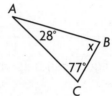

_____

Find the missing angle measure. Then classify the triangle
by its angles and by its sides.

4.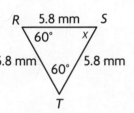

_____

5.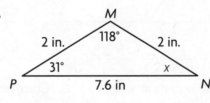

_____

Math Talk Explain why a
triangle that contains two
20° angles must be an obtuse
triangle.

On Your Own

Find the missing angle measure. Then classify the triangle
by its angles and by its sides.

6.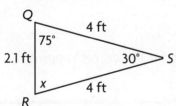

_____

7.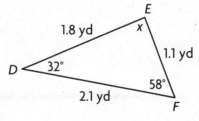

_____

8. **H.O.T.** **Sense or Nonsense?** The directions for building a triangular
table top state that the angles of the triangle should be 25°, 75°, and
70°. Are the directions sense or nonsense? Explain.

_____

UNLOCK the Problem

9. What is the measure of ∠B in the football pennant?

- (A) 24°
- (B) 48°
- (C) 78°
- (D) 156°

a. What do you need to find?

_____

b. What information in the figure can help you solve the problem?

_____

c. Describe the steps you will use to solve the problem.

_____

_____

_____

d. In the space below, write an equation you can use to solve the problem. Then solve the equation.

e. Complete the sentences.

The measure of ∠B is _____.

I can check my answer by making sure that

_____

_____

_____

f. Fill in the bubble for the correct answer choice above.

10. A triangle contains two angles that each measure 36°. What is the measure of the third angle?

- (A) 36°
- (C) 108°
- (B) 72°
- (D) 144°

11. Jared drew a triangle with a 30° angle and a 60° angle. Which of the following is a correct way to classify the triangle?

- (A) acute
- (C) obtuse
- (B) equilateral
- (D) right

Name _____

Quadrilaterals

Essential Question How can you find missing angle measures in quadrilaterals?

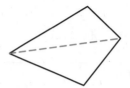

CONNECT As with triangles, the sum of the measures of the angles in any quadrilateral is always the same.

You can find the sum of the angle measures in a quadrilateral by dividing the figure into two triangles. The sum of the angle measures in each triangle is 180°. There are two triangles, so the sum of the angle measures in the quadrilateral is $2 \times 180° = 360°$.

Angles of a Quadrilateral

The sum of the measures of the angles in a quadrilateral is 360°.

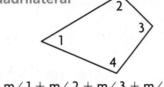

$m\angle 1 + m\angle 2 + m\angle 3 + m\angle 4 = 360°$

 UNLOCK the Problem REAL WORLD

A garnet is a type of mineral that is used to make gemstones. The photograph shows a face of a garnet crystal that is a quadrilateral. What is the missing angle measure?

Find m∠P.

The sum of the measures of the angles

in a quadrilateral is _____.

$m\angle P + m\angle Q + m\angle R + m\angle S =$ _____

Substitute the angle measures. $\quad x +$ _____ $+$ _____ $+$ _____ $=$ _____

Add. $\qquad x +$ _____ $=$ _____

Subtraction Property of Equality $\qquad x +$ _____ $-$ _____ $=$ _____ $-$ _____

Subtract. $\qquad x =$ _____

So, the missing angle measure is _____.

Math Talk Explain what must be true about the angles of a quadrilateral if all four of its angles are congruent.

Classifying Quadrilaterals There are several special types of quadrilaterals. Their names and properties are summarized in the table.

Quadrilaterals		
Name	**Figure**	**Properties**
Parallelogram		Opposite sides are parallel and congruent
Rectangle		Parallelogram with 4 right angles
Rhombus		Parallelogram with 4 congruent sides
Square		Rectangle with 4 congruent sides
Trapezoid		Quadrilateral with exactly two parallel sides

 Example Classify quadrilaterals

Give the most exact name for the figure.

A

The figure is a rectangle with 4

_____ sides and a rhombus

with 4 _____ angles.

So, the most exact name for the figure is

a _____.

B

The figure is a quadrilateral with opposite

sides that are _____ and

_____.

So, the most exact name for the figure is

a _____.

• **Describe** the relationship between rectangles and squares.

Name _____

Share and Show MATH BOARD •

Find the missing angle measure.

1. $x + 60° + 120° + 60° =$ [blank]

    $x +$ [blank] $=$ [blank]

    $x +$ [blank] $-$ [blank] $=$ [blank] $-$ [blank]

    $x =$ [blank]

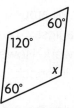

2.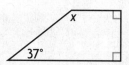

   _____

✓ 3.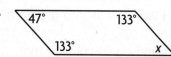

   _____

Give the most exact name for the figure.

4.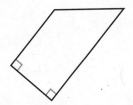

   _____

✓ 5.

   _____

> **Math Talk** Explain whether a trapezoid can also be a parallelogram.

On Your Own •

Find the missing angle measure. Then give the most exact name for the figure.

6.

   _____

7.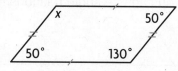

   _____

8. **H.O.T.** **What's the Error?** Jaclyn says that a rhombus can have four obtuse angles. Describe her error.

_____

_____

Jigsaw Puzzles

The first jigsaw puzzle was produced around 1760. By 1908, the United States was in the midst of a jigsaw-puzzle craze. These early puzzles often featured original artwork. However, unlike most of today's jigsaw puzzles, the pieces did not interlock.

Some artists still make jigsaw puzzles the old-fashioned way. They create pictures, reproduce them on wooden boards, and then cut the boards into puzzle pieces.

The figure shows several puzzle pieces that an artist is making.

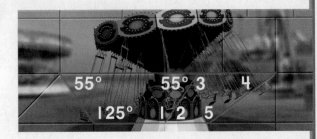

Find m∠1.

m∠1 + [   ] + [   ] + [   ] = [   ]   The sum of the measures of the angles in a quadrilateral is _____.

m∠1 + [   ] = [   ]   Add.

m∠1 + [   ] − [   ] = [   ] − [   ]   Subtraction Property of Equality

m∠1 = [   ]   Simplify.

So, the measure of ∠1 is _____.

Solve.

9. Explain how you can use angle relationships to find m∠2 and m∠3.

   _____

   _____

10. **H.O.T.** The artist knows that m∠4 = 40°. Explain how she can find m∠5.

   _____

   _____

Name _____

✓ Mid-Chapter Checkpoint

▶ Vocabulary

Choose the best term from the box.

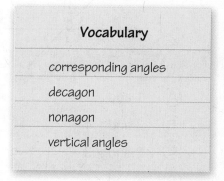
1. Angles that are in the same position in different figures are called

   _____. (p. 434)

2. A _____ is a polygon with nine sides. (p. 433)

3. _____ are angles formed by two intersecting
   lines. (p. 429)

▶ Concepts and Skills

Use a protractor to measure the indicated angle. (pp. 425–428)

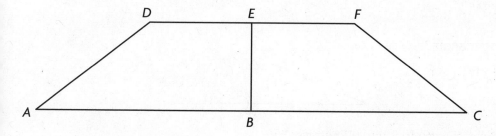

4. ∠DAB _____

5. ∠EBA _____

6. ∠CFE _____

7. ∠ABC _____

Use the figure above for Exercises 8–11. Classify the angle as *acute, obtuse, right,* **or**
straight. (pp. 425–428)

8. ∠DAB _____

9. ∠EBA _____

10. ∠CFE _____

11. ∠ABC _____

12. In the figure above, $\overline{DF}$ is parallel to $\overline{AC}$. Give the most exact name
    for *DFCA.* (pp. 441–444)

_____

Fill in the bubble for the correct answer choice.

13. Which pair of angles are complementary? (pp. 429–432)

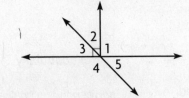

Ⓐ ∠1 and ∠2

Ⓑ ∠3 and ∠4

Ⓒ ∠2 and ∠3

Ⓓ ∠4 and ∠5

14. In the figure in Exercise 13, m∠3 = 45°. What is the measure of ∠5?
(pp. 429–432)

Ⓐ 45° 　　Ⓒ 90°

Ⓑ 55° 　　Ⓓ 135°

15. What is the value of *x* in the triangle? (pp. 437–440)

Ⓐ 71° 　　Ⓒ 131°

Ⓑ 109° 　　Ⓓ 289°

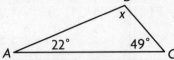

16. What is the correct way to classify the triangle in Exercise 15?
(pp. 437–440)

Ⓐ acute

Ⓑ right

Ⓒ obtuse

Ⓓ isosceles

17. Gary drew the quadrilaterals shown here. He found that
KLMN ≅ RSTU. Which of the following must be true? (pp. 433–436)

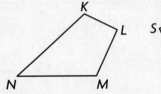 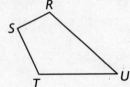

Ⓐ $\overline{KN}$ is congruent to $\overline{RS}$.

Ⓑ ∠M is congruent to ∠U.

Ⓒ ∠K is congruent to ∠S.

Ⓓ $\overline{LM}$ is congruent to $\overline{ST}$.

Name _____

Draw a Diagram · Polygon Angle Sums

Essential Question How can you find the sum of the angle measures of any polygon?

UNLOCK the Problem REAL WORLD

Hex is a board game that was co-invented by John Nash, the mathematician featured in the movie *A Beautiful Mind*. Players try to win the game by making a path from one side of the board to the other with their pieces. The board is made up of regular hexagons. What is the sum of the angle measures in a hexagon?

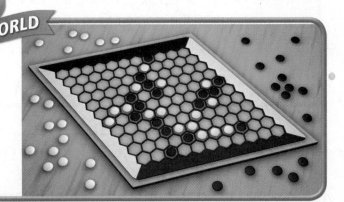

Read the Problem

What do I need to find?	What information do I need to use?	How will I use the information?
The sum of the _____ _____ of a hexagon.	A hexagon has _____ vertices. I can connect some of the vertices and find the angle sums of those smaller shapes.	I will use the strategy _____ to divide a hexagon into triangles.

Solve the Problem

Connect vertex *A* to all non-adjacent vertices.

Connect *A* to *C* to create Δ _____.

Connect *A* to _____ to create Δ *ACD*.

Connect *A* to *E* to create Δ _____ and Δ _____.

The hexagon has been divided into _____ triangles, and the sum of the angle measures in each triangle is

_____ degrees. To find the sum of all the angles in the hexagon, multiply the number of triangles by 180.

_____ × 180 = _____

So, the sum of the angle measures in a hexagon is _____ degrees.

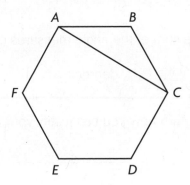

Math Talk Explain why you would get the same answer if you started with vertex *B*.

Try Another Problem

Engineers have designed several tires that have no air in them. Instead of air, the center of the tire is made with a web of supports. What is the sum of the angle measures of the red pentagon shown in this airless tire?

Read the Problem

What do I need to find?	What information do I need to use?	How will I use the information?

Solve the Problem

Use the copy of the pentagon at right and divide it into triangles. Then find the angle sum.

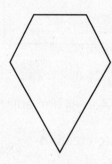

So, the sum of the angle measures of the pentagon

is _____ degrees.

1. **Explain** how you can justify your answer by using a protractor.

_____

_____

2. **Make a conjecture** about how to calculate the sum of the angle measures of a polygon with *n* sides, based on what you found for a pentagon and a hexagon and what you already know about triangles and quadrilaterals.

_____

_____

Name _____

Share and Show

UNLOCK the Problem Tips

√ Underline important facts.
√ Choose a strategy.
√ Solve the problem a second way to check your work.

1. What is the sum of the angle measures of the heptagon shown below?

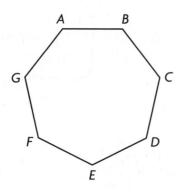

First, connect vertex *A* to all non-adjacent vertices.

Next, count the number of triangles formed by the connections and multiply that number by 180.

So, the sum of the angle measures in the heptagon

is _____ degrees.

2. **H.O.T.** **What if** one of the vertices of the heptagon points inward, like vertex *C* in the figure shown at right? (This is called a *concave polygon*.) Find the sum of the angle measures of this heptagon.

_____

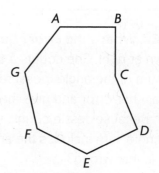

3. **H.O.T.** **Make a conjecture** about how the angle sums for polygons with the same number of sides but different shapes, like in Exercises 1 and 2, are related.

_____

_____

_____

_____

4. A variation of pool, called bumper pool, is often played on an octagon-shaped table. Draw an octagon like the table shown and find the sum of its angle measures.

_____

On Your Own.....................

Choose a STRATEGY

Work Backward

Solve a Simpler Problem

Choose an Operation

Use a Model

Use a Formula

Draw a Diagram

5. Karyn and her family are driving to visit family. The total trip is 137.6 miles. They leave home and drive 4.7 miles to the highway. They then drive 58.3 miles before stopping at a rest stop. How many more miles do they have left in their trip?

_____

6. Clayton deposits $39.78 in his savings account on Monday. Two days later, he withdraws $80.00. His balance after the withdrawal is $65.39. How much money did he have in his account before the deposit he made on Monday?

_____

7. Algebra An *enneadecagon* is a polygon with 19 sides. Use the formula $S = (n - 2) \times 180$, where n is the number of sides, to find the sum S of the angle measures of an enneadecagon.

_____

8. **What's the Error?** Jessie draws the diagram shown at right. She counts 5 triangles and concludes that the sum of the angle measures for the pentagon is 900°. Explain her error and give the correct angle sum. (*Hint*: Because Jessie counts the 5 triangles she's drawn, her angle sum includes the angles labeled 1 through 4. Why is that wrong?)

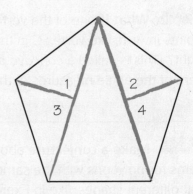

_____

_____

_____

9. ⭐ **Test Prep** What is the sum of the angle measures of the polygon shown?

Ⓐ 360°

Ⓑ 540°

Ⓒ 720°

Ⓓ 900°

Name _____

Figures on the Coordinate Plane

Essential Question How can you plot polygons on a coordinate plane?

🔑 UNLOCK the Problem > REAL WORLD

The world's largest book is a collection of photographs from the Asian nation of Bhutan. When opened, the book is a rectangle that is 7 feet wide by 5 feet tall.

A book collector models the shape of the book on a coordinate plane. Each unit of the coordinate plane represents one foot. The collector plots the points shown below. What is the missing vertex of the rectangle?

 Find the coordinates of the missing vertex.

Use the properties of a rectangle to find the missing vertex.

STEP 1

The opposite sides of a rectangle are _____.

Since the length of side $\overline{AB}$ is _____ units, the length of side

_____ must also be _____ units.

_____

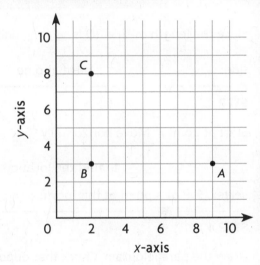

STEP 2

Start at point C. Move horizontally _____ units to the

_____ to find the location of the missing vertex,
D. Plot a point at this location.

_____

STEP 3

Draw the rectangle.

So, the coordinates of the missing vertex are _____.

---

1. Explain how you can check your answer by comparing the lengths of sides $\overline{BC}$ and $\overline{AD}$.

_____

_____

CONNECT You can use properties of quadrilaterals to help you find missing vertices. The properties can also help you graph quadrilaterals on the coordinate plane.

🔒 Example Find the missing vertex, then graph.

Three vertices of parallelogram PQRS are P(4, 2), Q(3, ⁻3), and R(⁻3, ⁻3). Give the coordinates of vertex S and graph the parallelogram.

Math Idea

The name of a polygon, such as parallelogram PQRS, gives the vertices in order as you move around the polygon.

STEP 1

Plot the given points on the coordinate plane.

_____

STEP 2

The opposite sides of a parallelogram are _____

and _____ .

Since the length of side $\overline{RQ}$ is _____ units, the length of

side _____ must also be _____ units.

_____

STEP 3

Start at point P. Move horizontally _____ units to the

_____ to find the location of the remaining

vertex, S. Plot a point at this location.

_____

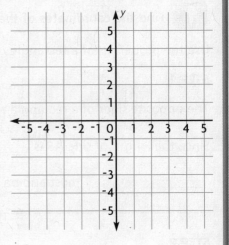

STEP 4

Draw the parallelogram. Check that opposite sides are parallel and congruent.

So, the coordinates of the vertex S are _____ .

2. **Explain** why vertex S must be to the left of vertex P rather than to the right of vertex P.

_____

_____

3. **Describe** how you could use a ruler to determine whether or not the parallelogram you graphed is a rhombus.

_____

Name _____

Share and Show

Give the coordinates of the missing vertex of rectangle *JKLM*.

1. The length of $\overline{JK}$ is _____ units.

The length of _____ must also be _____ units.

Start at point _____ and move _____ units to

the _____.

The coordinates of *M* are _____.

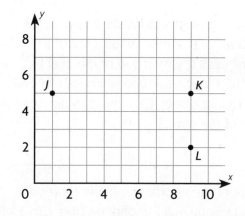

2.

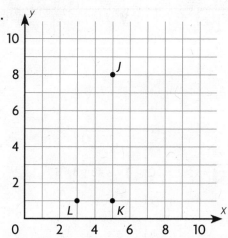

_____

3.

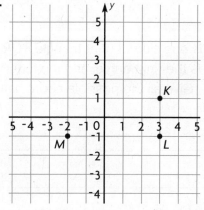

_____

On Your Own

Give the coordinates of the missing vertex of rectangle *PQRS*.

4.

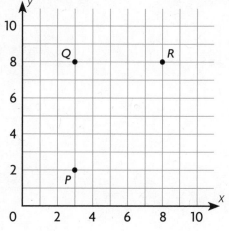

_____

5.

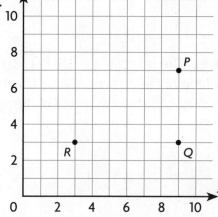

_____

Problem Solving REAL WORLD

**The map shows the location of some city landmarks.
Use the map for 6–7.**

6. A city planner wants to locate a park at the
   intersection of two new roads. One of the new
   roads will pass the mall and be parallel to Lincoln
   Street. The other new road will pass City Hall and be
   parallel to Elm Street. Give the coordinates for the
   location of the park.

   _____

7. Each unit of the coordinate plane represents
   2 miles. How far will the park be from City Hall?

   _____

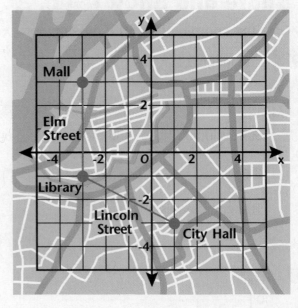

8. **H.O.T.** $\overline{PQ}$ is one side of right triangle *PQR*. In the
   triangle, $\angle P$ is the right angle, and the length of side
   $\overline{PR}$ is 3 units. Give all the possible coordinates for
   vertex *R*.

   _____

   _____

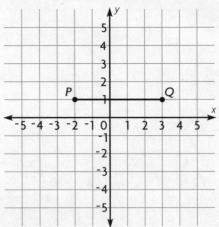

9. **Write Math** ▶ Quadrilateral *WXYZ* has vertices
   with coordinates $W(^-4, 0)$, $X(^-2, 3)$, $Y(2, 3)$, and
   $Z(2, 0)$. Classify the quadrilateral using the most
   exact name possible and explain your answer.

   _____

   _____

   _____

10. ★ **Test Prep** The points $(^-1, -2)$, $(^-1, 3)$, and
    $(4, 3)$ are three of the vertices of a square. What are
    the coordinates of the fourth vertex of the square?

    Ⓐ $(^-2, 4)$

    Ⓑ $(^-4, ^-2)$

    Ⓒ $(4, ^-1)$

    Ⓓ $(4, ^-2)$

FOR MORE PRACTICE:
Standards Practice Book, pp. P223–P224

Transformations

Essential Question How can you perform translations, rotations, and reflections on figures?

A transformation moves or changes a figure in some way. The figure that results is called the image of the original figure.

Three common transformations are called translations (slides), rotations (turns), and reflections (flips). These three transformations change the position or orientation of a figure, but they do not change the size or shape of a figure.

Translation	Rotation	Reflection

A translation slides a figure along a line without turning.	A rotation turns a figure around a point, called the center of rotation.	A reflection flips a figure across a line, called the line of reflection, to create a mirror image.

UNLOCK the Problem REAL WORLD

Each figure shows a stop sign and its image. Identify the transformation.

- Underline the sentence that tells you what you need to do.

🔒 **Identify the transformation.**

A

The transformation _____ the figure.

So, the transformation is a _____.

B

The transformation _____ the figure.

So, the transformation is a _____.

Drawing Transformations You can use tracing paper to help you draw the image of a figure under a transformation.

🔑 Example

Draw the transformation of the given figure.

Ⓐ Translation in the direction shown

Trace the triangle.

Slide the triangle in the direction of the arrow. The length of the arrow shows the distance to slide the triangle.

Draw the triangle in its new position.

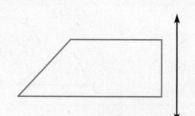

Ⓑ Reflection across the given line

Trace the trapezoid and the line of reflection.

Flip the tracing paper so that the line of reflection that you traced lies on top of the given line of reflection.

The image of the trapezoid should be on the other side of the line, the same distance from the line as the original trapezoid.

Draw the trapezoid in its new position.

> ⚠️ **ERROR Alert**
>
> When you draw a reflection, be sure the original figure and its image lie on top of each other if you fold along the line of reflection.

Ⓒ Rotation of 90° counterclockwise around the given point

Trace the rectangle.

Place the tip of your pencil on the point. Rotate the paper 90° counterclockwise.

Draw the triangle in its new position.

---

1. **Explain** what happens if you rotate a figure 360° around a point.

   _____

2. **Explain** whether you can change the shape of a figure by applying several translations, rotations, and/or reflections to it.

   _____

   _____

Name _____

Share and Show

Identify the transformation.

1.

The transformation _____ the figure.

So, the transformation is a _____.

2.

_____

Draw the transformation of the given figure.

3. Reflection across the given line

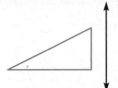

4. Rotation of 180° clockwise around point *A*

A

Math Talk Explain how you can use transformations to draw the petals of a flower.

On Your Own

Draw the transformation of the given figure.

5. Rotation of 90° clockwise around the given point

6. Reflection across the given line

7. Draw a figure of your own choosing and a 45° counterclockwise rotation.

Problem Solving 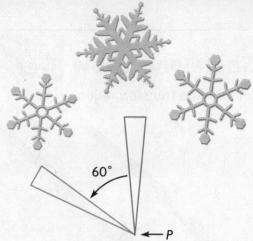 REAL WORLD

Snowflakes are formed when tiny droplets of water freeze into ice crystals. Frozen water molecules form hexagons, which is why many snowflakes have a hexagon shape in their centers and six arms growing out from that center.

8. You can draw a simple snowflake by rotating a triangle around point *P*, as shown. Use a protractor to complete the snowflake by performing four more rotations of 60° each.

9. **H.O.T.** **Make a Conjecture** In Exercise 8, you drew a snowflake with six arms using six 60° rotations. How many arms would the snowflake have if you used 45° rotations? Explain your reasoning.

_____

_____

_____

SHOW YOUR WORK

10. **Write Math** ▸ **Explain** how you can use transformations to create the pattern shown below.

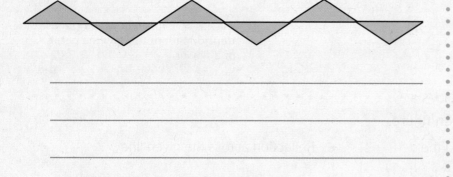

_____

_____

_____

_____

11. ⭐ **Test Prep** Which of the following shows a figure and its image after a reflection?

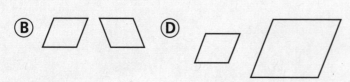

Name _____

Symmetry

Essential Question How can you identify line and rotational symmetry in plane figures?

<small>Connect</small> You can use transformations to describe properties of figures. A figure has **symmetry** if there is a transformation such that the image coincides with the original figure.

When you can draw a line through a figure so that the two halves are mirror images of each other, the figure has **line symmetry**. The line along which the figure is divided is called the **line of symmetry**.

 UNLOCK the Problem REAL WORLD

In 2009, an inventor in China developed a bicycle with a wheel that is rouhgly shaped like a regular pentagon. Because it takes more effort to pedal, the bike offers riders a better workout. Tell whether the wheel has line symmetry. If so, draw the lines of symmetry.

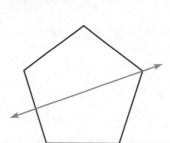

🔑 **Identify the lines of symmetry.**

The figure shows a regular pentagon.

When you draw a line through the pentagon as shown, the two halves are mirror images of each other.

So, the regular pentagon has _____.

The line shown is a _____.

Draw the remaining lines of symmetry.

So, a regular pentagon has _____ lines of symmetry.

> **Math Talk** Explain how line symmetry is related to reflections.

Try This!

Tell whether the square has line symmetry. If so, draw the lines of symmetry.

_____

A figure has **rotational symmetry** if, when it is rotated less than 360° around a central point, it coincides with itself. The central point is called the **center of rotation**.

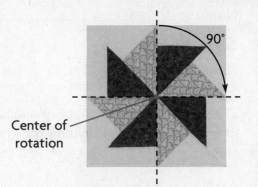
90°

The angle of rotational symmetry is the smallest angle through which a figure can be rotated to coincide with itself. The quilt block at right has rotational symmetry. The center of rotation is shown in blue. The angle of rotational symmetry is 90°.

Center of rotation

 Example

Tell whether a regular hexagon has rotational symmetry. If so, give the angle of rotational symmetry.

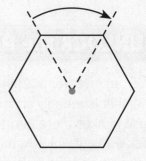

STEP 1

Trace the regular hexagon at right.

Place the tip of your pencil on the point shown in blue. Rotate the paper as shown by the arrow. The hexagon coincides with itself.

So, the hexagon has _____.

STEP 2

The amount of the rotation is ⬚/⬚ of a full turn.

To find the angle of rotational symmetry, multiply.

$$\frac{\boxed{}}{\boxed{}} \times 360° = \boxed{}$$

So, the angle of rotational symmetry is _____.

Remember
A full turn brings you back to your starting point. It is a rotation of 360°.

1. **Explain** why the definition of rotational symmetry states that the figure must be rotated *less than* 360°.

   _____

   _____

2. **Describe** a figure that has line symmetry, but that does not have rotational symmetry.

   _____

   _____

Name _____

Share and Show

Tell whether the figure has line symmetry. If so, draw the lines of symmetry.

1.

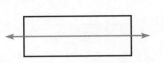

One line of symmetry is shown. Draw another.

_____

2.

_____

3.

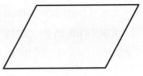

_____

Tell whether the figure has rotational symmetry. If so, give the angle of rotational symmetry.

4.

_____

5.

_____

Math Talk Explain how you can use paper folding to decide if a figure has line symmetry.

On Your Own

Tell whether the figure has line symmetry. If so, draw the lines of symmetry.

6.

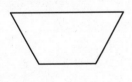

_____

7.

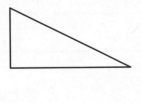

_____

8.

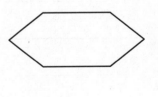

_____

9. Tell whether the figure has line symmetry. If so, draw the lines of symmetry. Then tell whether the figure has rotational symmetry. If so, give the angle of rotational symmetry.

Line symmetry? _____

Rotational symmetry? _____

© Houghton Mifflin Harcourt Publishing Company

Problem Solving REAL WORLD

A store sells ceramic tiles in the shapes shown in the figure. Use the figure for 10–12.

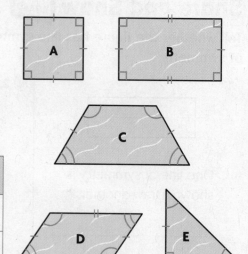

10. Complete the table. Give the most exact name for each tile. Then tell whether the tile has line symmetry and rotational symmetry by writing *yes* or *no* in the appropriate column.

Tile	Name	Line Symmetry?	Rotational Symmetry?
A			
B			
C			
D			
E			

11. A customer orders a tile that has at least two lines of symmetry. Which tile(s) could the customer have ordered?

_____

12. **Write Math** ▶ **Explain** how you can use the figure at right and rotations to make a design with rotational symmetry. Use the space at right to make the design.

_____

_____

_____

13. ⭐ **Test Prep** Which of the following figures has exactly 3 lines of symmetry?

(A) isosceles triangle

(B) equilateral triangle

(C) regular hexagon

(D) regular pentagon

Name _____

 Chapter 11 Review/Test

▶ **Vocabulary**

Choose the best term from the box.

1. A polygon with 7 sides is called a _____. (p. 433)

2. If you can draw a line through a figure so that the two halves are

   mirror images, the figure has _____. (p. 459)

3. If you can turn a figure less than 360° and it appears the same, the

   figure has _____. (p. 460)

Vocabulary
heptagon
line symmetry
nonagon
rotational symmetry

▶ **Concepts and Skills**

4. A dodecagon is a 12-sided polygon. The figure shows a regular dodecagon. What is the sum of the angle measures in a dodecagon? (pp. 447–450)

   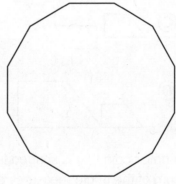

   Angle sum = _____

5. What is the missing angle measure in the quadrilateral? (pp. 441–444)

   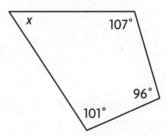

   x = _____

6. The coordinates of three of the vertices of parallelogram *QRST* are *Q*(2, 2), *R*(4, 5), and *S*(7, 5). What are the coordinates of vertex *T*?

   _____

Fill in the bubble for the correct answer choice.

7. Mitchell draws a figure in which ∠1 and ∠2 are vertical angles. The measure of ∠1 is 64° and the measure of ∠2 is (x − 22)°. What is the value of x? (pp. 429–432)

    (A) 22

    (B) 42

    (C) 64

    (D) 86

8. What is the angle of rotational symmetry for the figure? (pp. 459–462)

    (A) 30°   (C) 60°

    (B) 45°   (D) 90°

9. Which of the following shows a figure and its image after a rotation? (pp. 455–458)

    (A) 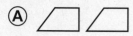   (C)

    (B) 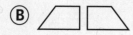   (D)

10. The nation of Tuvalu has a one-dollar coin that is shaped like a regular nonagon. What is the sum of the angle measures of this coin? (pp. 447–450)

    (A) 1,080°

    (B) 1,260°

    (C) 1,620°

    (D) 2,520°

11. A triangle has two angles that each measure 66°. What is the measure of the third angle of the triangle? (pp. 437–440)

    (A) 33°

    (B) 48°

    (C) 114°

    (D) 132°

12. Which is the best estimate for the measure of the angle? (pp. 425–428)

TEST PREP

(A) 30°   (C) 110°

(B) 80°   (D) 160°

13. The two polygons are congruent. Which angle is the corresponding angle for ∠M? (pp. 433–436)

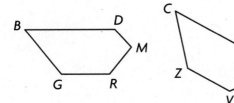

(A) ∠J   (C) ∠V

(B) ∠P   (D) ∠Z

14. Quadrilateral *UVWX* is a square. Which of the following is NOT another correct way to classify quadrilateral *UVWX*? (pp. 441–444)

(A) parallelogram

(B) rectangle

(C) rhombus

(D) trapezoid

15. What are the coordinates of the missing vertex of rectangle *ABCD*? (pp. 451–454)

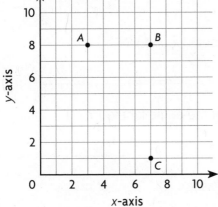

(A) (0, 1)   (C) (2, 1)

(B) (1, 3)   (D) (3, 1)

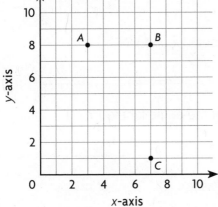

▶ **Short Answer**

16. The figure shows a ramp that is part of a miniature golf course. What is the missing angle measure in the figure? (pp. 437–440)

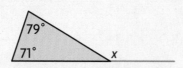

$x =$ _____

17. Draw a figure that looks the same after a reflection across a vertical line. (pp. 455–458)

▶ **Performance Task**

18. Roberto is making a stained-glass window. He has already made a regular pentagon. Next, he wants to cut a triangular piece of glass to fit next to the pentagon as shown, but he's not sure what the angle measures y and z should be.

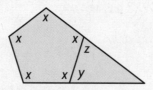

Ⓐ What is the angle sum of the pentagon? _____

Ⓑ Write and solve an equation to find the measure of one interior angle, labeled x in the diagram.

_____

Ⓒ What kind of angle pair is formed by the angles labeled x and y?

_____

Ⓓ Write and solve an equation to find the measure of the angle labeled y.

_____

Ⓔ Explain why angle z should be the same measure as y.

_____

_____

Show What You Know ✓

Check your understanding of important skills.

Name _____

▶ **Perimeter** **Find the perimeter.**

1.

$P =$ _____ units

2.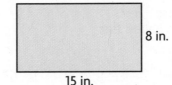
8 mm   15 mm

17 mm $P =$ _____ mm

▶ **Evaluate Algebraic Expressions** **Evaluate the expression.**

3. $5x + 2y$ for $x = 7$
and $y = 9$

_____

4. $6a \times 3b + 4$ for $a = 2$
and $b = 8$

_____

5. $s^2 + t^2 - 2^3$ for $s = 4$
and $t = 6$

_____

▶ **Area** **Find the area.**

6.

13 cm

13 cm

$A = s \times s$

Area = _____

7.

8 in.

15 in.

$A = b \times h$

Area = _____

8.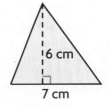

6 cm

7 cm

$A = (b \times h) \div 2$

Area = _____

MATH DETECTIVE

WITH

CARMEN SANDIEGO™

Ross needs to paint the white boundary lines of one end zone on a football field. The area of the end zone is 4,800 square feet, and one side of the end zone measures 30 feet. One can of paint is enough to paint 300 feet of line. Be a math detective and find out if one can is enough to line the perimeter of the end zone?

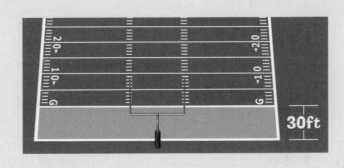

30ft

Vocabulary Builder

▶ **Visualize It** •••

Sort the checked words into the Venn diagram.

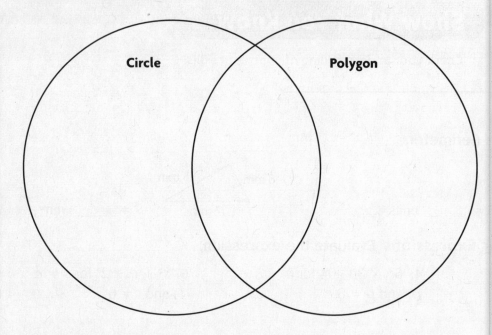

Circle   Polygon

▶ **Understand Vocabulary** •••••••••••••••••••••••••••••

Complete the sentences using the preview words.

1. The distance around a circle is called the _____.

2. The ratio of the circumference of a circle to the length of

   its diameter is called _____.

3. A(n) _____ is the product of a number and
   itself.

4. Half of a circle is called a(n) _____.

5. A number that is multiplied by itself to form a product is called

   a(n) _____ of that product.

6. A(n) _____ is made up of more than one shape.

GO Online • eStudent Edition • Multimedia eGlossary

Name _____

Estimate and Find Perimeter

Essential Question How can you find the perimeter of a polygon?

 UNLOCK the Problem REAL WORLD

Alex took his dog for a walk on the trail around the park. To find the distance he walked, he counted his steps and used the map to chart his progress. Each of Alex's steps measures 2.8 feet. How many yards did Alex walk?

Find the distance in yards Alex walked.

To find the distance Alex walked, find the perimeter of the pentagon. **Perimeter** is the distance around a closed plane figure. The perimeter is equal to the sum of the lengths of the sides.

P = sum of side lengths

$P = 335 + 317 + 376 + 404 + 333$

$P =$ _____ steps

To find the distance Alex walked, multiply the number of steps by 2.8 feet.

_____ $\times$ 2.8 = _____ feet

Then convert from feet to yards.

_____ ft $\times \dfrac{1 \text{ yd}}{3 \text{ ft}}$ = _____ yd

So, Alex walked _____ yards.

317 steps
376 steps
335 steps
404 steps
333 steps

---

1. Tell how you could use estimation to check your answer.

_____

_____

2. Explain how to find the perimeter of a regular polygon if you know the length of one side.

_____

_____

🔑 Example 1

The perimeter of the figure is 25 cm. Find the unknown side length.

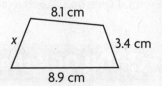

8.1 cm

x 3.4 cm

8.9 cm

Use what you know about perimeter.	P = sum of side lengths
Substitute 25 for P, and add the side lengths.	$25 = x + \underline{\hspace{1cm}} + \underline{\hspace{1cm}} + \underline{\hspace{1cm}}$
Add. Use Subtraction Property of Equality.	$\begin{array}{r} 25 \\ -20.4 \end{array} \quad \begin{array}{l} = x + 20.4 \\ -20.4 \end{array}$
Solve the equation.	$\underline{\hspace{1cm}} = x$

So, the unknown side length is _____ cm.

Perimeter of a Rectangle The opposite sides of a rectangle are equal in length. You can add all the side lengths to develop a formula for the perimeter of a rectangle where l is the length and w is the width.

$$P = l + l + w + w = 2l + 2w$$

l

w w

l

🔑 Example 2 Find the perimeter of the rectangle.

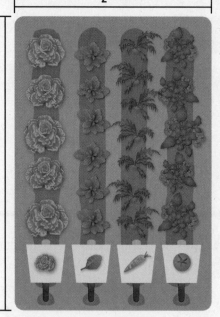

$3\frac{1}{2}$ feet

Roderick's garden is $3\frac{1}{2}$ feet wide. The length of the garden is $1\frac{1}{2}$ ft longer than the width. What is the length of the garden, and how many feet of fencing does Roderick need to put a fence around the perimeter of the garden?

Find the length.	$l = w + 1\frac{1}{2}$
Substitute $3\frac{1}{2}$ for w.	$l = 3\frac{1}{2} + 1\frac{1}{2}$
Solve for l.	$l = \underline{\hspace{1cm}}$

Find the perimeter.

Write the formula.	$P = 2l + 2w$
Substitute 5 for l and $3\frac{1}{2}$ for w.	$P = 2 \times 5 + 2 \times 3\frac{1}{2}$
Multiply.	$P = \underline{\hspace{1cm}} + \underline{\hspace{1cm}}$
Add.	$P = \underline{\hspace{1cm}}$

So, the length of the garden is _____ feet, and Roderick needs

_____ feet of fencing.

Math Talk Write a formula you could use to find the perimeter, P, of a square with side length s.

Name _____

Share and Show . . . .

Find the perimeter.

1.
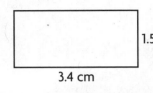

$P = 2l + 2w$

$P = 2 \times$ _____ $+ 2 \times$ _____

$P =$ _____ $+$ _____

$P =$ _____ cm

2.
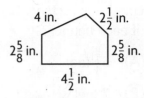

$P =$ _____

3. The perimeter is 207 cm. Find the length of the unknown side.

$x =$ _____

4. The width of a rectangular garden is 5 ft. The length is twice the width. Find the length and the perimeter of the garden.

$l =$ _____ $P =$ _____

Math Talk Explain how you can find the width of a rectangle if you know its perimeter and length.

On Your Own . . . .

The perimeter is given. Find the length of the unknown side.

5.
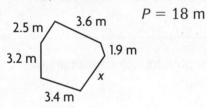

$P = 18$ m

$x =$ _____

6.
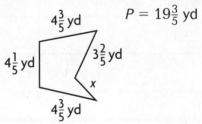

$P = 19\frac{3}{5}$ yd

$x =$ _____

7. A pentagon has a perimeter of 34.6 inches. Rafael knows the lengths of 4 sides: 6.2 in., 7.4 in., 8.1 in., and 5.8 in. How long is the fifth side?

_____

8. A square tile has a perimeter of 39.6 cm. Find the length of one side.

$s =$ _____

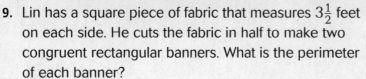
9. Lin has a square piece of fabric that measures $3\frac{1}{2}$ feet on each side. He cuts the fabric in half to make two congruent rectangular banners. What is the perimeter of each banner?

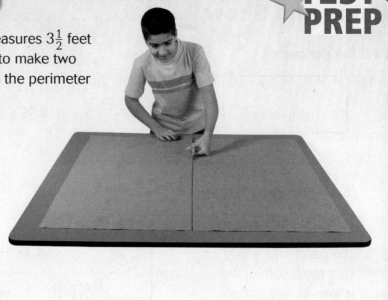

(A) $5\frac{1}{4}$ feet

(B) 7 feet

(C) $10\frac{1}{2}$ feet

(D) 14 feet

a. What is the length of the longer side of each rectangle?

_____

b. What is the length of the shorter side of each rectangle? Explain how you found your answer.

_____

_____

_____

c. What formula can you use to find the perimeter of each banner?

_____

d. What is the perimeter of each banner?

_____

e. Fill in the bubble for the correct answer choice above.

---

10. A triangle has a perimeter of 32.7 meters. Two of its sides have lengths of 12.1 meters and 7.9 meters. What is the length of the third side?

(A) 4.2 meters

(B) 12.7 meters

(C) 20 meters

(D) 52.7 meters

11. The width of a rectangle is 5 yards less than its length. If its dimensions are integers, which could be the perimeter of the rectangle?

(A) 14 yards

(B) 10 yards

(C) 8 yards

(D) 6 yards

Name _____

Estimate Circumference

Essential Question How does the diameter of a circle relate to the circumference?

CONNECT Recall that the **radius** of a circle is a line segment with one endpoint at the center and the other endpoint on the circle. A **diameter** is a line segment that passes through the center and has both endpoints on the circle. The **circumference** is the distance around the circle. You can use a ruler and string to estimate the circumference of a circle.

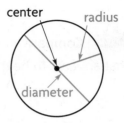

center   radius

diameter

Investigate

Materials ■ compass ■ centimeter ruler ■ string ■ calculator

A. Use a compass to draw a circle. Mark the center of the circle. Use a ruler to draw a diameter of the circle. Remember that the diameter passes through the center of the circle.

B. Measure the diameter of the circle to the nearest millimeter. Record your measurement.

_____

C. Lay the string around the circle. Mark the string where it meets itself.

D. Use the ruler to measure the string from its end to the mark you made. Measure to the nearest millimeter. Record your measurement.

E. Use a calculator to divide the circumference of your circle by the diameter. Record your result.

_____

F. Display your results on the board with those of other students in the class by making a table like the one below.

Circumference (*C*)	Diameter (*d*)	*C* ÷ *d*

Draw Conclusions

1. The length of the circumference of your circle is about how many times the diameter?

_____

2. **H.O.T.** **Compare** your results with those of other students. What appears to be the approximate ratio $\frac{C}{d}$ for any circle?

_____

Make Connections

1. Find the diameter of the circle.

   _____

2. Multiply the diameter of the circle by 3.

   $3 \times$ _____ = _____

3. **Estimate** the circumference of the circle. Explain how you made your estimate.

   _____

   _____

4. **Decide** whether the actual circumference of the circle is greater than or less than your estimate. Explain your reasoning.

   _____

   _____

5. Estimate the circumference of a circle with a radius of 7 cm. **Describe** your method.

   _____

   _____

   _____

   _____

   _____

Math Talk Describe the relationship between the diameter of a circle and the circumference.

Name _____

Share and Show [MATH BOARD] ·

Use a compass and a ruler to draw a circle with the given radius.
Estimate the circumference of the circle by using a string and a ruler.

1. radius = 4 cm

circumference: _____

2. radius = 8 cm

circumference: _____

3. radius = 6.5 cm

circumference: _____

4. radius = 7.5 cm

circumference: _____

Estimate the circumference of the circle.

5.

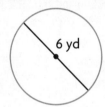

6 yd

circumference: _____

⊘ 6.

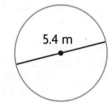

5.4 m

circumference: _____

⊘ 7.

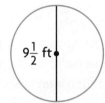

$9\frac{1}{2}$ ft

circumference: _____

8.

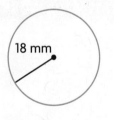

18 mm

circumference: _____

9.

25 in.

circumference: _____

10.

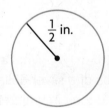

$\frac{1}{2}$ in.

circumference: _____

11. [Write Math] ► Explain how you could estimate the circumference
of a circle using only a ruler.

_____

_____

12. Explain how you could estimate the circumference of a circle if you
knew the radius of the circle.

_____

_____

Problem Solving

REAL WORLD

Use the table for 13–14.

13. Estimate the circumference of the clock on the face of Big Ben in London.

_____

14. The Cevahir clock at a shopping mall in Turkey may be the world's largest working clock. A football field is 100 yd long. How does the circumference of the Cevahir clock compare with the length of a football field?

_____

_____

Big Ben

Famous Clocks		
Name	**Location**	**Diameter (ft)**
Big Ben	London, England	23
Cevahir	Istanbul, Turkey	118
Colgate	Jersey City, New Jersey	50
Floral	Niagara Falls, NY	40

15. The minute hand on the Floral clock weighs 500 pounds. The minute hand on the Colgate clock weighs 1.1 tons. Find the difference in the weights.

_____

_____

_____

SHOW YOUR WORK

16. **Write Math** ▶ **What's the Error?** Keith measured the radius of a silver dollar and found it to be $\frac{3}{4}$ in. He estimated the circumference as $3 \times \frac{3}{4} = \frac{9}{4}$ in., or $2\frac{1}{4}$ in. What error did he make?

_____

_____

_____

17. ⭐ **Test Prep** Use the table above. Which is the best estimate of the difference between the circumferences of the Colgate clock and the Floral clock?

Ⓐ 5 feet

Ⓑ 10 feet

Ⓒ 15 feet

Ⓓ 30 feet

FOR MORE PRACTICE:
Standards Practice Book, pp. P235–P236

Name _____

Find Circumference

Essential Question How can you use a formula to find the circumference of a circle?

CONNECT In the last lesson, you found that the ratio $\frac{C}{d}$, is approximately 3. The actual ratio is called **pi**. It is represented by the symbol π. So, for any circle, $\frac{C}{d} = \pi$. The value of π is often approximated as 3.14 or $\frac{22}{7}$. To find a formula for the circumference of a circle, you can multiply both sides of the equation $\frac{C}{d} = \pi$ by d.

> **Circumference of a Circle**
>
> $C = \pi d$,
> where d is the diameter

UNLOCK the Problem — REAL WORLD

Five Sixty is a circular revolving restaurant located at the top of Reunion Tower in Dallas, Texas. It is 50 stories high and has a diameter of 118 feet. How far does a person seated 3 feet from the edge of the restaurant travel in one revolution?

 Find the circumference.

Find the diameter of the circular path the person is traveling.	$118 - 6 = 112$
Write the formula.	$C = \pi d$
Replace π and d with their values.	$C \approx \frac{22}{7} \times$ _____
Multiply.	$C \approx$ _____

So, a person travels about _____ ft in one revolution.

• What is the problem asking you to find?

_____

_____

• How will you find the diameter of the circular path the person is traveling?

_____

_____

 ERROR Alert

When you solve problems using approximations of π, use the symbol $\approx$, which means "is approximately equal to," instead of the symbol $=$.

• **Explain** when it might be easier to use $\frac{22}{7}$ for pi.

_____

_____

CONNECT You know the diameter of a circle is twice the radius, so you can also write a formula for circumference in terms of radius.

> **Circumference of a Circle**
>
> $C = 2\pi r$,
> where r is the radius

🔒 Example 1 Jeanette has a circular tablecloth with a radius of $3\frac{1}{2}$ ft. She wants to trim the tablecloth with fringe. How many feet of fringe will she need?

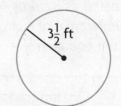

$3\frac{1}{2}$ ft

Write the formula. $C = 2\pi r$

Substitute the values for π and r. $C \approx 2 \times \frac{22}{7} \times 3\frac{1}{2}$

Rewrite 2 and $3\frac{1}{2}$. Simplify. $C \approx \frac{2}{1} \times \frac{22}{7} \times$ _____

Multiply. $C \approx$ _____

So, Jeanette will need about _____ ft of fringe.

🔒 Example 2 The circumference of a basketball hoop is 141.3 cm. What is the diameter of the hoop? Use 3.14 for π.

Write the formula. $C =$ _____

Replace C and π with their values.   _____ $\approx$ _____ d

Use the Division Property of Equality. $\dfrac{}{3.14} \approx \dfrac{d}{3.14}$

Simplify.   _____ $\approx d$

So, the diameter of the hoop is about _____ cm.

- **Explain** when it might be easier to use 3.14 for pi.

Math Talk **Explain** how you can check your answer after you find the diameter.

_____

_____

478

Name _____

Share and Show

Find the circumference. Use 3.14 or $\frac{22}{7}$ for π.

1. $C = \pi d$

$C \approx$ _____ × _____

$C \approx$ _____ cm

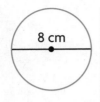
8 cm

2.

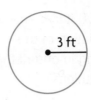
3 ft

_____

3.

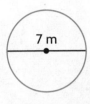
7 m

_____

4.

$17\frac{1}{2}$ yd

_____

5.

2.8 cm

_____

6. Juan measures the circumference of a fountain and finds it is 39.25 ft. What is the diameter of the fountain? Use 3.14 for π.

diameter = _____

Math Talk Explain how you can find the radius of a circle if you know its circumference.

On Your Own

Find the circumference. Use 3.14 or $\frac{22}{7}$ for π.

7.

20 in.

_____

8.

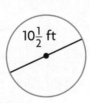
$10\frac{1}{2}$ ft

_____

9.

6.7 mm

_____

10.

4.5 km

_____

11.

$12\frac{1}{4}$ yd

_____

12.

1.8 m

_____

13. Randi measures the circumference of a hat box and finds it is $7\frac{6}{7}$ ft. What is the radius of the hat box?

_____

14. George W.G. Ferris built the first Ferris wheel in 1892. This wheel was 250 ft in diameter. Which is the best approximation of the distance that a person sitting in one of the cars would travel in 3 revolutions?

A about 750 feet

B about 1,178 feet

C about 2,355 feet

D about 4,710 feet

a. How do you know that the answer cannot be choice A?

_____

_____

_____

_____

c. What is the distance that a person sitting in one of the cars would travel in 1 revolution?

_____

_____

d. What is the distance that a person sitting in one of the cars would travel in 3 revolutions?

_____

_____

b. How can you find the distance that a person sitting in one of the cars would travel in 1 revolution?

_____

_____

_____

e. Fill in the bubble for the correct answer choice above.

15. A metal band encircles the top of a barrel with a diameter of 18 inches. Which measure is the best approximation of the circumference of the band?

A 45 inches

B 50 inches

C 57 inches

D 108 inches

16. Which method could you use to find the diameter of a circle if you knew C, the circumference of the circle?

A Divide C by π.

B Divide C by 2π.

C Multiply C by π.

D Multiply C by 2π.

Name _____

Area of Rectangles, Squares, and Parallelograms

Essential Question How can you find the area of a rectangle, square, and parallelogram?

The **area** of a figure is the number of square units needed to cover it without any gaps or overlaps. The rectangle shown has an area of 12 square units. The area is the product of the length and the width: 4 units $\times$ 3 units $=$ 12 square units.

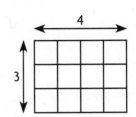

For a rectangle with length l and width w, $A = l \times w$, or $A = lw$.

🔓 UNLOCK the Problem REAL WORLD

Trampolining has been an Olympic sport since 2000. Athletes perform on a rectangular trampoline with a length of 14 ft and an area of 98 ft². What is the width of an Olympic trampoline?

🔑 **Find the width of a rectangle with area 98 ft² and length 14 ft.**

Write the formula.	$A = lw$
Replace A and l with their values.	$98 = 14w$
Use the Division Property of Equality.	$\dfrac{98}{} = \dfrac{14w}{}$
Solve for w.	_____ $= w$

So, an Olympic trampoline is _____ ft wide.

A square is a special rectangle in which the length and width are equal. For a square with side length s, $A = l \times w = s \times s = s^2$, or $A = s^2$.

🔑 Example 1 Find the area of a square with sides measuring 9.5 cm.

Write the formula.	$A = s^2$
Substitute 9.5 for s. Simplify.	$A = ($_____$)^2 =$ _____

So, the area of the square is _____ cm².

🔑 Example 2 Estimate the area of the parallelogram.

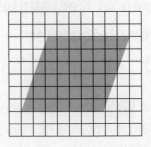

Count the shaded squares. There are _____ full squares.

There are _____ almost-full squares.

There are _____ squares that are about half-full. These

combine to make _____ full squares.

Total number of full squares: _____ + _____ + _____ = _____

So, the area is about _____ square units.

🔑 Activity Investigate the area of a parallelogram.

Materials • grid paper • scissors

- Draw the parallelogram on grid paper and cut it out.
- Cut along the dotted line to remove a triangle.
- Move the triangle to the right side of the figure to form a rectangle.

- What is the area of the rectangle? _____

- What is the area of the parallelogram? _____

- base of parallelogram = _____ of rectangle

  height of parallelogram = _____ of rectangle

  area of parallelogram = _____ of rectangle

- For a parallelogram with base b and height h, $A =$ _____

height (h)
4 units

base (b) 9 units

width (w)
4 units

length (l) 9 units

🔑 Example 3 Use the formula $A = bh$ to find the area of the parallelogram.

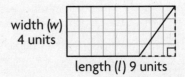

2.1 m

6.3 m

Write the formula.	$A = bh$
Replace b and h with their values.	$A = 6.3 \times$ _____
Multiply.	$A =$ _____

So, the area of the parallelogram is _____ square meters.

Math Talk Explain the difference between the height of a rectangle and the height of a parallelogram.

Name _____

Share and Show

Find the area of the figure.

1. $A = lw$

$A = 8.3 \times 1.2$

$A =$ _____ m²

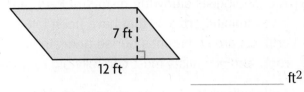

1.2 m

8.3 m

2.

7 ft

12 ft

_____ ft²

3. 2.5 mm

2.5 mm

_____ mm²

4.

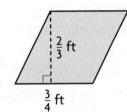

$\frac{2}{3}$ ft

$\frac{3}{4}$ ft

_____ ft²

Find the missing side length of the figure.

5. Area = 11 yd²

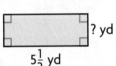

? yd

$5\frac{1}{2}$ yd

_____ yd

6. Area = 36 yd²

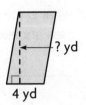

? yd

4 yd

_____ yd

> **Math Talk** Explain how the areas of some parallelograms and rectangles are related.

On Your Own

Find the area of the figure.

7.

6.4 m

9.1 m

_____ m²

8.

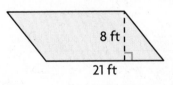

8 ft

21 ft

_____ ft²

Find the unknown measurement for the figure.

9. square

$A =$ _____

$s = 15$ ft

10. rectangle

$A = 36$ m²

$l =$ _____

$w = 9$ m

11. parallelogram

$A = 51\frac{1}{4}$ in²

$b = 8\frac{1}{5}$ in.

$h =$ _____

12. rectangle

$A = 121$ mm²

$l = 11$ mm

$w =$ _____

13. The height of a parallelogram is four times the base. The base measures $3\frac{1}{2}$ ft. Find the area of the parallelogram.

_____

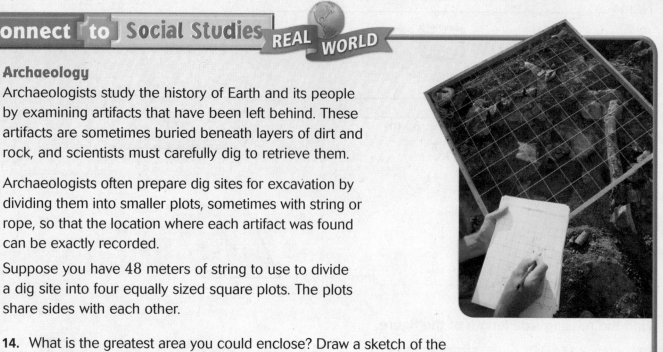

Connect to Social Studies — REAL WORLD

Archaeology

Archaeologists study the history of Earth and its people by examining artifacts that have been left behind. These artifacts are sometimes buried beneath layers of dirt and rock, and scientists must carefully dig to retrieve them.

Archaeologists often prepare dig sites for excavation by dividing them into smaller plots, sometimes with string or rope, so that the location where each artifact was found can be exactly recorded.

Suppose you have 48 meters of string to use to divide a dig site into four equally sized square plots. The plots share sides with each other.

14. What is the greatest area you could enclose? Draw a sketch of the area and explain your reasoning.

_____

_____

_____

_____

_____

_____

15. What would the perimeter of the site be? Explain.

_____

_____

_____

16. Juan used 20 m of string to mark off a dig site in the shape of a quadrilateral. The site has the greatest possible area. Name the kind of quadrilateral he used and its area.

_____

484   FOR MORE PRACTICE:
Standards Practice Book, pp. P239–P240

Name _____

Squares and Square Roots

Essential Question What is the relationship between the area of a square and the square root?

CONNECT Recall that the area of a square can be written as $A = s \times s$ or s^2. When a number is multiplied by itself, we say that it is squared.

$A = s^2$

s

Investigate

Materials ■ grid paper

How can you use grid paper to model the relationship between the side length of a square and its area?

A. Draw squares with side lengths of 1, 2, 3, and 4 on the grid paper.

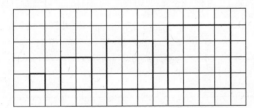

B. Use the squares you drew on the grid paper to complete the table.

Side Length of Square	Area of Square
1	
2	
3	
4	

> **Math Talk** Why do you think the numbers 1, 4, 9, and 16 are called perfect squares?

C. Continue drawing squares on the grid paper and filling in the table for side lengths up to 10.

A **perfect square** is the product of a number and itself. Since $5^2 = 25$, we say that 5 is the **square root** of 25. This is written $\sqrt{25} = 5$. A square with an area of 25 has a side length of 5.

D. Use your table to find $\sqrt{36}$, $\sqrt{49}$, $\sqrt{64}$, $\sqrt{81}$, and $\sqrt{100}$.

$\sqrt{36} =$ _____ $\sqrt{49} =$ _____ $\sqrt{64} =$ _____

$\sqrt{81} =$ _____ $\sqrt{100} =$ _____

Chapter 12   485

Draw Conclusions

1. **Tell** why you think squaring 4 and finding the square root of 16 are called inverse operations.

   _____

   _____

2. **Explain** how you know if the square root of 20 is a whole number.

   _____

   _____

3. **Generalize** Can the area of any parallelogram be found by squaring one of the sides? Explain.

   _____

   _____

   _____

Make Connections

Find the side length of the square. Explain how you found your answer.

Area = 225 square units

Use the formula for the area of a square.	$A = s^2$
Substitute 225 for A.	$225 = s^2$
Think: What number multiplied by itself equals 225?	____ $= s$

So, the side length of the square is _____ units.

- **Describe** the relationship between the area of a square and its side length.

   _____

Name _____

Share and Show

Find the side length of the square.

1.

Area = 144 units²

_____

2.

Area = 196 units²

_____

3.

Area = 361 units²

_____

Complete the equation.

4. $\sqrt{} = 16$

5. $\sqrt{324} = $

 6. $\sqrt{} = 13$

Solve.

7. Janet wants to make a square wall hanging from 16 square quilt blocks. How many blocks will be in each row?

_____

8. Jerrod's room is square with an area of 121 square feet. What is the length of one side of the room?

_____

9. Find two perfect squares with a sum of 25.

10. Find two perfect squares with a sum of 100.

_____

11. **H.O.T.** Craig covered his square patio with tiles. The area of the patio is 196 square feet. How many 6-inch square tiles are along one side of the patio? **Explain** how you found your answer.

_____

_____

Problem Solving 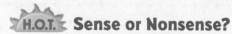 REAL WORLD

H.O.T. Sense or Nonsense?

12. Christina and Andrew are building a square patio. The area of the patio will be 256 square feet. Christina and Andrew each calculated the length of one side of the patio. Whose calculation makes sense? Whose calculation is nonsense? **Explain** your reasoning.

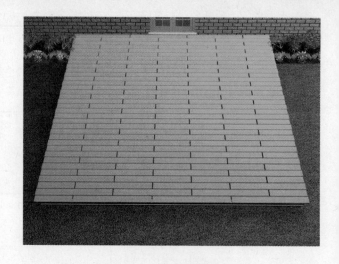

Christina's Calculation

$$256 = 2s$$
$$\frac{256}{2} = \frac{2s}{2}$$
$$128 = s$$

So, the length of one side of the patio is 128 ft.

_____

_____

_____

_____

_____

_____

Andrew's Calculation

$$256 = s^2$$
$$16 = s$$

So, the length of one side of the patio is 16 ft.

_____

_____

_____

_____

_____

_____

- For the calculation that is nonsense, how could you change it so that it makes sense?

_____

_____

- What would be the side length of a square with an area of 400 cm^2? **Explain** how you found your answer.

_____

_____

FOR MORE PRACTICE:
Standards Practice Book, pp. P241–P242

✓ Mid-Chapter Checkpoint

▶ **Vocabulary**

Choose the best term from the box.

Vocabulary
area
circumference
perfect square
perimeter
pi
square root

1. The distance around a closed plane figure is called the

   _____. (p. 469)

2. The number of square units needed to cover a surface without any

   gaps or overlaps is called the _____. (p. 481)

3. The ratio of the circumference of a circle to the length of its diameter

   is called _____. (p. 477)

4. A number that is multiplied by itself to form a product is called a

   _____ of that product. (p. 485)

5. The distance around a circle is called the _____. (p. 473)

▶ **Concepts and Skills**

The perimeter is given. Find the length of the unknown side. (pp. 469–472)

6. A rectangular painting has a width of 19 in. and a perimeter of 91 in. What is the height of the painting?

   _____

7. A pentagon with perimeter 97 cm has side lengths of 17 cm, 18 cm, 24 cm, and 23 cm. What is the length of the fifth side?

   _____

Solve. (pp. 477–480, 481–484, 485–488)

8. Find the circumference of a circle with a radius of 35 mm. Use $\frac{22}{7}$ for π.

   _____

9. The height of a parallelogram is 3 times the base. The base measures 4.5 cm. Find the area of the parallelogram.

   _____

10. A square rug has an area of 144 ft². What is the length of one side of the rug?

    _____

11. Rodney is building a foundation for a square storage building. The area of the foundation is 225 yd². What is the length of one side of the foundation in feet?

    _____

Fill in the bubble to show your answer.

12. An official table-tennis court is a rectangle with a perimeter of 28 feet and a width of 5 feet. How long is a table-tennis court? (pp. 469–472)

Ⓐ 4.5 feet

Ⓑ 9 feet

Ⓒ 14 feet

Ⓓ 23 feet

13. A round pizza has a diameter of 16 inches. Which is the best estimate of the circumference of the pizza? (pp. 473–476)

Ⓐ 32 inches

Ⓑ 48 inches

Ⓒ 64 inches

Ⓓ 96 inches

14. In a 3-ring circus, performers appear in 3 rings, each having a diameter of 30 feet. To the nearest foot, what is the total length of the material needed to construct the 3 rings? Use 3.14 for π. (pp. 477–480)

Ⓐ 94 feet

Ⓑ 188 feet

Ⓒ 283 feet

Ⓓ 565 feet

15. Rugs sell for $8 per square foot. Beth bought a 9-foot-long rectangular rug for $432. How wide was the rug? (pp. 481–484)

Ⓐ 6 feet

Ⓑ 48 feet

Ⓒ 54 feet

Ⓓ 72 feet

16. A square painting has an area of 324 square inches. What is the perimeter of the painting? (pp. 485–488)

Ⓐ 18 inches

Ⓑ 36 inches

Ⓒ 72 inches

Ⓓ 144 inches

Name _____

Area of Triangles and Trapezoids

Essential Question How can you find the area of triangles and trapezoids?

Any parallelogram can be divided into two congruent triangles. The area of each triangle is half the area of the parallelogram, so the area of a triangle is half the product of its base and its height.

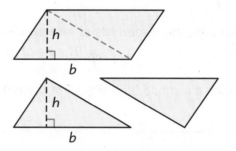

> **Area of a Triangle**
>
> $A = \frac{1}{2} bh$
>
> where b is the base and h is the height

🔑 UNLOCK the Problem REAL WORLD

The Flatiron Building in New York is well known for its unusual shape. The building was designed to fit the triangular plot of land formed by 22nd Street, 23rd Street, and Fifth Avenue. The diagram shows the dimensions of the triangular foundation of the building. The area of the foundation is 7,514.5 square feet. What is the height of the triangle?

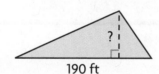

190 ft

🔑 **Find the height of the triangle.**

Write the formula. $A = \frac{1}{2} bh$

Substitute 7,514.5 for A and 190 for b.   _____ $= \frac{1}{2} \times$ _____ $\times h$

Multiply.   _____ $=$ _____ $\times h$

Use the Division Property of Equality. $\dfrac{7{,}514.5}{} = \dfrac{}{} h$

Simplify.   _____ $= h$

So, the height of the triangle is _____ feet.

Math Talk Explain how the area of a triangle relates to the area of a rectangle with the same base and height.

🔓 Activity

Materials grid paper • scissors

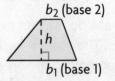

1. Trace two copies of the trapezoid on a sheet of grid paper. Label both trapezoids using h, b_1, and b_2, as shown. Cut them out.

2. Arrange the trapezoids to form a parallelogram. The length of the parallelogram is $b_1 + b_2$. The height is h.

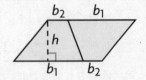

3. Write a formula for the area of the parallelogram.

   _____

4. How does the area of one trapezoid relate to the area of the parallelogram?

   _____

   _____

5. Write a formula for the area of a trapezoid.

   _____

🔓 Example   Find the area of the trapezoid.

Write the formula.

$$A = \frac{1}{2}(b_1 + b_2)h$$

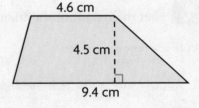

Substitute 4.5 for h, 9.4 for b_1, and 4.6 for b_2.

$$A = \frac{1}{2} \times (\underline{\quad\quad} + \underline{\quad\quad}) \times 4.5$$

Add.

$$A = \frac{1}{2} \times \underline{\quad\quad} \times 4.5$$

Multiply.

$$A = \underline{\quad\quad} \times 4.5 = \underline{\quad\quad}$$

So, the area of the trapezoid is _____ cm^2.

• **Explain** how to find the height of a trapezoid if you know the area and the length of both bases.

   _____

   _____

Name _____

Share and Show

1. Find the area of the triangle.

$A = \frac{1}{2}bh$

$A = \frac{1}{2} \times 14 \times$ _____

$A =$ _____ cm²

8 cm
14 cm

2. The area of the triangle is 132 in². Find the height of the triangle.

$h =$ _____

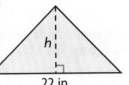
h
22 in.

Find the area of the trapezoid.

3.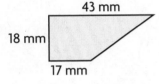
43 mm
18 mm
17 mm

$A =$ _____

4.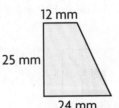
12 mm
25 mm
24 mm

$A =$ _____

Math Talk Explain how the area of a trapezoid is related to the area of a parallelogram with the same height and a base equal to the sum of the bases of the trapezoid.

On Your Own

Find the area.

5.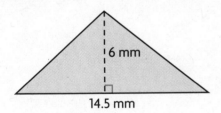
6 mm
14.5 mm

$A =$ _____

6.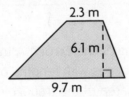
2.3 m
6.1 m
9.7 m

$A =$ _____

Find the missing dimension.

7.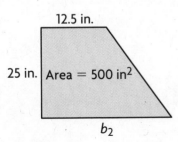
12.5 in.
25 in. Area = 500 in²
b_2

$b_2 =$ _____

8.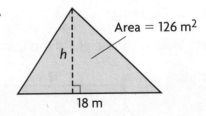
Area = 126 m²
h
18 m

$h =$ _____

Problem Solving  REAL WORLD

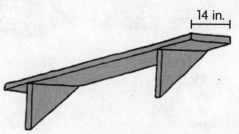

14 in.

9. Sarah is building a set of 4 shelves. Each shelf will have 2 supports in the shape of isosceles right triangles. Each shelf is 14 in. deep. How many square inches of wood will she need to make all the supports?

_____

SHOW YOUR WORK

10. A pattern used for tile floors is shown. A side of the inner square measures 10 cm, and a side of the outer square measures 30 cm. What is the area of one of the yellow trapezoid tiles?

_____

11. The formula for the area of a rhombus is $A = \frac{1}{2}d_1d_2$, where A is area and d_1 and d_2 are the lengths of the diagonals. Find the area of a rhombus with diagonals of length 10 m and 5 m.

_____

12. **Write Math** ▸ **What's the Error?** A trapezoid has a height of 12 cm and bases with lengths of 14 cm and 10 cm. Tina says the area of the trapezoid is 288 cm². Find her error and the correct area.

_____

_____

13. ★ **Test Prep** What is the height of the trapezoid?

Ⓐ 2.5 inches

Ⓑ 3 inches

Ⓒ 5 inches

Ⓓ 27 inches

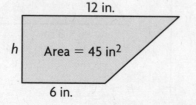

12 in.

h | Area = 45 in²

6 in.

© Houghton Mifflin Harcourt Publishing Company

Name _____

Area of Circles

Essential Question How can you use a model to estimate the area of a circle?

Investigate

Materials ■ compass ■ scissors ■ construction paper

A. Use a compass to draw a circle on construction paper.

B. Cut out the circle and fold it in half three times as shown.

C. Unfold the circle and trace the folds. Shade one half of the circle.

D. Cut along the folds. Fit the pieces together to make a figure that looks approximately like a parallelogram.

E. Compare the height of the parallelogram-like figure with the radius of the circle. What conclusion can you draw?

_____

_____

F. Compare the base of the figure with the circumference of the circle. What conclusion can you draw?

_____

_____

G. Since the circle and the parallelogram are made from the same pieces, they have the same area. So, to find a formula for the area of the circle, find the area of the parallelogram.

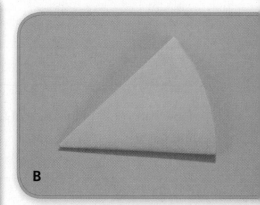

B

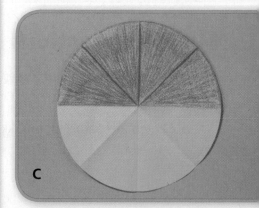

C

D

Write the formula for the area of a parallelogram.

$A = $ _____ × _____

Substitute half the circumference for the base and the radius for the height.

$A = \frac{1}{2}($ _____ $) \times$ _____

Simplify $\frac{1}{2}(2\pi r)$.

$A = $ _____ $\times r$

Simplify further, using the fact that $r \times r = r^2$.

$A = $ _____

So, the formula for the area of a circle with radius r is $A = \pi r^2$.

Remember

The formula for circumference of a circle is $C = \pi d$. Since $d = 2r$, the formula $C = 2\pi r$ can also be used to find circumference.

© Houghton Mifflin Harcourt Publishing Company

Draw Conclusions

1. **Explain** how you can use the formula for the area of a parallelogram to help write a formula for the area of a circle.

   _____

   _____

   _____

   _____

2. How can you find the area of a circle if you know the radius of the circle?

   _____

   _____

Make Connections

1. Imagine that you folded and cut this circle like the one in the investigation.

   8 cm

   a. Sketch the parallelogram-like figure and label the length and width.

   b. Write an equation to find the area of the parallelogram-like figure.

   _____

   c. Find the area of the circle. Use 3.14 for pi.

   _____

2. **Suppose** you had drawn a larger circle in the investigation. Would you have obtained the same result? Explain.

   _____

   _____

   _____

Math Talk Describe the relationship between the area of a circle and the radius.

Name _____

Share and Show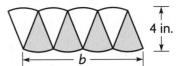

A circle is cut into 8 pieces. The pieces are rearranged to form the figure shown.

Answer these questions about the original circle and the figure. Use 3.14 for π.

1. What was the radius of the circle? _____

2. What is the value of b, the base of the figure? _____

3. What was the area of the circle? _____

Find the area of the circle with the given radius to the nearest whole number of units. Use 3.14 or $\frac{22}{7}$ for π.

4.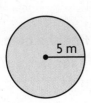

5 m

_____

5.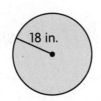

18 in.

_____

6.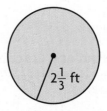

$2\frac{1}{3}$ ft

_____

7. A circular window has a radius of $2\frac{1}{2}$ feet. What is the area of the glass needed to fill the window?

_____

8. Alan rolls out pizza dough to form a circle with a diameter of 12 in. Find the area of the dough when it is rolled out.

_____

9. The pitcher's mound on a professional baseball field is 18 ft in diameter. What is the area of the circular pitching area?

_____

10. Rhonda uses a sprinkler to water her garden. The sprinkler waters a circular area with a radius of 14 ft. What is the area of the garden watered by the sprinkler?

_____

11. **Write Math** ▶ Explain how the area of a circle is related to the radius of the circle squared.

_____

Problem Solving

What's the Error?

12. Monica wanted to find the area of a circle with a diameter of $2\frac{4}{5}$ m.
She used $\frac{22}{7}$ for π.

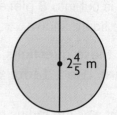

Monica solved:

$$A = \pi r^2$$

$$\approx \frac{22}{7} \times 2\frac{4}{5} \times 2\frac{4}{5}$$

$$\approx \frac{22}{7} \times \frac{14}{5} \times \frac{14}{5}$$

$$\approx \frac{22}{\underset{1}{7}} \times \overset{2}{\cancel{14}}{5} \times \frac{14}{5}$$

$$\approx \frac{616}{25}$$

$$\approx 24\frac{16}{25}$$

The area is about $24\frac{16}{25}$ m^2.

Find and describe Monica's error.

Show how to correctly find the area of the circle. Use $\frac{22}{7}$ for π.

So, the area of the circle is _____ m^2.

Describe the error that Monica made and how to correct it.

_____

_____

_____

Name _____

Area of Circles

Essential Question How can you find the area of a circle?

 UNLOCK the Problem REAL WORLD

Reflecting telescopes form images by reflecting light from the night sky off mirrors. Many of the mirrors are circular. The largest circular reflecting mirror in the United States is located at Mauna Kea Observatory in Hawaii. It has a diameter of 8.2 meters. What is the area of the mirror?

- Which formula should you use to solve the problem?

  _____

- How do you find the radius when you know the diameter?

  _____

Find the area of a circle with a diameter of 8.2 m. Use 3.14 for π.

Find the radius. $r = 8.2 \div 2 =$ _____

Write the formula. $A = \pi r^2$

Substitute the values for π and r. $A \approx$ _____ $\times ($_____$)^2$

Square the radius. $A \approx$ _____ $\times$ _____

Multiply. $A \approx$ _____

So, the Mauna Kea mirror has an area of about _____ m².

Try This! The Hale Telescope at Palomar Observatory in California uses a circular mirror with a diameter of 200 in. Find the area of the mirror. Use 3.14 for π.

Find the radius. $r = 200 \div 2 =$ _____

Write the formula. $A = \pi r^2$

Substitute the values for π and r. $A \approx$ _____ $\times ($_____$)^2$

Square the radius. $A \approx$ _____ $\times$ _____

Multiply. $A \approx$ _____

So, the mirror has an area of about _____ in².

🔑 Example 1
A circular skating rink has a circumference of 88 meters. What is the area of the rink? Use $\frac{22}{7}$ for π.

Use the formula for circumference to find the diameter.	$C = \pi d$
Substitute the values for C and π.	$88 \approx \frac{22}{7} \times d$
Use the Division Property of Equality.	$\frac{88}{\frac{22}{7}} \approx \frac{\frac{22}{7}}{\frac{22}{7}} \times d$
Multiply by the reciprocal of $\frac{22}{7}$.	$\overset{4}{\underset{1}{\frac{88}{1}}} \times \frac{7}{\underset{1}{22}} \approx d$
Simplify.	$28 \approx d$
Find the radius.	$r \approx 28 \div 2 \approx \underline{\hspace{1cm}}$
Write the formula for the area of a circle.	$A = \pi r^2$
Substitute the values for π and r.	$A \approx \underline{\hspace{1cm}} \times (\underline{\hspace{1cm}})^2$
Square the radius.	$A \approx \underline{\hspace{1cm}} \times \underline{\hspace{1cm}}$
Multiply.	$A \approx \underline{\hspace{1cm}}$

ERROR Alert

Be sure to divide the diameter by 2 before using the area formula.

So, the area of the rink is about _____ m^2.

🔑 Example 2
The sprinkler at the edge of Mrs. Brown's yard only rotates halfway around. It waters a semicircle, one half of a circle, rather than a full circle. Find the area of the semicircle with a diameter of 14 ft. Use $\frac{22}{7}$ for π.

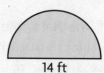

14 ft

Find the radius.	$r = 14 \div 2 = \underline{\hspace{1cm}}$
Write the formula.	$A = \pi r^2$
Substitute the values for π and r.	$A \approx \underline{\hspace{1cm}} \times (\underline{\hspace{1cm}})^2$
Square the radius and simplify.	$A \approx \frac{22}{\underset{1}{7}} \times \frac{\overset{7}{49}}{1} \approx \underline{\hspace{1cm}}$
Divide by 2 to find the area of the semicircle.	$A \approx \underline{\hspace{1cm}} \div 2 \approx \underline{\hspace{1cm}}$

So, the area of the semicircle is about _____ ft^2.

Math Talk How would you change the formula for the area of a circle to make it a formula for the area of a semicircle?

Name _____

Share and Show

Find the area to the nearest whole number. Use 3.14 for π.

1. $A = \pi r^2$

$A \approx 3.14 \times$ _____^{2}

$A \approx$ _____ or _____ cm^2

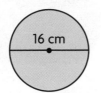
16 cm

2.

7 yd

_____

3.

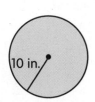
10 in.

_____

4.

12.2 m

_____

5.

22 in.

_____

Math Talk Explain how to find the area of a circle if you know the diameter.

On Your Own

Find the area to the nearest whole number. Use 3.14 or $\frac{22}{7}$ for π.

6.

15 m

_____

7.

21 ft

_____

8.

40 mm

_____

9. The Manicouagan crater in Quebec, Canada, was formed more than 200 million years ago by a meteor that impacted Earth. The diameter of the original crater was approximately 62 miles. What

was the area of the original crater? _____

10. The yellow circle in the center of the archery target has a circumference of 37.68 cm. What is the area of the yellow circle?

_____

11. H.O.T. The radius of the circle including the yellow and red rings

is 12 cm. What is the area of the red rings? _____

Problem Solving  REAL WORLD

Music has been recorded on at least four types of circular discs. Use the data in the table to solve. Use 3.14 or $\frac{22}{7}$ for π.

12. The earliest discs are called 78s because they make 78 revolutions per minute (rpm). What is the area of a 78?

_____

13. **H.O.T.** The 45-rpm disc has a hole in the center measuring $1\frac{1}{2}$ in. in diameter. How much of a 45s area remains after the hole is cut out?

_____

14. Johnny wants to figure out how far a point on the edge of a $33\frac{1}{3}$-rpm disc travels in 5 revolutions.

a. Should Johnny use circumference or area to solve the problem?

_____

b. Solve the problem.

_____

15. **Write Math** ▶ **What's the Error?** Mike said the area of a CD is about 18.84 cm². Describe his error and find the correct area. Use 3.14 for π.

_____

_____

16. ⭐ **Test Prep** Tammy has a square piece of cardboard that measures 18 inches by 18 inches. What is the approximate area of the largest circle she can cut from the piece of cardboard?

(A) 28.26 in² **(B)** 56.52 in²

(C) 254.34 in² **(D)** 1,017.36 in²

Recording Formats		
Name (rpm = "revolutions per minute")	Year Invented	Diameter
78 rpm	~1900	10 in.
$33\frac{1}{3}$ rpm	1948	12 in.
45 rpm	1949	7 in.
CD	1982	12 cm

······ **SHOW YOUR WORK** ······

FOR MORE PRACTICE:
Standards Practice Book, pp. P247–P248

Name _____

Composite Figures

Essential Question How can you find the perimeter and area of composite figures?

A **composite figure** is made up of two or more simpler figures, such as triangles and quadrilaterals.

🔑 UNLOCK the Problem REAL WORLD

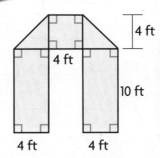

The new entryway to the fun house at Happy World Amusement Park is made from the shapes shown in the diagram. It will be painted bright green. Juanita needs to know the area of the entryway to determine how much paint to buy. What is the area of the entryway?

 Find the area of the entryway.

STEP 1 Find the area of the rectangles.

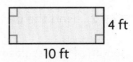

Write the formula. $A = l \times w$

Substitute the values for *l* and *w* and evaluate. $A = 10 \times$ _____ = _____

Find the total area of two rectangles. $A = 2 \times$ _____ = _____ ft^2

STEP 2 Find the area of the triangles.

Write the formula. $A = \frac{1}{2} \times b \times h$

Substitute the values for *b* and *h* and evaluate. $A = \frac{1}{2} \times 4 \times$ _____ = _____

Find the total area of two triangles. $A = 2 \times$ _____ = _____ ft^2

STEP 3 Find the area of the square.

Write the formula. $A = s^2$

Substitute the value for *s*. $A = ($_____$)^2 =$ _____ ft^2

STEP 4 Find the total area of the composite figure.

Add the areas. $A = 80$ ft$^2 +$ _____ ft$^2 +$ _____ ft$^2 =$ _____ ft^2

So, Juanita needs to buy enough paint to cover _____ ft^2.

Math Talk Discuss other ways you could divide up the composite figure.

🔑 Example 1   Find the area and perimeter of the composite figure shown. Use 3.14 for π.

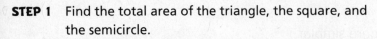

STEP 1   Find the total area of the triangle, the square, and the semicircle.

area of triangle $A = \frac{1}{2}bh = \frac{1}{2} \times 16 \times$ _____

$= $ _____ cm²

area of square $A = s^2 = ($ _____ $)^2$

$= $ _____ cm²

area of semicircle
(*half* of circle) $A = \frac{1}{2}\pi r^2 \approx \frac{1}{2} \times$ _____ $\times ($ _____ $)^2$

$\approx$ _____ cm²

total area $A \approx$ _____ cm² + _____ cm² + _____ cm²

$\approx$ _____ cm²

STEP 2   Find the perimeter of the figure.

length of blue segments $20 + 16 +$ _____ $+$ _____ $=$ _____ cm

length of red semicircle
(*half* of circumference, C) $\frac{1}{2}C = \frac{1}{2}\pi d \approx \frac{1}{2} \times$ _____ $\times$ _____

$\approx$ _____ cm

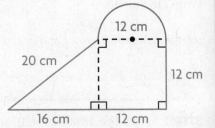

total perimeter $P \approx$ _____ cm + _____ cm $\approx$ _____ cm

So, the area is about _____ cm² and the perimeter is about _____ cm.

🔑 Example 2   Find the area of the shaded region.

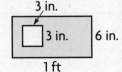

STEP 1

Find the area of the rectangle.
(1 ft = 12 in.)

$A = lw =$ _____ $\times$ _____

$A =$ _____ in²

STEP 2

Find the area of the square.

$A = s^2 = ($ _____ $)^2$

$A =$ _____ in²

STEP 3

Subtract the areas.

$A =$ _____ in² $-$ _____ in²

$A =$ _____ in²

So, the area of the shaded region is _____ in².

> **Math Talk**   Can you find the perimeter of the figure in Example 1 by adding the perimeter of the triangle, the square, and the semicircle? Explain.

504

Share and Show

1. Find the area of the figure.

area of one rectangle $A = l \times w$

$A = $ _____ $\times$ _____ $= $ _____ ft^2

area of 2 rectangles $A = 2 \times $ _____ $= $ _____ ft^2

length of base of triangle $b = $ _____ ft $+$ _____ ft $+$ _____ ft

$= $ _____ ft

area of triangle $A = \frac{1}{2} bh$

$A = \frac{1}{2} \times $ _____ $\times$ _____ $= $ _____ ft^2

area of composite figure $A = $ _____ ft^2 $+$ _____ ft^2 $= $ _____ ft^2

(figure at right: 8 ft, 3 ft, 10 ft, 5 ft, 5 ft)

Find the area and perimeter of the figure. Use 3.14 for π.

2.

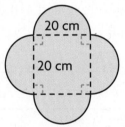

20 cm
20 cm

_____

3.

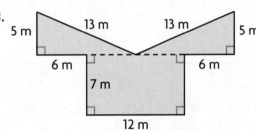

5 m   13 m   13 m   5 m
6 m   6 m
7 m
12 m

_____

> **Math Talk** Explain how to find the area of a composite figure.

On Your Own

4. Find the area and perimeter of the figure. Use 3.14 for π.

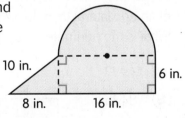

10 in.   6 in.
8 in.   16 in.

_____

5. Find the area of the shaded region.

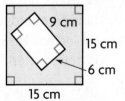

9 cm
15 cm
6 cm
15 cm

_____

6. The flag of the nation of Guyana is shown. What is the area of the yellow shape?

Ⓐ 360 square inches

Ⓑ 540 square inches

Ⓒ 720 square inches

Ⓓ 1,080 square inches

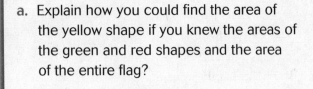

15 in.

24 in.

15 in.

48 in.

a. Explain how you could find the area of the yellow shape if you knew the areas of the green and red shapes and the area of the entire flag?

_____

_____

_____

b. What is the area of the entire flag? Explain how you found it.

_____

_____

_____

c. What is the area of the red shape? What is the area of each green shape?

_____

d. What equation can you write to find A, the area of the yellow shape?

_____

_____

e. What is the area of the yellow shape?

_____

f. Fill in the bubble for the correct answer choice above.

7. Four photographs each measuring 8 in. by 10 inches are pinned on a rectangular bulletin board measuring 20 inches by 24 inches. How much of the bulletin board is not covered by photos?

Ⓐ 80 square inches

Ⓑ 160 square inches

Ⓒ 320 square inches

Ⓓ 400 square inches

8. The figure shows an arrow on a road sign with the given dimensions. The arrow is composed of an equilateral triangle and a rectangle. What is the perimeter of the arrow?

Ⓐ 76 in.

Ⓑ 84 in.

Ⓒ 92 in.

Ⓓ 100 in.

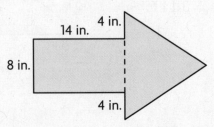

14 in.   4 in.

8 in.

4 in.

© Houghton Mifflin Harcourt Publishing Company

Name _____

Find a Pattern · Changing Dimensions

Essential Question How does changing the dimensions affect the perimeter and area of a polygon?

UNLOCK the Problem REAL WORLD

Jason has created a 3 in. by 4 in. rectangular design to be made into mouse pads. To manufacture the pads, the dimensions will be multiplied by 2 and 3. How will the perimeter and area of the design be affected?

3 in.

4 in.

Read the Problem

What do I need to find?	What information do I need to use?	How will I use the information?
I need to find how _____ _____ will be affected by changing the _____.	I need to use _____ of the original design and _____ _____.	I can draw a sketch of each rectangle and calculate _____ of each. Then I can look for _____ in my results.

Solve the Problem

Sketch	Dimensions	Multiplier	Perimeter	Area
	3 in. by 4 in.	none	$P = 2(3) + 2(4) = 14$ in.	$A = 3 \times 4 = 12$ in^2
6 in. 8 in.	6 in. by 8 in.	2	$P = 2(\underline{\hspace{1cm}}) + 2(\underline{\hspace{1cm}})$ $= \underline{\hspace{1cm}}$ in.	$A = \underline{\hspace{1cm}} \times \underline{\hspace{1cm}}$ $= \underline{\hspace{1cm}}$ in^2
9 in. 12 in.				

How are the perimeter and area affected when the dimensions are multiplied by 2? by 3?

_____

_____

Try Another Problem

A stained-glass designer is reducing the dimensions of an earlier design. The dimensions of the triangle shown will be multiplied by $\frac{1}{2}$ and $\frac{1}{4}$. How will the perimeter and area of the design be affected? Use the graphic organizer to help you solve the problem.

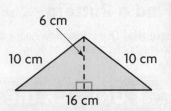

Read the Problem

What do I need to find?	What information do I need to use?	How will I use the information?

Solve the Problem

Sketch	Multiplier	Perimeter	Area
	none	$P = \underline{\hspace{1cm}} + \underline{\hspace{1cm}} + \underline{\hspace{1cm}}$ $= \underline{\hspace{1cm}}$ cm	$A = \frac{1}{2} \times 16 \times \underline{\hspace{1cm}}$ $= \underline{\hspace{1cm}}$ cm^2
3 cm 5 cm 5 cm 8 cm	$\frac{1}{2}$		

So, when the dimensions are multiplied by $\frac{1}{2}$, the perimeter is multiplied

by _____ and the area is multiplied by _____. When the dimensions

are multiplied by _____, the perimeter is multiplied by _____ and the

area is multiplied by _____.

Math Talk Explain what happens to the perimeter and area of a triangle when the dimensions are multiplied by a number *n*.

508

Name _____

Share and Show MATH BOARD . . . .

Tips

🔑 UNLOCK the Problem

✓ Plan your solution by deciding on the steps you will use.

✓ Find the original perimeter and area and the new perimeter and area, and then compare the two.

✓ Look for patterns in your results.

✓ 1. The dimensions of a 2 cm by 6 cm rectangle are multiplied by 5. How are the perimeter and area of the rectangle affected?

First, find the original perimeter and area:

perimeter: _____ area: _____

Next, find the new perimeter and area:

perimeter: _____ area: _____

So, the perimeter is multiplied by _____ and

the area is multiplied by _____.

SHOW YOUR WORK

✓ 2. 🔺**H.O.T.** What if the dimensions of the original rectangle in Exercise 1 had been multiplied by $\frac{1}{2}$? How would the perimeter and area have been affected?

_____

_____

_____

3. Evan bought two square rugs. The larger one measured 12 ft square. The smaller one had an area equal to $\frac{1}{4}$ the area of the larger one. What fraction of the side lengths of the larger rug were the side lengths of the smaller one?

_____

4. On Silver Island, a palm tree, a giant rock, and a buried treasure form a triangle with a length of 100 yd and a height of 50 yd. On a map of the island, the three landmarks form a triangle with a length of 2 ft and a height of 1 ft. How many times the area of the smaller triangle is the area of the larger triangle?

_____

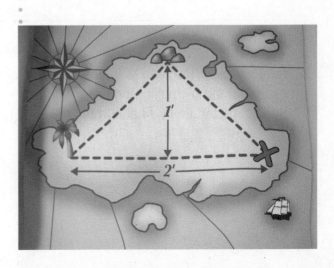

On Your Own...

Choose a STRATEGY

Work Backward
Solve a Simpler Problem
Choose an Operation
Use a Model
Use a Formula
Draw a Diagram

5. A square game board is divided into smaller squares, each with sides one-ninth the length of the sides of the board. Into how many squares is the game board divided?

_____

6. **H.O.T.** Flynn County is a rectangle measuring 9 mi by 12 mi. Gibson County is a rectangle with an area 6 times the area of Flynn County and a width of 16 mi. What is the perimeter of Gibson County?

_____

SHOW YOUR WORK

7. Carmen left her house and drove 10 mi north, 15 mi east, 13 mi south, 11 mi west, and 3 mi north. How far was she from home?

_____

8. **Write About It** Bernie drove from his house to his cousin's house in 6 hours at an average rate of 52 mi per hr. He drove home at an average rate of 60 mi per hr. **Explain** how you could find how long it took him to drive home.

_____

_____

_____

9. ⭐ **Test Prep** The dimensions of a rectangle are reduced by $\frac{1}{3}$. The area of the reduced rectangle can be found by multiplying the area of the original rectangle by what number?

Ⓐ $\frac{1}{3}$

Ⓑ $\frac{1}{6}$

Ⓒ $\frac{1}{9}$

Ⓓ $\frac{1}{12}$

Name _____

✓ Chapter 12 Review/Test

▶ Vocabulary

Choose the best term from the box.

1. A _____ is half of a circle. (p. 500)

2. The ratio of the circumference of a circle to the length of its

   diameter is called _____ (p. 477)

3. A _____ is made up of more than
   one shape. (p. 503)

4. A _____ is the product of a number
   and itself. (p. 485)

▶ Concepts and Skills

Find the circumference and area of a circle with the given measure. Use 3.14 or $\frac{22}{7}$ for π. (pp. 477–480, 499–502)

5. radius = 7 ft

6. diameter = 9.4 cm

_____

_____

Find the unknown measure. (pp. 485–488, 491–494)

7. triangle

   $A = 40$ in^2

   $b =$ _____

   $h = 5$ in.

8. trapezoid

   $A = 55$ m^2

   $b_1 = 9$ m

   $b_2 = 13$ m

   $h =$ _____

9. square

   $A = 169$ mm^2

   $s =$ _____

10. A racetrack is formed by a rectangle and two semicircles.
    What is the perimeter of the racetrack? Use 3.14 for π.
    (pp. 503–506)

    100 yd

    • 25 yd •

_____

Fill in the bubble to show your answer.

11. Newton County, Mississippi, is a square county with a perimeter of 95.2 miles. Find the length of one side of Newton County.
(pp. 469–472)

Ⓐ 9.8 miles

Ⓑ 23.8 miles

Ⓒ 47.6 miles

Ⓓ 380.8 miles

12. A beetle sits on the outer edge of a merry-go-round with a radius of 10 yards. Which is the best estimate of the total distance that the beetle will travel in 5 complete revolutions of the merry-go-round?
(pp. 473–476)

Ⓐ 30 yards

Ⓑ 60 yards

Ⓒ 150 yards

Ⓓ 300 yards

13. Curved tiles shaped like portions of a circle are each 6.28 inches in length. A complete circle can be formed by placing 12 tiles end-to-end. What is the radius of the circle? Use 3.14 for π. (pp. 477–480)

Ⓐ 24 inches

Ⓑ 18 inches

Ⓒ 12 inches

Ⓓ 6 inches

14. A rectangular rug is 9 feet in width and has an area of 108 square feet. What is the length of the rug? (pp. 481–484)

Ⓐ   6 feet

Ⓑ 12 feet

Ⓒ 24 feet

Ⓓ 972 feet

15. Ellen's living room is square and has an area of 400 square feet. What is the perimeter of the room? (pp. 481–484)

Ⓐ 20 feet

Ⓑ 80 feet

Ⓒ 400 feet

Ⓓ 800 feet

Fill in the bubble to show your answer.

16. A pattern block in the shape of an equilateral triangle has a base of 2 centimeters and an area of 1.7 square centimeters. Find the height of the block. (pp. 491–494)

Ⓐ 0.85 centimeter

Ⓑ 1.7 centimeters

Ⓒ 2.55 centimeters

Ⓓ 3.4 centimeters

17. A circle is drawn inside a square so that the circle touches the square at the midpoint of each side. The area of the square is 100 square inches. What is the area of the circle? (pp. 495–498)

Ⓐ 10π

Ⓑ 20π

Ⓒ 25π

Ⓓ 100π

18. Two semicircles are cut from a circular piece of cloth with a diameter of 14 centimeters. What is the area of each semicircle? Use $\frac{22}{7}$ for π. (pp. 499–502)

Ⓐ 11 square centimeters

Ⓑ 22 square centimeters

Ⓒ 77 square centimeters

Ⓓ 154 square centimeters

19. A wall in Stanley's living room measures 9 feet by 20 feet. There are two windows in the wall, each measuring 4 feet by 4 feet. If he paints the wall, how much area will he have to cover? (pp. 503–506)

Ⓐ 100 square feet

Ⓑ 116 square feet

Ⓒ 148 square feet

Ⓓ 160 square feet

20. The dimensions of a rectangle are multiplied by 9. How is the area of the rectangle affected? (pp. 485–488)

Ⓐ It is multiplied by 3.

Ⓑ It is multiplied by 9.

Ⓒ It is multiplied by 18.

Ⓓ It is multiplied by 81.

21. Explain how you could estimate the radius of a circle if you knew the circle's circumference. (pp. 477–480)

_____

_____

_____

22. Explain how you could find the height of a triangle if you knew the length of the base and the area of the triangle. (pp. 491–494)

_____

_____

_____

► **Performance Task**

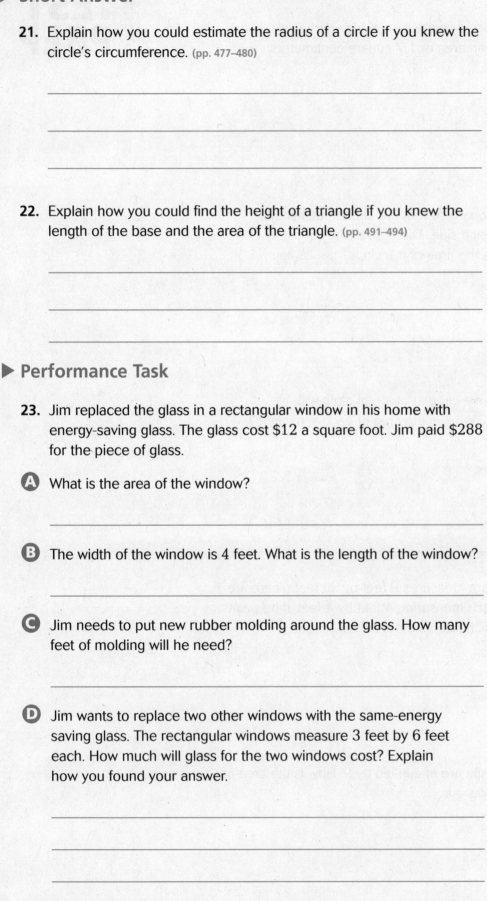

23. Jim replaced the glass in a rectangular window in his home with energy-saving glass. The glass cost $12 a square foot. Jim paid $288 for the piece of glass.

Ⓐ What is the area of the window?

_____

Ⓑ The width of the window is 4 feet. What is the length of the window?

_____

Ⓒ Jim needs to put new rubber molding around the glass. How many feet of molding will he need?

_____

Ⓓ Jim wants to replace two other windows with the same-energy saving glass. The rectangular windows measure 3 feet by 6 feet each. How much will glass for the two windows cost? Explain how you found your answer.

_____

_____

_____

Show What You Know

Check your understanding of important skills.

Name _____

▶ **Volume** **Multiply to find the volume.**

1. length = _____

   width = _____

   height = _____

   _____ cubic units

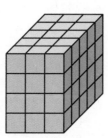

2. length = _____

   width = _____

   height = _____

   _____ cubic units

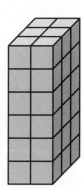

▶ **Solid Figures** **Identify the figure.**

3.

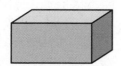 _____

4.

 _____

▶ **Faces, Edges, and Vertices** **Write the number of faces, edges and vertices for the figure.**

5. Use the figure in problem 3.

   _____

6. Use the figure in problem 4.

   _____

MATH DETECTIVE

WITH

CARMEN SANDIEGO™

Jerry is building an indoor beach volleyball court.
He has ordered 14,000 cubic feet of sand.
The dimensions of the court will be 30 feet by 60 feet.
Jerry needs to have a 10-foot boundary around the
court for safety. Be a math detective and determine
how deep the sand will be if Jerry uses all the sand.

Vocabulary Builder

▶ **Visualize It** •

Complete the bubble map. Use the review terms
that name solid figures.

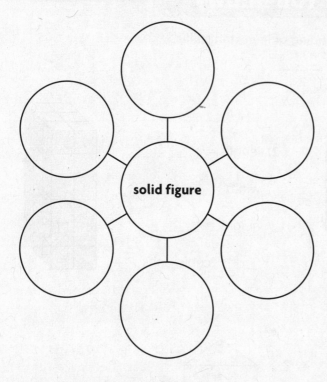

solid figure

▶ **Understand Vocabulary** •

Complete the sentences using the checked terms.

1. A three-dimensional figure having length, width, and height is

   called a(n) _____.

2. A two-dimensional pattern that can be folded into a

   three-dimensional figure is called a(n) _____.

3. _____ is the sum of the areas of all the faces,
   or surfaces, of a solid figure.

4. Any surface of a solid figure other than a base is called a(n)

   _____.

5. _____ is the measure of space a solid figure
   occupies.

GO Online • eStudent Edition • Multimedia eGlossary

Name _____

Solid Figures and Nets

Essential Question How can you identify solid figures and draw their nets?

A **solid figure** has three dimensions—length, width, and height. Solid figures can be identified by the shapes of their bases, the number of bases, and the shapes of their lateral faces, or surfaces.

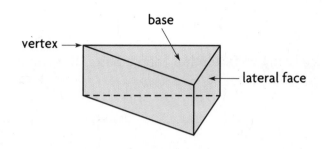

base

vertex →

— lateral face

Triangular Prism

UNLOCK the Problem · REAL WORLD

A designer is working on the layout for the cereal box shown. Identify the solid figure and draw a net that the designer can use to show the placement of information and artwork on the box.

- How many bases are there? _____
- Are the bases congruent? _____
- What shape are the bases? _____

 Identify the solid figure.

Recall that a prism is a solid figure with two congruent, parallel bases. Its lateral faces are rectangles. It is named for the shape of its bases.

Is the cereal box a prism? _____

What shape are the bases? _____

So, the box is a _____.

 Draw a net for the figure.

A **net** is a plane figure that can be folded into a solid figure.

STEP 1

Make a list of the shapes you will use.

top and bottom bases: _____

left and right faces: _____

front and back faces: _____

STEP 2

Plan how the shapes will connect to each other. Then draw the net. One possible net is shown.

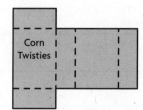

🔒 Example 1 Identify and draw a net for the solid figure.

Describe the bases of the figure.

_____

The **lateral surface** is any surface other than a base. Describe the lateral surface.

_____

So, the figure is a _____.

Shapes to use in the net:

Net:

top and bottom bases: _____

lateral surface: _____

🔒 Example 2 Identify and draw a net for the solid figure.

Describe the base of the figure.

_____

Describe the lateral faces.

_____

The figure is a _____.

Shapes to use in the net:

Net:

base: _____

lateral faces: _____

• **Compare** the net of a prism and a cylinder.

_____

_____

_____

Math Talk Compare the bases and lateral faces of prisms and pyramids.

518

Name _____

Share and Show ....

Identify and draw a net for the solid figure.

1.   <u>Net</u>

base: _____

lateral faces: _____

figure: _____

2.

_____

3.

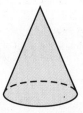

_____

4.

_____

Math Talk Describe the characteristics of a solid figure that you need to consider when making its net.

On Your Own ....

Identify and draw a net for the solid figure.

5.

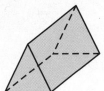

_____

6.

_____

Problem Solving  REAL WORLD

Solve.

7. Crystals of ice often form prisms with six rectangles as lateral faces. Describe the bases of the crystals.

_____

ice crystals

8. The lateral faces and bases of crystals of the mineral galena are congruent squares. Identify the shape of a galena crystal.

_____

· · · · · · · · · · · · · · SHOW YOUR WORK · · · ·

9. Julie makes and sells pentagonal-prism-shaped boxes for hats. Box tops are sold separately. Sketch a net for a hatbox without a top.

10. 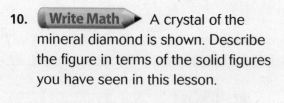 **Write Math** ▶ A crystal of the mineral diamond is shown. Describe the figure in terms of the solid figures you have seen in this lesson.

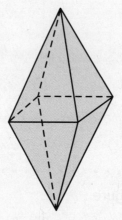

_____

_____

_____

_____

11. ⭐ **Test Prep** Jesse made a triangular prism from paper. What shapes did she use?

(A) 3 triangles only

(B) 3 triangles and 2 rectangles

(C) 4 triangles only

(D) 2 triangles and 3 rectangles

Name _____

Surface Area

Essential Question How can you find the surface area of a solid figure?

The **surface area**, S, of a solid figure is the sum of the areas of its faces, or surfaces. You can use a net to find the surface area of a figure.

 UNLOCK the Problem REAL WORLD

Alex is designing wooden boxes in which to store his books. Each box measures 15 in. by 12 in. by 10 in. To know how much wood to buy, he needs to find the surface area of each box. What is the surface area of each box?

🔑 **Use a net to find the surface area.**

- What is the shape of each face?

_____

- What are the dimensions of each face?

_____

_____

```
              12 in.
  10 in.  ┌────────┐
  10 in.  │   1    │
          │        │         10 in.   12 in.
  ┌───────┼────────┼────────┬────────┐
  │       │        │        │        │
  │   2   │   3    │   4    │   5    │  15 in.
  │       │        │        │        │
  └───────┼────────┼────────┴────────┘
  10 in.  │   6    │
          └────────┘
```

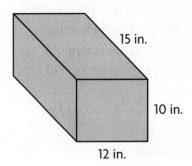

STEP 1 Find the area of each numbered face.

Face 1: $12 \times 10 = 120$ in^2 Face 2: $15 \times 10 =$ _____ in^2

Face 3: _____ $\times$ _____ = _____ in^2 Face 4: _____ $\times$ _____ = _____ in^2

Face 5: _____ $\times$ _____ = _____ in^2 Face 6: _____ $\times$ _____ = _____ in^2

STEP 2 Find the sum of the areas of the faces. $S =$ _____

So, the surface area of each box is _____.

Math Talk Describe What do you notice about the opposite faces of the box that could help you find its surface area?

Example 1 Use a net to find the surface area of the triangular prism.

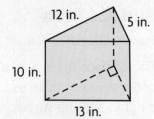

The surface area equals the sum of the areas of the three rectangular faces and two triangular bases. Note that the bases have the same area.

area of bases A and E: $A = \frac{1}{2}bh = \frac{1}{2} \times 5 \times$ _____ = _____

area of face B: $A = lw = 5 \times 10 =$ _____

area of face C: $A = lw =$ _____ $\times$ _____ = _____

area of face D: $A = lw =$ _____ $\times$ _____ = _____

Surface area: $S = 2 \times$ _____ + _____ + _____ + _____ = _____

So, the surface area of the triangular prism is _____.

Math Talk Explain why the area of one triangular base was multiplied by 2.

To find the surface area of a cylinder, think of its net. The top and bottom are circles. The lateral surface is like a label on a soup can. The length of the rectangle is equal to the circumference of each base.

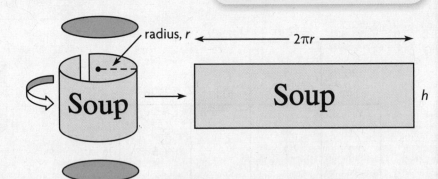

Example 2 Use a net to find the surface area of the cylinder.
Use 3.14 for π.

Write the formula. $S = 2 \times$ (area of base) + area of lateral surface

$A(\text{base}) = \pi r^2$
$A(\text{rectangle}) = l \times h$ $S = 2 \times (\pi \times r^2) + (l \times h)$

rectangle length = circumference $S = (2 \times \pi \times r^2) + (\text{circumference} \times h)$

$C = 2\pi r$ $S = (2 \times \pi \times r^2) + (2 \times \pi \times r \times h)$

Replace π with 3.14, r with 7, and h with 16. $S = [2 \times 3.14 \times ($ _____ $)^2] + (2 \times$ _____ $\times$ _____ $\times$ _____ $)$

Simplify within grouping symbols. $S =$ _____ + _____

Add. $S =$ _____

So, the surface area of the cylinder is about _____.

Name _____

Share and Show [MATH BOARD] ·

Use a net to find the surface area. Use 3.14 for π.

1.
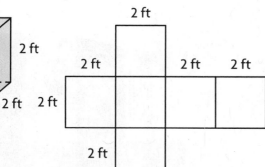

area of each face: _____ × _____ = _____

number of faces: _____

surface area = _____ × _____ = _____ ft²

2.
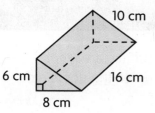

10 cm

6 cm   16 cm

8 cm

_____

3.
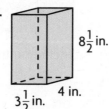

$8\frac{1}{2}$ in.

$3\frac{1}{2}$ in.   4 in.

_____

> **Math Talk** Explain how to find the surface area of a cylinder with a radius of 3 ft and a height of 8 ft.

On Your Own ·

Use a net to find the surface area. Use 3.14 for π.

4.
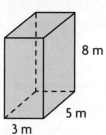

8 m

5 m

3 m

_____

5.
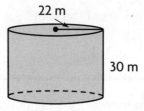

22 m

30 m

_____

6. Emma covers the surface of a cube-shaped box with wrapping paper. The length of one side of the cube is 5 in. How much wrapping paper will Emma need to cover the cube?

_____

7. The Vehicle Assembly Building at Kennedy Space Center is a rectangular prism. It is 218 m long, 158 m wide, and 160 m tall. There are four 139 m tall doors in the building, averaging 29 m in width. What is the building's outside surface area when the doors are open?

- Ⓐ   536 m²
- Ⓑ   138,640 m²
- Ⓒ   154,764 m²
- Ⓓ 5,511,040 m²

a. Draw a net of the building not including the floor.

b. What are the dimensions of the 4 walls?

_____

_____

c. What are the dimensions of the roof?

_____

d. Find the building's surface area (not including the floor) when the doors are closed.

_____

e. Find the area of the four doors.

_____

f. Find the building's surface area (not including the floor) when the doors are open.

_____

g. Fill in the bubble for the correct answer choice above.

---

8. A rectangular prism measures 4 centimeters by 5 centimeters by 6 centimeters. What is its surface area?

- Ⓐ   74 square centimeters
- Ⓑ 120 square centimeters
- Ⓒ 148 square centimeters
- Ⓓ 240 square centimeters

9. Lynn will use a closed glass tube for an art project. The tube is 45 centimeters high with a radius of 4 centimeters. What is the surface area of the tube?

- Ⓐ   590.32 square centimeters
- Ⓑ 1,180.64 square centimeters
- Ⓒ 1,230.88 square centimeters
- Ⓓ 2,361.28 square centimeters

Name _____

Volume of Prisms

Essential Question How can you find the volume of a prism?

Volume is the number of cubic units needed to occupy a given space without gaps or overlaps. Volume is measured in cubic units, such as cubic feet (ft^3) or cubic meters (m^3).

UNLOCK the Problem REAL WORLD

A bento is a single-portion meal that is common in Japan. The meal is usually served in a box. A small bento box is a rectangular prism that is 5 inches long, 4 inches wide, and 2 inches high. How much food can the box hold?

- Underline the sentence that tells you what you are trying to find.
- Circle the numbers you need to use.

Find the volume of a rectangular prism

Find the number of 1-inch cubes that are needed to fill the box.

STEP 1

Sketch the rectangular prism.

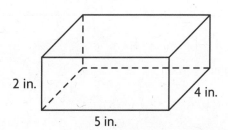

STEP 2

Fill the base with 1-inch cubes.

It takes _____ × _____ or _____ cubes to fill the bottom layer.

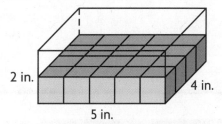

STEP 3

Add another layer of cubes to completely fill the prism.

There are _____ layers, so the total number

of cubes is _____ × _____ = _____.

So, the bento box can hold _____ in^3 of food.

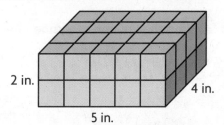

Math Talk Describe What shortcut could you use to find the volume of the rectangular prism instead of counting each cube.

CONNECT You know that the volume of a rectangular prism is the product of its length, width, and height. Since the product of the length and width is the area of one base, the volume is also the product of the area of one base and the height. This gives a general formula for the volume of any prism.

> ## Volume of a Prism
>
> Volume = area of one base × height | $V = Bh$

🔒 Example 1 Find the volume of a triangular prism

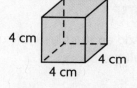
5 cm   12 cm
6 cm

STEP 1

Find the area of one base, B.

The area of the triangle is $\frac{1}{2}bh$,

where $b =$ _____ and $h =$ _____.

$B = \frac{1}{2} \times$ _____ $\times$ _____

Multiply.

$B =$ _____

_____

STEP 2

Use the volume formula.

Write the formula. $V = Bh$

Substitute _____ for B and _____ for h. $V =$ _____ $\times$ _____

Multiply. $V =$ _____

So, the volume is _____ cm^3.

> **⚠ ERROR Alert**
>
> When you find the volume of a triangular prism, be sure to use one of the parallel faces as the base. The bases of a triangular prism are not necessarily the top and bottom of the figure.

🔒 Example 2 Find the volume of a cube

Write the formula. The area of the square base is s^2. $V = Bh = s^3$
The height of a cube is also s, so $V = Bh = s^3$.

4 cm
4 cm
4 cm

Substitute _____ for s. $V =$ _____

Simplify. Use 4 as a factor 3 times. $V =$ _____

So, the volume is _____ cm^3.

> **Math Talk** Describe the difference between the units used to measure area and volume.

Name _____

Share and Show

Find the volume.

1.

25 in.

15 in.

10 in.

$V = lwh$

$V =$ _____ × _____ × _____

$V =$ _____ in^3

2.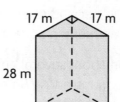

17 m   17 m

28 m

_____

3.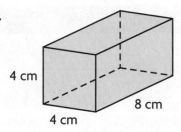

4 cm

8 cm

4 cm

_____

4.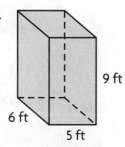

9 ft

6 ft

5 ft

_____

5.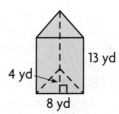

13 yd

4 yd

8 yd

_____

Math Talk Describe the steps for finding the volume of a triangular prism.

On Your Own

Find the missing dimension of the prism.

6. $V = 576$ ft^3

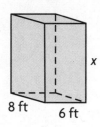

x

8 ft   6 ft

7. $V = 175$ m^3

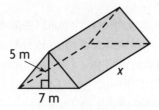

5 m

x

7 m

8. $V = 682.5$ cm^3

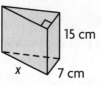

15 cm

x   7 cm

9. Wayne's gym locker is a cube with a side length of 14 inches. What is the volume of the locker? Explain how you found the answer.

_____

Connect to Science — REAL WORLD

Aquariums

Large public aquariums like the Tennessee Aquarium in Chattanooga have a wide variety of freshwater and saltwater fish species from around the world. The fish are kept in aquariums of various sizes.

The table shows information about several aquariums that are rectangular prisms. Use the formula $V = Bh$ or $V = lwh$ to find the missing values in the table.

Find the length of Tank 1.

$$V = lwh$$

$$52,500 = l \times \underline{\hspace{2cm}} \times \underline{\hspace{2cm}}$$

$$52,500 = l \times \underline{\hspace{3cm}}$$

$$\frac{52,500}{\underline{\hspace{1.5cm}}} = l$$

$$\underline{\hspace{2cm}} = l$$

So, the length of Tank 1 is _____.

Aquarium Tanks

	Length	Width	Height	Volume
Tank 1		30 cm	35 cm	52,500 cm³
Tank 2	12 m		4 m	384 m³
Tank 3	18 m	12 m		2,160 m³
Tank 4	72 cm	55 cm	40 cm	

Solve.

10. Find the width of Tank 2.

_____

11. Find the height of Tank 3.

_____

12. **H.O.T.** To keep aquarium fish healthy, there should be the correct ratio of water to fish. A recommended ratio is 9 L of water to 5 cm of fish. Find the volume of Tank 4. Then use the equivalencies 1 cm³ = 1 mL and 1,000 mL = 1 L to find how many centimeters of fish can be safely kept in Tank 4.

_____

13. Give another set of possible dimensions for Tank 2. Explain how you found your answer.

_____

_____

Name _____

 Mid-Chapter Checkpoint

▶ Vocabulary

Choose the best term from the box.

1. _____ is the sum of the areas of all the faces, or surfaces, of a solid figure. (p. 521)

2. A three-dimensional figure having length, width, and height is called a(n) _____. (p. 517)

3. _____ is the measure of space a solid figure occupies. (p. 525)

4. A _____ is any surface of a solid figure other than a base. (p. 518)

▶ Concepts and Skills

5. Identify and draw a net for the solid figure. (pp. 517–520)

_____

6. Use a net to find the surface area. Use 3.14 for π. (pp. 521–524)

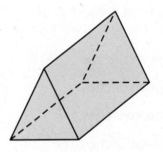

_____

7. Find the missing dimension of the prism if the volume is 315 cm³. (pp. 525–528)

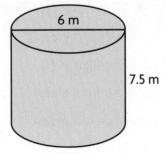

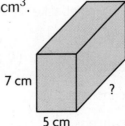

_____

8. A machine cuts nets from flat pieces of cardboard. The nets can be folded into cylindrical containers for party favors. Which is a complete list of the shapes that appear in the net? (pp. 517–520)

  (A) 2 circles and 1 rectangle

  (B) 2 circles and 2 rectangle

  (C) 2 squares and 4 rectangles

  (D) 6 rectangles

9. Fran's filing cabinet is 6 feet tall, $1\frac{1}{3}$ feet wide, and 3 feet deep. She plans to paint all sides except the bottom of the cabinet. Find the surface area of the sides she intends to paint. (pp. 521–524)

  (A) 26 square feet

  (B) 41 square feet

  (C) 56 square feet

  (D) 71 square feet

10. An aquarium is shaped like a triangular prism. The volume of the aquarium is 1,320 cubic inches. The height of the aquarium is 20 inches. What is the area of the triangular base of the aquarium? (pp. 525–528)

  (A) 33 square inches

  (B) 40 square inches

  (C) 66 square inches

  (D) 132 square inches

11. What is the surface area of a storage box that measures 15 centimeters by 12 centimeters by 10 centimeters? (pp. 521–524)

  (A) 450 square centimeters

  (B) 900 square centimeters

  (C) 1,350 square centimeters

  (D) 1,800 square centimeters

12. A wastebasket is a cube with sides that are 16 inches long. What is the volume of the wastebasket? (pp. 525–528)

  (A) 256 cubic inches

  (B) 512 cubic inches

  (C) 2,048 cubic inches

  (D) 4,096 cubic inches

Name _____

Volume of Cylinders

Essential Question How are the area of the base, the height, and the volume of a cylinder related?

Investigate

Materials ■ 2 sheets of centimeter grid paper ■ centimeter cubes ■ scissors ■ tape

A. Cut out a rectangle 12 cm long and 6 cm wide from one sheet of grid paper.

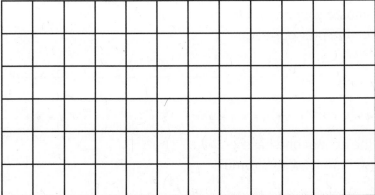

12 cm

6 cm

B. Without overlapping the edges, roll the rectangle horizontally and tape it to model a cylinder.

C. Stand the cylinder on the second sheet of grid paper. Trace one circular base of the cylinder.

D. Count the whole squares and the parts of squares inside the traced circle. How many cubes do you estimate will fit on the bottom layer of the cylinder?

_____ cubes

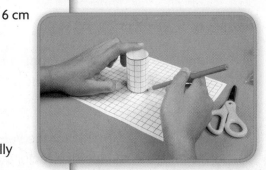

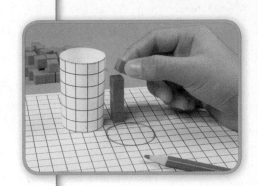

E. Stack the cubes to estimate the height of the cylinder. How many layers of cubes will it take to fill the cylinder?

_____ layers

F. What is the approximate volume of the cylinder? Explain how you found the answer.

_____

_____

_____

Proportions
   defined, 175
   equivalent ratios to solve, 179–182
   model, 175–178
   unit rates to solve, 183–186

Pyramid, 518

Q

Quadrilaterals
   classifying, 442–444
   graph on coordinate plane, 452–454
   parallelograms, 442–444
   rectangles, 442–444
   rhombi, 442–444
   squares, 442–444
   sum of angles, 441
   trapezoids, 442–444

Quart, 227–229

Quotients
   compatible numbers to estimate, 139–141

R

Random sampling, 277

Range, 259–262

Rates, 171–174
   defined, 171
   distance, rate, and time problems, 241–244
   unit rate, 171–175

Ratios
   defined, 167
   equivalent, 168–169
   percent as, 189
   probability as, 291, 296
   proportions, 175–178, 179–182, 183–186
   rates, 171–174
   writing, 167

Raven, dimension of egg, 52

Reading
   Connect to Reading, 402

Real World
   Connect to Science, 74, 240, 528
   Connect to Social Studies, 280, 484
   Problem Solving, 12, 16, 20, 30, 38, 42, 56, 66,
      70, 96, 124, 142, 146, 158, 170, 178, 182,
      186, 192, 200, 218, 226, 236, 244, 262, 272,
      284, 372, 376, 384, 388, 410, 411, 418, 428,
      454, 458, 462, 476, 494, 498, 520

Unlock the Problem, 5, 9, 13, 17, 21–22, 27, 31,
   34, 35, 39, 49, 57, 60, 63, 71, 75, 85, 88, 89,
   92, 93, 97, 100, 103, 106, 107–108, 120, 121,
   125, 128, 129, 138, 139, 143, 150, 151, 155,
   167, 171, 174, 179, 183, 189–190, 193, 197,
   201, 204, 205, 215, 219–220, 223, 227, 230,
   233, 237, 241, 251, 255, 258, 259, 263, 269,
   273, 277, 291, 295, 298, 305, 309, 321, 328,
   329, 337, 347, 351, 355, 359, 369, 377, 380,
   385, 389, 395, 399, 403, 407, 411, 415, 429,
   433, 437, 440, 441, 447, 451, 455, 459, 469,
   472, 477, 480, 481, 491, 499, 503, 506, 507,
   517, 521, 525, 535

Reciprocal
   defined, 143
   fraction division, 143–145

Rectangles
   area, 481–484
   graph on coordinate plane, 451–454
   perimeter, 470–471
   properties, 442

Rectangular prism, 525

Rectangular pyramid, 519

Redwood National Park, 226

Reflection, 455–457

Relative frequency table, 264

Remember!, 13, 50, 64, 71, 89, 93, 130, 136, 139,
   190, 260, 263, 269, 310, 351, 359, 460, 495

Repeating decimals, 86

Rhombus, 442

Right angle, 426–428

Right triangle, 438

River otter, water consumption, 56

Robin, dimension of egg, 52

Roller coaster speeds, 100

Rotation, 455–457

Rotational symmetry, 460–462

S

Sales tax, 206

Samples, 277
   bias and, 278

Sample space, 291

Sampling method, 277–279
   convenience, 277
   random, 277
   systematic, 277

Sand sculptures, 196

Saturn, 324

Table of Measures

METRIC | CUSTOMARY

Length

METRIC	CUSTOMARY
1 centimeter (cm) = 10 millimeters (mm)	1 foot (ft) = 12 inches (in.)
1 meter (m) = 1,000 millimeters	1 yard (yd) = 3 feet, or 36 inches
1 meter = 100 centimeters	1 mile (mi) = 1,760 yards,
1 kilometer (km) = 1,000 meters	or 5,280 feet

Capacity

METRIC	CUSTOMARY
1 liter (L) = 1,000 milliliters (mL)	1 cup (c) = 8 fluid ounces (fl oz)
1 kiloliter (kL) = 1,000 liters	1 pint (pt) = 2 cups
	1 quart (qt) = 2 pints, or 4 cups
	1 gallon (gal) = 4 quarts

Mass/Weight

METRIC	CUSTOMARY
1 gram (g) = 1,000 milligrams (mg)	1 pound (lb) = 16 ounces (oz)
1 gram = 100 centigrams (cg)	1 ton (T) = 2,000 pounds
1 kilogram (kg) = 1,000 grams	

TIME

1 minute (min) = 60 seconds (sec)	1 year (yr) = about 52 weeks
1 hour (hr) = 60 minutes	1 year = 12 months (mo)
1 day = 24 hours	1 year = 365 days
1 week (wk) = 7 days	1 decade = 10 years
	1 century = 100 years
	1 millennium = 1,000 years

TEMPERATURE

Celsius (°C) $C = \frac{5}{9}(F - 32)$

Fahrenheit (°F) $F = \frac{9}{5}C + 32$

SYMBOLS

$=$	is equal to	$(2, 3)$	ordered pair (x, y)
$\neq$	is not equal to	$\cong$	is congruent to
$\approx$	is approximately equal to	$\perp$	is perpendicular to
$>$	is greater than	$\parallel$	is parallel to
$<$	is less than	$\overleftrightarrow{AB}$	line AB
$\geq$	is greater than or equal to	$\overrightarrow{AB}$	ray AB
$\leq$	is less than or equal to	$\overline{AB}$	line segment AB
10^2	ten squared	$\angle ABC$	angle ABC
10^3	ten cubed	$m\angle A$	the measure of angle A
2^4	the fourth power of 2	$\triangle ABC$	triangle ABC
$\sqrt{4}$	the square root of 4	π	pi; $\pi \approx 3.14$ or $\pi \approx \frac{22}{7}$
$|{}^-4|$	the absolute value of ${}^-4$	$^\circ$	degree
$\%$	percent		

FORMULAS

Perimeter and Circumference

Polygon	$P =$ sum of the lengths of sides
Rectangle	$P = 2l + 2w$
Square	$P = 4s$
Circle	$C = 2\pi r$ or $C = \pi d$

Area

Rectangle	$A = lw$
Parallelogram	$A = bh$
Triangle	$A = \frac{1}{2}bh$
Trapezoid	$A = \frac{1}{2}h(b_1 + b_2)$
Circle	$A = \pi r^2$

Volume*

Prism	$V = Bh$
Rectangular Prism	$V = Bh$ or $V = lwh$
Cylinder	$V = Bh$ or $V = \pi r^2 h$

Surface Area*

Prism	$S = 2B +$ area of faces
Cylinder	$S = 2B +$ area of lateral surface

*$B =$ area of one base of a solid figure

Photo Credits

KEY: (t) top, (c) center, (b) bottom, (l) left, (r) right, (bg) background.

Cover Front: (bg) Purestock/Getty Images; (deer) David W. Hamilton/Getty Images; (owl) Brian Hagiwara/Brand X Pictures/Getty Images; (leaf texture) Image Gap/Alamy.

Cover Back: (leaves) Studio Ton Kinsbergen/Beateworks/Corbis.

Title Pages: Copyright page (bg) Purestock/Getty Images; (tl) Danita Delimont/Alamy; (br) Don Hammond/Design Pics/Corbis; iii altrendo nature/Getty Images; iv (bg) Purestock/Getty Images; (br) Daniel J. Cox/Getty Images.

Table of Contents: v Craig Tuttle/Corbis; vi (l) Oleg Boldyrev/Alamy; vii Garry Gay/Alamy; viii (l) Jonathan Daniel/Getty Images; ix Kelly-Mooney Photography/Corbis; x (l) Digital Vision/Getty Images; (r) Photo Disc/Getty Images; xi Digital Vision/Getty Images; xii (l) Richard T. Nowitz/Corbis; (r) Paul Souders/Corbis.

Big Idea 1: 1 Craig Tuttle/Corbis; 2 (bl) D. Hurst/Alamy; (t) Foodcollection RF/Getty Images; (br) Frederic Cirou and Isabelle Rozenbaum/PhotoAlto/Corbis; 5 Granger Wootz/Blend Images/Corbis; 8 Biomedical Imaging Unit, Southampton General Hospi/Photo Researchers, Inc.; 9 Robert Quinian/Alamy; 12 Image Source/Getty Images; 13 PhotoDisc/Getty Images; 17 Herbert Kehrer/Corbis; 20 Laurence Mouton/Alamy; 21 Mark Andersen/Getty Images; 22 Corbis; 24 (t) Artville/Getty Images; (l) Eyewire/Getty Images; (r) Digital Vision/Getty Images; 30 Dr. Paul Zahl/Photo Researchers, Inc.; 35 Stock4B/Getty Images; 38 Comstock/Getty Images; 39 Kevin Dodge/Corbis; 49 Rubberball/Alamy; 50 (t) Lee Dalton; (b) United States Mint; 52 David R. Frazier Photolibrary, Inc.; 53 Bryan Knox; Papilio/Corbis; 56 PhotoDisc/Getty Images; 57 SW Productions/PhotoDisc/Getty Images; 60 Comstock/Getty Images; 63 Alamy Images; 66 Mike Kemp/Getty Images; 67 Digital Vision/Getty Images; 70 Martin Ruegner/Getty Images; 71 Brand X Pictures/Getty Images; 74 M.I Walker/Photo Researchers, Inc.; 75 NASA Images; 85 brandi ediss/Getty Images; 88 Don Mason/Corbis; 89 Craig Tuttle/Design Pics/Corbis; 92 PhotoDisc/Getty Images; 93 Tom Vezo/Danita Delimont/Alamy; 100 Alamy Images Royalty Free; 103 Corbis; 106 John and Lisa Merrill/Corbis; 107 Macduff Everton/Corbis; 108 Phil Schermeister/Corbis; 120 Julie Dansereau/Getty Images; 121 Rob Melnychuk/PhotoDisc Green/Getty Images; 125 Anna Peisi/Corbis; 128 Jonathan Daniel/Getty Images; 129 Blend Images/Shalom Ormsby/Getty Images; 139 Amos Nachoum/Corbis; 147 Getty Images; 151 Plush Studios/Blend Images/Corbis; 154 ImageState/Alamy; 158 PhotoDisc/Getty Images.

Big Idea 2: 163 Tannen Maury/epa/Corbis; 164 Jonathan Daniel/Getty Images; 165 Image Source/Corbis; 167 Daniel J. Cox/Corbis; 174 GK Hart/Vikki Hart/Photodisc/Getty Images; 178 (t) Mark A. Schneider/Photo Researchers, Inc.; (bl) Charles D. Winters/Photo Researchers, Inc.; (br) Astrid & Hanns-Frieder Michler/Photo Researchers, Inc.; 179 Andersen Ross/Getty Images; 182 Darryl Leniuk/Corbis; 193 Victor Baldlzon/National Basketball Association/Getty Images; 196 J. Griffs Smith/Texas Department of Transportation; 198 Dinodia Images/Alamy; 200 (r, l) PhotoDisc/Getty Images; (c) Robert Glusic/PhotoDisc/Getty Images; 204 Thinkstock/Getty Images; 208 Corbis; 215 Corbis; 218 Corbis; 219 Yoav Levy/Phototake/Alamy; 223 PhotoDisc/Getty Images; 226 Vito Palmisano/Getty Images; 228 American School/The Bridgeman Art Library/Getty Images; 233 Bon Appetit/Alamy; 240 NASA Marshall Space Flight Center Collection; 241 John Zich/Stringer/Getty Images; 242 Frank Krahmer/Getty Images; 244 PhotoDisc/Getty Images; 249 Tony Garcia/Getty Images; 251 (t) Jose Luis Pelaez/Blend Images/Corbis; (b) Comstock/Getty Images; 254 Tim Pannell/Corbis; 265 Ben Blankenburg/Corbis; 266 David Davis Photoproductions RF/Alamy; 269 AMPAS/FilmMagic/Getty Images; 271 Stockdisc/Getty Images; 272 Veronique Krieger/Getty Images; 276 Corbis; 277 SW Productions/Getty Images; 278 Banastock/Jupiter Images; 280 Jim West/Alamy; 281 Bob Thomas/Corbis Images; 294 Adrian Thomas/Photo Researchers, Inc.; 295 Corbis; 302 Henry Horenstein/Corbis; 303 JupiterImages/Brand X/Alamy; 306 Plush Studios/Bill Reitzel/Blend Images/Corbis; 312 Digital Vision/Getty Images.

Big Idea 3: 317 Kelly-Mooney Photography/Corbis; 318 Nicola Angella/Grand Tour/Corbis; 324 Brand X Pictures/Getty Images; 328 Corbis; 329 Paul Souders/Corbis; 330 Corbis; 337 Corbis; 340 David Anthony/Alamy; 346 Ariel Molina/epa/Corbis; 354 Sindre Ellingsen/Getty Images; 355 henry owen/Alamy; 358 Peter Cade/Getty images; 359 Randy M. Ury/Corbis; 369 Concept by Beytan/Alamy; 372 Iain Masterton/Alamy; 376 Corbis; 377 Erik Isakson/Getty Images; 384 Joseph Sohm/Visions of America/Corbis; 387 Image Source/Corbis; 389 Digital Studios; 392 NASA/Johnson Space Center; 395 Gabe Palmer/Corbis; 399 PhotoDisc/Getty Images; 402 Franco Vogt/Corbis; 407 Tom Schierlitz/Getty Images; 411 Denis Scott/Corbis; 415 Van Hasselt John/Corbis Sygma; 418 nik wheeler/Alamy; 428 imac/Alamy; 430 Doug Pensinger/Getty Images; 437 Paul A. Souders/Corbis; 441 Greg C. Grace/Alamy; 451 Toru Ysmanaka/AFP/Getty Images; 455 (all) PhotoDisc/Getty Images; 457 (all) Image Ideas/Jupiter Images; 459 PhotoDisc/Getty Images; 467 Andres Rodriguez/Alamy Images; 468 MedioImages/Getty Images; 469 Richard Cummins/Corbis; 470 Corbis; 472 Stock Montage/Getty Images; 473 John Biever/Sports Illustrated/Getty Images; 476 Richard T. Nowitz/Corbis; 483 Frank Whitney/Getty Images; 493 Shigemi Numazawa/Atlas Photo Bank/Photo Researchers, Inc.; 501 Brand X Pictures/Getty Images; 520 Ted Kinsman/Photo Researchers, Inc.; 524 NASA; 525 Studio Eye/Corbis; 528 Comstock/Corbis; 534 Yellow Dog Productions/Getty Images; 537 Sinclair Stammers/Photo Researchers, Inc.

All other photos Houghton Mifflin Harcourt libraries and photographers: Guy Jarvis, Weronica Ankarorn, Eric Camden, Don Couch, Ken Kinzie, Steve Williams, Victoria Smith and Sam Dudgeon.